WORTHY OF THE NATION

WORTHY OF

Published by the SMITHSONIAN INSTITUTION PRESS City of Washington

THE NATION

The History of Planning for the National Capital

NATIONAL CAPITAL PLANNING COMMISSION

FREDERICK GUTHEIM Consultant

NATIONAL CAPITAL PLANNING COMMISSION HISTORICAL STUDIES

SAMUEL K. FRAZIER, JR., *Study Director*, National Capital Planning Commission
RUTH W. SPIEGEL, *Editor*, Smithsonian Institution Press

WORTHY OF THE NATION: The History of Planning for the National Capital

THE FEDERAL CITY: Plans and Realities

PLANNING WASHINGTON 1924–1976: An Era of Planning for the National Capital and Environs

WORTHY OF THE NATION ⓒ Copyright Smithsonian Institution 1977
Printed in the United States of America
Library of Congress Cataloging in Publication Data
appears on the last printed page of this book.

Photographic Essays by Robert C. Lautman
Typographic Design by Hubert Leckie
Production Supervision by Susan Lehmann

The value of planning has nowhere been so clearly demonstrated as in the development of the city of Washington, for the magnificence of our national capital today is in large part the heritage of the strong and enduring plan laid down by Major Pierre L'Enfant in 1791. In spite of changing social and technological priorities and needs, his concepts have continued for 186 years as the framework within which decisions have been made for the original central portion of Washington known as the L'Enfant city, and as the nucleus for generating ensuing development within the National Capital Region as a whole.

Implementation of L'Enfant's proposals began with individual building projects early in the nineteenth century and continued apace with the extension of the L'Enfant city street system throughout the District of Columbia in the 1890s, the far-reaching plans of the McMillan Commission for city and region at the turn of the century, and the rush of urban development of the post-Depression years. The L'Enfant plan remained essentially intact throughout all of this activity owing to the soundness of its broad concepts which were coupled with inherent flexibility in their details. The plan now continues in our own time to be the basis for our current planning efforts and, as such, it gives a continuity to the planning process and provides a strong sense of the value which that continuity creates.

The National Capital Planning Commission, including its predecessor agencies the National Capital Park Commission and the National Capital Park and Planning Commission, had the responsibility for overseeing this orderly development of the national capital since 1924 and has shared its city planning role with the mayor since the enactment of Home Rule for the District of Columbia in 1973. The rapid acceleration of change will make our task increasingly difficult in the future. But it is my hope that the publication of this historical study, by documenting the importance of the planning process in the past, will clearly demonstrate the even greater value it can hold for the future.

David M. Childs, *Chairman*
National Capital Planning Commission
Washington, D.C.
August 1977

CONTENTS

*View along the Eighth Street Cross Axis
from the National Archives across the Mall*

All unattributed photographs are by Robert C. Lautman.

To Charles Conrad who conceived this book, and Samuel Frazier who assumed the day-to-day responsibility of realizing it, on behalf of the National Capital Planning Commission, my first obligation is due; and behind them in various supporting capacities I must acknowledge the members of the staff of the commission. They recognized a significant moment, the fiftieth anniversary of the creation of the comprehensive planning agency, and the role of the national capital city in the 1976 Bicentennial celebration. But without their broad interpretation this could have become just another "official history." Others must also have played an important part, but I can only identify Paul Thiry, a member of the commission whose historical interest in the city over many years is unmatched.

As author I have been assisted by Antoinette J. Lee, whose collaboration in the research and editorial phases of the work has been indispensable. In the initial collection of data, in the interviews, and especially in the assembling of the visual elements of the study, Charity Vanderbilt Davidson played a similar role. At the Smithsonian Institution Press, Ruth W. Spiegel has labored to bring this work to a high standard of scholarly documentation and editorial clarity; and Hubert Leckie, once again a colleague, has endowed it with visual clarity in design.

I have been fortunate in knowing every chairman and all five directors of the National Capital Planning Commission, and the opportunity to meet them again and to receive their cooperation in the preparation of this work has been warmly appreciated. All have been interviewed and many provided access to personal papers and collections as well as reminiscences and answers to specific questions.

The decision to prepare an administrative history of the National Capital Planning Commission and a Register of commission members and principal staff should also be noted, both as these works are integral parts of this undertaking, and as this step relieved the present work of such specialized detail. The preparation and publication in the present series of a shorter and more popularly written work, *The Federal City: Plans and Realities*, should also be noted; and at this point I should like to acknowledge the services of Mrs. Davidson and Dr. Lee in this as well as the present work.

Washington as the planned capital city must occupy a special place in American urban history. Few of our cities have received detailed topographical study, and the present work is preeminently about the place rather than the people of the city. Washington has been fortunate in its general histories, that of Wilhelmus B. Bryan carrying the story from its origins to 1878; and that of my valued friend and colleague, the late Constance McLaughlin Green, addressing the subject in a more contemporary spirit and continuing it to the present. Hardly a page of the present volume is not indebted to these works, and I have had no intention of furthering what they have done so well. My more specialized study has been reinforced by two predecessors, another good friend and colleague, the late Elbert Peets, and John Reps; but the lasting impression I have gained from this effort is of its unexplored dimensions.

While accepting the larger and more particular obligations in a work of this nature, my personal aim has been to write a work that would be read as a companion volume to my earlier environmental history, *The Potomac*. And having done so to the best of my ability and under present circumstances of time and resources, I would like nothing so much as to start all over again.

FREDERICK GUTHEIM
Washington, D.C.
June 1977

The Washington Plan in Past and Present

Time itself has reinforced the prime enigma of the Washington plan: that such a city design could have been rejected, its creator dismissed, its very documentation lost, yet the plan itself, *on the ground*, have survived to guide and direct the growth of the national capital. The explanation escapes us of how an artist and military engineer, even if somewhat trained in architecture, could at his first essay have conceived so superlative a city plan that today the built city is recognized as one of the world's major planning achievements. Yet the greatness of the Washington plan is more than a tribute to L'Enfant's genius of synthesis and creation, or his ability to produce a city plan in so little time and in face of political and economic obstruction. The L'Enfant plan was unparalleled in its scale, scope, and complexity, and in its resolution of the problems—in process no less than in design—of creating out of bare landscape a new capital city. Despite crisis, criticism, and shortcoming, there was a correctness of vision that inspired and endured. And there is now in Washington, national capital city, the timeless beauty of rise and river, street and circle, dome and diagonal, monument and Mall, that fastens itself on the imagination and finds a place not just in history books but in our most creative thought.

The L'Enfant Plan: *Timelessness and Persistence*

To evaluate the L'Enfant plan one needs to recognize that it was incomplete as it came from the hand of its designer—soundly conceived in its fundamentals but still hardly more than a sketch, greatly lacking in significant details and soon compromised by physical deterioration of the manuscript itself. What is commonly referred to as the "L'Enfant plan" embraces not only the initial design by L'Enfant, but its transposition by Andrew Ellicott into the first official map of the city; the 1803 plats by the city surveyor, Nicholas King; various building regulations, by George Washington and others, to implement the plan; and several documents, particularly the manuscript map, that were drawn by L'Enfant and illustrate his intentions, permitting more detailed interpretation of his basic design.*

---

* On this and all other source and background materials alluded to in the text, see the Bibliographic Essay, pp. 373–403.

View of the Historic City from the Tomb of L'Enfant

1

The persistence of the plan is notable, even if it was ignored in major respects, such as the development of the Mall and location of certain federal buildings, and in minor dispositions as, for example, of open spaces within the city. One great change in the modern city has been the reclamation of the Potomac flats, adding the "made" land from the Washington Monument west to the Lincoln Memorial. Yet even more basic was the city's transition from the eighteenth-century scale of its original design to the Victorian scale of the later nineteenth century. This altered urban scale was accompanied by the still more significant increase in scale of major buildings and memorials in the monumental core of the city. So while the city has remained a "horizontal city," it has ultimately become filled with huge buildings.

WHO PLANNED WASHINGTON?

The question, "Who planned Washington at the start?" invites a multiple answer. George Washington decided its location and set its boundaries four-square to the compass points, and he decided that Alexandria and Georgetown should be included in the federal district. The president established and appointed the commissioners and supported their efforts to plan as well as to build the capital city and its principal buildings. Most significantly, the president appointed Pierre Charles L'Enfant —and kept him on a short rein during the period when negotiations with the original proprietors were under way, Washington himself assuming many of the most important planning decisions. Without doubt the president was looked to by L'Enfant (and everyone else) as the patron of the city's plan and its decisive formulator. As President Washington's secretary of state, Thomas Jefferson had significant administrative responsibilities, but as a talented designer and one of the nation's few architects, he followed his personal interest farther—as in his initial suggestions for a rectilinear city along the north bank of the Tiber and in proposals he offered to L'Enfant. Yet Jefferson's interest neither was a major factor nor was it sustained, and one suspects he realized that his own technical abilities as an architect and engineer would not allow him to compete successfully with L'Enfant. The commissioners could have played an important planning role, but there is no evidence that,

apart from deciding that the federal city should be called "City of Washington" and that streets should be designated by numbers and letters of the alphabet, they took any interest in the city's plan—as, on the contrary, they did in its development, in the sale of lots and construction of individual buildings.

Revolution, Reason... and Architecture

The year 1791 was a time of political revolution in the United States as well as in Europe, and particularly in France. The last half of the eighteenth century was the Enlightenment, the Age of Reason, the period that searched out its great men and called them immortal— not kings and rulers, but scientists, artists, and philosophers. Science, especially mathematics, then reigned, and all aspects of civilization and the arts responded to its leadership. In architecture, from the mid-eighteenth century on, neoclassicism had expressed absolute rationality in the work of Boullée and Ledoux in France, and the Adam brothers, Dance and Soane, in Great Britain. L'Enfant developed his artistic talents under these conditions; his art was inspired by these ideals and purposes. His plan for Washington, despite the derivation of certain elements from Versailles, was less the work of any late baroque style than it was a classically inspired design, fully characteristic of its time. Viewed in these terms the apparent contradiction between an urban design suited to a tyrannical Renaissance prince and his absolute state, and the needs and beliefs of a young democracy, vanishes. Instead one sees the revolutionary spirit that inspired L'Enfant to offer his services to the army of the young American republic, that sustained him through difficult military campaigns, that nourished his veneration of George Washington, commander-in-chief and president, for whom he would one day plan a great city.

NEOCLASSICISM AND THE MATHEMATICS OF THE AGE

By 1791, the characteristics of neoclassicism had been well established and translated not only into literature, painting, and sculpture but into landscape design and urban forms. Classical echoes of the earlier Renaissance and subsequent Greek revivals and forms of academicism are to be distinguished from this unique historical period with its sympathies toward reform and revolution, its endeavors to purify and simplify, its search for absolute values and ideal forms. This was the age L'Enfant knew in France, heartland of neoclassicism. It was to this that L'Enfant reoriented himself on his return to Paris in 1783, the same neoclassic impulse reflected in his plan for Washington. That the United States was an integral if distinct part of this artistic movement cannot be doubted when one examines the aspirations of Thomas Jefferson at Richmond, the achievements of Benjamin Latrobe in Baltimore, the paintings of Benjamin West, as well as the work of Houdon. Urban design shared the architectural aims enunciated finally in 1793 by Léon DuFourny in the statement, "L'Architecture doit se régénérer par la géométrie." The new architecture was based on cubes, cones, cylinders, pyramids, and other mathematical models. The design of cities was based no less on geometry. Indeed, urban design was inspired by the search for the ideal city, in which the fundamentally moral quest of the age would be expressed in elevating experiences: *the city would aim at making better citizens.* Such a city would be filled with great aesthetic experiences, with monuments commemorating great men and heroic acts, all set in a Virgilian landscape.

The mathematics of the age is fully expressed in the geometry of the L'Enfant plan with its evident roots in the principles of Descartes, and its perfect right angle formed by the Capitol, the President's House, and that prime expression of the great revolutionary personality and starting point of the plan, an equestrian statue of George Washington. The system of Cartesian coordinates to which L'Enfant's plan is fundamentally oriented establishes what has been called the gridiron element of his plan. A closer examination, however, discloses no affinities with that mechanical checkerboard element that disfigured Philadelphia and countless later cities to which it was applied. In L'Enfant's Washington plan there is instead a carefully worked out plaid (as Elbert Peets has called it) of differentially spaced streets, calculated to relate to the earlier selected sites for public buildings, to principal squares and functional places, and to intersections with the system of radial boulevards.

A political interpretation of the L'Enfant plan must commence with the dominant position assigned to that most representative body, the Congress. For all his veneration of George Washington, L'Enfant did not regard him as a divinely ordained ruler. Nor was L'Enfant's city designed to focus on a ruler and his palace. The planner's eighteenth-century view of the city showed a rich assortment of institutions assigned to key sites throughout the city. These institutions were popular as well as cultural in character: a nondenominational national church (literally a pantheon in which monuments to revolutionary heroes would be placed), colleges, academies, and learned societies—what could be more appropriate to the spirit of the age? While there is little evidence of the architecture that L'Enfant would have provided had he continued work according to his initial instructions, his collateral activities as an architect firmly establish his affinity with contemporaries.

The Historic City and the Continuing Plan

The city Washington became has certainly been influenced by its physical and social environment, but little has been written that explores in detail these influences and relationships. That kind of urban history is just beginning to appear. Meanwhile one is left with a pragmatic analysis of the city that in fact did come into being. There has been little hesitation by contemporary writers or subsequent historians to deal with urban shortcomings. Before the Civil War these deficiencies received widespread notice; later on a more exciting view of the modern city with its social and physical characteristics begins to appear. The growth of the metropolitan city has revived old questions about Washington's distinctive identity, its difference from other American, indeed, other modern cities. These analyses have centered chiefly on the social, economic, and political aspects of the city, and relatively little attention has been given the positive values of the planned city as these have been expressed since the beginning of this century and, indeed, the beginning of continuous official planning in 1924. Yet in the last fifty years the city has been among the fastest growing in the nation, and for all its uniqueness, Washington is expected to exemplify effective urban planning. As the literature of urban history unfolds, there inevitably will be some larger appreciation of the city's accomplishments, and greater attention to precisely what did emerge from the continuous and comprehensive planning efforts.

The new urban history teaches continuity for the contemporary city: growth, change, difficult problems, agonized decisions. From past planning efforts important lessons can be learned about new sources of urban vitality, new uses of existing resources, adaptations of buildings and districts, the professionalization of planning, and persistence of the city's vivid individuality.

More than other cities Washington explicates these lessons precisely because it has had two centuries of planned urban development. The history of Washington invites our sophisticated exploration of urban values: how and by whom were they formulated, interpreted, articulated, provided for, and maintained? What can we learn from the monumental buildings and the row houses, Capitol Hill and Oxon Hill, national capital and indigenous city, home town and metropolitan region? Through word, picture, and plan we may quarter the land in the rain with L'Enfant, walk up Pennsylvania Avenue from Capitol to White House with a president, or ride the Metro from Dupont Circle to Judiciary Square, and at last see for ourselves *this* Washington— national capital, planned city.

Inauguration Day Walk up Pennsylvania Avenue from the Capitol to the White House, 20 January 1977

PHOTOGRAPHIC ESSAY: THE NATIONAL CAPITAL CITY

Telephoto View of the River and Its Bridges, Showing the Naval Observatory Domes

Aerial View of Dupont Circle,
Looking South down Connecticut Avenue

Telephoto View of the Mall and the Monumental Core

8

Meridian Hill Park

9

Aerial View of the Capital City and Key Bridge

CHAPTER I THE PLANNED CENTRAL CITY 1790–1800

The Planned Central City 1790-1800

The New National Capital City and Its Potomac Site

Whether for historic or aesthetic reasons, Washington's plan has not failed to enlist its admirers. "At its formal best," as Ada Louise Huxtable has acknowledged, "Washington has a solemn, full-blown beauty. It is a sybaritic city in correct academic dress. Spring is a romantic overstatement. Summer is a surrealist nightmare as the cool temples shimmer and dissolve in steamy heat. Winter buries the proper palaces in snowdrifts, while the sun hints warmly and regeneratively of spring. There is an hour before twilight, with the glow of the sun still illuminating the horizon, when serene white buildings stand luminous against a clear sky, set stagily amidst the flowers or foliage of a warm spring evening or the bare benches of a crisp winter day. Then the city is touched with its own magic. In the Venetian light the art of politics recedes into the art of architecture. The eye rejoices and the soul expands. The experience is more than the pleasurable recognition of an impressive vista or a successful dialog between structures and spaces. It is an act of love between citizen and stone, and Wash-

ington has many lovers, in the tradition of all great cities that have captured the hearts of men." On balance, Huxtable concludes: "Washington succeeds as a city because of that plan . . . that unifies and binds the city with singular grace, character and charm."

The origins of this plan are as celebrated as the city's present form. In ancestry the plan of Washington points back to the heroic landscape designs of kings and emperors. The salient lessons of mathematics, triumphal architecture, and green avenues were absorbed by the city's designer, Pierre L'Enfant, and transplanted to the frontiers of democracy. Here, in a land previously dividing its allegiances between London, capital city of the British Empire, and the local colonial capitals, a new focus was demanded. The new national capital would embrace actual as well as symbolic importance in uniting the nation—and its potency, as reflected in its physical form, would predict the ability of this new capital to serve as a unifier of diverse sympathies.

THE FEDERAL DISTRICT

Well before the Residence Act was passed by Congress on 12 July 1790, and signed by the president four days

Telephoto View of the Historic White House Axis, Looking South down Sixteenth Street

later, a substantial legislative history of the proposed federal district had been written. The legislative maneuverings from 1783 to 1789 show a reasonably steady evolution and accumulation of concepts about the federal city. Outstanding among these was the notion of a federal "district," ultimately reflected in the language of the Constitution itself. The "district" concept has been traced to the 1783 debates of the Continental Congress on the proposed Delaware River site. The term "district" was repeatedly used after that and, despite the efforts of Jefferson and Madison to popularize the usage of 'territory," it is as the *District* of Columbia that the city has maintained its identity.

The Potomac site ultimately chosen by Congress for the national capital was the result of several years' deliberation. In addition to the primary competitor, the city of Philadelphia, the other site Congress had leaned most strongly toward was on the Delaware River in the vicinity of Trenton, not far from the government's onetime provisional location in Princeton. It was in the spring of 1784, however, that a congressional committee visited Georgetown and inspected several alternative sites in the vicinity before concluding that the most desirable of these alternatives was the land north of Tiber Creek and west of where the White House now stands. While nothing came of this recommendation, unmarked even by legislative history, it established in Congress—and in the minds of the residents of the Georgetown locality—the possibility of the national capital city's being situated here. This further supported George Washington's efforts first in the designation of the Potomac as the seat of government and, second, in the later steps of acquiring the land and building the capital city.

A third element now was the realization that a substantial area of land was required for the proposed federal district. Having started with a minimal conception that embraced only sites required for federal buildings, Congress had gone on—in its authorization on 23 December 1784 of the Delaware River location—to describe an area of two to three miles square. Such an area was in President Washington's mind, apparently, when he commenced his consideration of the Potomac River site in 1790, and one of the notable factors in the evolu-

tion of the national capital city was Washington's decision to increase its size to ten miles square, the maximum allowed by the Constitution.

THE TEN-MILE SQUARE

The constitutional provision to create a national capital city is the beginning. Article I, section 8, provides that "Congress shall have power . . . to exercise exclusive legislation in all cases whatsoever, over such District (not exceeding ten miles square) as may, by cession of particular States, and the acceptance of Congress, become the seat of the government of the United States. . . ." Legislation to further this provision was enacted by Congress on 12 July 1790. This act specified a temporary location for ten years in Philadelphia, and the permanent location of the capital on the Potomac, at such point between the Eastern Branch and the Conococheague (a small Maryland stream near Hagerstown, in the Cumberland valley) as the president should designate.

No positive evidence has been found that George Washington influenced the provisions of this legislation, but much exists to document his long residence on the Potomac and his consequent familiarity with this region—not to mention what was probably of greater significance in the eyes of Congress, the *identification* of the Potomac region with the president. Moreover, the Potomac River site recommended itself to George Washington, and later to Jefferson, Madison, and others, because among the Atlantic port cities it appeared to offer the best access to the Ohio valley and the West, the key to territorial expansion and national unity. This was also the key to the widely disseminated ambitions and expectations of the Potomac Company canal—indeed, urban growth of the port cities of Georgetown and Alexandria appeared to support the same hope. The actual transaction between Alexander Hamilton and Thomas Jefferson that resulted in agreement on the Potomac site could have applied, however, to a number of different locations. When one searches for the reason for the location of the capital city on the Potomac, the most compelling thought is that it was put there because the president wanted it so.

Presidential responsibility for the specific location and boundaries of the city is more explicit. As the new nation made and shaped its capital city at Washington, several formative influences can be identified. The natural setting, the geography of rivers and streams; the soils, forests, and other resources; the shape of the land, its lowland marshes and heights; and, at finer detail, the springs, the places where streams could be crossed, the commanding views and other qualities of the landscape —all were influential in the decision to locate the city here, to give it specific boundaries and a certain size and shape. A second set of factors is associated with the earlier settlement of the area, the 10,000 years of aboriginal occupation by Indian tribes at various stages of their development, and nearly a century and a half of plantation life with its distinctive economy and culture. By 1790 this was largely a man-made landscape, not a raw frontier, and what was known of the land was the result of prior use. Most significantly, the land had been divided into plantations and towns and was held by private owners; both a way of looking upon land as an investment and a business, and a philosophy of urbanization had taken clear and firm shape.

There had also developed a strong awareness of the locality's regional position, especially as a place where travel and traffic north and south through the colonies could cross the broad tidal rivers that indented the coastal plain. The location commanded the chief route to the West with its rapidly developing agriculture and natural resources—and its potential industries. Finally, the city was a creation of its historical period. It incorporated not only the experience of building colonial towns but also the larger European view of urban design, amenity, architecture, and city life. As the barely articulated hopes took form for a democratic capital city to be deliberately created, these were the principal influences at work.

Plantations in the Potomac Valley. The traditional plantation system in the Potomac region paid immediate rewards but offered little for the future. Without the aid of fertilizers, crop rotation, and later agricultural improvements, the thin, sandy coastal soil became rapidly exhausted under the intensive single-cropping system. Fields would often be abandoned after only three years. While the typical large plantation may have embraced five hundred to a thousand acres, as little as thirty acres may actually have been in cultivation for tobacco. The rest was in woodland that was cleared as needed for fresh tobacco acreage. A variation of this system was the ownership of supplementary farms in the vicinity of the home farm, a practice illustrated by George Washington's land holdings at Mount Vernon.

In the vicinity of the federal city, lands had been settled in the latter half of the seventeenth century. Thus, by the time the national capital was moved here the traditional tobacco culture was in decline. Plantations were being farmed by second and third generation settlers. Many were poor and nearly all were eager to liquidate their real estate holdings. Urbanization provided an answer. A long history of "paper towns" in the Potomac valley, as John Reps referred to them in *Tidewater Towns*, had refined the technique of development. This experience, however, had also produced a quantity of abortive efforts to develop towns and of those that had achieved any settlement, few had flourished. What caused new hope for future increases in land values—as plantation acres would become town lots—was the interest of the national government in creating a capital city.

Planned Towns in the Potomac Valley. By common practice in the Potomac region, towns were established by an authorization from the colonial legislature designating both the site and the initial governors of the town. A survey would then determine more precisely the boundaries and the lots into which the town was divided, and would designate whatever public facilities or amenities might be considered part of the total development. In addition to these sites for public buildings, such tidewater town plans would provide for wharves, warehouses, and other commercial facilities.

Some small port cities were called into being by the tobacco trade; yet the ease with which cargoes could be collected from plantation wharves (often reached by "rolling roads" along which casks tightly packed with the weed were hauled), and the small number of towns

actually required, doomed the speculative efforts to failure. Nor were there feasible sites for such towns below
Alexandria on the Potomac. Even the requirement that
the exported tobacco be inspected and graded caused
only a moderate need for centralization in towns. In
contrast with the wide experience in land speculation
and such related work as surveying, there was little
understanding of the more complex and costly activities
of town building: the time needed, the skills required,
the financing obligated.

THE DELIBERATELY CREATED CITY

Deliberately created towns, whatever motives lay behind
their origin, had much in common with colonial urbanization elsewhere in the British Empire, not only in
America but especially in Ireland and the West Indies.
They also provided a marked contrast to the organic
growth of towns occurring gradually over long periods
of time and circumferentially around a center, often a
river crossing, a concentration of transportation routes,
or some single industry or economic activity like a port
or source of power. Whatever might be the environmental deficiencies, for example, of Boston and New
York, they were reasonably complete towns at each stage
of their growth. So, for that matter, was William Penn's
more carefully planned "green country town," Philadelphia. By rejecting the organic, unplanned pattern of
urban creation and growth, Washington had to accept
nearly a century as a half-formed city in which the contrast between its aspirations and its urban reality were
a continual subject of ridicule and satire.

Yet, as a deliberately created city—and in contrast to
many other cities of this kind—Washington did succeed.
It grew. Its growth followed the earlier expectations and
the original plan. And unlike the myriad other deliberately planned cities and capitals (as illustrated in certain capital cities of South America), Washington managed to divest itself of its earlier colonial origins and
definitely assert the identity of the new nation and its
capital city. More than a century later—in 1930—Washington became the city of 500,000 which L'Enfant had
envisioned and provided for, the capital of the coast-to-
coast nation of imperial scale which he had foreseen.

Only now, and for the first time, was the significance of
the 1791 plan fully recognized, and the greatness of its
designer appreciated.

Pierre Charles L'Enfant

The selection of Pierre Charles L'Enfant as the city's
planner tells something about city planning at the end
of the eighteenth century, that it could be considered
the province of "the artist of the army." This aside, it is
more reasonable to look upon the expectations of the
creators of the capital city as hopes that would be realized in ceremonial arrangements and the symbolism of
architecture and garden art, rather than in any products
of engineering and economics.

That L'Enfant had been the architect of Federal Hall,
where Congress met in New York City, a building widely
regarded as the most beautiful of its time and place, was
a further recommendation for him as a planner. Nor
should it be overlooked that part of L'Enfant's commission to design the capital city was that he propose
designs for its principal buildings. At the time he undertook the design of the new capital city he was firmly
established in New York and evoked the admiration and
respect of Charles Bulfinch and other leading architects
—whatever one thinks of the claim he later made of
being "able of commanding whatever business I liked."
Finally among L'Enfant's qualifications was the fact
that he was French. That Americans owed their independence to the French intervention—and that France
(as against England) hoped to reestablish in the New
World the hegemony that had ended in 1759 with the
loss of the Caribbean and Quebec—brought France to
a peak of popularity in the United States that favored
all things French.

With all his conspicuous French origins (an impression reinforced by his erratic command of the English
language), L'Enfant, it needs to be remembered, by the
time of his Washington commission in 1791 had been
resident in the United States fourteen years, had served
in the army, had practiced architecture in New York
City, and in other ways had assimilated himself into the

American scene. That he reflected his artistic background is to be expected, but it is also true that he translated this into language of the New World. Nowhere is this more evident than in his respect for the landscape and its treatment, and the buoyant confidence and optimism with which he viewed the expansion of this nation and the growth of its capital city. This is true despite the more obvious contrast between Jefferson, who "accepted" nature in the New World fashion, and L'Enfant who boldly restructured nature—especially water—in the fashion of Lenôtre. In the heavily forested river bottom, sparsely settled with modest plantation dwellings, L'Enfant envisioned a *new* kind of city, suited to the American space and reflecting the conditions of its national growth. It was new by contrast to the contemporaneous densities of Paris (before the boulevards of Haussmann and the growth and improvements of the nineteenth century), as new as the Garden District of New Orleans was by contrast to the Vieux Carré.

The mandate that L'Enfant received to design a new capital city was hardly original. Many new capitals had been carefully laid out in the colonies and states; many other nations in the New World had been provided with new or transformed capital cities; and European nations and principalities were liberally furnished with examples of capital cities created *de novo*. In these backgrounds, however, there was nearly always the factor of concentrated power. Thus, L'Enfant might be forgiven for expecting from President Washington the autocratic will, just as he had expected and received from him the patronage L'Enfant considered necessary to create the new city.

L'ENFANT AND WASHINGTON

The selection of L'Enfant is most easily explained by asking the question, Who else? In the selection of architects to design the Capitol and the White House, public competitions were held and numerous applicants submitted designs. In choosing the planner of the capital city, it was difficult even to establish required qualifications. L'Enfant's desire for the commission, his military record and acquaintance with President Washington, Jefferson, and other political leaders, his previous experi-

ence as an architect in New York City were all important, but more significant appears to have been his generally acknowledged design abilities—in engineering and landscape design as well as in architecture and the decorative arts. In fine, about L'Enfant's commission to design the city it can be said that he sought it; that George Washington appointed him; that the commission was vaguely defined by Washington and Jefferson; that the planner's relationship to the commissioners appointed to be in charge of building the city was poorly described; and that no businesslike contractual agreement defining the work to be done, the schedule, or the fee was ever concluded. Throughout the initiative remained L'Enfant's.

George Washington's selection of L'Enfant has found many defenders. What has been less noticed is that he kept the French designer on a short leash. Washington's first concern was to secure the capital on the Potomac—to secure it against those who were intent upon keeping it in Philadelphia, or relocating it in New York City, or moving it elsewhere amongst numerous other rival sites. President Washington was steadfastly aware of the thin margin of legislative victory that had finally placed the capital city on the Potomac. And as the difficulties of that decision increased they seemed to strengthen those who would have liked to see the capital located elsewhere.

A CAPITAL CITY WORTHY OF THE NATION

Certainly a great and glorious city plan, "worthy of the nation," as the phrase would run for many decades, would strengthen the Potomac's claim. That L'Enfant could provide this better than any other designer was President Washington's initial motivation. But as general and as president Washington had experienced L'Enfant's temperament, had little confidence in his judgment or tact (particularly in negotiation), and thought him extravagant, overoptimistic, egocentric, and prickly.

L'Enfant's biographers have been intent on using him for their own purposes. Elizabeth Kite presents him as an exemplar of French artistic genius; H. Paul Caemmerer aims at strengthening the claim of the designers of the McMillan Park Commission, and their advocate Charles Moore, that L'Enfant's plan formed the basis of the 1901–1902 plan* and of the modern city; Fiske Kimball reinforces L'Enfant's professional and technical stature. And while the facts about L'Enfant's life are both few and clear, they do not provide much illumination of his inner life nor as much direction of his career as a biographer would wish. For this direction one must search in the man's lifetime of rich experience.

THE EARLY YEARS

Pierre Charles L'Enfant was born in Paris on 2 August 1754, the son of a court painter, a decorative artist. He knew Paris and Versailles, the cities whose formal influence upon the Washington plan is most apparent. He received training in architecture and military engineering, and at the age of twenty-three was a lieutenant in the French army when he was recruited as one of a clandestine group of French military engineers, artillery, and cavalry officers whose mission was to aid the American Revolutionary movement and embarrass the British. L'Enfant's ambition was rewarded by a creditable military career and advancement to captain and then major. While he undertook the design and construction of fortifications and other engineering works, he achieved greater distinction from artistic odd jobs: he illustrated Von Steuben's drill manual, designed medals and insignia, drew portraits of colonial military leaders, and devised appropriate ceremonies. After Yorktown, L'Enfant was well remembered by his comrades and took a leading part in the organization of the politically powerful veterans' organization, the Society of the Cincinnati; in converting Federal Hall in New York City as the scene of Washington's first inaugural; and in other tasks required by the young republic and its political leaders.

Whatever may have been the influence of L'Enfant's Versailles boyhood or the Paris he knew when he left it at the age of twenty-three, a more proximate experience would have been his visit to Paris from December 1783

to March 1784. At this point he would be facing both the architectural and urban problems of the new nation and the matter of his own professional career as an architect. Here one wishes to relate such awareness as he may have had to Père Marc-Antoine Laugier's *Essai sur l'architecture* (1753) with its emphasis on urban squares and the straight, wide avenues explicitly derived from the hunting rides of the royal forests. Equally germane are the later designs by Pierre Patte, whose *Monuments* (1765) reproduced the detailed plans of Boffand, Hazon, and others, and expressed a design philosophy based on the development of important squares connected by wide avenues or circles from which avenues radiated. But since too little is known of L'Enfant's activities in 1784, one can but point to the obvious stylistic resemblance between contemporary proposals for Paris at this most important period in its urban development and the L'Enfant plan for Washington formulated eight years later. The urban designers of this period were concerned with creating more than urban landscapes: they dealt with the new urban agenda of commerce, waterfronts, and transportation, the new social architecture of hospitals, prisons, and educational institutions, and the new design of entire industrial towns. Amongst such urban designers L'Enfant was one.

THE PLANNING BEGINS

As L'Enfant addressed the planning of Washington, fully recognizing its importance, the ambitious scope had many consequences. It obliged him to rationalize a development strategy based on multiple centers of growth. More than anything else it was this that brought him into conflict with the commissioners. The large-scale investment needed to provide the extensive infrastructure for the multicentered city led L'Enfant to the quixotic recommendation of a large bond issue, a further point of conflict with the commissioners and the pay-as-you-go policy to which they were committed.

Over longer periods of time the decentralized multicentered city encouraged a diffusion of industrial and commercial location, and the growth of distinctly separate communities in each of which were found diverse income and ethnic groups. The walk-to-work city affected rich as well as poor—although from the start there were

---

* The term "1901–1902 plan" is used throughout in reference to the Washington plan published in January 1902 by the Senate Park Commission formed in 1901 during Senator James McMillan's chairmanship of the Senate District Committee. While the work of the McMillan Commission is correctly dated to 1901, publication of the commission's report and plan occurred in 1902: hence the run of dates 1901–1902. For further details, see Chapter V.

some individuals like Benjamin Latrobe, who was willing to travel on horseback from his residence in Kalorama to his work in the Navy Yard, six miles distant. If wealth and ethnicity did not shape Washington as they had shaped the older and larger cities of the East Coast, some distinctly separate character was given parts of the city that were predominantly oriented to trade, manufacturing, shipping, or certain government functions and installations, like the Navy Yard.

L'Enfant did not come on as an imperious figure—but he was. He did appear to some as truculent and obstinate. He had difficulty in getting people to accept him at his own estimate. With other architects and engineers his relations were better, but to them as to his political employers he appeared first and foremost an artist. As an artist, capable and confident in resolving problems, he boldly assumed that his solutions were the right ones. This sort of self-confidence may have been just what a new and still shaky nation required, but there were times when the nation did not seem to appreciate it. What he was most confident about was the urban programme, and since *that* had not been given to him—not by Washington or Jefferson, and not by the commissioners—he made it up: churches, embassies, universities, monuments, gardens, public buildings and all, the large public functions and the small domestic details, all delivered with a charming French accent, and without hesitation. Thus, the biography of its designer was translated into the form of the city.

The Land and the Watercourses

At the time of L'Enfant's appointment, Congress had agreed on a location on the Potomac River at the head of navigation *of*—as specified in the Constitution—*as much as ten miles square to be organized as a federal district*. The land to be occupied by L'Enfant's city comprised the river "flats" (the flood plains both of the Potomac and of the Anacostia northward to the Talbot terrace) and the Wicomico terrace, a step higher, extending from just north of the Mall to the boundaries of the formal city at the Wicomico-Sunderland escarpment as later generally defined by Boundary Street

(Florida Avenue). The subject of L'Enfant's design was defined, therefore, by the Potomac and its Eastern Branch, the Anacostia, and the hills that framed the basin city to the north. In its future growth, the city would expand upward into the higher lands surrounding the initial core, in all directions save down the Potomac.

These old river terraces, north of the flats, were further slashed by the stream valleys, most notably Rock Creek. In the larger geographical context, the site embraced the fall line at Little Falls, where the coastal plain meets the Piedmont Plateau, and thereby symbolically linked the tidewater plantation life with the Piedmont farming areas. Like London, Washington was located at the extreme end of a navigable water, far enough inland to be protected from sea attack but accessible to a flourishing sea trade.

PLAIN, PIEDMONT, AND TIDEWATER

Apart from the small but growing ports of Alexandria and Georgetown, the site selected for the city contained but few agricultural clearings and plantation houses in its predominantly wooded expanse. The varied geology, ranging from the flood plains to the palisades of the Potomac and the steep ravines of Rock Creek, combined with highly differentiated climates within a small radius, allowed a wide range of plant species. The environmental detail accurately reflected the fundamental condition of the site: the conjunction of coastal plains and Piedmont. L'Enfant's Washington was framed at Boundary Street by the first evidences of the Piedmont, the Talbot escarpment. Within this boundary the old sea beds with their layers of sediment and their susceptibility to erosion were clothed in sweet gum, oak, and hickory forests. Sycamore, willow, and birch filled the stream valleys of the flood plain of the Anacostia and the Potomac. The higher lands of the Piedmont offered a more complex geology with a greater variety of soils and rocky outcrops on its characteristic terraces. Here the forest cover was composed of oak and tulip poplar, sassafras, beech, and basswood.

Given the tidewater character of the area, the outstanding natural resource was the Potomac fishery, particularly the herring, shad, salmon, sturgeon, and other anadromous varieties that seasonally teemed to spawn in the river at the falls. This fishery together with the shell-fish—oysters, clams, and crabs—supported the relatively dense population of Indians and their characteristic village life, and until nearly the end of the nineteenth century sustained the local community and also provided an important economic activity. Associated with the fishery as an element of the local economy as well as the ecology, and expressing equally the underlying geographical character of the area, was the bird life. The migratory waterfowl were an outstanding element, and turkeys, quail, and other game birds were also abundant.

These characteristics of the Potomac at the head of navigation, where that geological factor known as the fall line presents a distinctive topographical feature, have received much comment. Perhaps no one has better summarized it than Henry Fleet, who in 1631 eulogized: "This place without all question is the most pleasant and healthful place in all this country, and most convenient for habitation, the air temperate in summer and not violent in winter. It aboundeth with all manner of fish. The Indians in one night commonly will catch thirty sturgeons in a place where the river is not above twelve fathom broad. And as for deer, buffaloes, bears, turkeys, the woods do swarm with them and the soil is exceedingly fertile." Other observers noted the abundant water power and excellent mill sites, the ease with which the river as it narrowed could be crossed by ferries and bridges, and additional desirable conditions for settlement and urban growth.

THE DRAINAGE SYSTEM AND HYDRAULICS

The drainage patterns of the area included the primary elements of the Potomac and the Anacostia Rivers; the important boundary between Georgetown and the federal city, Rock Creek; and the large tidal inlet, Tiber Creek. This estuary, also called Goose Creek, originated in an extensive watershed, the upper part of which had been named Tiber Creek nearly a hundred years earlier by a settler who had entitled his plantation "Rome." (Tiber Creek is not, as some historians have assumed, a name that derived from the neoclassicism that engulfed the early city.) Major tributaries of Rock Creek—notably Pine Creek, now Piney Branch—reached north and east through the city, and important streams like Reedy Branch and Slash Run were topographical features noted on early maps.

As they presented initial obstacles to travel (because they created important flood plains), as they determined forest species and plant communities, and as their steep banks were easily eroded, these watercourses had important effects upon later development. They also had significance as water supply, and parts of the drainage system, such as Rock Creek, supported significant water power mills, or, like the Tiber and lower Rock Creek, were navigable to the river craft of the day. Much of L'Enfant's extensive canal system simply straightened out and rationalized the natural stream locations, improving their use for navigation, while still allowing them to serve their primary purpose of drainage.

As will be seen, however, L'Enfant would not be satisfied simply to solve the city's drainage problem; he wanted to use water in the form of fountains, reflecting pools, and—his most spectacular proposal—in a cascade that was to emerge from the base of the Capitol and flow down to join the projected City Canal in a carefully designed reflecting pool that formed an integral element in the functional canal system. It is in such proposals that L'Enfant's debt to European landscape design is most evident, echoing the great Renaissance tradition of cascade design.

Yet, while the aim was aesthetic, the hydraulics was entirely practical. Something had to be done with the waters of Tiber Creek, and the cascade was an ornamental and dramatic means of carrying it to tidewater. In the great cascades of the Renaissance, important iconographic themes were involved. L'Enfant here, however, appears content to use water for its dramatic effect. He can hardly have been oblivious, however, of its potential to echo the stairs that would be needed to provide access to the Capitol, and there is no doubt he envisioned a truly monumental building on this site.

Travelers' Descriptions of Early Washington

The approach to Washington from the north offered travelers a synoptic view of the town and its natural setting from the hills above the Bladensburg road. The view reached to Georgetown and showed both the Anacostia and the Potomac Rivers framing the beginnings of the federal city. Many travelers commented on the panorama from this point—and indeed the progress of the city's growth could be described by the evolution of the Capitol and others of its principal buildings. In the spring of 1797, the French traveler La Rochefoucauld-Liancourt set down in his journal characteristic details of the city at this time.

The La Rochefoucauld-Liancourt journal is the most comprehensive account by a contemporary traveler of the creation and development of the city to this date. It embraces the city's legislative authorization, land acquisition, financing, and administration. The author takes the measure of the speculation in land and identifies the effect of this activity in stimulating the initial urbanization around the Capitol, the several competing port areas along the Potomac and the Eastern Branch, and other early urban growth nuclei. Despite La Rochefoucauld-Liancourt's approval of the location and commercial prospects of the city, his expectation for its future was gloomy, taking into account its overlarge size, its widely separated centers of urban development (he mentioned particularly the distance from the Capitol to the President's House), and the land speculation and influence of mercantile interests. He correctly foresaw a long period of inconvenience and physical discomfort for the city's inhabitants. The adverse impact of this condition upon the federal establishment and on official visitors to the city seemed to La Rochefoucauld-Liancourt to imperil the entire venture. "One cannot say that [visitors] are pushing the idea of 'comfort' to extremes when they wish to be preserved from falling into mud holes for lack of paved roads, or from breaking their necks for lack of street lights. This sort of inconvenience will endure here for many years, given the size of the city's plan and the great distance between the two centers of public affairs," he concluded.

Yet, over time, this disbelief that "the Federal City will ever develop to the point where it will become a pleasant place to live for the kind of people who are destined to inhabit it" proved as wrong as the author's larger expectation that the federal union itself would soon dissolve.

THE TIMELESS HYPNOTIC CHARM

That the French visitor should have totally ignored the contribution of his countryman to the city is surprising. Without mentioning L'Enfant by name, his most direct comment is: "The plan has been well conceived and cleverly, even magnificently drawn; as a matter of fact, it is the very magnificence of the conception that gives it its dreamlike quality." But in that single insight he perfectly expresses the timeless hypnotic charm of L'Enfant's drawing, deliberately designed to touch the imagination.

The densely wooded character of the land to be occupied by the city was remarked by travelers. The stage from Baltimore passed through an almost uninterrupted forest, and the arrival at Washington was announced by the sound of trees' being lopped to facilitate the work of surveyors. In limited areas in the center of the projected city, the woods had been more fully and systematically cleared. Here the sites for public buildings were to be found, and whatever construction there was was evidenced. Isaac Weld, Jr., reported in 1796 that "excepting the streets and avenues and a small part of the ground adjoining the public buildings, the whole place is covered with trees." A few locations, wrote Thomas Twining in the same year, "assumed more the appearance of a regular avenue, the trees having been cut down in a straight line." Francis Baily thought that perhaps half of the area projected for the city had been cleared of trees by the fall of 1796, and perceived the site as "broad avenues in a park bounded on each side by thick woods."

THE PORT TOWNS: ALEXANDRIA AND GEORGETOWN

Two towns, Alexandria and Georgetown, were already to be found at the head of Potomac navigation. Both closely resembled what, in fact, they had been created in the image of, the British provincial town. Red brick and green trees pleasantly and closely arranged themselves along the waterfront. Here one found on a limited scale the amenities of eighteenth-century urban life: homes close to occupations and recreation, inns, and taverns; lively streets and markets crowded with cattle, sheep, hogs, poultry, produce, and eager buyers and curiosity-seekers. Of public buildings and churches there were, as yet, few. Theaters and concert halls were unknown, and the mansions of the rich and influential were still built on a small scale and with rudimentary taste. The parks and pleasure grounds of the city plan had not yet appeared, but a short walk brought the hunter into woods or open fields, and the river teemed with fish for the angler.

Like all port cities, Georgetown and Alexandria were cosmopolitan, and whatever transpired or was produced in the world soon found its way here. The waterfronts bristling with masts and the warehouses announced the purpose of these towns, to ship and receive goods. These port functions were recorded in hogsheads of tobacco and flour exported, and goods of every description gathered in from Bristol, Glasgow, and other British ports. The population of Georgetown and Alexandria from the start had been predominantly composed of Scots; their names were stamped on plantations, streets, landmarks, business firms, and establishments of every sort, and their accent marked the place along colonial towns.

Whatever their shortcomings, the towns were distinctly urban creations, complete with town governments, public works, courts, prisons, and other municipal institutions. Here also one found the early water-power industries, the flour and grist mills, foundries and forges, sawmills and lime furnaces, distributed along lower Rock Creek and lesser streams. The Potomac port towns were regularly laid out, with streets at right angles. Although travel was still mainly by horseback, the streets were wide and modern, with no trace of the winding lanes of some older cities. The river was crossed by ferries; the single bridge proposed at Georgetown was still in prospect.

It was possible in 1791 to entertain the highest hopes for the "Potomac route to the West," and its stimulus to urban growth at the fall line. Expectations for Washington's growth were being sustained by the improvement of river navigation and by canals around the falls. Downriver traffic five years later took the form of narrow barges loaded with tobacco, flour, and other commodities that passed Great Falls on an inclined plane down which the cargoes of hogsheads were lowered, and, afloat again, passed Little Falls via a canal on the Maryland side of the river.

L'Enfant's Survey: March 1791

In such a Potomac region Pierre Charles L'Enfant arrived on Wednesday, 9 March 1791, at Georgetown, and immediately started his reconnaissance. Quartering the river bottom and ridges of the site of the future city on horseback he came quickly to an appreciation of its streams and marshes, its uncertain and fragile river edges, the few really commanding heights of land, the ridges and terraces, and the strategic importance of a few feet in elevation. These factors had already determined the drainage, roads, and stream crossings, the existing and prospective settlement, and the siting of many individual plantation houses.

L'Enfant had been directed by President Washington to commence his reconnaissance "at the lower end and work upwards." He continued his work as weather allowed over the next ten days. He carefully noted the approaches to the city from Baltimore and the north, and the few but important ferries, fords, bridges, and stream crossings. Starting at the point where the Potomac and the Anacostia come together, he traveled north toward the height of land where the future Capitol would stand. Turning east he examined the shoreline of the Anacostia as high as the ferry road that led into the future city. Here he turned west and passed Jenkins Hill on the north side, continuing along the Wicomico ridge to the crossing of Rock Creek that led into Georgetown.

L'Enfant noted that the days were cold and rainy. The landscape was obscured by a heavy fog, but he managed to see sufficient of its principal features to form an immediate and important opinion: the high flat land to the east of Jenkins Hill offered far greater opportunity for urban development than the more constricted area north of Tiber Creek on which Jefferson and Washington had been concentrating. He also decided that Jenkins Hill, the highest spot in the land between the Potomac and the Anacostia, was the most desirable location for the Capitol.

Nearly one hundred fifty years had passed since the first explorers had passed through the region, and it had long been divided into plantations, large in acreage but typically occupied only by a small dwelling and accommodation for a few black farm workers. Only the largest plantations could command a Potomac headland for a mansion site. This was an agricultural frontier. Signs of change were witnessed in the growth of the port towns of Alexandria and Georgetown and there was evidence, however frustrated, of urban aspiration in the platted but still unoccupied riverside towns of Hamburg and Carrollsburg. It was the end of the tobacco boom. The soils of the immediate locality could not support a thriving colonial agriculture. Where port towns at the head of Potomac navigation were growing, as in Georgetown and Alexandria, it was because they had tapped a more distant hinterland of wheat farming deep in the Piedmont and had become exporting centers for the Atlantic trade. The future growth of this business depended upon the improved access provided by new turnpikes, canals, improvements in river navigation, and the large expansion of grist and flour mills.

PRESIDENT WASHINGTON'S STRATEGY FOR THE PROPRIETORS

L'Enfant's initial reconnaissance had been craftily specified by President Washington in order to confuse the proprietors, particularly Robert Peter and others who had been bidding up the price of real estate in the initially favored site north of Tiber Creek immediately east of Georgetown. This strategy Washington disclosed to Francis Deakins and Benjamin Stoddert. Noting in his letter of 2 March 1791 to Deakins that L'Enfant was "directed to begin at the lower end and work upwards," Washington added that "*nothing further is communicated to him.*" This cat and mouse game backfired. Not many days passed before Washington had greatly enlarged his conception of the amount of land required for the federal city, and accepted L'Enfant's estimation of the greater desirability of the land between Jenkins Hill and the Anacostia. Within a week of L'Enfant's first view of the site, Washington was writing Deakins and Stoddert that he intended to view this part of the federal district on his next visit. How this changed attitude came about is not known, but in addition to some meeting, or letter now lost, or other direct message from L'Enfant to Washington, the French planner's enthusiasm may have been communicated to young Daniel Carroll who owned the largest tract of

land commencing with Carrollsburg and reaching north, to the east of Goose Creek, to the tract owned by Deakins, with whom Washington was in close touch.

Through the wet, early spring months, L'Enfant pressed his survey. Before March had ended Washington enlarged his instructions to embrace more fully the task of planning the city. In his letter of 31 March 1791 to Jefferson, Washington confirmed his enlarged oral instructions to L'Enfant, and further described his expanded view of the size of the city, now seen as "containing from three to five thousand acres," the whole of which "shall be surveyed and laid off as a city (which Major L'Enfant is now directed to do)." The same letter, written from Mount Vernon, also described for the first time a new arrangement with the proprietors that promised to solve the major financial problems posed by the necessity of purchasing sufficient land for the future city.

The Proprietors Enter Partnership with the Government. The new arrangement provided that the proprietors should convey their lands to the federal government, and after the city plan had been prepared they would receive back, in exchange, every other one of the platted lots. For a set price of twenty-five pounds per acre, the proprietors would be compensated for federal building reservations as well as for the unplatted lands required for public use as squares, walks, and similar elements. The land required for streets and alleys would be dedicated by the proprietors without charge. At one stroke, this new arrangement placed the proprietors in partnership with the federal government—and with each other —in urban development.

This partnership departed from the way in which the development of those earlier "paper towns" of the Potomac had been attempted. In these towns, the original owner sold outright to a new party who proposed to undertake the tasks of urbanization. Where, then, did the new arrangement come from? The research of Louis Dow Scisco attributes the concept to George Walker, a small businessman of Georgetown who also owned one tract of land and part of another in the valley of the Anacostia, the prime center of L'Enfant's city. The overwhelmingly Scottish character of the towns of

Georgetown and Alexandria and of the proprietors themselves, however, suggests that the scheme may well have reflected the real estate and legal experience in realizing James Craig's "New Town" in Edinburgh in 1767.

The details of the arrangement were also very congenial. The planters were left in possession of their homes, the sites of which were excluded from the partnership arrangement. Family burying grounds were left undisturbed. And, for the other side, the decisive factor was that the developers of the federal city secured the land substantially without cost, thus allowing their limited funds to be devoted to the heavy expenses of building.

PLANNING ON A VISIBLY GRAND SCALE

In his important meeting with the proprietors on 29 March 1791 at Suter's Tavern in Georgetown, described by Washington in his diary, the president reviewed: the need to enhance the feasibility of the city building project, and thus counter the still-present threat that the capital might not be moved from Philadelphia at all; the desirability of planning on a visibly grand scale; the absolute necessity of overcoming the limited financial resources available for building the city; the self-defeating competition for public building sites among the proprietors, particularly as between those of Georgetown and Carrollsburg; and the need for a tract of land so large that it would embrace both Alexandria and Georgetown, the two established urban centers at the head of Potomac navigation, whose commercial success appeared to assure the future of the national capital city. Above all, Washington urged recognition of the "common cause" to build the city that would stretch from Georgetown to the Anacostia. It was a successful meeting, and on the following day the eighteen proprietors signed the agreement to convey their lands by the proposed deeds of trust.

The terms of the agreement certainly were conducive to a liberal view of the city's size. Since the land acquisition costs had been drastically reduced, the earlier restraint no longer obstructed Washington's increasingly expansive view of the city's boundary, which now moved steadily northward. First the boundary was seen as the Bladensburg-Georgetown road; then it moved to what is now Massachusetts Avenue; and ultimately it moved to what is now Florida Avenue, along the rugged base of the old river terrace called the Wicomico-Sunderland escarpment. These changes caused perturbation among the proprietors, for L'Enfant's personal view of the city en grand was now being affirmed by the expansionist views of his patron, and, despite the uncertainties about land acquisition, L'Enfant proceeded steadily with his planning work. By 27 June 1791, all difficulties with the landowners had been resolved and deeds of trust were executed with fifteen of the proprietors.

L'Enfant's Memorandum: Urban Design, Landscape Image, and a Strategy for Development

By June 22 L'Enfant was prepared with an initial plan which he took to Mount Vernon and discussed with the president at what must have been a decisive encounter. While minor changes were incorporated in this plan —prior to the version of it, dated August 19, which Washington accepted in Philadelphia and used as the basis for the sale of lots and other decisions—it is remarkable that so complete and detailed a conception could have been arrived at in such a brief period of time and under such uncertainties. From March 9, when L'Enfant arrived in Georgetown and commenced work, to June 22, when his preliminary plan was completed, less than three and a half months had elapsed. To be sure, his efforts were accelerated by frequent reminders from Washington and Jefferson, as well as the commissioners, of the need for dispatch. But by contrast to the concerns expressed about the city's boundaries and the negotiations with the proprietors, almost no attention appears to have been given the plan itself, nor did Washington mention the meeting of June 22 in his diary. Fortunately, both the plan itself (in the August 19 outline version known as the "Map of Dotted Lines") and a memorandum to accompany it were prepared by L'Enfant and have survived. The memorandum describes how the planner went about his work as well as the plan he created.

"Map of Dotted Lines," the Outline Plan Produced by L'Enfant to Keep President Washington Informed of Progress in Surveying Sites for Major Public Buildings, 1791

After some preliminary qualifications as to the nature of this initial design—the limited time available, the unfinished graphic presentation, the small scale of the plan which precluded much detail — L'Enfant then moved to the positive character of his proposal, "correct only as it respects the situation and distance of objects"

but adequately reflecting the topography and illustrating the major features of the proposed city, as well as emphasizing the unity of its several parts. The President's House was sited on a rise just north of the Tiber Creek. From this site major radial avenues stretched outward and crossed grid streets and other radials at points intended by L'Enfant as nodes of urban development. The major radial avenue commenced at Rock Creek and was traced by L'Enfant through the President's House; it then ran southeast where it met the foot of Jenkins Hill, site for the Capitol, and ended at the Anacostia River. Thus, Pennsylvania Avenue became the city's principal avenue—and eventually the nation's great ceremonial and processional route.

L'ENFANT'S STREETS AND AVENUES: "THESE I MADE BROAD"

"Having determined some principal points to which I wished to make the others subordinate," L'Enfant's memoir explained, "I made the distribution regular with every street at right angles, north and south, east and west, and afterwards opened some in different directions, as avenues to and from every principal place, wishing thereby not merely to contract [contrast?] with the general regularity, nor to afford a greater variety of seats with pleasant prospects, which will be obtained from the advantageous ground over which these avenues are chiefly directed, but principally to connect each part of the city, if I may so express it, by making the real distance less from place to place, by giving them reciprocity of sight, and by making them thus seemingly connected, promote a rapid settlement over the whole extent, rendering those even of the most remote parts an addition to the principal, which without the help of these, were any such settlement attempted, it would be languid, and lost in the extent, and become detrimental to the establishment. Some of these avenues were also necessary to effect the junction of several roads to a central point in the city, by making these roads shorter, which is effected [by directing them] to those leading to Bladensburg and the Eastern Branch—both of which are made above a little shorter, exclusive of the advantage of those leading immediately to the wharves at Georgetown. The hilly ground which surrounds that place the growth of which it must impede, by inviting settlements

25

on the city side of Rock Creek, which cannot fail soon to spread along all those avenues which will afford a variety of pleasant rides, and become the means for a rapid intercourse with all parts of the city, to which they will serve as does the main artery in the animal body, which diffuses life throughout the smaller vessels, and inspires vigor, and activity throughout the whole frame.

"These avenues I made broad, so as to admit of their being planted with trees leaving 80 feet for a carriage way, 30 feet on each side for a walk under a double row of trees, and allowing 10 feet between the trees and the houses. The first of these avenues and the most direct one begins at the Eastern branch and ends over Rock Creek at the wharves at Georgetown, along the side of which it is continued to the bridge over to the Virginia shore, and down to the lower canal to the Potomac, along the sides of which it may be of great advantage to have such a road extended to the upper canal to facilitate dragging the boats up and down."

L'ENFANT'S UNIFIED VIEW

Throughout his presentation L'Enfant urged "embracing in one view the whole extent from the Eastern branch to Georgetown, and from the banks of the Potomac to the mountains [the hills surrounding the city]." While not understating his concern with the urban design, L'Enfant stressed consistently his aim to generate development of the city throughout its entire large area, and the simultaneous development of its several major districts. What L'Enfant offered was not simply the urban design that has survived and attracted admiration over the centuries, but a theory of urban growth and development that was both original and far in advance of its time. It was this growth strategy that brought him into conflict with President Washington and the commissioners, and eventually caused his downfall and his dismissal. The man was rejected, but never his plan.

By his system of avenues, L'Enfant the planner thought both to unify the vast extent of the city and its many well-distributed functional centers of development, and to provide a means of directing the development effort. This development, he believed, would occur initially along the avenues and later in the more intensive local growth of the various districts around their centers, these to be established by major public buildings. He also considered that by such disposition he could engender competition among the several key points of the multinucleated city. Nor did he evade the designation of what he regarded as the principal artery of initial development, "across the Tiber above tidewater"—or approximately Pennsylvania Avenue. "Where the tidewater comes into Tiber Creek, is the position the most capable of any within the limits of the city, to favor those grand improvements of public magnitude which may serve as a sample for all subsequent undertakings."

In favoring this spot as the principal focus for initial development, L'Enfant was influenced by the alignment of his proposed City Canal. This canal was a means both of draining the low-lying marshland to either side of Tiber Creek and at its head, and of supplying a means of transportation for goods into the heart of the city. The canal would "facilitate a conveyance" which would stimulate the growth of markets to supply the city.

THE CAPITOL AND THE PRESIDENT'S HOUSE

Here within the principal focus, too, L'Enfant located the Capitol, for as his memorandum explains, he could discover no other location as advantageous as the one he first identified at the top of Jenkins Hill, "which stands as a pedestal waiting for a superstructure." Balancing this, he proposed a site for the presidential "palace" on the edge of the Wicomico terrace, shrewdly reminding President Washington that it was precisely this location "which very justly attracted your attention when first viewing the ground which is upon the west side and near the mouth of the Tiber." Minor adjustments in the site, he explained, would provide a more extensive view down the Potomac and connecting with the Capitol through the system of public walks, gardens, and avenues. Finally L'Enfant's memorandum described the Mall, "the vast esplanade," in whose center—at the point where the views from the Capitol to the west and the President's House to the south intersected—he found the appropriate site for an equestrian monument, with suitable landscape embellishments.

Anticipating the objection (reflecting Jefferson's and other earlier and more limited conceptions of the city) that the Capitol and the President's House should be closer together, L'Enfant argued that the distance between the two buildings was not all that great in his plan, and further that "no message to nor from the President is to be made without a sort of decorum which will doubtless point out the propriety of Committee waiting on him in carriage should his palace be even contiguous to Congress." In addition, L'Enfant noted, the interest and delights provided by the gardens and walks of the President's House and the Capitol, and the development of the connecting avenue with "play houses, rooms of assembly, academies, and all such sort of places as may be attractive to the learned and afford diversion to the idle" would make the apparent distance less.

The City of Illusion. Following out the theory expressed in L'Enfant's multinuclear city plan, appropriate sites were designated for the major capital city functions; it was expected that around these, functional districts would develop. Thus, along the most desirable waters for navigation, the Navy Yard, the marine hospital, the arsenal, and the city's commercial waterfront with its wharves, warehouses, and industries were situated. By contrast to these working elements disposed along the north bank of the Anacostia, that part of the capital oriented to the Potomac was proposed as the monumental, residential, and official quarter. The critical location of the City Hall immediately south of the Capitol was closely linked to the location of the commercial heart of the city along the Eastern Branch and the expectations for the City Canal as a commercial waterway. In the over-all conception, the federal and local functions were closely interwoven. There was no sense of economic or social class segregation. If the city as a whole was to function as it was planned, L'Enfant was correct in asserting that its various functional elements should be simultaneously developed and be able to interact with each other.

The city of illusion was reinforced in its architecture and urban design by provisions for the landscaping. Functional elements of the city, such as the canal, were to become decorative features as well, their turning basins and port features being used as reflecting pools.

The grounds of major public buildings were designed as gardens and as parks and promenades. At the Capitol a magnificent cascade forty feet high and a hundred feet wide, of a size that would permit it to be seen from the President's House, was proposed by L'Enfant to carry the water of the Tiber from its bed beyond the city to its ultimate destination at the base of Jenkins Hill, where it would augment the waters of the canal and urge them towards the Potomac. In these features of his plan L'Enfant is most clearly the child of the great Lenôtre, whose ingenious use of water is a compelling feature of L'Enfant's boyhood home, Versailles.

L'ENFANT'S LANDSCAPE DESIGN

L'Enfant's masterly and brief memorandum concluded with the vividly expressed landscape image: "the whole will acquire new sweetness being laid over the green of a field well level and made brilliant by the shade of a few trees artfully planted." In this comment on the open central composition, L'Enfant reflects the spirit of the age that was creating Saint Petersburg and other princely capitals, that age in which the French designers were achieving their renown. It was a period when the divorce of engineering from architecture and landscape design had not yet materialized; so, in the work of L'Enfant, is it impossible to determine where one set of professional interests ceases and another begins.

In two distinct ways Washington was conceived as a landscape design. It looked forward in its recognition and adaptation of the natural features of the riverfront, the surrounding hills (especially across the Potomac to the west), and the spacious river meadows to be occupied by the city. Yet, it expressed continuity with the formal tradition of landscape design. This tradition L'Enfant knew best from the work of Lenôtre at Versailles and the great chateau gardens of the Loire valley, but it was also part of the larger body of renaissance garden art of Italy and indeed informed the deliberately planned princely cities of the Rhineland. In the formal landscape tradition, the modern distinction between landscape design, urban design, and architecture had not appeared, however, particularly in the crucial matter of siting the principal buildings. In this, as L'Enfant knew, practical considerations of drainage were as important as the commanding prospect or the prominent situation.

The Formal City. To later generations, the Washington plan in its formal characteristics has seemed a paradoxical echo of old-world baroque autocracy in the design of the capital city of a democracy. Such a judgment not only projects Jacksonian democracy two generations ahead of its advent, but attributes to the late eighteenth century design alternatives that only a more sophisticated, historically later period possessed. In plain fact, Washington and Jefferson as well as L'Enfant saw only one form of excellence in urban design—that of the age—*the formal city.* It could be accepted or ignored, as it had been in the gridiron cities. It could express a standard of excellence. But there was no alternative. Historical criticism has allowed the present day to see the design of Philadelphia and Savannah, with their regular plan, their park squares, and their waterfronts, as key representatives of a native town planning tradition. They were not so regarded at the time of the planning of Washington, however, and the civic virtues that today they are seen as having were little appreciated at the earlier time.

MEANINGS OF THE L'ENFANT PLAN

In the view of contemporaries, when the plan of Washington was first exhibited in Paris in 1793 it was correctly received by a culture immersed in the rationalism of the neoclassic, and was compared with Pierre Patte's paradigmatic assemblage of proposals for the city's reconstruction rather than with any actual cities or their plans. It was immediately set into the broader canvas of the world's cities, of urban thought, and of the contemporary search for the ideal city—in the case of Washington, a city oriented to a new nation and a new continent, and to the future.

What L'Enfant intended, what he proposed, what survived Andrew Ellicott's translation of his plan, what the 1901–1902 plan recognized and continued, and what has endured to the present day are all important and interesting problems. They have been analyzed from time to time by careful and intelligent students among whom Elbert Peets, Fiske Kimball, William Partridge,

and John Reps are the leaders. This analysis is being continued by the National Capital Planning Commission, the Commission of Fine Arts, and by others, working with still unpublished sketches and documents. One can therefore expect revisions in what has been thought in the past. In the end, however, a large measure of judgment and interpretation will be required to answer the questions posed by the L'Enfant plan. How large a building did L'Enfant intend the Capitol or the President's House to be? Were his squares intended as paved and built-up urban designs, or leafy green intervals in the man-made city? In further detail, were the urban trees proposed by L'Enfant to take the naturalistic forms of the elms and maples found along the streets of Washington and other American cities, or the more geometrical shapes of the pruned and trimmed plane trees, limes, and other trees indigenous to European cities? Was the Mall essentially a visual conception as a line of sight, or was it seriously and functionally intended as a pedestrian walk and carriage drive?

The L'Enfant Plan: Beginnings of Built Washington

L'Enfant's sketch plan of 22 June 1791 was laid before the proprietors by George Washington the next week and their approval was noted in the president's diary. There is disappointingly little evidence, however, of Washington's own appreciation of the creative dimensions of this work; on the contrary, his expressed concern was the city's boundaries and the procurement of deeds from the landowners. Hence, Washington's participation in such changes as were made by L'Enfant in the plan between its presentation to the proprietors and its subsequent development must remain unknown. One can only conjecture that L'Enfant made these changes, incorporating Washington's wishes as he understood them. That the plan had secured the measure of approval that would allow it to be translated immediately into building activity is evident. And, as L'Enfant had recommended, the work of clearing and building commenced with the system of avenues he had planned. It was along these avenues that he anticipated the initial development of the national capital city would take place.

If detailed response of President Washington to L'Enfant's plan was obscure, the commissioners to whom the development of the city was entrusted were equally silent. And if Jefferson's sole substantial comment was a suggestion of draftsmanship, the commissioners in commenting on the plan confined themselves to deciding that the federal city should be called Washington, that the streets of the gridiron system should be designated by numbers and letters, that river soundings be specified on the plan, and that the plan itself be entitled "A Map of the City of Washington in the Territory of Columbia." Attention of all officials from the president to the commissioners was concentrated upon the pragmatic issue of the promotion and sale of the

Andrew Ellicott's Plan of the City of Washington in the Territory of Columbia, 1792

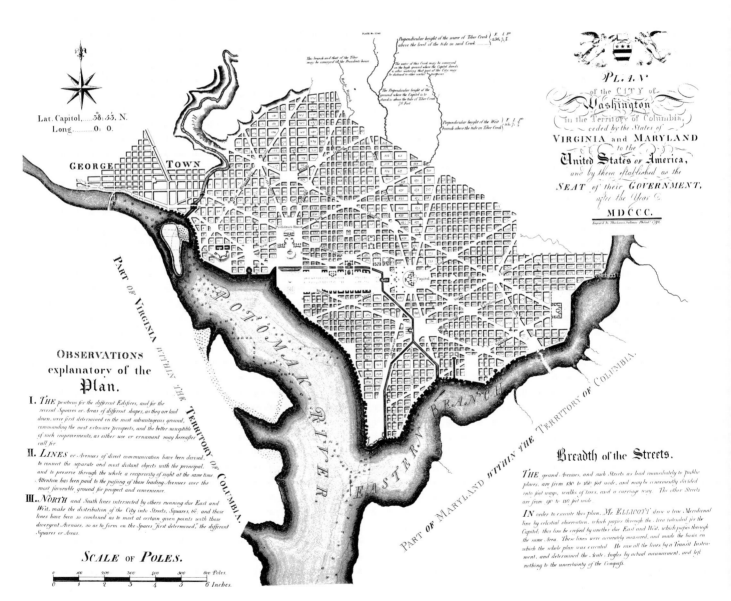

29

Andrew Ellicott's Topographical Map of the Territory of Columbia, 1793

city lots, since this provided the entire source of funds for urban development and the construction of public buildings. For this the officials needed quantities of engraved copies of the city plan, at a scale that would show both the lots to be sold and the principal streets and public improvements proposed. Intent upon perfecting his conception, L'Enfant did not produce the engraved plans, and chose to withhold his manuscript plan. The work of producing the engraved plans was handed over by President Washington to Andrew Ellicott, the city's surveyor, who followed L'Enfant's earlier plans with little change.

The Work of Andrew Ellicott. With his own surveyor's notes and some direct or indirect access to L'Enfant's work as well as his own memory of the designer's plan, Andrew Ellicott in 1792 produced the plan that was transformed into the "official city plan" of streets and lots. This map (shown here) was engraved by Thackara & Vallance of Philadelphia, and published in October 1792. Ellicott did not alter the major physical features of the plan L'Enfant had proposed, nor did he resolve its major problems. Sites for major buildings, radial avenues, gridiron streets, open spaces, and environmental features—all are approximately as L'Enfant proposed. Ellicott straightened several radial avenues and eliminated others, and, as instructed, provided information on the depths of the navigable waters. Ellicott also numbered the blocks so that the necessary land sales could be efficiently carried on. "Observations explanatory of the Plan," abbreviated from the L'Enfant manuscript plan, appear in the margins of the Ellicott version. In 1793, Ellicott also drew a topographical map which defined the land formations, the major land routes, and the water routes around the L'Enfant city. In this drawing Ellicott followed the suggestion Thomas Jefferson had earlier made to L'Enfant that the map should be oriented to the northwest in order to bring the rectangular boundaries of the planned city into congruity with a rectangular sheet of paper.

The Work of William T. Partridge. In 1926, William Partridge, chief draftsman of the 1901–1902 McMillan Commission design staff, was retained by the National Capital Park and Planning Commission to interpret and reconstruct the L'Enfant design of the federal city. Among other study drawings, Partridge prepared a drawing showing the comparative plans of L'Enfant and Ellicott. On this comparison map, the major deviation is the straighter course taken by Massachusetts Avenue on the Ellicott plan. Without doubt Washington endorsed L'Enfant's plan and wished only to translate it into a form that met the practical requirements of de-

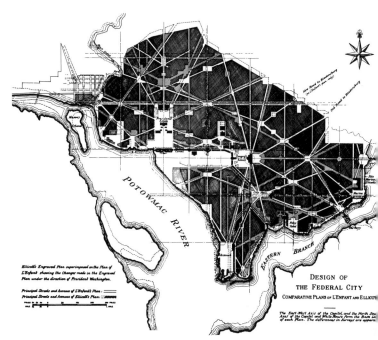

Comparative Plans of L'Enfant and Ellicott As Shown in William T. Partridge's Study of the Design of the Federal City, 1926

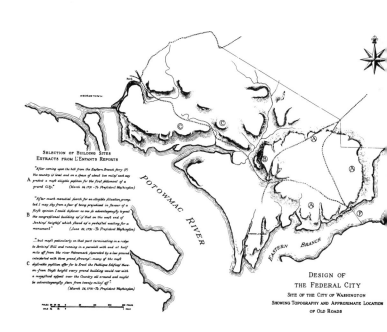

Topography and Approximate Location of Old Roads As Shown in William T. Partridge's Study of the Design of the Federal City, 1926

31

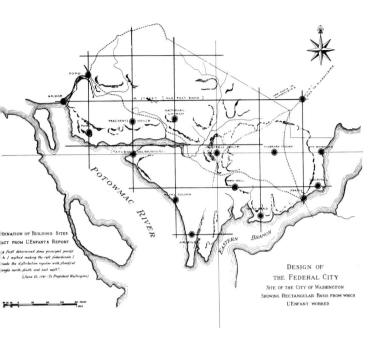

DESIGN OF
THE FEDERAL CITY
SITE OF THE CITY OF WASHINGTON
SHOWING RECTANGULAR BASIS FROM WHICH
L'ENFANT WORKED

The Rectangular Basis from Which L'Enfant Worked, As Shown in William T. Partridge's Study of the Design of the Federal City, 1926

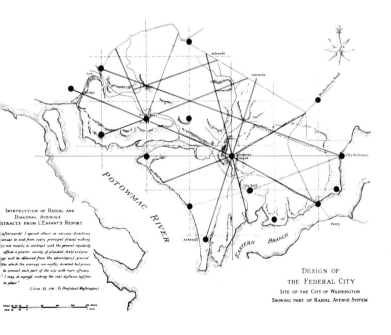

INTRODUCTION OF RADIAL AND
DIAGONAL AVENUES
TRACTS FROM L'ENFANT'S REPORT

DESIGN OF
THE FEDERAL CITY
SITE OF THE CITY OF WASHINGTON
SHOWING PART OF RADIAL AVENUE SYSTEM

Part of the Radial Avenue System, As Shown in William T. Partridge's Study of the Design of the Federal City, 1926

velopment. Ellicott himself had neither the time nor the inclination to prepare any significant planning alternatives. Consequently, what resulted legitimatized the plan—despite the dismissal of its creator—and justified L'Enfant's later claim that his work had been used without his being compensated.

THE MANUSCRIPT MAP AND THE RECONSTRUCTIONS

Of the many versions of early Washington plans that are in common reference, only the one entitled "Plan of the City intended for the Permanent Seat of the Government of the United States . . . By Pierre Charles L'Enfant" (undated but prepared in 1791)—*the manuscript map*—can be accepted as showing L'Enfant's intentions. The manuscript map was the most complete version of the Washington plan prepared by the designer himself. L'Enfant also provided "Observations" and "References" for the various features he noted on the map. L'Enfant clearly defined on this map the sites intended for the President's House and the Congress House, or Capitol. These two sites were connected by a public walk, the "Grand Avenue."

L'Enfant likely completed his drawing late in 1791. The manuscript map thus does not incorporate subsequent revisions and developments made by the designer. The faded manuscript drawing was copied in 1887 by the United States Coast and Geodetic Survey and was then varnished over. This map, as shown here, is now in the Library of Congress and reproductions are available from the National Ocean Survey, Department of Commerce. During the map's handling by the commissioners in Washington's time and by the Army Corps of Engineers and unknown others later on, and then the varnishing and other measures taken in the effort to preserve the manuscript original, certain features appear to have become obscured. These include some of the most significant architectural details of critical areas, such as the Capitol grounds, the Municipal Center, the White House, and the public market. Various efforts at "reconstruction" have been made, most notably by William Partridge in 1926 and by Elbert Peets.

The Reinterpretation by Elbert Peets. In 1932, Elbert Peets published the essay, "The Lost Plazas of Washington," in which he sketched what L'Enfant likely had envisioned for the President's House, a large building with a strongly silhouetted dome. Such a building would have helped to unify a city that stretched over L'Enfant's "magnificent distances." Pennsylvania Avenue, traced southeast toward the Capitol, was to have been lined, Peets thought, with "low vernacular buildings," also shown in the drawing.

Peet's reconstruction of L'Enfant's intentions is most persuasive, enlightened as it is by a broader view of urban design, the origins and probable motives of the designer, and contemporary eighteenth-century usages. Yet all the reinterpretations contribute to understandings of the original plan for Washington. Among the important considerations that have emerged from these efforts at reconstruction is the greater integration of urban design and architecture, as in the siting of buildings, the use of arcades and other civic design features, and the embellishment of the plan with such details as fountains and sculpture. We can understand and sympathize with L'Enfant's reluctance to regard his plan as complete when we appreciate how gripped he was by creative fervor. Certainly no estimation or appreciation of the L'Enfant plan could ever be complete without weighing in the reconstructions and interpretations made of the plan through all the decades.

THE REAL CITY AND THE ENDURING PLAN

L'Enfant's advice respecting the sale of lots and the simultaneous development of dispersed centers was not followed. Wholesale speculation in land and lots escalated—until inevitable collapse of the inflated land values. As early as 1800 and the removal of the government to Washington, this downward trend in land values put its stamp on the city. At that, the effect of the speculative boom would be seen for a century in the ragged, dispersed character of urban development ridiculed by several generations of visitors and commentators on the city's form. Thus appeared the dichotomy between the real and the ideal city, the former revealing the immediate facts of poverty and the slow pace of urban development, and the latter the artistic and unified intent of its planner. This intent of L'Enfant's, however, as well as the comprehensiveness of his design for Washington would not become evident for another century. In the

early years the city's few key structures, the Capitol and the White House, seemed hardly more than isolated monuments, without sufficient urban connection. Indeed, the urban activity contained by the plan responded chiefly to the operations of the private real estate market and other dimensions of private enterprise. The speculative pressures unleashed by the desperate if misguided effort to finance the building of the city was nevertheless responsible for the location and building of significant improvements such as bridges over the Potomac, the Anacostia, and Rock Creek, roads and turnpikes, churches, wharves, public buildings—civic undertakings that were influenced by the interest of major landholders and speculators and in turn shaped the further development of the city. This pattern is most clearly illustrated by the development of the area south of the Capitol, an area initially significant because of the merging here of the two broad tidal streams, the Potomac and its Eastern Branch (the Anacostia). In this area were focused the commercial interests of Daniel Carroll of Duddington and the activity of the real estate speculator Thomas Law and his associates in the firm of Morris, Nicholson, and Greenleaf. What was lost in the conflict was not only the topographical significance of the rivers' merging, but the importance of the entire sector designated from the very beginning by L'Enfant as the most explicitly municipal element of his over-all plan.

Development of the waterfront facing the deepwater channel of the Potomac, from its junction with the Anacostia upstream for nearly a mile and a half, was naturally handicaped by a shoreline bluff fifteen to twenty-five feet in height. Only at Sixth and Eleventh Streets could traffic descend to the level of marine commerce, and it was at these points and between them that development was topographically favored. Here, then, in spite of the greater inherent advantages of the Anacostia shoreline, and contrary to the specific expectations of Pierre Charles L'Enfant, was the principal commercial waterfront of the city located and deliberately developed.

As the street system proposed by L'Enfant was laid out with only slight modifications, so were the canals described in his plan also built with but small changes.

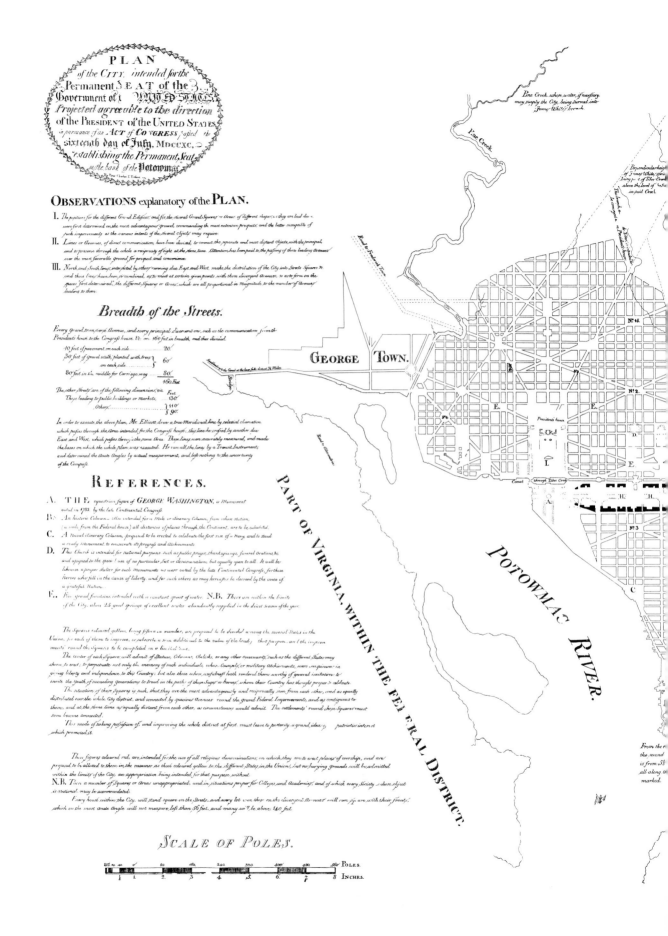

PLAN of the CITY, intended for the Permanent SEAT of the Government of the UNITED STATES. Projected agreeable to the direction of the PRESIDENT of the UNITED STATES, in pursuance of an ACT of CONGRESS passed the sixteenth day of July, MDCCXC, establishing the Permanent Seat on the bank of the Potowmac.

OBSERVATIONS explanatory of the PLAN.

Breadth of the Streets.

REFERENCES.

SCALE OF POLES.

GEORGE TOWN.

PART OF VIRGINIA, WITHIN THE FEDERAL DISTRICT.

POTOWMAC RIVER.

Lat. Congrefs Houfe, 38. 53. N.

Long. 0'. 0'.

PART OF MARYLAND, WITHIN THE FEDERAL DISTRICT.

EASTERN BRANCH.

New Road to Bladensburg.

References.

F. Grand Cascade, formed of the Water from the sources of the Tiber

G. Public walk being a square of 1200 feet, through which Carriages may ascend to the upper Square of the Federal house.

H. Grand Avenue, 400 feet in breadth, and about a mile in length, bordered with Gardens, ending in a slope from the houses on each side. This avenue leads to the Monument A, and connects the Congress Garden with the

I. Presidents park, and the

K. Well improved field, being a part of the square of the Presidents house, of about 1800 feet in breadth, and ½ of a mile in length. Every lot deep coloured red, with green plots, designates some of the situations which command the most agreeable prospects, and which are the best calculated for spacious houses and gardens, such as may accommodate foreign Ministers, &c.

L. Around this Square, and all along the

M. Avenue from the two bridges to the Federal house, the pavement on each side will pass under an arched way, under whose cover, Shops will be most conveniently and agreeably situated. This Street is 160 feet in breadth, and a mile long.

By the Civil War the City Canal entered the city directly south of the White House and continued east along present Constitution Avenue to Sixth Street. Here it had been changed from the more graceful alignment proposed by the city's designer. Instead it turned directly south to the center of the Mall, where it again turned due east. At the foot of Capitol Hill it again turned south and, closely following L'Enfant's proposed route, divided at Virginia Avenue into the two sections leading to the Anacostia. Above the main Potomac inlet, an extension connected the City Canal to the Chesapeake & Ohio Canal at Rock Creek by extending the design to include a protected waterway along the shoreline.

The Destiny of L'Enfant and His Plan for Washington. The full story of L'Enfant's dismissal and of his subsequent career belong to a still unwritten biography. But it may be said that the planner was a perfectionist who resisted to the end halting the creative process by an imposed deadline; that he refused to recognize the authority of the commissioners or anyone other than the president; that he may have followed his pecuniary as well as his professional interest; and that he steadfastly maintained his position that the city should be developed simultaneously from many centers and along the principal avenues. Although in all of this Pierre Charles L'Enfant stood alone, posterity has surely tended to sustain his views—and his plan for Washington.

L'Enfant's Intention for the Design of the President's House, As Envisioned by Elbert Peets, 1932

CHAPTER II THE PORT CITY 1800–1860

The Port City 1800-1860

The City of Washington in 1800

The place that greeted the federal government in 1800 restated its sylvan origins, but held the promise of a city commensurate with the country's foremost urban centers. The vision of the new capital could not fail to inspire. Its growth depended in large part on governmental commitment to provide public buildings, grounds, public services, and other improvements. This commitment was at best haphazard, timid, and in many respects unmindful of L'Enfant's larger concepts. A regional infrastructure was important to the growth of the river city; a transportation network was needed from sources of raw or manufactured materials to various public and private building sites as well as the city markets. The port cities of Georgetown and Alexandria, whose early commercial prosperity and rivalry had argued for the present site of Washington, found a new rival in the commercial growth of the capital city and expectations of future growth. Tripartite rivalry among the cities forced many compromises in the government's willingness to invest in Washington's commercial future. In the long run, however—as in the beginning—the fates of the three cities were seen to be inextricably intertwined, especially in the effects of the physical changes in the river and in attempts to tap the riches of the western hinterland. Nonetheless, Washington, newest of the three cities, was never the commercial giant L'Enfant had intended.

The city survived crisis, failure, and threat: the many recurring thoughts about removal of the national capital to a more western location, the halfhearted attempts to build a canal and drainage system through the city's center as planned by L'Enfant, the increasingly hazardous environmental conditions in the lowlands caused by an altered river, and the upheavals of the British invasion in 1814. Yet, by the eve of the Civil War, the city would emerge with its own identity, distinct from the nearby urban centers. With classical-styled public architecture, pleasure grounds, distinctive private dwellings and gardens, and a modern water supply system, Washington by the 1850s would begin to present an image of the nation's capital powerful enough to subdue future uncertainties.

THE BUCOLIC CITY

In 1800 both termini of L'Enfant's ceremonial avenue, the President's House and the Capitol, were unfinished.

*The Port: Maine Avenue Piers in
Washington's Redeveloped Southwest*

Small public and private buildings were scattered widely throughout the settlement, clustering near these two major federal centers and near the arsenal and Navy Yard. Open fields, pastureland, and produce gardens spread out over the land in between. Tiber Creek stretched lazily toward the Capitol, but its natural winding form was on the verge of man's improvement. This bucolic city, while offending the notion of a city as compact, dense, and defined by mortar, masonry, and wood, nonetheless appealed to many of Washington's newcomers. One of these early settlers, Margaret Bayard Smith, was favorably impressed by the romantic beauty of the natural landscape, watered by the Tiber, Potomac, and Anacostia Rivers, their banks shaded by trees and wildflowers. "Indeed the whole plain was diversified with groves and clumps of forest trees which gave it the appearance of a fine park." Her friend, Thomas Jefferson, resided at Conrad's Boarding House on Capitol Hill so that he would be able to "enjoy the beautiful and extensive prospect described above." In his appreciation of the countrylike surroundings, Jefferson shared regrets at the tree felling necessary for clearing the land and for fuel.

Early real estate investments made by entrepreneurs like James Greenleaf produced scattered clusters of row houses in the Southeast and the Southwest quadrants of the city, close to the employment centers of the arsenal and Navy Yard and also to the anticipated thriving wharves. The rush to the waterfront sites verified the strategic location of Carrollsburg along the Eastern Branch as well as L'Enfant's siting of the arsenal point —and with it the commercial orientation of much of the city east of the Capitol. The speculative building activities were envisioned by prominent men primarily as commercial investments rather than as locations for their in-town residences, but all such prospects became clouded as the prime riverfront land fell victim to the uncertain shoreline.

Almost as quickly as the area became settled, the shoaling process appeared in both the Potomac River and the Eastern Branch, the lifelines to the city's commercial health. As deforestation of Washington City proceeded, and as the Potomac River watershed upriver was cleared of forest cover, the Little River causeway

The Bucolic City: Watercolor by Nicholas King of Downtown Washington, Showing Blodgett's Hotel and the President's House, 1803

became dammed, its narrow channel suddenly forced into a wider channel at the foot of Twenty-seventh Street. Sediment carried by freshets became deposited along the riverfronts downriver. A more intensified version of this shoaling process from Bladensburg downriver filled the channel of the Eastern Branch and produced extensive marsh areas along its shores. Communication across the land between the riverside developments and the rest of the city was hampered by the natural terraces, some sharply defined as bluffs measuring as high as thirty feet and only occasionally pierced by dirt roads. The uneven landscape had yet to be flattened by successive cycles of development and renewal. As late as 1830, the lower sections of the Carrollsburg settlement were dotted with "simple wharves and shacks about the shore."

THE INDIGENOUS CITY: ROW HOUSES AND MANSIONS

Looking to the form and architectural style of the row houses of Philadelphia, Georgetown, and Alexandria, the investors in residential developments both in the riverfront areas and in other sections of Washington clearly anticipated a compact city inhabited by a cosmopolitan citizenry. Georgian-styled Wheat Row, a multifamily complex named after one of its early residents, was completed in the Southwest quadrant in the mid-1790s, induced by Greenleaf's investments. The rowhouse vernacular sprang up in the Northwest quadrant along Pennsylvania Avenue (the anticipated heavily traveled route between Georgetown and the President's House), although not all developers reflected complete confidence in the quick development of a major city. In addition to row houses, single houses with generous gardens also were commissioned. Within the context of L'Enfant's plan, a villa architecture began to flourish and a new kind of villa life established the style. Large houses surrounded by flower and vegetable gardens were so prevalent in this dispersed city of the early nineteenth century that, according to the historian Wilhelmus Bogart Bryan, "the cultivated gardens and lawns about the houses in Washington were regarded as one of the distinctive features of the city." In the earliest years of the capital city, the best qualities of the regional life of the Potomac plantation aristocracy were being transplanted

to urban conditions and given new form. Thus, an indigenous city from the beginning paralleled the official city and contributed to its character.

In the early turn-of-the-century city there were a significant number of mansions, their owners in most cases having been attracted to the city by its distinctive role as the seat of government. Some of the most prominent of these mansions were built as townhouses by planters from nearby Maryland and Virginia. The Octagon, built for Colonel John Tayloe in 1798–1800 to a design by William Thornton, first designer of the Capitol, was complete with kitchen garden, smokehouse, and other plantation features, as well as a stable, carriage house, and dependencies. The house itself in shape presented a novel façade, while its interior woodwork testified to the family's tastes acquired in the genteel tidewater tradition—and to the early attractiveness of the city to men of means.

Many newcomers to Washington, especially congressmen, viewed the city as a temporary home during their short sessions here. Housing was adapted to this transient population in the way of boarding houses, hotels, and taverns. Temporary accommodations for related residential activities revealed a remarkably flexible use of existing structures. The only church on Capitol Hill was fashioned from a tobacco barn that once belonged to Daniel Carroll. Religious services were held in the Capitol, a popular center for socializing and entertaining, cultural as well as political activities. Despite its scattered and transient pattern, the less than 9,000 population in the entire District made Washington an intimate city. Especially among the affluent and politically prominent, houses were not just shelter; they bespoke the inhabitant's penchant for a social life of formalities and rigorous etiquette.

THE CITY OF GEORGETOWN

The city of Georgetown, platted in 1751, exhibited some of the desired indications and physical results of advanced urbanization. Rising to prominence in the eighteenth century, first as a tobacco port and then as a milling center, Georgetown reached its commercial peak just before removal of the government to Washington. Serious environmental difficulties, however, barred fur-

Lithograph of the Port City of Georgetown and the University, Mid-Century

ther development of this port city at the head of ocean-going navigation. Deforestation and cultivation of the land upriver along the Potomac silted up the shoreline between Analostan Island and the Georgetown wharves. As sandbars formed, dredging machines were used and causeways for diverting the water current were attempted in order to resolve these hazards to navigation. Nevertheless, in the early decades of the nineteenth century, because of its faltering port capabilities as well as changes in agricultural production in Maryland, Georgetown was well advanced in its gradual transition from a tobacco port to a flour milling center.

In Georgetown itself, the years as a profitable port had produced a sizable concentration of warehouses along the Potomac River, with commodious residences extending northward up the steep hill toward M Street.

Around this nucleus of trade, related commerce developed: produce, game, fish markets, and diversified goods attested to the tastes of a more affluent society. Then, with the construction of the Potomac Canal by the Potomac Company, George Washington attempted further to improve the town's commercial health. Although the Potomac Company venture failed, the canal route from Harpers Ferry past the falls of the Potomac and into Georgetown presaged Benjamin Latrobe's 1802 "Plans and Sections of the Proposed Continuation of the Canal at the Little Falls of the Potomac," and ultimately the actual route of the Chesapeake & Ohio Canal. Despite Georgetown's difficulties as a port, the turn of the city's fortunes was such that in 1800 it contained excellent brick houses and prosperous business establishments—advantages that early on led many congressmen and affluent Washingtonians to live in Georgetown and commute to Washington City.

THE CITY OF ALEXANDRIA

Further downstream lay Alexandria, formally incorporated in 1748. Notable in the colonial era for its associations with George Washington, it thrived as a collecting point of several tobacco roads. As in Maryland's tidewater and Piedmont agriculture, so also in northern Virginia tobacco lands gave way to wheat—and Alexandria became the accessible port for the lower Shenandoah valley. Thus, the city became a wheat export center, reaching far into the western lands through the gaps in the first ranges of the Appalachians. Alexandria's most prosperous decades were the wheat boom years of the late eighteenth century and the early nineteenth century. A distinctive Federal architecture blossomed during Alexandria's heyday and endured as the city's trademark long after national architectural styles evolved into the romantic revivals.

Building the City: First Four Decades

In the first four decades of public improvements in Washington, the government concentrated on completing the President's House and the Capitol, building the City Hall, initiating construction of its illustrious buildings to house the executive functions (such as the Treasury, the Post Office, and the Patent Office), and developing the Navy Yard and arsenal along the Anacostia. In the early years of this period, the talents of Thomas Jefferson and Benjamin Latrobe were definitive, while the later years were dominated by Robert Mills. The city's physical face was affected by private interests: clients for the genteel homes designed by Latrobe and George Hadfield, and spirited business groups that financed and developed markets, mills, and manufactories that supplied city and government needs. In the process of growth, the city survived the severe test of the 1814 burning of its main buildings by the British, a shattering experience that, in Margaret Bayard Smith's words,

Sketch of the Port City of Alexandria, Showing a Steam Ferryboat, 1844

"gave civic spirit to the people of Washington" and reinforced the public and private sector's commitments to the city's rebuilding. The national capital, only a decade and half old, had acquired distinctive enough characteristics to stand on its own, a symbol of patriotism that not even major devastation could destroy.

BENJAMIN LATROBE AND THE CAPITOL BUILDING

Benjamin Latrobe's initial government commission came in 1802 when President Jefferson invited him to Washington to design drydocks for the Navy Yard. Although the drydocks plan was never carried out, Jefferson had found an intellectual kindred spirit in Latrobe, and it was in the following year that Latrobe was commissioned to design and build the south wing of the Capitol. To this commission, Latrobe brought considerable architectural and engineering background. Born in Yorkshire, England, Latrobe had studied architecture under Samuel Cockerell and engineering under John Smeaton, both among England's outstanding practitioners of the day. Grieved by the death of his wife, Latrobe emigrated in 1796 to Norfolk, Virginia, where he was quickly engaged in architectural and navigation projects in the Richmond and Norfolk area. In the next six years, Latrobe worked on a great variety of architectural and engineering projects in America's large cities.

In 1803, Latrobe was appointed Surveyor of Public Buildings, which included superintending the construction of the south wing of the Capitol Building. The Capitol was from the start the scene of architectural controversy — not least among its successive architects. William Thornton provided the winning design but construction of the south wing was supervised by a succession of architects including, besides Latrobe, Stephen Hallett, James Hoban, and later George Hadfield. Strong-minded designers like Hallett attempted to redesign Thornton's plan in order to overcome technical deficiencies, to provide details where Thornton had offered none, and to place their personal stamp on this important public building. Because Thornton also served as one of the three city commissioners and was thus directly responsible for the building of the Capitol, he was in frequent conflict with the architects who superintended construction.

During the construction of the south wing, Latrobe—over strenuous objection by Thornton—was able to make some alterations to interior arrangements. It was Latrobe's stature as the architect and engineer personally selected by Jefferson that enabled him to overrule Thornton. After the completion of the south wing in 1807, Latrobe then began alterations to the Capitol's north wing, the two sections being joined by an inappropriate but temporary "hyphen." After the Capitol was burned by the British in 1814, Latrobe supervised its rebuilding with zest, incorporating at this time the famous tobacco and corncob column capitals. Latrobe's other public building commissions included alterations to the President's House, design of the entrance gate at the Navy Yard, and construction of the "fireproof" building—intended for archives—abutting George Hadfield's Treasury Building.

THE WASHINGTON CITY CANAL

In the private sector, the versatile Latrobe was commissioned in 1802 by the Washington Canal Company, incorporated by an act of Congress, to engineer construction of the City Canal. Operating under severe financial constraints, Latrobe was obliged to route the canal in a straight line along the north side of the Mall, taking then an abrupt bend in front of the Capitol, and continuing southward toward the arsenal where it met the Eastern Branch at Buzzard Point. In the canal's passage through the city's interior, many aesthetic and drainage features planned by L'Enfant were denied by reason of financial considerations. Omitted were L'Enfant's turning basin at Eighth Street, the cascade down Capitol Hill, and the settling basin at the foot of the Capitol. Still, the cutting of the canal did affirm the northern boundary of the "Grand Avenue" as defined by L'Enfant. Wood served as lining for the canal as well as for the locks. As a result the canal enclosed water often too shallow and silted for navigation. It also lost its locks and linings during heavy storms, and the frequent repairs repeatedly forced grudging congressional appropriations.

The failure of the City Canal to fulfill L'Enfant's or even Latrobe's expectations for a major commercial route was an indication in part of the federal government's unwillingness or inability to commit sufficient funds for the building structures to endure. To be sure, the roving congressmen were more often preoccupied with their own constituencies back home than with the economic health of their Potomac River abode. Congressional decisions were sometimes swayed by the rivalrous business sentiments of the competing port cities of Georgetown and Alexandria that still argued against the emergence of a major commercial center in Washington City. The canal project was further hampered by the more remote turnpike interests that fought any new schemes to siphon off land trade.

THE YOUNG CAPITAL: JOEL BARLOW'S PLACE AT KALORAMA

At the less material end of the spectrum, there were others in the young city who responded to the ideals which the founders had institutionalized in provisions like those for a national nonsectarian church and a university. Enterprise and advancement were combined, for example, in one of the most attractive of Washington's developers, Joel Barlow, settler of Kalorama and close friend of Latrobe. In Barlow's mind the great national university "should be the center of a national educational system. It should include a school of mines, a school of roads and bridges, a conservatory of art, a national library and museum of painting and sculpture, a military school, a mint, a veterinary college, an observatory." The vision was characteristically of Napoleonic origin, but the inception—the felt need to which it responded — was characteristically American. Barlow, a friend also of Robert Fulton, creator of American internal waterways, reflected the national taste for the mechanical arts. Intellectual and educational in intent, Barlow's conception of the city's development incorporated practical measures: "Washington must be the center of a network of national highways and canals linking all the rivers."

At Kalorama, at the edge of town, overlooking the Potomac and Rock Creek, Joel Barlow established himself in a country house remodeled by Benjamin Latrobe, and became—in the Jefferson and Madison administrations—a social fixture of the city, his house being "the place to go in the swampy young capital for good company and good talk." The retired diplomat-poet's taste

for homegrown vegetables and fruit from his own orchard paralleled Jefferson's as did the style of his house. The close friendship of Barlow and Latrobe took explicit form when the architect moved to a house at the edge of Kalorama and a connecting gravel path was laid down. The heights of Kalorama did not discourage Jefferson and others from visiting, nor Latrobe from walking to his work at the Capitol. "We reside on the top of the range of beautiful eminences that surround the cities of Washington, Georgetown, and Alexandria on every side. . . . By the aid of a good telescope, my wife sees me ascend Capitol hill, three miles distant, and can trace me on the whole of my return home," Latrobe wrote in 1816. A romantic landscape painting by Charles Codman shows a bit of meadow ornamented with a large urn, and the rather sheltered cove at the mouth of Rock Creek; beyond, the Barlow house appears perched on a terrace behind which rises the more dominant Wicomico escarpment. It is possible that this view shows the pond Barlow created by damming Rock Creek so that his friend Fulton might have a suitable place for his steamboat experiments. That conjecture, however, like the event itself, awaits further documentation.

LATROBE'S WASHINGTON: DOMESTIC ARCHITECTURE

In addition to remodeling the house for Barlow, Latrobe designed several of the capital city's outstanding residential and religious structures in a style so representative of the early affluence of the constituent city that the era can rightfully be called "Latrobe's Washington." The capital was indebted to Latrobe for his classical public buildings as well as the City Canal designs. In 1816, Latrobe designed a grand mansion at Seventeenth and B Streets—just north of the City Canal's first lock—for John Peter Van Ness. The Van Ness House, sited adjacent to the modest childhood home of Mrs. Van Ness, the former Marcia Burnes, was the largest house Latrobe had ever designed. It was a handsome residence, described by Talbot Hamlin as "its author's domestic masterpiece. . . . The house was worth waiting for. Its exterior was deceptively simple, with all the restraint and originality of which Latrobe had become such a master. Thin, guttered eaves, supported on pairs of widely spaced wooden brackets, replaced the usual cornice." The interior design moved the principal rooms to the second floor level, and offered a separation—new in the United States—of the activities of the owner's family from those of the servants. Considered to be "more elaborately finished than any private home in the District," the Van Ness House and its carefully laid grounds epitomized the country-estate quality of the city's affluent residential areas. Around Lafayette Square, Latrobe designed for the naval hero, Stephen Decatur, a stately residence with spacious grounds, and Saint John's Episcopal Church, which served the president as well as congregants from the residential district sprouting up in the immediate area.

GEORGE HADFIELD: CITY HALL, 1820

The architecture of George Hadfield echoed the clean classical lines that were Latrobe's signature. Although an accomplished designer, Hadfield was a tragic figure. Among the succession of superintending architects on the construction of the Capitol, Hadfield—like Stephen Hallett—had also succumbed to the tirades of William Thornton. British-educated, Hadfield began a brilliant career in London, promising to rival John Nash as court architect. Refused membership in a prestigious architectural club, however, Hadfield emigrated to Washington where his mentors thought he might find a more immediate outlet for his considerable talents. After a few painful years under the strain of the "rogues then employed in the construction of public buildings," Hadfield enjoyed a relatively successful career as a private architect, designing, for example, a home for Commodore David Porter on Sixteenth Street just at the northern boundary of L'Enfant's city, the location later called Meridian Hill. Hadfield also designed the Custis-Lee mansion at Arlington, the Van Ness mausoleum in Oak Hill Cemetery, and the home for John Mason on Analostan Island.

Washington's City Hall, constructed in 1820, was Hadfield's greatest commission. Located a few blocks northwest of the Capitol at Fourth and D Streets, at a site identified by L'Enfant to accommodate some monumental building, City Hall signaled a major departure from the functions outlined in the original Washington plan. L'Enfant had intended the municipal functions to develop not to the northwest but facing the south leg of the canal, far enough from the federal functions to assert an independence but near enough to the port-

Elevation of George Hadfield's Original Design of Washington's City Hall As Drawn in 1832

industrial area and major arteries to play an integral part in the life of the city. Thus, in its location, City Hall—seed of what would much later become the sprawling Municipal Center that is now called Judiciary Square—revealed the lack of a comprehensive scheme for the siting of public buildings, and this uncertainty was to endure for the rest of the nineteenth century.

In itself, Hadfield's building bespoke the simplicity and economy desired in buildings constructed with public funds. Its quiet exterior, a central Ionic portico flanked by two Ionic-columned wings, enclosed interiors that were notable for their stark simplicity. The building, much admired in the first half of the nineteenth century, inspired a new appreciation in the early twentieth century as it conformed to Classical Revival tastes. The construction of City Hall in effect provided the initial link connecting and making visually comprehensible the long distance between the Capitol and the President's House, although in fact the building is located several blocks north of Pennsylvania Avenue, the planned visual connection.

ROBERT MILLS: PATENT OFFICE, TREASURY, AND POST OFFICE

The burning in 1834 of the Hadfield-designed Treasury Building east of the President's House pointed up the inadequacy of the city's water system. The event also occasioned the designing of a new structure on a larger scale as compared to the modest dimensions Hadfield had given the initial structure. Sited on Fifteenth Street directly in front of the President's House as viewed from the Capitol, the new Ionic-styled Treasury Building was designed by Robert Mills, who reigned as the government's Architect of Public Buildings between 1836 and 1851. A Latrobe protégé, Charleston-born Mills brought to the capital city considerable experience in both public and private architectural and engineering works. He had worked in Philadelphia, Richmond, and Baltimore, and for ten years was State Engineer and Architect of South Carolina. In the Treasury Building, Mills achieved what he considered a "good common building" constructed of masonry vaulting derived from groined arches cemented and coated with the newly perfected "hydraulic cement." Owing to financial constraints, the building as completed in 1840 was much smaller than

Mills had intended. In its subsequent enlargement according to the designs by Thomas U. Walter between 1855 and the mid-1870s, the completed building presented what later planners termed a "spoliation" of the view inasmuch as it blocked the vista between the Capitol and the President's House.

Seven blocks to the west—on the site L'Enfant actually had designated for the national nonsectarian church—Mills superintended construction of the Patent Office, commencing in 1836, after the designs by William P. Elliott. Having himself, however, designed many public buildings and developed in the process a well-grounded philosophy of the design priorities that applied, Mills proceeded to alter this building according to his own tastes. The large building, constructed with bold vaulted galleries, presented a powerful Doric façade extending beyond the original building lines along F and G Streets. At the building's completion just prior to the Civil War, the white granite exterior resembling the Parthenon faced the axis of Eighth Street toward the Central Market, across the canal, and through the Southwest quadrant to the waterfront, at least partially fulfilling L'Enfant's intentions for a compelling visual experience.

One block from the Patent Office, the Corinthian-styled Post Office designed by Mills rose according to no formal plan on a site facing E Street between Seventh and Eighth Streets. Initiated in 1839, the original section was completed in the mid-1840s. Thomas U. Walter designed the northern extension, completed by 1855, facing F Street and the Patent Office. Articulate exponent of economy in public architecture, Robert Dale Owen praised the Post Office as "a graceful example [of the Italian style], creditable to the architect who designed it." The construction of these buildings indicates what was seen as the grandeur of the government's presence in the city, as expressed in individual structures. Before long, however, the thickening up of the central core with government edifices forced a broader than architectural view of these individual structures. Now there was growing concern with the larger environment surrounding public buildings, the relationship of the buildings to each other, and the structures and functions that clustered around them.

The Navy Yard and the Omnibus to Georgetown. The federal presence was felt in the southern quadrants too. A major employment center along the Anacostia River was the Navy Yard, whose shipping activities, functional buildings, and wharves attracted numbers of craftsmen and laborers as well as midshipmen attending the navy's training school. The nearby federal arsenal on Greenleaf Point acted as the storage center for weapons manufactured at Harpers Ferry and the Foxhall foundry near Georgetown. A large volume of trade was generated between these government installations and manufactories in the area and between the workers and small businesses serving this neighborhood. The opening in 1830 of an omnibus line between the Navy Yard and Georgetown created a route by which the ties between the waterfront communities and the developing monumental core as well as Georgetown were strengthened. This linkage of communities to each other by an expanding transportation network followed the essential growth pattern predicted by L'Enfant, who had visualized distinct communities, developed around multiple centers of growth, eventually merging as the population increased—and producing a continuous if diversified urban fabric. The ability of these centers to be closely tied to the rest of the city's prosperity rather than to function as competing centers depended on the fortunes of the transportation networks.

THE CANAL NETWORK: THE CITY CANAL AND THE C & O

By the 1820s, the Potomac River's channels had become so silted and impassable that neither Georgetown nor Alexandria could survive on river navigation alone. The two port cities looked to a large canal scheme. In 1828, construction of the Chesapeake & Ohio Canal commenced. Its route began in Georgetown and ran parallel to the Potomac westward to Harpers Ferry. From Georgetown, the canal was extended eastward, entering the Washington City Canal at Seventeenth and B

Lithograph of Aqueduct Bridge, Constructed to Carry the Water of the Chesapeake & Ohio Canal across the Potomac to Virginia, 1850s

Streets. According to the plan, Alexandria also was to benefit from the new canal by means of the Aqueduct Bridge and Alexandria canal constructed between 1833 and 1843 and located just west of Georgetown to carry the Virginia trade southward; there the canal emptied through an outlet lock into the Potomac. By the mid-1830s, the system was completed from Harpers Ferry to the Washington City connection. The southern route to Alexandria, barely realized in fact, proved commercially unprofitable.

The canal system as a whole never lived up to its expectations. Not only did the three cities thwart each other's portions of the scheme, but any state investment in the project was compromised by commitments to other urban centers, as for example Maryland's interest in Baltimore's thriving port. Nevertheless, even in the act of visualizing the canal as a large commercial artery linking western Maryland counties with the urban depots that clustered along the Potomac, the three cities realized that solutions to their economic problems lay beyond their local boundaries. Regional economic viability clearly depended on strengthening the intercity physical linkages in canals, bridges, and ferries.

The canal network and bustling ports oriented the city toward the river. The river basin flatlands were occupied by urban functions; the highlands remained devoted to farms and country or summer residences. The orientation to the city's waterpower resources saw the development of manufacturing centers along Rock Creek, the stream that defined Georgetown's eastern borders, where the rushing waters could be harnessed. The falls of the C & O Canal within Georgetown offered that port city an additional cheap power source for flour milling. The prosperity brought by the water power on two borders and the change of goods at the canal created a Georgetown filled with a sense of self-sufficiency reflected in the large Italianate residences on the terraces facing the waterfront.

THE COMING OF THE RAILROAD: THE B & O

This river orientation was diminished by the coming of the railroad. Abetting the later removal of the affluent population from the lowlands river city, the railroad displayed its easy conquest of larger, highland areas and its emphasis on intercity links. At the same time that the Chesapeake & Ohio Canal was commenced and hailed as generator of the city's future prosperity, the Baltimore & Ohio Railroad was inaugurated with a direct line to Washington City. As soon as the railroad opened for travel, it was established that rails were destined to become *the* transportation mode of the future, dominating the area's landscape and settlement patterns for the next century—and orienting the city to a stronger regional context. Baltimore, in fact, offered strong competition to the Potomac port cities. In connecting the city to the rich western lands, the railroad paralleled the Chesapeake & Ohio Canal and offered a speedier transit of goods and passengers between urban centers. Another intercity line radiated from Baltimore, reaching the District line in 1835. This line cut in half the travel time normally required by the stagecoach.

BRIDGES, ROADS, AND FERRIES

Roads and turnpikes, the earliest transportation routes through the region, were swept from their focus on Alexandria and Georgetown to Washington City itself. Fourteenth Street and Seventh Street were the major roads from the Maryland counties into the northern sections of the city. The Southeast quadrant housing the bustling Navy Yard was serviced by bridges over the Eastern Branch. The Potomac River was traversed by ferries and by the 1810 Chain Bridge above Georgetown. Long Bridge, constructed in 1809 between the Virginia shore and Fourteenth Street in Washington City, served as a major turnpike and later a railroad access into the city. Often damaged by high water and ice, this bridge was subject to frequent repairs. Its wide piers hampered the rush of water from upstream, exacerbating the silting of the river, preventing large ships from entering Georgetown's harbors, and throwing off excess water onto the already marshy lowlands south of Pennsylvania Avenue.

THE POTOMAC FISHERIES

The prosperity of the three cities did not depend on the exchange of raw and manufactured goods at the canals, turnpike, and railroad depots alone. The rich fisheries of the Potomac River strengthened the river

Wash Drawing by August Köllner of Pennsylvania Avenue and Seventh Street, 1839

orientation and wharf facilities appended to the three cities. The abundant supply of fish had for thousands of years attracted aboriginal settlement, and only two centuries earlier had astonished the first white explorers in the area. In the 1830s, the Potomac and its tributaries counted a hundred and fifty fisheries. Those along the Eastern Branch produced such huge fish hauls that farmers from the surrounding rural counties came to the city in order to sell their produce and, in the process, took away quantities of the fish for use as fertilizer. While deforestation and settlement upriver drastically changed the Potomac as it flowed past the District, so the riverine life was gradually destroyed by the growing residential centers within the District.

Washington Panorama: The Year 1840

As the mile-and-a-half stretch between the Capitol and President's House became linked by new Mills-designed

public buildings, the residential areas clustered about these two major termini also merged. By 1840, a major residential corridor spread northward from Pennsylvania Avenue within this mile-and-a-half distance as far north as K Street. Indicators of this residential configuration were the new churches constructed to serve the nearby population. The President's House inspired the clustering of aristocratic residences of the diplomatic corps and important government officials. The Capitol Hill neighborhood generated less stately mansions and a more transient population. The business district formed along Pennsylvania Avenue from the foot of Capitol Hill to Ninth Street. Thus, along Pennsylvania Avenue, where L'Enfant had intended a cultural-ceremonial thoroughfare, banks defined the strip, filled in with newspaper offices, hotels, eating houses, and small retail establishments.

THE SURGE OF WASHINGTON CITY

By 1840, the District—numbering over 33,000 in population—became clearly definable. The once autonomous

50

port cities of Alexandria and Georgetown were about to be eclipsed by the surging giant of Washington City. Henceforth, the two older cities would become neighborhoods or suburbs of the large capital city center. In its evolving image, Washington City gathered strength from the new public buildings and installations, the adjoining residential clusters, and the river, canal, turnpike, and rail arteries of trade and communication. In the beginning of the period from 1800 to 1840 the city depended on the prosperity of the older port cities. At the end of this period, attention was now focused on Washington itself. Moreover, public and private decisions about its physical future would now affect the region outside the original L'Enfant borders.

RETROCESSION: THE QUESTION OF ALEXANDRIA
AND GEORGETOWN

In the two decades prior to the Civil War, Washington City would dominate and direct physical growth in the region. The decline of Alexandria and Georgetown, plus the increasing control of Congress exerted now over all the settlements within the District, inspired calls in the two port cities for retrocession to their respective states. In this Alexandria was successful, as the physical barrier of the Potomac River argued for much inconvenience in communication with the District as a whole, and thus poor prospects for physical improvements. Georgetown never succeeded in separating but rather remained tied to the city, in both physical and social terms. The highlands and opulent residences of Georgetown created an enclave for the fashionable set, many of whom were still rooted in the surrounding plantation life. The new District, although shorn of its Virginia lands, prospered beyond the rural outlines suggested at the time of its early occupancy, and indeed doubled its population in the short twenty-year span between 1840 and 1860.

WHITE MASONRY AND RED BRICK: THE FEDERAL PRESENCE
IN THE CONSTITUENT CITY

The government's commitment, while not nearly at the scale required had L'Enfant's canal and drainage plan been executed, did bear the predictive stamp of a strong federal presence. In 1840, Mills's three major public buildings were either completed or well on their way. Their white masonry façades would dwarf the structures of the constituent city and serve as visual landmarks of national capital grandeur set amid the red brick façades of the residential city. New or expanded federal functions clamored for accommodation in equally dignified surroundings, necessitating construction of new public buildings and extensions of the old. The attention of Congress was now directed to the Mall.

The Mall and the Monumental Core

Prior to construction of the privately financed Washington Monument, begun in 1848, and the Smithsonian, in 1849, the Mall was used as grazing and agricultural lands. Several years earlier, the Columbian Institute had set up greenhouses at the Mall's east end. The land itself undulated between hills and swamps. The siting of the obelisk off the President's House–Washington Monument axis was the result of fears about uncertain foundations. The monument was built on higher ground, thus presenting a geometric problem later for tidy planners preoccupied with "true" vistas. Nevertheless, the building of the towering monument, although not completed for nearly four decades, did provide a major interest in retaining the Mall for the ceremonial purposes intended by L'Enfant. In concept and function, however, the Mall gradually changed; instead of L'Enfant's intended site for ambassadorial residences, the Mall became the setting for cultural institutions.

The cornerstone laying for the Smithsonian Institution in 1849 created a benchmark in the city's history. Small but assertive, the building centered concerns for the larger environment, beyond the immediate structure and grounds. The future character of the entire Mall was at stake. The acceptance in 1838 of James Smithson's bequest of slightly more than half a million dollars had set into motion a lengthy period of discussion as to the nature of the Institution, its location in the capital city, and an appropriate design for the building. From 1840 to 1841 at the request of General Joel R. Poinsett, who was associated with the budding Institution, Robert Mills prepared a plan for the building and grounds. Breaking from his Classical Revival trademark, Mills presented a building designed in the Norman

Robert Mills's Design for the Washington Monument, Mid-Century

style, likely in honor of the British scientist Smithson and "our associations with great literary institutions . . . assimilated with the Saxon style of architecture," as Mills expressed it in a letter to Robert Dale Owen. Mills considered the site of the Smithsonian Building to be the entire "Public Mall" itself, from the foot of the Capitol to the Potomac River, affording large acreage for horticultural and botanical experiments as well as zoological buildings. The Smithsonian Building was planned by Mills to be located on a slight rise at the Twelfth Street axis and would afford a view of the rolling land, the varied plantings, and a "good variety of rural scenery." The waterways—canal and river—defining the Mall's edges offered the prospect of fountains and other water displays. Reflecting some continuity with L'Enfant's residential intentions for the area, Mills anticipated the construction of adjacent houses for the "officers of the Institution."

Mills's plans were not executed, but they were not

Ink Sketch of Robert Mills's Design for the Smithsonian Institution Building, 1841

irrelevant to the ultimate fate of the Smithsonian. Further discussion ensued in Congress, which by 1844 defined the Institution to embrace a display area for natural history and geological specimens, a library, a laboratory, and a lecture hall, all of which were to appeal to the general audience. Two years later, James Renwick's turreted Norman-styled designs for the building were accepted, with the grounds question seemingly a separate matter. In any case, the siting of the building longitudinally along the axis of the Mall, leaving an "open corridor [of] 600 feet," as Daniel Rieff documents, insured the retention of the long vista from the Washington Monument to the Capitol.

DOWNING'S PLAN FOR THE MALL AND THE "MUSEUM OF LIVING TREES"

In 1850, Andrew Jackson Downing, America's pioneer "landscape gardener," was invited by President Millard Fillmore to design the grounds on the Mall as well as the parks north and south of the President's House. Downing had already gained nationwide recognition as a landscape designer. His commission on this national project was an outcome of conversations between the Washington banker William W. Corcoran and Joseph Henry, Secretary of the Smithsonian, and discussion with city officials about improvement of the grounds around the Smithsonian. A strong botanical focus had

Ink Sketch of Robert Mills's Plan of the Mall, 1841

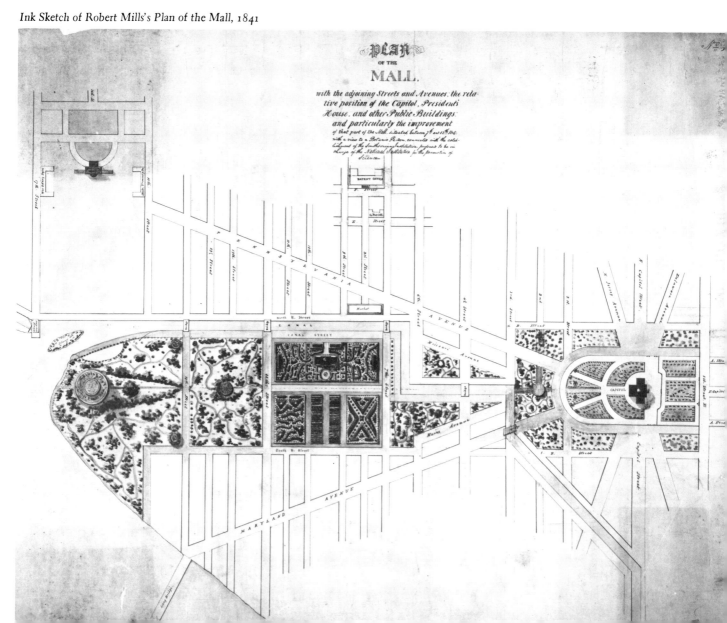

Lithograph of the Smithsonian Institution's "Castle" on the Mall, Completed 1855

been a tradition of the Mall area, especially with the founding in 1820 of the Botanic Garden at the foot of Capitol Hill. The gardens located here were seeded by the Columbian Institute and also incorporated exotic specimens recovered from the Wilkes Arctic Expedition.

Downing's 1851 plan for the Mall and adjoining parks outlined three objectives: 1) "to form a National Park," 2) "to give an example of the natural style of Landscape Gardening which may have an influence on the general taste of the country," and 3) to create a "public museum of living trees and shrubs." These three objectives were applied to six separate major reservations linked by connecting curvilinear walks and drives. The spaces between were to be filled with trees, pleasure grounds, and lakes, while a decorative wire suspension bridge would

connect the Mall with the President's Park south of the White House. The hard geometric lines of each reservation's boundaries were thus offset by the emphasis on undulating ground surfaces and roadways, as if in a man-made artifact recalling the sylvan glories of the city's first decade. Downing's plan softened the sharp bend of the canal in front of the Capitol into a smooth diagonal along Missouri Avenue, thereby consolidating more ground for public park purposes. Like L'Enfant, Downing envisioned water displays as critical to the aesthetic fulfillment of the city. Under Downing's plan, Fountain Park, to the east of the Smithsonian Pleasure Grounds, would be supplied from a reservoir in the Capitol with the overflow pumped into a lake that was to be carved out. The execution of this 1851 plan met

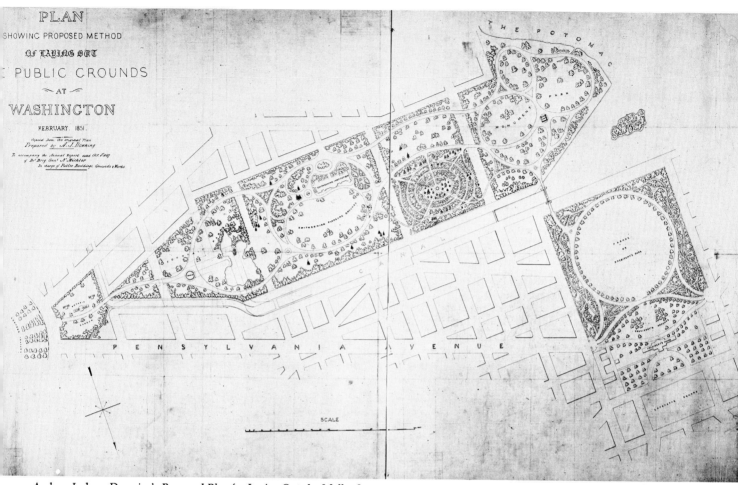

Andrew Jackson Downing's Proposed Plan for Laying Out the Mall, 1851

financial and political obstacles reminiscent of L'Enfant's time. As a matter of fact, the Smithsonian's immediate grounds were the only element to benefit from the over-all plan, the other reservations being left to piecemeal improvements. Nonetheless, Downing did succeed in creating a design ideal that influenced the physical realization of Washington's scattered parklets in the post–Civil War era. The continuing influence was then reflected in the frequent revivals of the complete Downing landscape plan by various members of the Army Corps of Engineers—and by wistful mapmakers.

THE CAPITOL EXTENSIONS AND THE NEW DOME

The growth of the nation (and consequently of the number of congressmen) necessitated an enlarged Cap-

itol Building. Architect of the extension to the Mills-designed Treasury Building and Post Office, Philadelphian Thomas U. Walter now was appointed Architect of the Capitol Extensions. To accommodate new and larger chambers for the House and Senate, extensions were to be added to the original wings, with the original space given over to other uses. But "extension" of the Capitol embraced much more than this work, commenced in 1851. The new cast-iron dome, designed to crown the completed building, was an accomplishment in terms of both technology and aesthetics. The dome was only partially constructed at the outbreak of the Civil War, but after a lapse of a few months, work was resumed—that the new dome might serve as a patriotic symbol of the Union.

The City's Waterways and the Design of a Modern Water Supply

In becoming a more compact city and losing its country-like appearance, Washington was experiencing more and more serious water problems. The water supply that initially depended on springs was becoming clearly inadequate, and in fact, to some extent the construction of new public buildings was an outcome of their predecessors' having burned to the ground. When Army Engineer Montgomery Meigs recommended to Congress the feasibility of a water system originating at Great Falls, Congress appropriated the largest outlay of funds for a single project since monies had been appropriated for its own Capitol. For the new water system Meigs was appointed chief engineer. An important designer in creating several of the city's post–Civil War architectural monuments, Meigs had entered the Engineers Corps of the United States Army following his graduation from West Point. Possessing a highly inventive mind, Meigs designed engineering structures, integrating mechanical and ornamental fixtures into his large creations.

GREAT FALLS TO CITY PIPES: MEIGS'S COSMOPOLITAN VISION

For the city aqueduct ground was broken at Great Falls in 1853, although interruptions in the funding would retard completion of the system until nine years later. From a point just above Great Falls, the diverted water was conveyed to the receiving reservoir near Little Falls at Dalecarlia. From this point, at the District line, the settled water was carried to the distributing reservoir just west of Georgetown at Drover's Rest where it was then piped to the city users. In carrying the water twelve miles over the jagged topography, Meigs designed the famous masonry single-arched Cabin John Bridge to convey the conduit over the Cabin John valley. To bridge Rock Creek Meigs designed the Pennsylvania Avenue Bridge constructed of cast-iron arches. Meigs's objectives were more than merely to supply water to households and fire hydrants; his cosmopolitan vision saw an increased water supply as feeding into fountains which were necessary health and aesthetic provisions in a congested city.

The immediate effect of Meigs's water system was an abundant water supply necessary to a modern city, even if this supply was not yet consistently clear or healthy. Loose earth rushing downriver from the agricultural lands gave the water a turbid appearance. The design of the system, however, was basically sound. Further improvements were made only in the way of extensions or minor corrections of Meigs's original design; no major changes were undertaken until the twentieth century.

SOCIAL EFFECTS OF THE NEW WATER SUPPLY: SECTORING

In the long run, the water supply system had a profound effect on the city's social configurations, particularly on its residential areas. Since the water came in from the west, it served the western sections of the city first before being piped to the eastern quadrants. This predictability of supply in the city's western quadrants tended to draw the affluent to those areas by reason of the superior services available. The eastern sections, often threatened with water shortages, were left to the less affluent. To be sure, this sectoring of the city along social lines had commenced prior to the coming of Meigs's water system. There had already occurred clustering of the blue-collar classes close to the Navy Yard while the affluent had early settled near the President's House and westward into Georgetown. This sectoring was now given enormous reinforcement by the allocation of public services, and the pattern persists to the present time.

In terms of planning for the water system—as also for the interurban canal and the railroad systems—success depended on more than technological achievements. The functions of the city's vital arteries depended on the cooperation and resources of an area much larger than the local boundaries—in this case the ten-mile square. The Maryland legislature, in response to a federal request, granted to the United States right of way for the route of the water mains and support structures through Maryland territory along the Potomac. Later improvements made to the system were necessitated by change occurring miles away and again solutions had to be found on a regional basis.

While in terms of water supply the city now benefited from serious commitments on the part of the federal government, Washington's waterfront prosperity was adversely affected by the changed river conditions. The pattern for Washington was the same as for Georgetown. Repeated silting and poor conditions of the canal boat basin at Rock Creek and the Washington City Canal forced the city to yield the greater part of the coal and lumber business to Alexandria with its deep-water wharves above Hunting Creek. The decline of the Washington City Canal was partly attributable to the sewage that flowed directly from the city to the canal's basins. The canal, a major determinant of the city's commercial core—Center Market and the Pennsylvania Avenue business strip—was by 1860 of little commercial use. It was in fact foul, dangerous, and unhealthy. Water-oriented industries suffered a similar decline. Shipbuilding at the Navy Yard was seriously curtailed by the silting of the Eastern Branch. Manufacturing of armaments at the government arsenal at Greenleaf Point ceased. The important mid-century flour milling business in the environs of Georgetown declined. And although water-oriented industries did decline, the value of manufactures of the District of Columbia actually increased from $2,690,000 in 1850 to $5,500,000 in 1860, evidence of increasing reliance on new rail transportation facilities.

Buildings Beyond the Boundary. Location of new government centers away from the river and even outside of the L'Enfant city contributed to the decline of city waterways. In 1851 the United States Soldiers' Home, two miles north of the Capitol, was established. In 1852 the Government Hospital for the Insane, now Saint Elizabeths Hospital, was located on the former farm of Thomas Blagden along the Anacostia. In 1857 Congress began to support Amos Kendall's Columbia Institution for the Instruction of the Deaf, Dumb and Blind—now called Gallaudet College—a mile northeast of the Capitol. The siting of these new institutions in widely separated areas of the District outside the boundary of the city was a significant factor in the city's pattern of suburbanization in the pre–Civil War era.

Mud Machines and Ferryboats. Despite fading prospects for commercial success of the city's waterways, the rivers were by no means ignored. Investment both public and private, although generated piecemeal, worked to remold the river edges. As early as 1805, "mud machines" had been employed to remove the sedimentation that adhered to the Potomac riverfront. Throughout this first half of the century, various mechanical devices could be found on or in the river, in the continuing attempt to manipulate the flow of water and to scoop away obstructive marshes. Watercraft could be observed plying the Potomac and Eastern Branch; various vantage points in the region gave view to white sails and vertical masts cutting across the horizontal waterscape. By 1852 steamboats served all parts of the lower river and the Chesapeake Bay; ferries ran hourly between Washington and Alexandria, daily to Aquia Creek, weekly to Baltimore and Norfolk. Tolling bells as they saluted Mount Vernon, they added smoke and noise to the environment.

Toward a More Cosmopolitan City: The 1850s

The local government contributed to the momentum of urban improvements. The City Council's 1852 prohibition of new cemeteries within the city of Washington; installation in 1853 of gas lamps on major streets and avenues; introduction of modern street signs; inauguration of the city's first system of house numbering in 1854: all these are distinct moves away from a country-like settlement to a modern city.

Southern habits set the tone of residential life in the antebellum city, a reflection in part of the many presidents who were from the South. Many of Washington's oldest families were descendants of the tidewater planter class, and most Washingtonians retained strong familial ties to the agricultural societies of Maryland and Virginia. "The gentry," as an English observer termed the citizens belonging to the social set, "are thoroughly Virginia in sentiment." Such sentiment and inclination were played out in the rural pastimes at the several race-tracks located outside the perimeter of Boundary Street, played out also in the rhythmic life clocked to the sessions of Congress, creating the Washington cycle of social seasons. Opulent French Renaissance and Italianate residences served as set pieces for the urban-oriented winter seasons, while country residences only a short distance away in the unsettled District served as havens of relief from summer heat and the "miasma" of the basin city.

An important indicator not just of congressmen's increased residential stability and affluence but of the attractiveness of the city itself for residences was the increased number of legislators who now made Washington their home. In 1845, only a little more than 2 percent of the United States senators occupied single-family homes in the capital city. By 1860, the percentage of senators living in single-family units had grown to forty. Many built their own houses—sometimes in the unsettled portions of the city beyond Boundary Street—and thus became more sympathetic to physical improvements needed in the region.

The First Suburbs: Uniontown and the Rail Settlements. Working people residing near the Navy Yard and arsenal could spend leisure time in activities oriented to the Eastern Branch which offered the recreational pleasures of swimming, boating, and fishing. The river-oriented blue-collar community was bolstered in 1854 by the establishment of Uniontown across the Eastern Branch from the Navy Yard. Uniontown is often considered to be the first suburb in Washington. It may, however, have been preceded by settlements along the railroad lines since, according to the historian Bryan, "by 1853 so many people were living along the Baltimore and Ohio Railroad, whose business required their daily presence in the city, that the railroad company was requested to have the trains stop at way stations for their accommodation." The growth of suburbs as signified by Uniontown and the rail settlements enlarged the physical dimensions of the city and produced the first inklings of the commuter life-style.

THE CULTURAL CITY

The growth of cultural institutions gave the leisurely life-style of Washington an extra dimension and bestowed a unique image upon the city's physical form. The Smithsonian Institution, itself an architectural creature of evolving notions about taste and economy, attracted scientists and other intellectuals who had earlier gathered around the Patent Office and similar agencies. The first permanent argument for the Mall area as a cultural corridor, the Smithsonian was joined in 1855 to the east—on the site of the present National Air and Space Museum—by an armory intended to exhibit military artifacts. While the significant decades of such growth still lay ahead, the constituent city of the 1850s continued to enjoy lectures, concerts, and religious services in the federal buildings, using the space after hours and providing for bustling round-the-clock activities in the city's central core. The city also produced its own cultural landmarks, most notably the assertive Corcoran Gallery (designed in French Renaissance style by James Renwick) facing the Georgian, Hadfield-designed State Department Building. And in the popularity of steamboat service to Mount Vernon in the 1850s, cultural exploration again tied the city to a larger region and ushered in the city's major source of income made in private enterprise: tourism, and its accompanying mirror of the unique capital city, the guidebook.

Conflicts between the interurban centers within the federal district had been hushed by 1860 with the projection of Washington City as the decisive voice. That city's own intracity clusters that formed about major public installations and buildings had by the period's end merged, all still framed largely by the L'Enfant boundaries. And just when the capital city had overcome its interurban rivalries and had at last become physically unified, it was faced with a disunited and warring country.

CHAPTER III THE CIVIL WAR 1860–1865

The Civil War 1860-1865

Washington in Wartime: The Military City

Any indecisiveness of the federal government concerning the capital city's future was swept aside at least temporarily in the emergencies of war. The city was a salient; projecting into the northern Virginia front, it was surrounded by southern sympathizers. Washington needed to be protected and in the process a vast area was swept into the defenses. The city became an armed camp and later a vast hospital. With its prominent architectural and urbanistic features, the city also produced patriotic symbols of an ever-united country. The city's defenses encompassed not only military posts but new methods of acquiring food, housing, and raw and manufactured materials necessary to the military and civilian functioning. These requisite goods and services were acquired forthright by the Military District of Washington, identifying the federal government as the dominant force in the city's daily existence. In the military control of the city, it can be said that the government dedicated itself to the city's survival as never before or since, even if later on it could be said that in many respects the military never left the city. Rather, utilizing the city's extant buildings and grounds to suit wartime needs, the government subsequently provided a new physical pattern upon which the city would rise.

Military preparedness had been an integral part of L'Enfant's plan for the city. The long expanse of the Potomac River downstream was intended to act as a buffer to sea attack. The Eastern Branch, site of the Navy Yard and the arsenal, was the first face of the city to accost any water-borne invasion. Fort Washington, constructed in 1809 opposite Mount Vernon on the Maryland side of the Potomac, had served as the only defense on the river prior to the Civil War. Little else had been planned in the interim and by all standards the city's defenses were meager. The decline of the Eastern Branch installations had accompanied the growth of similar facilities in other locations, such as the federal arsenal at Harpers Ferry. Although national sectional differences had been endemic during the settling of the country, the designers of Washington never anticipated a civil war and therefore had not planned for defense against attack from surrounding settlements.

John Brown's raid on the Harpers Ferry arsenal was translated into serious doubts about the capital's ability

A Fantasia of the Wartime Capital City by an Anonymous Artist, 1861

to defend itself. The transportation routes leading to the heart of the city had earlier functioned as vital links to the city's communications with Virginia and Maryland. Now these routes defined its vulnerability. The area's natural topography, a ring of hills surrounding the basin city, offered easy command of the central core.

SHELTER AND FOOD FOR THE TROOPS

When Fort Sumter was attacked in April of 1861, signaling the commencement of hostilities, fear gripped a capital city unsure of its future course. Southern sympathizers dominated the ruling groups, and thus at first no clear indication could be made of the government's commitment to the Potomac River city. In a few days, however, tens of thousands of troops for defense entered the city at the command of President Lincoln. Over the next few years, the District's population would nearly double, taxing beyond limit the city's resources. At the

opening of the war, the armory on the Mall and the barracks at the arsenal were the only places actually designed for the use of troops. Soon after, the government leased and occupied new sites of open space and buildings. Wooden stables and barracks were located on the grounds north of the Capitol and west of Seventeenth Street near the President's House. In a few months, other sites were occupied by troops, changing drastically the physical appearance of the city. Whole regiments were quartered in the Capitol, the Patent Office, and the Treasury Building, on the Georgetown College grounds, in the Center Market, in warehouses, churches, and hotels, and inside the White Muslin Palace of Aladdin which had been built for Lincoln's inaugural ball. Temporary barracks were erected in the open spaces planned by L'Enfant, on the Mall and at Observatory Hill.

Beyond N Street, both inside and outside L'Enfant's

city boundaries, the open fields were occupied, filling in the original city limits and settling the suburbs north of Boundary Street. Meridian Hill, site of antebellum racetracks, country mansions, and the Columbian College grounds, became a small town of its own, formed about hospitals and barracks. Country estates, such as William Corcoran's Harewood near the present neighborhood of LeDroit Park, were filled with troops. Other estates became hospitals. Engineer of the Washington aqueduct, Quartermaster Montgomery Meigs took over the unfinished but highly visible Corcoran Gallery of Art as his headquarters and set up the nearby army clothing department.

Grounds not devoted to troop accommodations were shifted to new functions, with the concentration of food production in the core of the city and the growth of localized industries replacing earlier reliance on goods shipped in from secessionist settlements. Under the stress of war, Washington acquired industrial characteristics that had been foreign to it before and would again be foreign afterwards.

Blacksmith Shops and Bakeries. The Washington Monument grounds became pasture land for cattle, with a slaughterhouse nearby to provide fresh meat for the soldiers. The vault in the Capitol Building, originally intended for George Washington's tomb, served as the army bakery. Within a year's time, a major center for army equipment and supplies spread over several acres of Foggy Bottom, easily serviced by the river wharves south of G Street. Here corrals and harness and blacksmith shops were located. George Washington Young's mansion on Giesboro Point, located on the Maryland side of the Potomac just south of Uniontown, was leased to the government in 1863. This strategic 624 acres of land in full view of river traffic became the major cavalry remount depot, alleviating the desperate crowding of the corrals near the Naval Observatory. Described as the largest animal depot ever organized by the army, the Giesboro Point installation accommodated as many as 30,000 horses at a time.

In order to transport food and other strategic goods to the city, the military took control of the region's

The Beef Depot Monument Where Cattle Awaiting Slaughter Are Enclosed by a Wooden Fence around the Monument Grounds, 1860s

Troops Quartered at the Treasury Building, 1861

63

DEFENSES OF WASHING
Extract of
MILITARY MAP
OF
N.E. VIRGIN

SHOWING FORTS AND ROAD
Engineer Bureau War Departr
1865.
Scale one inch to the mile

NOTE
The Coast Survey Maps were used in the c
North of the Potomac outside of the Dist of
Roads marked thus ——— were used i
military purposes

major ports. From the Georgetown flour mills and ships at the wharves flour was directed to the army bakeries. Alexandria was occupied because of its railroad connections to the South and, like Young's Giesboro Point, because of its commanding situation on the Potomac. Much of the riverfront along the Potomac and the Eastern Branch was thus devoted to military purposes, a usurpation of civilian port facilities which commercial interests would never succeed in fully regaining after the end of hostilities.

THE RING OF HILLS

To build defenses for Washington required a larger view of the city than was to be gained from ground-level maneuvering. In the summer of 1861, the Secretary of the Smithsonian, Joseph Henry, sponsored a number of balloon ascensions by Thaddeus Lowe above the city and over many battlegrounds. From such balloon flights, detailed sketches of the region could be made, affording comprehensiveness and current descriptions that were unprecedented. Then for the first time, military strategists could grasp the entirety of the natural topography: its ring of hills surrounding the basin city and the gaps facilitating roads into the city's core. New military roads began to be built, cut long and straight, by the end of the war measuring thirty-two miles in total. These new lines of communication preempted those that in the past had been focused upon Alexandria and Georgetown. Thus, the ascendancy of Washington as the primary urban center was now augmented and defined.

In order to secure the ring of highland vantage points surrounding the basin city, a chain of forts was constructed, reinforcing these points throughout that portion of the District located in Virginia and tying together these once disparate areas into a comprehensive defense design. Built to serve as temporary structures, the earth forts were constructed of timber and some masonry, surrounded by trenches, and flanked by abatis of newly felled timber. Materials to build the abatis were gathered from the woodlands along many parts of the ring. The woods were cleared for several miles in front of the military works to provide for what was described at the time as a "clear field of fire from the forts, batteries, and infantry redoubts." In fact, every movable object in front of the forts was shaved away, including houses and barns. In the course of the war, the military constructed over sixty forts and over forty supporting batteries. The location of the forts was determined both by the views offered and by proximity to important arteries. For example, Fort Reno on the heights of Tenallytown commanded three roads. Fort Foote, on a stretch of land jutting out into the Potomac, was constructed on a bluff 100 feet above the Maryland shore with full view of the channel south as far as old Fort Washington. Complementing the new Fort Foote on the Virginia shore, Battery Rogers was constructed in the corporate limits of Alexandria.

Even with this control over hills and roads, potential weaknesses existed in the line of fortification. A connecting system was therefore devised whereby enclosed field forts were sited at intervals of 800 to 1,000 yards. Field gun batteries covered the depressions in the ground between the major forts. The entire line of defense was linked by rifle trenches that also provided a vast network of strategic openings in the line for the passage of troops and artillery.

TELEGRAPHS AND MAPS

Communication between these far distant sites was facilitated by the telegraph. Reels of insulated wires were unrolled to link the War Department, housed in the Winder Building at Seventeenth and F Streets, with critical government centers within the region. A telegraph wire connected to the President's House was taken aboard a balloon flight by Professor Thaddeus Lowe in his reconnaissance of the city. Employees of the Pennsylvania Railroad worked as telegraph operators, headed by Thomas A. Scott, charged with the government railways and telegraphy. In the use of the telegraph, messages could be relayed with greater ease than by messenger. Thus, it was no longer necessary for federal bureaus to be physically close to one another. And as much as the telegraph permitted speedier communication between war strategists, it also greatly improved the relaying of news to newspaper reporters— and to the nation. Furthermore, as an adaptation, flags and the blinking of colored lights permitted long-dis-

Bird's-Eye View of Alexandria, 1863

tance communication. Similarly, a signaling method devised and taught by Colonel Albert J. Myer in Georgetown utilized the techniques of ciphering and coding as well as telescopic observation. His method having proved successful, Myer prepared a manual on signaling. In 1863, a much-impressed Congress appropriated funds to create the United States Signal Corps.

In this same period, the increasingly intense preoccupation of strategists with the natural and man-made topography fostered map-making activities, intended to clarify the outlines of military action in general and in particular to plan coastal blockades and amphibious operations. In order to hold intact his scientific staff, Alexander Dallas Bache, superintendent of the United States Coast and Geodetic Survey Office, cooperated with high-ranking military officers in preparing charts, maps, and data. Such information may have been decisive in precluding the use of the Potomac River as an easy military route into the city. Although in the short run the military evaluations most immediately affected

the problems of defense and supply, the new and vivid familiarity with the region as a whole and in detail was to have significance for the future. Many crucial peacetime decisions about the city would later on be made by men experienced in the wartime city. Among these men were Quartermaster Montgomery Meigs and United States Sanitary Commission official Frederick Law Olmsted.

PHOTOGRAPHING WASHINGTON

Photography also increased familiarity with the city. The most famous recorder of wartime Washington, Mathew Brady, photographed the important balloon experiments and the map-making activities of the topographical engineers. Brady's former partner, Alexander Gardner, was also a major wartime photographer, publishing in 1863 his *Catalogue of the Photographic Incidents of the War*. Both photographers supplied *Harper's New Monthly Magazine* and *Frank Leslie's Illustrated Newspaper* with photographs and daguerreo-

66

types from which woodcut illustrations were made. Through such illustrations, the reading population of the nation was given an unprecedented and immediately compelling view of the wartime city. New personnel policies were dramatically depicted by illustrations of female civil servants working in the Treasury Department. Photographs also revealed the war's effect on the physical city, with clean parallel rows of wooden barracks shown in front of the uncompleted Washington Monument. Revealing the new role of the Army Corps of Engineers, the official photographs of the war for governmental records were made by members of the Corps.

FREEDMEN AND THE FREEDMEN'S BUREAU

During the war years former slaves, encouraged by the 1862 act of Congress that emancipated the 3,100 slaves in the District, migrated to Washington—a safe haven. Within one year, the population of freedmen increased to approximately 10,000. Charged in 1862 was easing the plight of the incoming black population, the Freedmen's Bureau set up several "contraband villages" in the unsettled lands within the fortified region. One such settlement, opened by the Contraband Department of the Military District of Washington, was located in the bottom lands of Arlington. In exchange for housing,

View of Cattle on the Monument Grounds As Photographed by Mathew Brady from the Corner of Fourteenth Street and the Mall, 1861–62

Freedmen's Barracks in Alexandria, 1860s

the freedmen in this settlement raised hay and vegetables for the army.

Washington in Wartime: The Civilian City

The civilian city was able to adapt to the rapid physical changes brought on by the war largely because during the preceding decade, it had already been undergoing extensive change, with basic alterations being wrought by increased private and government investment. For example, the intercity railroad connections of the 1850s initiated the radial configurations of the future city. Interest had already been expressed in intracity street railroads to transport local commuters between residential neighborhoods and employment centers. And the water supply, crucial to the growth of a city, was underway.

Further municipal improvements were an outcome of the federal government's preoccupation with military demands. In his annual report of 1863, Secretary of the Interior John P. Usher suggested that the federal government share expenses of paving the city streets. Although his suggestion bore no immediate results, a congressional act passed in the following year allowed for streets to be lit, paved, and provided sewers without consent from or subsequent taxation of the abutting property owners. A general tax fund was created to finance such improvements, enabling the city government simply to order the work done. Although only little more than half the improvements ordered were actually executed, the law cleared the way for massive improvements in the postwar era.

Land and Transportation Lines. By the second year of war, Washington was a boom city, inviting investors in real estate and public services. Competition for buildings and land had become so intense that during the war assessments for real estate property increased markedly in proportion to market value. The population had become so enlarged and far-flung that many residential areas already were more than a comfortable walk from the downtown. In 1862, Henry Cooke persuaded Congress to grant him a charter to build and operate the city's first street railroad system. In July of that year, the streetcar line between the Capitol and the Willard Hotel at Fourteenth Street and Pennsylvania Avenue was opened, serving the major downtown strip along the Avenue. In the fall of 1862, the main line from Georgetown to the Navy Yard via the Capitol was opened, with lateral branches along Seventh Street and Fourteenth Street added later. The initial handsome profits made by Cooke's line inspired the chartering in 1864 of a new streetcar line, the Metropolitan Railroad Company. This new company constructed its line on the first terrace above the lowland city along F Street, predicting that thoroughfare's eventual emergence as the city's desirable shopping area.

Threat of Fire, Disease, and Disorder. The congested city filled with roving military men and other newcomers raised questions about daily security. As early as 1860, city officials had asked Congress for a larger police force than the day patrol of fifty officers. In the following year Congress, acknowledging widespread social problems in the swollen city, created the metropolitan police department. At its inception, the force consisted of a superintendent, ten sergeants, and one hundred and fifty patrolmen. Fire on the scale of the conflagrations that devastated many American cities became a near reality in Washington when massive fires broke out at the government stables. Such fires killed hundreds of animals, and those that survived panicked and stampeded through the startled city. Emergencies of this magnitude were beyond the capabilities of the eight hook, hose, and ladder companies then in existence. In 1864, a consolidated and salaried fire department was created and outfitted with three steam engines, a fire alarm, and a police telegraph. The congestion of the city also threatened its occupants with disease. Smallpox struck in Washington in the winter of 1862. The metropolitan police, instructed to be on the lookout for conditions contributing to contagion, made inspections for discarded refuse close to crowded quarters and removed obvious nuisances. Not until the following year did the War Department begin to bear responsibility for the waste accumulated by its own overwhelming presence in the city. By summer of 1863, municipal garbage carts were making regular rounds, at last providing inhabitants with public services befitting a modern city.

The Triangle. One product of the wartime city that defied police action and protection was the notorious area around "Murder Bay" and "Hookers' Division." Formed as a triangle by the canal, Pennsylvania Avenue, and Fourteenth Street, the area's transformation during the war into a crime-ridden neighborhood signaled the twilight of the Avenue as Washington's desirable shopping area. Although this triangle had begun its history of decay with increased use of the canal for sewer purposes, it began to live up to its name of Murder Bay with transient military men—and also the unemployed or underemployed—frequenting its various abodes of entertainment. All types of criminals, thieves, and prostitutes collected in dilapidated housing, often using the euphemism "oyster houses," presenting such a concentration of vice that the police were powerless to defend innocent victims. Even so, military officers and government officials frequented this area to patronize its gambling and game houses, the best of which were located near Fourteenth Street and Pennsylvania Avenue. By the war's end, the triangle presented a distinct image, notorious, dangerous, and isolated from the rest of the surrounding city.

In this wartime city, other forms of recreation and amusement could be found. The resumption of the Marine Band concerts within a few months after the outbreak of the war projected a reassuring air of normalcy in the heavily guarded city. In this secured atmosphere, moreover, three new theaters were established. They were joined by an amusement hall redesigned from the former Odd Fellows Hall on Louisiana Avenue and renamed Canterbury Hall, suggesting the arrival of "high culture" in Washington.

Washington in Transition: The War's End

At the war's end, the reunited Congress viewed a changed city. While much of the transient military population left, the number of permanent residents in the city jumped 50 percent. Some of the government installations found their wartime locations suitable for the future defense of the city. Services offered and new functions inaugurated by the government during the

war could not suddenly be halted. The "temporary settlements" outside the city for which the government had had no plans became the nuclei of future permanent neighborhoods. The open spaces within the old city —the Mall and the series of smaller parks—had earlier been planned for special functions; these spaces were slowly returned to their prewar state. The rapid municipal improvements that had been implemented to accommodate population influx would continue as the wartime growth proved permanent.

POSTWAR CHANGES IN MARYLAND, VIRGINIA,
AND THE DISTRICT

Suburban Maryland and Virginia were now oriented to Washington rather than to their respective state capitals. And critical to the future management of the city and its environs was the efficiency in government that had been demonstrated by the Military District of Washington. Here was a model for directness and scope in metropolitan government, a standard of governmental operation difficult to emulate even as late as mid-twentieth century.

In the public sector, the government retained the large installation at Giesboro Point (the present Bolling Anacostia Tract). The federal government also retained ownership of many of the wartime fort sites. The ring of forts was dismantled, but the lands with their mossy ruins were not reclaimed as farmland. These lands were available, therefore, for acquisition later on by the National Capital Park and Planning Commission for park development. Today these forts are historic landmarks, artifacts expressing the natural topographical defenses exploited by military strategists.

Nearly all of the Virginia side of the defended city was returned to civilian uses. Exceptions were the green hills opposite the basin city. Part of the former Robert E. Lee plantation was also retained in federal ownership. Dedicated as the Arlington National Cemetery, the Lee plantation would serve the nation as a new symbol of national unity, a burial place for both Union and Confederate soldiers.

The Freedmen's Bureau continued into the postwar era, converting Campbell Hospital at the head of Sixth Street, NW, into Freedmen's Hospital. A new residen-

Panoramic Views of Washington from the Tower of the Smithsonian Institution Building, Early 1870s

tial area provided by the bureau was carved out of the old Barry Farms between Saint Elizabeths Hospital and Uniontown (Anacostia). The federal government provided further commitment to the black population in the establishment of Howard University, chartered in 1866 and located on a commanding bluff on Seventh Street just north of Boundary Street.

The leisurely southern persuasions of the prewar civilian city of Washington survived the Union triumph, although the physical accoutrements of the distinctive life-style were never recovered. The large country seats, taken over by the government during the war years, had attracted small settlements and thus opened the way for exploitation of these areas as suburban residential neighborhoods. In much of this nearly cleared metropolitan land, northerners settled, while southern sympathizers tended to move west or south to other parts of the country. In the metropolitan area itself, the farming activities originally organized to serve military needs now served the growing urban population.

Suburbanization. Seen both in far-flung black settlements and in the subdivision of land tracts, suburbani-

zation was made possible by extension of the streetcar system. New postwar routes were established along major commercial and transportation corridors extending from the central city to Georgetown via Connecticut Avenue and P Street, north along Seventh and Fourteenth Streets. They made large newly subdivided tracts accessible to streetcar commuters. As in the twentieth-century city to come, development patterns would be strongly influenced by the location and extent of transportation facilities. The railroad, indispensable to supplying the wartime city, was given a greater visual presence as well as symbolic linkage to the government's fortunes in the new Baltimore & Ohio train depot and tracks fronting Capitol Hill. Rail traffic would dominate the transportation and communication networks of the peacetime city, further decreasing water-borne traffic. Still, the river was accessible to many of the region's localities that were virtually untouched by the railroad, and so it would continue to serve as a carrier of passengers and produce between riverfront settlements for many years to come.

The View from the Tower. By the end of 1865, tents

and other signs of wartime military activity had largely disappeared from the Mall and other nonmilitary areas of the city. New streetcar tracks imposed their pattern and attendant activity across the city. As viewed from the central tower of the original Smithsonian Institution Building, the uncompleted Washington Monument and tidal swamps beyond to the west seemed to be waiting for the transition to end. From the same

tower vantage point, a completed Capitol dome was visible. The dome overlooked the awakening city and symbolized the national unity President Lincoln had striven to establish. This new unity would have a permanent effect on the shape and character of the national capital city, affording a clearer vision of new directions for Washington.

CHAPTER IV   THE POSTBELLUM CITY   1865–1900

The Postbellum City 1865-1900

The Winds of Peace: Demilitarized City

The salvation of the Union was assured but Washington's future as the capital city was less certain. The earlier failure of the federal government to make the necessary commitment in public improvements—and of the commercial city itself to develop an enduring mercantile trade—relegated the river basin city to severe environmental degradation. In the postwar era, the affluent residents would turn away from the river city to higher ground, as both the search for healthier living conditions and the new mobility of the transit system motivated them. At the same time, the low-lying areas of this basin city would be taken over by blue-collar workers, who occupied the older houses or moved into the new and relatively cheap row houses and alley dwellings. In this pattern, a future polarization of the city was foretold along social and racial lines as well as by locality. Given the abandonment of the basin city by many newly mobile residents, some reaffirmation by the federal government to the city was of primary importance. In the provision of public services—water, sewers, the park system, and street planting—the initial federal con-

cern was environmental quality. No strong comprehensive policy as yet ruled public improvement. Decisions about parks, public buildings, and the sitings of public projects were made on an ad hoc basis, leaving the way open at the century's end for a more systematic approach to the city's physical future.

As the winds of peace blew over Washington, the inhabitants—numbering over 100,000—were faced with the immediate challenge of demilitarizing the city. In the transition, some hospitals constructed for the care of wartime casualties were retained for permanent use. Lumber and other building materials used in temporary structures were recycled for use in public and private building. Lands confiscated in and around Washington for military encampments were returned to private use. Samuel C. Busey, whose farm at Belvoir had been surrounded during the war years by troops, observed the return to peacetime conditions: "The soldiers, camps, barracks, parade-grounds, and hospitals disappeared, and labor, help, and hirelings returned in some measure to the accustomed ways and pursuits of former days. But a new era had come, and with it new methods, new enterprises, and a new impetus to thought and ambition."

Restoring confidence in the reunited country was a

*Interior View of the Pension Building
As It Looks Today*

symbolic task as well as a concern of political substance. Not only did the physical scars of the former military presence need to be removed, but the city's essential public services—as initiated by Montgomery Meigs's aqueduct before the war—needed modernization. Federal and municipal officials faced along B Street a stinking canal that served as an unofficial sewer. The lowlands to the south of the President's House resembled an untamed marsh, its westernmost sections merging into the Tiber Creek as it fed the canal. Wide-piered Long Bridge, the main route connecting the North and the South, acted as a barrier to the free flow of water downstream, silting up the Potomac River along the shores of Washington and Georgetown. Development of a powerful commercial depot at the capital city's wharves was thus precluded—a gloomy future for those of the upriver port. Inland, public squares that had been set aside as parks by the L'Enfant plan were instead covered by houses.

THE CENTRAL BUSINESS DISTRICT

Center Market had served as the focal point for commercial activity along Pennsylvania Avenue ever since it located there, on Market Square, in the early years of the nineteenth century. The location was fixed by the crossing of Pennsylvania Avenue and Seventh Street, the principal connection between the waterfront and Bladensburg Road, a turnpike and post road leading to Baltimore and points further north. Here at the crossing L'Enfant had provided a turning basin for canal boats that brought produce into town. Market stalls within Market Square proper contained a large and diversified range of goods. More specialized functions defined the markets that grew up nearby. The area along Eighth Street between the market and the Patent Office was devoted to clothing, with secondary lines of other marketing activities along Seventh and Ninth Streets and northeast along Indiana Avenue. Center Market had been a powerful magnet, attracting the best of the produce and household goods and commanding a competitive position over the localized neighborhood markets, like Western Market, the market at O Street, NW, and the market on Capitol Hill. Out of Center Market evolved the central business district, Washington's re-

tailing core. At the same time, other localized markets would assume a more important position in the expanding residential areas, marking the general trend: transformation of the capital city from small town to large city. This strong nodal structure of urban growth, hinged on functions like markets, is precisely the pattern predicted by L'Enfant—as his provision for future growth generated from a number of strategic points attests.

PERMANENCY FOR WASHINGTON, CAPITAL CITY

The preponderance of individual enterprise and initiative over that of the federal government for at least a decade following the war set up great uncertainty about Washington's future, especially its future as the nation's capital city. Potential sites for a new "Seat of Empire" included Philadelphia, an old city which had profited handsomely from supplying war materials. Other invitations came from midwestern states with offers of major cities like Saint Louis and Cincinnati as sites for the federal establishment.

Advocates of removal of the capital city from Washington could not, however, overlook the distinctive social and physical city that had blossomed during nearly seven decades. The comings and goings of politicians, foreign dignitaries, and civil servants created a culture unique to Washington. The city was the focal point in a cycle of social seasons. By 1881, *Harper's New Monthly Magazine* was describing the fascinated caravan of "rich or energetic and inquiring inhabitants of other places" who came to live in Washington periodically, so that "Washington may be called the winter end of New York, as Newport is the summer extension of the metropolis." The point is that the highly structured Washington winter season—commencing at New Year's Day with a reception given by the president and his wife, and ending at Lent—encouraged these "inhabitants of other places" to invest in opulent residences in Washington.

Just as important to the growth of cultural and scientific institutions in the city (and the nation) was the large number of brilliant men who came to Washington during the Civil War, rose quickly through the wartime ranks, and then found in the intellectual and professional opportunities of the government and other public institutions a reason for staying. The Smithsonian Institution, for example, attracted scientific-minded intellectuals, and the various departments of the executive branch of government were staffed by distinguished professionals. Federal bureaus like the Patent Office, the Geological Survey, and the National Observatory also served as magnets to draw the nation's outstanding scientists and social scientists to Washington. Leading architects and artists, attracted to the capital city by major public building projects, also enhanced the intellectual climate. With this concentration of accomplished citizens, Washington through this period was known as the "paradise of a poor man with brains." Indeed the presence as well as the general tastes of these highly mobile intellectuals of modest means was evident in the distinctive row houses of restrained proportions nevertheless embellished in a style analogous to the grandeur of the millionaires' mansions in Washington.

PERMANENCY FOR THE L'ENFANT PLAN

This same promise of magnificence was felt in a far more essential way. Critical to Washington's salvation as the capital city, the still unfinished original city plan had a recognized grandeur, whereas a new site could offer only accommodation to an extant set of urban conditions or else the creation of some new and undefined plan. In 1875, a reporter for *Harper's New Monthly Magazine* writing about the partially executed L'Enfant plan recounted the relationship of the plan to the symbolism of the major public buildings and to the natural topography. By the third quarter of the century, as the article observed, development over the land's irregular surface had proceeded in such a way that the major public buildings and adjacent development on highland sites, as well as on the hilly terrain of Georgetown and the Eastern Branch heights, rose from the river bottom settlement to create a city "somewhat like Quebec, an upper and lower town." The writer ascribed the irregularities of the land to the "soil friable under the action of water, and affected by three brooks or creeks," the Tiber, Rock Creek, and the Eastern Branch.

With the advantages of the city reaffirmed, the strat-

egy in retaining the Potomac River site was based on completing and thus giving permanency to the L'Enfant plan. In error is a common belief that L'Enfant's plan was "lost" for much of the nineteenth century, only to be "found" and revived for the McMillan Commission in 1901. In fact, retention of the essential elements of the L'Enfant plan—the sweeping avenues, the chain of park areas along the Mall area, the public spaces at the conjunction of the radials and the grid, and the locations of the major branches of government as developed between 1792 and the Civil War—dominated public improvements of the postwar city, even if certain major changes in the plan had been made in the decades immediately following the issuance of L'Enfant's plan.

L'Enfant's original map, the manuscript plan of 1791, imprinted by the Office of the Commissioner of Public Buildings, was recopied in 1887 under the direction of F. M. Thorn of the United States Coast and Geodetic Survey as evidence of the title of the United States to the reclaimed lands along the Potomac River. This evidence was brought to bear in the Potomac flats suit, *Martin F. Morris et al. vs. United States*. One can assume from the plan's availability and use in legal proceedings that it was consulted by both federal and municipal officials engaged in public improvements. The Mall, to cite the most obvious focal point of L'Enfant's intentions, was subjected to many grand embellishments throughout the last quarter of the nineteenth century, from the reclaimed finger of land (now East Potomac Park) to the layout and plantings along the Mall proper. The implementation of improvements to the old city was more than cosmetic. A new city steadily emerged. Largely based on L'Enfant's scheme, this city was seen to be worthy of federal commitment to its future as the capital city—and thus worthy also as city of residence for those who had made their fortunes elsewhere but would be attracted to the seat of federal power.

THE CONSTITUENT CITY

The distinction between the public city and the private city was not always clear. One depended on the other. Residents of the constituent city depended on the federal and municipal governments to provide a clean water supply, to lay out and pave streets, to define and develop public parks, to provide sites for public markets, and to maintain the city according to up-to-date sanitation standards. In return, the public city counted on the private residents to support its public works projects, to fill its labor demands, and to build and reside in residential structures befitting the nation's capital city.

While much public effort was spent on extensive tidying up of federal reservations and buildings in the flatlands, public improvements also carved out new roads into the highlands rising in a crescent of settlements about the antebellum city. In these newly accessible areas, the government found prime lots of land for federally supported institutions. Among these was Howard University, started in 1866, as mentioned, on hills to the north of the city center, along Seventh Street. New residential areas were also carved out in the highlands, providing after-office-hours escape from the heat and foul air of the lowlands and establishing new patterns of residential activity.

Public Works: The Army Corps of Engineers

In 1867, even before the question of the capital's ultimate future was resolved, the United States Army Corps of Engineers shouldered the federal government's responsibilities for the creation and upkeep of public works, buildings, and grounds, responsibilities previously discharged by the Office of the Commissioner of Public Buildings. The first of a long list of remarkable and versatile engineers who fulfilled these responsibilities as Officer in Charge of the Corps was Nathaniel Michler. Born in Easton, Pennsylvania, in 1827, Michler had achieved recognition in the battle of Petersburg, Virginia, and was brevetted brigadier general.

MAJOR PUBLIC WORKS PROBLEMS AND THE WORK OF
NATHANIEL MICHLER

Four major and closely related problems facing Michler reflected the immediate public works needs of the postwar city: 1) paving and adornment of Pennsylvania

Avenue, with special consideration of the President's House, and at the same time 2) inspection of alternative highland sites that might be suitable for a new presidential residence; 3) dredging of the Potomac River not only to improve navigation and reclaim the lowland marshes, but also to render the Tiber Creek flood plain and the land south of Pennsylvania Avenue floodproof; and 4) clearer definition of the city's public parks starting with the sprawling magnificence of a "National Park" along Rock Creek and including many smaller triangular neighborhood greens planned throughout the L'Enfant city.

PENNSYLVANIA AVENUE AND ITS ENVIRONS

At the end of the war, Pennsylvania Avenue remained the city's principal street, although its physical appearance did not in any way connote the grandeur of an urban "ceremonial way." On the north side of this lively street, one found hotels and many boarding houses patronized by members of Congress and their staffs during the short legislative sessions. A brick sidewalk provided the environment for fashionable promenades even if the Avenue itself was largely unpaved. Shops lined the way, most of them occupied above by residential apartments. A principal feature of Pennsylvania Avenue was the horse omnibus tracks, following the shortest line from Georgetown to the Capitol and on to the Navy Yard. (The other omnibus route led up Seventh Street.)

The City Canal. The south side of the Avenue reflected the low estate of the area south of the City Canal. Washingtonians generally called this area "the Island." Here the decaying City Canal presented a barrier, a marshy area, bridged at Maryland Avenue and at Seventh, Tenth, Twelfth, and Fourteenth Streets. Heavy rains and high tides brought the waters to Pennsylvania Avenue proper, particularly where the old bed of the Tiber Creek crossed it at Second Street. To the south, the decline of the waterfront area had been accelerated by the wartime port of embarkation on the southwest waterfront at the Sixth and Seventh Street wharves, a concentration point for both troops and civilians. Around this population center, gambling places, houses of pros-

View from Pennsylvania Avenue down Eleventh Street to the Mall and the Smithsonian Institution Building, 1874

titution, theaters, cheap entertainment spots, bars, eating houses, and places of amusement clustered, showing their distinctive faces on the south side of the Avenue. Here on "the Island," illicit activities formed themselves into "Hookers' Division." To the west, near Fourteenth Street, the area was called Murder Bay, a freedmen's settlement.

The low-lying topography contributed the popular name to the city's central market: "Marsh Market." At this strategic spot had grown up not only the produce market, but a brisk trade in dry goods, books, stationery, and the banking and business establishments of the antebellum capital city. In the postbellum era, as the city spread beyond pedestrian limits, Center Market was also transformed; no longer serving just the daily needs of city inhabitants, it now provided for more specialized wants. General Michler, in the 1868 *Annual Report of the Chief of Engineers*, took a dimmer view of the mar-

ket atmosphere, describing the area around the canal as "overrun by market stalls, piles of lumber, and junk shops."

THE PRESIDENT'S HOUSE

The President's House stood to the west of this bustling market area. To the south, the mansion faced sewerlike conditions of the flats and City Canal, the notorious "B Street Main." Smells and malarial mosquitoes became a nuisance and hazard, especially in the hot summer months, forcing even presidents to flee to highland country estates such as Anderson Cottage at the Soldiers' Home. Moreover, comfort and health conditions aside, the south side of the President's House grounds was clearly an inappropriate conclusion to the parks surrounding the mansion. Set apart in the midst of swirling city life, the Executive Mansion could offer the president little in the way of a haven from the "active

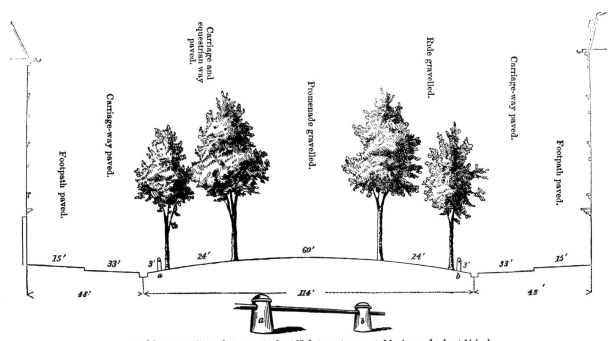

Carriage and
equestrian way
paved.

Carriage-way paved.

Footpath paved.

Promenade gravelled.

Ride gravelled.

Carriage-way paved.

Footpath paved.

15' 33' 3' 24' 60' 24' 3' 33' 15'

48' 114' 48'

a and *b* represent lines of stone posts about 15 feet apart, connected by iron rods about 1¼ inch.

Montgomery Meigs's Sketch of Unter-den-Linden, Berlin, from a *Letter by Meigs to General Nathaniel Michler Written* 27 July 1867

Montgomery Meigs's Sketch Showing Plan for the Improvement of Streets and Avenues in the City of Washington, 1868

Sketch showing Plan for the Improvement of Streets and Avenues in the City

OF

WASHINGTON.

Asphalt
9'
Gravelled

Asphalt
9'
Gravelled

FROM AVENUE DES CHAMPS ELYSÉES, PARIS, 240' WIDE.
reduced to 160'

MacAdamized

50' 60' 50'

A: Gas; B: Water; C: Sewer.

Accompanying Report of N. Michler, Maj. of Eng.rs & Brig. Gen.l U.S.A. dated Sep.t 30th 1868.

cares and business of his high office"—as the *Annual Report of the Chief of Engineers* for 1867 noted—"where he can secure that ease, comfort, and seclusion so necessary to a statesman."

Planning, Paving, and Adorning the Avenue. Now Pennsylvania Avenue needed to be paved and adorned—but patterned after what model? In his travels through Europe in 1867 to recover his health, Montgomery Meigs sent a letter to Michler describing the paving of streets in cities of Germany, Denmark, and Prussia. With reference to the brick paving of Pennsylvania Avenue, Meigs observed: "Sidewalks here [in Europe] are never paved with brick." European pavements were created primarily of Belgian blocks or flagstones, laid out at right angles to the line of travel, or with cobblestones and gravel packed closely in a bed of sand. In Berlin, fountains and statues were surrounded by fine mosaic work created out of colored Belgian blocks and marble fragments. Meigs suggested that natural stones available in the Washington area might be readily adaptable to this vivid presentation of street adornment: red and gray sandstone from the Seneca, Maryland, quarries and blue- and white-veined limestone from the Potomac.

THE WASHINGTON STREET SYSTEM

As for an ideal street layout, Meigs studied Unter-den-Linden in Berlin, and sent home his sketch of it showing a wide gravel central walk, four rows of shade trees, and wide sidewalks next to the houses. Berlin's principal hotels and shops faced the parklike street. This arrangement generated much foot traffic during the day while at night the wide walks attracted promenaders, making the street a resort for business and recreation. Viewing the success of the physical layout of this Berlin street, Meigs hoped it would serve as "authority in introducing improvements as yet novel in Washington."

One year later, in his 1868 report on the improvement of Washington's streets and avenues, Michler presented his own street scheme, patterned after the Champs Elysées. Whereas Meigs had suggested broad paved areas extending out from the houses, Michler placed a row of trees against the houses with a broad paved area separating the residential trees from the street trees. Michler's macadamized central thoroughfare replaced Meigs's graveled promenade. In both designs, however, the width of the paved streets was dramatically narrowed, a necessary prerequisite if all of Washington's streets were to be modernized under the press of time and financial constraints.

Paving and planting Pennsylvania Avenue would go far to reclaim the street from its postwar undeveloped condition. On the other hand, its vulnerability to the periodic freshets of the Potomac River discouraged the federal government from building any major public buildings along or south of the Avenue. For example, in the early 1880s during the planning stages of Meigs's Pension Building, the original site in proximity to Pennsylvania Avenue (at the old intersection of Ohio and Louisiana Avenues) was rejected in favor of a higher site at Judiciary Square because of concern over the unpredictable behavior of the river. Thus, if Pennsylvania Avenue were to realize development, reclamation of the flats to floodproof the land to the south was essential.

PLANS FOR DREDGING THE POTOMAC

Beyond the benefits that would accrue to Pennsylvania Avenue from river improvements, General Michler viewed the dredging of the river in the process of reclamation as an improvement to navigation and an impetus to expanded commercial trade in Washington and Georgetown. Not having relinquished the expectation that Washington might yet become a major commercial center, Michler suggested the dredging of two channels—along the city's shores and along those of Virginia—to a depth of twelve feet. The removal of Long Bridge, functioning more as a dam than a bridge, as it "contracted the current and obstructed the flow of the tide," would aid in releasing large volumes of water, scouring the obstructions and securing adequate depths of water for navigation. Breakwaters should be constructed, Michler thought, to deflect water into the new channels, and a cut be opened for the Tiber to allow strong currents of deep water to scour the sewerage, which otherwise was left to spread over the flats and "generate pestilential vapors." So wrote Michler in the 1868 Annual *Report of the Chief of Engineers.* Despite Michler's urgings and those of his immediate successors, little serious attention was paid by the congressional Committee on Public Buildings and Grounds to the improvement of the Potomac until after the massive flood of 1881.

SHALL THE PRESIDENT'S HOUSE BE MOVED?

The proximity of the President's House to the uncompleted Pennsylvania Avenue and the hazards of the Potomac flats encouraged some members of Congress to seek out potential new sites for the mansion, most preferably in the countryside. In ordering Michler to study these sites, the Committee on Public Buildings and Grounds implied some readiness to make a dramatic departure from L'Enfant's site selection, which in the case of the President's House had been made in accordance with President Washington's wishes. Michler, in his *Annual Report of the Chief of Engineers* for 1867, proposed four alternative locations. The first site was at Meridian Hill. "On the first range of hills bounding the limits of the City of Washington," but only one and a half miles from the Executive Mansion, it was too near to the city, Michler thought, and would be exposed to the "miasmic influences" rising from the marshes of the Potomac. In addition, the Meridian Hill site offered little as a haven from urban cares. In 1867, "already the street railroad approached, and numerous houses [were] being built on all sides" of Sixteenth Street, reflecting the accelerating real estate activity in Washington just two years after the close of the Civil War. The remaining three sites, at least three miles away from the present President's House, were situated in the northeast section of the District on former estate grounds with commanding views of the environs of Washington City. Michler argued strongly for the northeast sites, but no further action was taken on the matter.

PUBLIC PARKS AND THE MALL

In the realization of Washington as a city much like London, Philadelphia, and New York, public parks were now viewed as an urban necessity. Recently established and immediately celebrated park areas totaling thousands of acres graced these other cities. In 1865, over seven and a half million visitors entered New York's Central Park. All classes of Washingtonians desired and deserved their own large preserve of greenery for healthy recreation, and the expected expansion of the city in the future envisaged little open space left unless it was procured in the public interest. Only one portion of the Mall, that fronting the Smithsonian, was "tastefully" laid out. The partially developed Lafayette Square to the north of the President's House suffered from grading-induced drainage problems as in the undeveloped marshes to the south. On the east side of the Capitol grounds, croquet games and band music attracted citizens, although the gradual rise of the ground away from the Capitol concealed both these activities and views of the entire Capitol Building from the northeast and southeast sections of the city. The city's other major parks—squares, circles, and triangles—had yet to be cleared and formed.

Rock Creek Park. Nathaniel Michler's suggestions for what he termed a "National Park," vividly described by him, were ultimately his most enduring contribution to the physical appearance of the city. The valley of Rock Creek, a "wild and romantic tract," wound as a serpentine canyon through the northwest section of the city and thus acted as a barrier to extensive settlement west of the creek, except for Georgetown, which was connected to the rest of Washington by the Pennsylvania Avenue Bridge that Montgomery Meigs had built to carry water into the city. The lower creek valley, the site of mills and light industry, was divided among several large property owners with land parcels extending up to higher farming land to either side. The combination of rushing waters, deep ravines, and varied greenery—the landscape taste of the times—appealed to Michler who envisioned winding roads and paths, and ornamental lakes and ponds created from the creek's waters. This picturesque tract was in a central position to both Washington and Georgetown and was adaptable to many uses: zoological and botanical gardens, playgrounds, and a processional route. Looking forward to the city's expansion, General Michler suggested in his *Annual Report* for 1867 that the Committee on Public Buildings and Grounds "purchase at once a sufficient

*Detail of the A. Boschke Topographical Map
of the District of Columbia, 186*

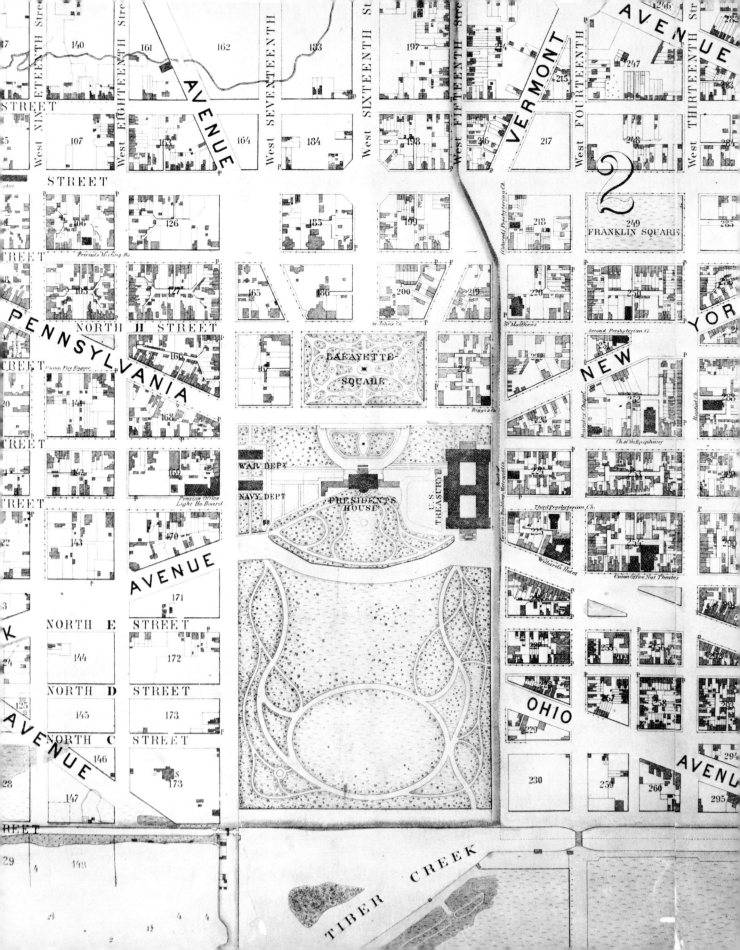

number of acres bordering on Rock Creek to anticipate the further growth of the city and its increased population," an area of 2,540 acres embracing the forts in the area constructed during the Civil War for the defense of the city.

Hopes for a Unified Mall. Michler recommended that the adjoining open areas or reservations making up the then irregular Mall should be made to correspond in appearance with the Downing-designed portion fronting the Smithsonian. Foretelling their ultimate agglomeration, the open areas should be "laid out in carriageways, paths for equestrians, and walks for pedestrians, as if the different parts formed a unit." A major hindrance to forming a unified public parkland out of the separate reservations was the Baltimore & Potomac Railroad Station, later called the Pennsylvania Railroad Station, a scene of great activity and noise. As Michler wrote in his *Annual Report* for 1868, "the running of the trains is now distinctly heard within the halls of the Senate, and shrill screams of the engine must frequently interfere with debate." Yet in 1868, partial fulfillment of Michler's efforts in the Mall area was at hand: the thirty-five acres of experimental gardens fronting the Department of Agriculture Building were designed to serve as an instructional exhibit with ornamental flowers and shrubbery.

THE SQUARES AND CIRCLES

To the north and east of the public reservations, other public park areas and connecting avenues also faced substantial improvement reflecting the maturation of the surrounding residential developments. Two blocks northwest of Lafayette Square was Farragut Square, adorned by trees and shrubbery, with water pipes laid in anticipation of a fountain. On K Street between Thirteenth and Fourteenth Streets, was Franklin Square with its undulating terrain, about to be landscaped in treatment similar to that of the Downing-planned Smithsonian grounds. This square was described by Michler in his *Annual Report* for 1871 as comparing favorably with Lafayette Square. To the east of the Capitol, at Lincoln Square, miniature lakes were planned. The grounds of the Capitol itself were in need of clearance, however, as the northern boundary of these grounds still held a stonecutter's yard while the southern boundary remained covered with stables and sheds. Other unimproved public squares and reservations restated the Capitol grounds situation: Scott Circle was studded with frame buildings, and Massachusetts Avenue was described in the *Annual Report of the Chief of Engineers* for 1868 as having "remained closed [for many years], houses, gardens, brick kilns, and other obstructions preventing it from being used."

The system of romantic and picturesque public parks as envisioned by Nathaniel Michler remained incomplete when he left his Washington position in 1871; it was for his successors to expand on his work. The extension of these projects revealed by the end of the century the makings of a continuous and unified park system, composed of the massive Rock Creek Park and the Mall and its appendages. The two major parks were laced together by wide avenues which in turn were threaded through the smaller squares, circles, and triangles.

The Territorial Government of Washington: 1871-1874

In the years immediately following the Civil War, a critical issue was the form that municipal government would take and the commitment to it that Congress would guarantee. The future of the city was at stake. In 1871, the problem appeared to be resolved. In that year Congress created a territorial form of government which, while touted throughout the following decades as "self-government" by Washington citizenry, was actually a blend of local and federal participation, the most powerful positions being dependent on presidential appointment. The Organic Act provided that citizens elect twenty-two members to a house of delegates and a nonvoting delegate to the United States House of Representatives. The governor, governing council, and heads of administrative departments were to be appointed by the president. The Board of Public Works was created to deal with the city's public improvements and was to be advised by a panel of notable engineers, architects, and landscape designers, including Montgomery C. Meigs and Frederick Law Olmsted, Sr.

In the three years of territorial government, three men worked feverishly—and brilliantly—to improve the face of the city and thus secure Washington's future as the national capital city: Alexander R. Shepherd as prime mover in the municipal Board of Public Works, Orville E. Babcock both as major in the Corps of Engineers in charge of public buildings and grounds and as a member of the advisory panel to the Board of Public Works, and Alfred B. Mullett as Supervising Architect of the Treasury Department and architect of the great State, War and Navy Building.

ALEXANDER R. SHEPHERD AND THE BOARD OF PUBLIC WORKS

Of the three men, Shepherd was the best known. Thrust into supporting his family at the age of thirteen, Shepherd began a career in business that very early projected him as an exceptional man. Accumulating a small fortune while working for J. W. Thompson's plumbing and gas fitting company, Shepherd made many business and political friends on his way up. Backed by a powerful group of supporters, Shepherd forced through Congress the territorial form of government that promised federal support for long-deferred public works. Although Henry D. Cooke, brother of financier and railroad baron Jay Cooke, was appointed governor, Shepherd was appointed to the municipal Board of Public Works, a position he made more powerful than Cooke's.

The blending of federal and municipal interests was especially prominent in the public works projects. Federal officials served on the Board of Public Works, presumably to oversee federal interests. Projects undertaken by Shepherd, however, including planting of trees, construction of sewers, filling in of the Washington City Canal, and laying of streets, were distinctly different from the tasks of the Corps of Engineers. The Corps's primary concerns, as already noted, encompassed dredging the Potomac River for both navigation and reclamation purposes, improving the water supply, and improving and maintaining not only Pennsylvania Avenue but associated public parks, reservations, and buildings. For the public buildings, the Supervising Architect of the Treasury Department or the Architect

of the Capitol took primary responsibility, except that in the case of the State, War and Navy Building, Alfred Mullett was specially retained by Secretary of State Hamilton Fish. In the three years of rapid public improvements under territorial government, friendships between federal and municipal officials played an important role—to the benefit of the city, if also in some cases to the personal financial benefit of the officials involved.

The Sewer System and the City Canal. Planning and laying gas and sewer pipes, and afterwards grading and paving the streets, marked Shepherd's most dramatic improvement activity in the city. Attention was paid to the central part of the city, the business sections, and especially Pennsylvania Avenue, Seventh Street, and Fourteenth Street. Two major sewers running parallel to the Washington City Canal were laid: one, running from Sixth Street to Third Street, emptied into the sluggish waters of the City Canal, while the other, running from Seventh Street to Seventeenth Street, emptied into the Potomac River. Later the City Canal itself was filled, and a sewer pipe was laid along its route to serve as an outlet. Once paved the canal was renamed B Street (now Constitution Avenue) and adorned as other Washington streets, its completion and proximity to the President's South Park and the Washington Monument foretelling its later monumental functions.

Pennsylvania Avenue, already conceived as a ceremonial way, demanded special treatment. It was paved with wooden blocks, a material in wide use in other American cities. Lesser streets did not always benefit from an agreed upon system of grading, however, and in some cases improvements plowed through settled areas where houses had been constructed according to the natural contours of the land, now leaving some buildings either perched on the new bluff or half-sunken below the new grade. Hills in unsettled areas were leveled and valleys filled in, providing a flat terrain for development. To crown these completed streets, Shepherd arranged for trees to be planted—as ornamentation, shade, and, as it was popularly inferred, to decrease erosion and provide for ventilation.

The frantic pace and high expenditures, which resulted in a debt of $10,000,000 by the end of 1872, invited congressional investigation and public discredit on Shepherd. His forthright actions in tearing down the public market at Mount Vernon Square, for example, and in removing the Baltimore & Ohio Railroad tracks at Second Street and Pennsylvania Avenue characterized Shepherd as all the more controversial. Although the territorial form of government was abolished in 1874, after three and a half years of existence, and Shepherd's reputation was too clouded for him to be offered further governmental positions, Shepherd did envision a physical plan that had exceeded in scale anything undertaken in the city since L'Enfant. Shepherd's legacy to the city was of consequence. In his concentration of efforts on the business section of the city and on residential neighborhoods west of Capitol Hill, the eastern section of the city was ignored, reinforcing the pejorative characterization of that sector as limited to middle- and lower-income dwellings. This negative reputation the area was to bear for years to come.

The central business district improvements caught the eye of congressmen, residents, and visitors, persuading them that the city was indeed worthy of the nation. The 1875 *Harper's New Monthly Magazine* article on Washington enthusiastically alludes to the up-to-date status of the sewer, water, and gas systems servicing the city. In particular the streets, upgraded by Shepherd's efforts, merited special attention, being "covered with the most noiseless and perfect pavements in the world, and embowered in the greenest borders of grass-plots, inclosed with panels of post and chain or graceful paling, and planted with trees. . . . At all points of junction new squares and circles appeared, their verdure relieved with flashing fountains, or bits of statuary, or effects in sodded terraces, all ready for the sculptor. . . ." The city, with its new physical appearance and attendant social and cultural "remodeling," shared with the industrial cities to the north a sudden revival of confidence. Washington had "clothed itself anew, thrown away its staff, and achieved a transformation bewildering to its old residents, but very grateful to the patriotic sense

which had so long felt the stigma of a neglected and forlorn capital apparently without a destiny." As a final compliment, the newly formed commission system of federally controlled municipal government, adopted in 1874, pledged itself to support and continue the public improvements that had been initiated by Shepherd.

MAJOR ORVILLE E. BABCOCK

Major Orville E. Babcock of the Army Corps of Engineers rose to a key position in public works between 1871 and 1877, his work thus adding to and complementing the municipal improvements. At least as controversial as Shepherd, Babcock began his military career upon graduation from West Point in 1861. His Civil War record, which included building pontoon bridges at Harpers Ferry, taking part in an engagement at Yorktown, and witnessing the surrender at Vicksburg, was marked by brilliance. Attracting the esteem of General Ulysses S. Grant, he became aide-de-camp to the leader of the Union army and made the first contact with General Lee prior to the treaty at Appomattox. Babcock, continuing to serve as an aide and secretary to Grant, accompanied him to the Executive Mansion when Grant became president in 1869.

In 1871 Orville Babcock had been given responsibility for public buildings, grounds, and works. To this end he pursued a thorough study of the public reservations. Elevating himself above Nathaniel Michler, his predecessor, Babcock complained in the *Annual Report of the Chief of Engineers* for 1871 that "no provision has been made for water in many of the squares and parks." In the next six years, under Babcock's direction, the city's public parks were drained, gas pipes were laid for lamps, water pipes were laid for irrigation, drainage, and drinking purposes, the walks traversing the parks were graveled, and grounds were planted and augmented with rustic furniture.

The Drainage System and the Monument Grounds. The apparatus for drainage was constructed on the Washington Monument grounds, which Babcock described as a "primary recipient" of the Potomac's overflowing at high tide. Prior to his 1877 departure, Babcock in the *Annual Report* for 1876 referred to the newly drained and adorned monument grounds as follows: "The forming of these lakes, the roadway between them, and the extension of Virginia Avenue, amounting in all to about fifteen acres, has, without doubt, been very beneficial to the general health of the vicinity. Sheets of pure water, green lawns, and roadway now occupy the space formerly a marsh overgrown with vegetable matter. . . ." The ground removed in grading the hills surrounding the unfinished monument was transported to the developing park south of the President's Mansion, creating an image of a flat plain stretching into the horizon.

Standing in front of the monument on the newly created public park and looking directly east, Babcock envisioned the mile-and-a-half stretch from the Capitol to the President's House as a unified landscape system. In the 1875 *Annual Report of the Chief of Engineers*, after reporting on the graveling of Armory Square, the plot of green fronting the Pennsylvania Railroad yards, Babcock wrote that "the walls and roads [of Armory Square] harmonize with those in the Smithsonian grounds, the idea being to make the line of the reservation extending from the Capitol to the Executive Mansion one continuous park." Two years later, the public reservations defined by Third Street, Four-and-a-half Street, Maine Avenue, and Missouri Avenue were drained, graded, and serviced by water and gas pipes. Thus the last gaps in the continuous chain of parks were filled in.

Parks, Squares, and Ellipses. The existing smaller public parks that were scattered throughout the rest of the city as satellites to the Mall also benefited in detail from Babcock's attentions. As an experiment, Babcock attempted to flatten the coarse unscreened gravel forming the public walkways in Lafayette Square with a 3,600-pound roller, only to replace the walkway later on with a finer grade of gravel. Rawlins Square to the west of the President's House was created in 1873 and subjected to the usual process of drainage, grading, laying of pipes, planting, and furnishing. It also received topsoil from the excavations of the new State, War and Navy Building. To the east of the President's House, Judiciary Square, used as a dumping ground by contrac-

tors and punctuated by wooden buildings that once housed a government hospital—and later (until 1874) was used by the YWCA—was cleared by Babcock as dramatically as his friend Shepherd had removed the Northern Liberty Market from Mount Vernon Square in 1872. An ellipse was carved into Farragut Square in anticipation of a statue, honoring the Civil War admiral, for which Babcock designed the pedestal. The trees and plants adorning all of these squares were gathered throughout the nation by George H. Brown, long-time landscape gardener for the Corps of Engineers. In addition, Babcock himself planned and stocked several mini-zoos made up of birds, deer, and prairie dogs.

THE HARBORS OF WASHINGTON AND GEORGETOWN

Babcock's fellow military engineer, S. T. Abert, was responsible for improving the Washington and Georgetown harbors and integrating them as parts of a permanent, year-around park along Babcock's envisioned "continuous" Mall. In the process of dredging the Potomac, depositing the material onto the flats, and thereby giving sharper definition to land south of the Washington Monument, Abert envisioned deepwater ports necessary to the commercial viability of the city and the extension of the city itself to the waterfront. The freshet of 1873 made it clear to the Board of Survey, created by Congress only one year earlier, that a permanent solution was needed to stabilize the wide expanse of land where the city gradually merged into the river. The general plan as adopted by the Board of Survey was to create a channel sufficiently deep for navigation on the east side of the river between Georgetown and Gravelly Point, the land reclaimed affording approximately "455 acres of land, most advantageously located, for Government purposes," as quoted in the *Annual Report of the Chief of Engineers* for 1875.

Abert also suggested that "much will be saved by making nature an auxiliary" in guiding the natural flow of the river, hindered at that time by Easby's Point (just below Rock Creek's juncture with the Potomac), by Analostan Island, and by the obstruction of Long Bridge. The effort to clear the river was commenced in 1874, when an appropriation was made to continue the dredging operation (initiated in 1869) above Long Bridge, with the material to be deposited on the flats behind the bulkhead of the proposed Washington wharves. Two years later, in 1876, and for several years thereafter, Abert supervised the splitting and removal of several large rocks in the Georgetown harbor by drilling and using nitroglycerine. This initial work, while predicting a radical improvement in the city's waterfront and parks system, remained of minor scope at Babcock's departure from Washington.

ALFRED B. MULLETT, SUPERVISING ARCHITECT

While Shepherd and Babcock worked strenuously to re-shape existing lands and by reclamation furnish new lands upon which the postbellum city would rise, Alfred B. Mullett provided the city with a major public building, an architecturally decisive indication of the federal government's commitment to the city of Washington and—as its rich façades and powerful physical form took shape between 1871 and 1888—a symbol marking the end to any further agitation to remove the capital city. Although Mullett was already working full time as Supervising Architect of the Treasury, having succeeded his former associate Isaiah Rogers in 1865, he consented to take on the design for the new State, War and Navy Building in addition to his Treasury duties because of the persuasive powers of Assistant Secretary of State J. C. Bancroft Davis. Davis had seen Mullett's French Renaissance–designed Post Office and Treasury Building in Boston and (according to architectural historian Donald Lehman) "declared it a specimen of what he wanted for the State Department."

THE STATE, WAR AND NAVY BUILDING

In 1870, Mullett at age 36 thus found himself the much sought after designer of this public building. Born in Somerset County, England, he had emigrated with his parents to Cincinnati, Ohio, when he was eleven years old. Prior to his architectural work for Rogers's Cincinnati office, Mullett had traveled through Europe, at that time considered a prerequisite for the architectural profession. In 1863, Mullett was appointed as a clerk in the Office of Construction under the Supervising Architect while Rogers held that position. In the next two

years, Mullett traveled widely throughout the country inspecting custom houses and was during this time appointed Assistant Supervising Architect. In 1874, after serving for nine years as Supervising Architect, Mullett resigned that position because of poor relations with then Secretary of the Treasury Benjamin Bristow. Mullett continued to work on the State, War and Navy Building, however, until the following year when delays in the construction schedule prompted the War Department to take control of the project. Secretary of War William Belknap and his ally Orville Babcock managed to oust Mullett during a disagreement over funding, bringing in Colonel Thomas Lincoln Casey of the Corps of Engineers and his assistant Richard von Ezdorf to supervise the building's completion over the next twelve years.

The State, War and Navy Building designed by Alfred Mullett was not the first French Renaissance building in the city, as it faced directly across Pennsylvania Avenue the James Renwick–designed Corcoran Gallery of Art built in the late 1850s. Unlike the Renwick building, however, Mullett's large and rich façades achieved a heightened sense of dominance and power in the city. The iron structural framework allowed increased floor-to-ceiling heights, giving the entire building a new sense of architectural scale. The tall mansard roof intensified this impression which was further elaborated by the cast-iron crestings and iron sculpture work in the pediments. Designer Richard von Ezdorf provided the interior furnishings and decor with as rich and artistic a flavor as the exterior, creating "intricate designs," as Lawrence Wodehouse has written, that were straight out of the baroque palaces of Austria and Germany." In the State, War and Navy Building, the executive end of Pennsylvania Avenue acquired a palatial public building that both stimulated and fed the nation's post-war preoccupation with symbols of luxury.

The New Municipal Government: By Commission

Because of concern about the enormous unauthorized municipal debt accumulated by Alexander Shepherd

State, War and Navy Building (Now Called the Old Executive Office Building) at Pennsylvania Avenue and Seventeenth Street, Completed 1888

during his term as a member of the Board of Public Works and the financial benefits reaped by his friends in the process, Congress—by an act passed on 20 June 1874—transferred local authority to three temporary commissioners. The commissioners were responsible for general administration of the city while the territorial government was being phased out and a permanent system of municipal government was being developed. Based on the work of the temporary Board of Commissioners, a permanent board was established by

the Organic Act of 11 June 1878. Among other things this act provided for the federal government to contribute 50 percent of the municipal revenues needed to operate the city, a funding arrangement necessitated by the rising debts and municipal needs that had been created by Shepherd.

The new municipal government continued, through its various departments, to play an active role in upholding livability in the physical city. Its Board of Health, Office of Engineer Commissioner, Office of Surveyor, and Parking Commission directed teams of municipal employees in maintaining and cleansing the city; reported accomplishments on an annual basis to the Commissioners of the District of Columbia; prepared special reports; and promulgated regulations covering such subjects as building codes and sanitation standards for public markets. Under the direction of the commissioners, an officer of the Corps of Engineers, detailed by the President, was charged (as the 1874 *Annual Report of the Commissioners of the District of Columbia* stated) with the "work and repair and improvement of all streets, avenues, alleys, sewers, roads, and bridges of the District of Columbia," as well as performance of "all the duties heretofore devolved upon the Chief Engineer" of the territorial Board of Public Works.

The Board of Public Works was abolished only two days after President Grant named Lieutenant Richard L. Hoxie as a board member. To assure administrative and locational continuity between the defunct territorial government and the new commission form of government, the 1874 act provided that one of the three commissioners should be an army engineer. This position of Engineer Commissioner as an integral part of Washington's municipal government endured for more than eighty years. Hoxie was immediately appointed to the post of Corps officer detailed to the commission and the newly arrayed commissioners occupied the former quarters of the Board of Public Works in the building at 214–216 John Marshall Place.

Thus the Corps continued to be instrumental in planning new large-scale public work projects, creating the modern floodproof city, and insuring the future desirability of the city for residential purposes in terms of clean water, the continuous system of parklands, and public edifices with which a nationwide citizenry could identify.

The Water Supply for Washington, Abundant and Clear

The Washington aqueduct, conceived and built by Montgomery Meigs in the 1850s, remained little changed in its essentials through to the early 1880s. The reservoirs fed by force-pump systems allowed the water network to accommodate residential expansion north of Florida Avenue, above the route of direct flow, and to increase the capacity of the network as the city grew. Water serviced not only the needs of the residential population but the fire hydrants, drinking fountains, and ornamental fountains as well. Although observers recorded high praise for the city's water, the location, quantity, and quality of the supply were increasingly called into question. Because of the western source of the water and distributing system, water reached the parts of the city west of the Capitol first, often providing much inferior service to the residual areas east of the Capitol. And to be sure, as the city's western residential sections swelled and made increased demands on the existing water system, these western residents, too, complained of an inadequate and muddy water supply.

THE MCMILLAN RESERVOIR AT HOWARD UNIVERSITY

Supplying Capitol Hill and the eastern sections of the city with water had first priority. In 1883, Major G. J. Lydecker began work on a new distributing reservoir on the heights of Washington, the site of Smith Spring, just east of Howard University. A large direct-line tunnel was drilled through solid rock under Rock Creek Park to the new reservoir. It was Lydecker's intention that water distributed from the new reservoir at Howard would flow directly to the eastern sections of the city at a greater elevation than was possible from the old reservoir. Work on the Howard University Reservoir, as well as its receiving and distributing mains, continued until 1888—when all activity at the site stopped for fifteen years. The system was not placed in full service until 1903. Renamed McMillan Reservoir, the new castellated structure utilized a slow sand filtration system for water purification.

The lack of water improvement activity for so many years partially abated in 1890 when the Corps of Engineers laid a large 30-inch main along East Capitol Street, servicing housing developments as far east as the Anacostia River. While this new main opened sections of the city to the east of the Capitol to denser populations, the pattern of the most desirable residential areas in the western half of the city had secured itself by the momentum of public commitments and private investment.

THE DAM ABOVE GREAT FALLS

While new extensions to the existing system addressed the eastern section of the city, increasing the over-all supply of water depended on raising the height of the water's fall at Great Falls. In 1881, Thomas Lincoln Casey, then a lieutenant colonel and engineer in charge of the Washington aqueduct, had recommended that the dam built from 1863 to '67 halfway across the Potomac above Great Falls be completed in order to control the depth of water in the pool above. Casey's recommendation was echoed by Major Lydecker, who three years later urged that the dam be extended across Conn's Island (in the middle of the Potomac just above Great Falls) and the Virginia channel to the Virginia shore. By 1889, the dam was completed, inspiring Lieutenant Colonel George H. Elliott to declare (as quoted in the *Annual Report of the Chief of Engineers* for 1889) that the city was now "abundantly supplied with water," except where corrosion or the small size of city mains impeded its flow. In 1896, however, the demands of the city again outran the supply, forcing the raising of the Great Falls dam to "an elevation of 148 feet above mean tide at the Washington Navy Yard and its extension at that height across Conn's Island and the Virginia channel of the river," as D. D. Gaillard noted in the 1896 *Annual Report of the Chief of Engineers.*

Abundant water was not enough to insure resident satisfaction with the city's supply. A study of Washington's water supply written by Thomas W. Symons in 1886 led him to declare that other American cities had cleaner water; he also reprinted testimonial letters from prominent physicians as to the urgent need for clean water in Washington. Viewing the extant system in its entirety, Symons observed that the 550 miles of the Potomac River, draining principally from the north and south branches, the Cacapon, the Shenandoah, and the Monocacy, collected pollutants from the cultivated and fertilized lands along its route. Deforestation along the river had loosened earth that now flowed into the river, especially during storms and heavy snows. In fact, the

drainage from the watershed, estimated to number nine million acres, had so polluted the waters that in the spring of 1888 the Dalecarlia receiving reservoir was thrown out of operation.

The effect of the muddy and impure water on the city's future extended beyond citizen reactions; it was viewed as a significant hindrance to the growth and development of the city. In summer, the weather was at its calmest, the water at its clearest—but the city was at its emptiest. As Lydecker said in the 1886 *Annual Report of the Chief of Engineers:* "It is during the period of the year that the water presents the worst appearance that the city is at its best, Congress is in session, all the Executive Departments are full-handed, and people from all over the country and the world flock to the Capital for the purpose of transacting business and enjoying its social pleasures."

THE DALECARLIA RESERVOIR AND DAM

In 1886, Symons suggested three cures to the water quality ills of Washington: aeration of the water with a hydraulic ram, cleaning and paving the Dalecarlia receiving reservoir, and chemical purification. Four years later, Lieutenant Colonel George H. Elliott saw the problem more in terms of the water's turbid appearance than its fitness for human consumption. The most important improvement needed at the aqueduct was "to furnish the city with better water; or, since the water of the Potomac as brought from Great Falls is, I am convinced, perfectly wholesome at all times, it would be more correct to say with clearer water." So states the 1891 *Annual Report of the Chief of Engineers.* With the view that the mingling of the drainage water from surrounding lands at the reservoir was the primary fault, Elliott constructed three diversion dams outside the Dalecarlia Reservoir, one each across Little Falls Branch, Mill Creek, and East Creek, in order to catch and throw off these waters from the cleaner waters received from Great Falls. By the end of the century, Washington's water supply was judged to be abundant, clear, and wholesome, a public improvement essential to the physical growth of the city.

Reclamation of the River Flats and the Creation of Public Parks

While the upper Potomac supplied the growing city with water, the portion of river fronting the city proper detracted from the city's waterfront appearance, health, and commercial prospects. The dredging of channels and removal of rocks near the Georgetown harbors initiated by Nathaniel Michler in 1870 and continued by S. T. Abert for several years from 1876 on, received little serious attention from Congress and even less serious effort toward a permanent solution. Even the major freshet of 1877 that forced the coal merchants of Georgetown to dredge a temporary channel did not bring a change in the policy of temporary patchwork activity despite exhortations of the various army engineers charged with river improvements. Above and below Long Bridge nearly three hundred acres of bare land extended, created by the sedimentation brought in by the seasonal freshets. These flats, alternately exposed and covered by the daily tides, were especially noxious near the south end of Seventeenth Street where the sewer main discharged into the Potomac. In 1879, Army Engineer Abert recommended that the flats be reclaimed by raising the ground one foot above the freshets, using dredged material; he also recommended that the street system be extended to the newly usable land. In Abert's plan, wharves constructed along the extended riverfront would be serviced by water depths of at least sixteen feet.

THE UNTAMED POTOMAC AND THE FLOOD OF 1881

The flood of February 1881 swept aside congressional hesitancy. The melting following a severe winter caused the Potomac to rise more than two feet over Long Bridge, pushing out three spans of the bridge onto the flats below. Although the low-lying portions of the city were accustomed to periodic flooding, as was noted in the 1881 *Annual Report of the Chief of Engineers*, "to an unprecedented extent, the low portion of the city along the Mall and extending across Pennsylvania Avenue was flooded, and a large amount of damage was caused by the flooding of the cellars and first floors." The flood waters swept ominously close, just three blocks south of the President's House, and over as far east as the Botanic Garden at the western edge of the Capitol grounds.

In a spectacular display the untamed Potomac thus surged in full view of the executive and legislative branches. Added incentive to a radical departure from governmental indecision came in a report on the inferior and unsafe sanitary conditions of the President's House. In November of the flood year, the nationally reputed sanitary and public parks engineer, George E. Waring, reported that the improvement of the river and reclamation of the flats would be an essential condition to improving the drainage and sanitary requirements of the mansion. The nearly 1,000 acres of flats that served as a lodging ground for sewage, the "low and saturated conditions of much of the city lying south of Pennsylvania Avenue," and the drainage from dwellings in the higher parts of Washington to the sewage swamp of the lowlands were seen by Waring as part of the entire problem of improving the Executive Mansion. Referring to the little-understood disease, malaria, Waring urged that the Corps of Engineers be "guided by our suspicions" and "accept as a common-sense guide of action the rule that all land in or near a town should be kept clean and dry." In filling the flats out to the Michler-proposed line of wharves, Waring envisioned a new public recreational area.

PETER C. HAINS AND THE ELLICOTT MAP

Rising to the task of taming the Potomac, Civil War hero Major Peter Conover Hains studied the river with engineer's and historian's eyes and undertook to direct the river's improvements over the next eight years. In 1883, reviewing the legislative history since 1804 with yearly appropriations of only tens of thousands of dollars for piecemeal improvements, Hains could readily detect the alarmed response of Congress to the 1881 flood, for suddenly began the appropriation of hundreds of thousands of dollars to the reclamation process. More important, Hains looked at the history of the river as revealed in the historical maps, so that he could—as stated in the *Annual Report of the Chief of Engineers for 1883*— "form an idea of the changes that have taken place in the river during a period of less than a century." Referring to Andrew Ellicott's 1792 map, Hains pronounced it "the oldest map of the Potomac River in this vicinity," and noted that "the original is now preserved in the office of the Commissioner of Public Buildings and Grounds, but copies of it have been made at various times." The Ellicott map revealed three navigable channels fronting the city. Comparing this map with the 1834 map drawn by Lieutenant Colonel James Kearney of the Corps of Topographical Engineers, Hains detected a rapid shoaling process that had already erased two of the three channels. Summarizing additional studies and Potomac River surveys, Hains stated in the 1883 *Annual Report*: "The surveys enumerated here are themselves a history of the river. On the Ellicott map we trace the Washington or City Channel, not deep, it is true, though even above Seventeenth Street a stream of water large enough to be dignified by the name of a channel. . . . In a similar manner the growth of the flats may be traced."

THE WASHINGTON CHANNEL AND THE SLUICING PONDS

Against this legislative and topographical background of the river, Hains outlined the projected improvements as provided in the congressional act of August 1882, which appropriated $400,000. The 1872 plan of the congressional Board of Engineers that had guided Nathaniel Michler recommended that one all-purpose channel be dredged between Georgetown and Giesboro Point with the material simply dumped on the flats. In 1879, Major William J. Twining, the Engineer Commissioner of the District of Columbia, modified the 1872 plan by leaving the Washington Channel open as far as Long Bridge and (as Hains stated in the 1883 *Annual Report*) constructing "sluicing basins for the purpose of purifying the water in that channel, which would otherwise become stagnant and offensive." Thus, the traditional and natural channel fronting Washington would be preserved and cleansed. Twining envisioned the purifying sluicing basins as ornamental, and projected hundreds of acres of parkland to be created out of the flats. Abert's recommendations of 1881 differed from those of Twining's only in details: the reclaimed land would rise six feet above low water and be enclosed by both a masonry wall resting on piles and riprap along its edges. As with

other low-lying parkland throughout the city, this reclaimed land was to be drained by pipes. In 1882, the Board of Engineers recommended to Congress that the permanent improvement be a combination of Twining's and Abert's plans—Twining's sluicing ponds and Abert's filling and embankments.

RECLAMATION OF THE POTOMAC FLATS: 1882, THE PROJECT BEGINS

In the late summer of 1882, Hains began the vast reclamation project according to recommendations of the congressional Board of Engineers, providing in the following year a map of the areas to be reclaimed. Four irregularly shaped flushing lakes were to be joined by meandering walkways, extending from B Street south to the farthest end of the reclaimed area, the ground to be landscaped by clusters of trees. As the dredging process continued, a temporary railroad was built from the outer edge of the fill to the sewer canal so that the dredged material could be deposited on the flats. Four years later, in 1886, Hains modified Twining's four lakes to one large tidal reservoir between Long Bridge and the sewer canal. This reservoir, later named the Tidal Basin, measured "not less than 8 feet deep" and was intended to supply fresh water to the Washington Channel. A smaller reservoir was constructed near the foot of Seventeenth Street to flush the sewer canal. The Tidal Basin was provided with inlet and outlet gates in order to flush sewage accumulated along the Washington Channel to the open waters of the Potomac. By the end of the decade, most of the reclaimed area—appended to the Washington Monument grounds—was filled in, awaiting the construction of embankments and landscaping. Dredging activity along the channel and the Tidal Basin continued to the end of the decade and afterwards.

Litigation Begins: Morris et al. v. United States. As early as 1882 when Congress was discussing appropriations to be made for the reclamation work, it anticipated that individuals and corporations would claim rights to the land. John L. Kidwell and his family owned 49 acres of marshland, "Kidwell's Meadows," just south of the Naval Observatory at Twenty-third Street. Representing more than fifty claimants including Kidwell's

Reclamation of the Potomac Flats Using the McNee Dredge, 1891

family and the descendents of Chief Justice John Marshall, the case of *Martin F. Morris et al.*, appellants, v. *United States* began in the District courts in 1886. The case persisted in the courts for the next dozen years, causing both sides to scrutinize carefully the legislative and topographical history of the District's land holdings and subdivisions. Finally, in 1898, the United States Supreme Court made the definitive decision sustaining the government's rights to the lands south of Water Street. The Supreme Court also referred to the 1886 congressional appropriation for the reclamation work and its additional provision for compensation to be made for "the private property of individuals situated within the lines of the Government improvement." These compensations, to be settled by the District courts according to estimated values of the land exclusive of improvements, were made possible by the 1896 District appropriation bill which included over $26,500,-000 to be paid to the Potomac flats claimants.

THE RECLAIMED LAND AND CREATION OF POTOMAC PARK

As the government's authority over the land neared this confirmation, discussion arose over the use of the land. The push by private real estate interests for subdivision was supported by the example of Boston's Back Bay, which had been similarly reclaimed and transformed

into a residential enclave. Commercial interests also argued for such a subdivision of land in Washington because the profits from the sale would reimburse the government for the cost of reclamation. In the civic atmosphere then current, however, when Rock Creek Park and the Mall, not to mention the many neighborhood parks, were gaining clearer definition as vital elements in the capital city, Charles Glover and other Washington leaders pushed successfully for designation of the reclaimed land as parkland. In 1897, shortly before the final Supreme Court decision, Congress set aside the 621 acres of reclaimed flats and the 118 acres of tidal reservoirs as "Potomac Park . . . to be forever held and used as a park for the recreation and pleasure of the people." (This designation was duly recorded in the *Annual Report of the Chief of Engineers* for 1897.)

The Beginning of the Modern City. Historically, the creation of Potomac Park marked a major departure from the pattern of original public reservations as provided by L'Enfant and elaborated by the Corps of Engineers up to 1874. It was the beginning of the modern city. The filling in of the original boundaries of Washington City inside Boundary Street and the growth of suburban tracts in the District of Columbia, Maryland, and Virginia encouraged the Corps of Engineers to respond to major community interest and seek new areas for landscaped park development. This would maintain the garden city character of the capital and secure the balance between open space and built-up area. Thus, the search for new expanses of parkland outside the L'Enfant city paralleled a significant tidying up of the parkland within the original city.

The founding of Howard University in 1866, and its location on a bluff along Seventh Street's extension, had cordoned off nearly twelve acres just south of the university grounds fronting the unfinished distributing reservoir. In creating the Howard University Park in 1896, Colonel John M. Wilson saw its use by both city and suburban residents. The park, as described in the *Annual Report of the Chief of Engineers* for 1896, was "within a few squares of the terminal sections of four of our city and suburban street railroad lines, by which any part of Washington and its chief outlying suburban villages can be reached from the park in a comparatively short period of time." Unfortunately all of this park has been lost.

The creation in 1888 of the National Zoological Park on the western bank of Rock Creek revived Michler's and the community's hopes for the great park along the creek. A congressional bill also inspired by the banker Charles Carroll Glover passed two years later, allowing for the purchase of 2,500 acres. In the following years, more acreage was acquired, greatly satisfying President Theodore Roosevelt and encouraging the philanthropic Glover in the twentieth century to create for public use similar strips of parkland in other sections of the city.

FEDERAL FUNCTIONS IN VIRGINIA

Although Congress had ceded the Virginia section of the original ten-mile square District of Columbia back to the Commonwealth in 1846, the area had proved of little interest to Richmond. On the other hand, federal occupation of this southern position of the original ten-mile square District of Columbia during the Civil War —and thereafter in the form of military posts and Arlington National Cemetery—served to define the general area within which federal functions were maintained.

From Aqueduct Bridge down the Potomac to Mount Vernon, the traditional tidewater landscape still exhib-

ited plantation houses on headlands overlooking the river. The home and tomb of George Washington had been preserved by the efforts—beginning in 1856—of Ann Pamela Cunningham and her Mount Vernon Ladies Association of the Union. In 1889, Congress directed Colonel Hains to survey this historic area in search of an appropriate "National Road."

Since the new boundary established in 1846 between the District of Columbia and Virginia was located on the Virginia shoreline of the Potomac River at the high water mark, any reclaimed land along the Virginia shoreline would be under federal jurisdiction. Thus of the three main routes surveyed by Hains, one was along the river. That route could be viewed as a precursor to what became the George Washington Memorial Parkway. Like Lake Shore Drive in Chicago, this also would be one of the major parkway projects constructed in America symbolizing the conquest of space along powerful natural features. No matter which route was selected along the Potomac, Hains intended it to be always in the process of development and embellishment. Envisioned as having a monumental character, the proposed "National Road" was a symbolic link between the Mount Vernon estate, the site so closely associated with George Washington, and the city that bore his name.

THE MALL: ROMANTIC VISION OR COMPREHENSIVE PLAN?

The romantic vision of the Mall as a continuous string of informal parks enunciated by Downing in 1851, and reinforced by Michler and Babcock, persisted to the end of the century, when the 1901–1902 McMillan plan proposed a return to the L'Enfant vision of a broad, formal greensward extending from the Capitol to the monument. By 1900, from the Botanic Garden eastward to the monument grounds, the parks developed in response to this romantic vision were considered to be separate public areas that comprised the Mall as a whole: the Botanic Garden, a trapezoidal configuration at the foot of the Capitol; Seaton Park, two smaller trapezoids; Armory Park, a rectangular park flanked on the east by the Pennsylvania Railroad yards; the Smithsonian Pleasure Grounds, those carefully landscaped grounds that served as a model for public parks citywide; the Depart-

United States Capitol Grounds Prior to Implementation of the Olmsted Plan for Landscaping, Late 1860s

ment of Agriculture grounds of landscape quality approaching that of the Smithsonian grounds; and the monument grounds, a rectangular park centered (by 1885) by the completed memorial shaft and merging at its southern end into the area being developed into what was to become the Tidal Basin and Potomac Park.

Frederick Law Olmsted, Sr., familiar with the city from his position on the United States Sanitary Commission during the Civil War, had been appointed to design the Capitol grounds. Existing parks on the Mall represented many bureaus, each employing its own architects, surveyors, and gardeners, each bureau responsible to independent congressional committees. This situation seemed to Olmsted "absurd and wasteful." Olmsted urged his most steadfast congressional supporter, Senator Justin Morrill, that "before anything more is done in regard to any particular ground an effort should be made to simplify and consolidate the present organizations and bring all these grounds into subordination to a comprehensive scheme." Such a scheme would remain elusive for the next quarter century.

THE OLMSTED PLAN FOR THE CAPITOL GROUNDS

While the Mall's reservations would be subject to changing notions as to their over-all design, Olmsted's new grounds and terracing of the Capitol's west front has remained admired and survived challenges by later arbiters of taste—including his son, whose proposals would be contained in the McMillan plan. Conceived as an adjunct to the Capitol Building, the grounds as designed by Frederick Law Olmsted, Sr., were cleared of the dense forest of decaying trees that had obscured the building from full view. The grounds were refurnished with symmetrically placed and winding walks, with a thin shield of trees ringing the base of the building's new display platform. A grand architectural terrace was completed in 1892, resembling Olmsted's Bethesda terrace in New York's Central Park. The terrace in front of the Capitol served as an unfolding invitation to the building itself and as an improved platform from which to view the expanse of the city. With Olmsted's design for the west front, the Mall could no longer serve as the "backyard" of the Capitol. Until the reclamation process solved what Olmsted termed the "miasma" problem, he proposed a thick belt of trees placed south of the Capitol grounds, as "an efficient means of protection to the Capitol from malarial poison originating on the banks of the Potomac."

In planning for the expansion of public parks into new physical areas beyond the borders of the city of Washington, as well as rethinking the forms and functions of park areas within the city, the Corps of Engineers absorbed new types of public properties and sites, then designated simply as public buildings. Present terminology would classify these properties as historic landmarks, and even when they were acquired in the 1890s they were already seen as objects evoking great patriotic sentiment. In 1893, when Ford's Theatre collapsed, the Engineers took on their first property. Subsequently, the Peterson House, scene of Lincoln's death, the monument to George Washington at Wakefield, Virginia, and the national military park at Gettysburg, Pennsylvania, were added in response to citizens' landmark preservation efforts. The acquisition of these buildings and sites, responding initially to a preservation motive, inaugurated the federal government's more explicit commitment to properties of historical value, later institutionalized in the National Park Service.

THEODORE A. BINGHAM AND THE PUBLIC SPACES

By the end of the decade, the Corps's responsibility for public buildings and grounds as defined by Congress had expanded well beyond the Mall and the satellite parks, growth centers envisioned by L'Enfant. This expansion demanded a new comprehensive policy and program so that parks and other public properties would become an integrated part of the city's image. Colonel Theodore A. Bingham thought himself equal to the development of new plans and policies. Bingham was born in Andover, Connecticut, on May 14, 1858. Graduating from West Point in 1879, he rose through the military ranks, serving as an engineer officer in various locations. Important for his later Washington work, he was military attaché at the United States legation in Berlin from 1890 to 1892, and in Rome the two years following. Transferred to the Corps of Engineers' Public Building and Grounds post in 1897, he remained there until 1903.

Reporting on public grounds in the District of Columbia, Bingham revealed new interests in a dramatic change from the preoccupations with mere maintenance that were characteristic of many of his predecessors. In a sense, Bingham's interests presaged the work of the 1901 McMillan Commission. In Bingham's view (as quoted in the *Annual Report of the Chief of Engineers* for 1897), "Washington [was] not the most beautiful and attractive city in America." He was dissatisfied with the appearance of the city's public and monumental spaces and with the lack of a strong commitment by the federal government to allocate adequate funds for embellishing its green "breathing spaces." Moreover, officials from park agencies in other cities voiced similar disappointment with the capital city's system of parks which should rightly be a "model in what pertains to the development, improvement, and maintenance of parks." Washington's park system was expected to provide both model and inspiration for improved park systems in cities throughout the nation, to elevate the taste of all visitors. On the local level, park improvements were also important amenities for the city's resident population. Echoing the often repeated needs for parks, Bingham stated in the 1897 *Annual Report* that parks were crucial in the "promotion of mental growth and cultivating a love for horticulture, arboriculture, and floriculture among our people, who congregate here from all sections of our country." Bingham's style and rhetoric were impressive even if the ideas were already a half-century old.

"A Little Touch of the Outside Country." Colonel Bingham's reports on the shortcomings of the capital's park system reflected the ideals of the national progressive movement that viewed the physical environment as critical in determining social behavior. By the end of the century, urban life could be depicted by the crowding together of toiling masses, suffering "intellectual degradation and physical degradation" from the demands of city life. In an atmosphere of charity and good will, however, enlightened public officials attempted to resolve these social problems by providing "a little touch of the outside country," in much the same spirit that public servants concerned themselves with "the study and conquest of epidemic diseases, the increase and purification of [the] water supply, and the introduction

and improvement of drainage systems" as prerequisites to moral improvement. So went the prose of the *Annual Report of the Chief of Engineers* for 1898.

Anticipating a bright future for the resolution of social problems as the new century dawned, Bingham made specific suggestions on Washington's parks, economy dictating that "the parks in and around Washington should form a systematic and well considered whole." The newly created Potomac flats should form, Bingham thought, "the western end of the beautiful system planned by the originators of the city, to extend from the Capitol to the Potomac River," unifying the Mall area. Bingham recommended in the *Annual Report* for 1899 that the Botanic Garden be "thrown open, improved by walks and drives, and made a part of [the Mall]." The much neglected eastern section of the city, especially the Anacostia flats, deserved development as a balance to the formally designed western sections. Washington's "subtropical climate" demanded more public fountains, Bingham thought, not only as a respite to the summer weather but as "a rest to mind and body." And, further justifying increased governmental funding for park development and embellishment, Bingham called attention to the fact that, when compared to expenditures by other cities the size of Washington, the capital city's expenditures for parks were meager indeed.

Recognition of L'Enfant as the First City Surveyor. A Senate resolution passed in January of 1898 directed the Chief of Engineers to assess the "numbers and locations of all lots in the District of Columbia the title to which the records in the Office of the Commissioner of Public Buildings and Grounds show to be in the United States," in order that legal issues over property rights might be resolved. Among all the pertinent documents collected was L'Enfant's 1791 manuscript plan. This manuscript plan was listed by Bingham in 1900 as only one in a long list of documents transferred, under the terms of the 2 March 1867 act, from the Commissioner of Public Buildings to the Chief of Engineers.

In reviewing the papers in the custody of the Chief of Engineers, especially the early records of the city, Bingham was the initial member of the Corps of Engineers

explicitly to credit L'Enfant with the role as "first United States city surveyor" and the first to lay out the city. Any similar recognition by Bingham's predecessors in the Corps during the years after the Civil War must be assumed from the actual fulfillment of many L'Enfant plan proposals regarding streets and public parks. Further evidence of interest in the plan was demonstrated in popular publications such as *Harper's New Monthly Magazine*, which acknowledged the origins and brilliance of the plan. With this renewed interest in L'Enfant's design, especially among those in government circles, began the twentieth century's reverence for the city's first planner and the original intentions of his plan, standards against which all future improvements to the city would be compared.

The Corps of Engineers' responsibilities for public buildings in the post–1874 era were primarily maintenance and improvement of the President's House, with the Government Printing Office and the historic landmarks or shrines as later concerns. As for construction of new public buildings, in the case of the State, War and Navy Building (see page 88, above), the Corps entered the project after Mullett's plan had been approved and after the War Department had taken charge of the project. While Colonel Casey as superintendent of construction did little to change the building's design, his assistant, Richard von Ezdorf, did leave his mark on the interior details and furnishings.

Public Buildings in the Century's Last Decades

Three additional major public buildings constructed in the post–Civil War era reflected the vision of members of the Corps of Engineers. By special invitation, Montgomery Meigs provided designs for the new National Museum (now the Arts and Industries Building) south of the Mall adjoining the original Smithsonian Building, and the Pension Building in the Judiciary Square complex. In both instances, Meigs was chosen for these projects because his diligent public work had won him a good professional reputation among members of building committees. Contrasting with the white classicism

Library of Congress, First Street and Independence Avenue, Showing the Capitol Grounds As Redesigned by Frederick Law Olmsted, Sr., and Horatio Greenough's Controversial Statue of the Seated George Washington, Late 1890s

of Washington's public buildings constructed prior to the Civil War, these monumental structures were of red brick. The National Museum's design as adapted by the German-born architect-engineer Adolph Cluss exemplified the polychromatic possibilities of glazed brick, while the Pension Building was embellished by Casper Buberl's continuous terracotta frieze depicting a procession of Civil War soldiers and sailors. The construction of the Library of Congress in the last three years of the century represented a return to the light-hued classical model for public buildings, although the library's design involved greater elaboration than was characteristic of the pre–Civil War era. The execution of this building involved the talents of private architects J. L. Smithmeyer, Paul J. Pelz, and Edward Pearce Casey, as well as the latter's father, Colonel Thomas L. Casey of the Corps of Engineers.

GROWTH OF THE FEDERAL BUREAUCRACY

With the construction of these major public buildings, the federal government committed itself to the future of Washington as the national capital city. By the end of the century, conditions were ripe for further amplifi-

cation of the built city by Colonel Bingham, and later on by the McMillan Commission. In fact, in Bingham's 1900 report—as quoted in the *Annual Report of the Chief of Engineers* for that year—he stated that, as of June 1900, he was instructed to the "work of making an examination and reporting plans for the treatment of [the newly floodproofed lowlands] section of the District of Columbia situated south of Pennsylvania Avenue and north of B Street, S.W." Improvement of this area had already begun a few years earlier when the new Romanesque Post Office, designed after the plans of Supervising Architect Willoughby J. Edbrooke, rose out of the deteriorated commercial neighborhood at Pennsylvania Avenue and Twelfth Street.

The relatively small number of public buildings of enduring symbolic quality masked the actual growth of the federal bureaucracy in Washington after the Civil War. For example, between 1881 and 1891 the total number of federal employees in Washington rose from 13,124 to 20,834. Department and bureau employees spilled over into many private buildings originally constructed for private commercial functions. Indeed, the federal government's high rent bills served as a powerful

Pennsylvania Avenue at Seventh Street, Showing the Bank of Washington/Central National Bank (left) and the Apex Building (right), 1890s.

impetus for new public building construction in the following century.

COMMERCIAL STRUCTURES AND RETAIL THOROUGHFARES

Private commercial structures, often housing public functions, clustered along the north side of Pennsylvania Avenue and stretched further northward to G Street, eastward to Judiciary Square, and as far west as Fifteenth Street. The major streets devoted to the retail trade, Pennsylvania Avenue, Seventh Street, and F Street, were served by the streetcar system, described by an observer in 1875 as "neutralizing the magnificent distances." Pennsylvania Avenue was the first street in the city devoted to commercial purposes, but its low and

Constitution Avenue and Tenth Street at the Almost-Completed National Museum of Natural History of the Smithsonian Institution, 1909

often flooded location caused its more prosperous merchants and the builders of office blocks to seek higher ground, notably along F Street, the first ridge of highland rising from the lowland basin. Moreover, while the activity surrounding the Center Market at Seventh Street and Pennsylvania Avenue had spawned the thriving business thoroughfares to the north along Seventh Street, the noise and congestion led many business establishments to leave the Avenue. Along the city's major new retail thoroughfares, structures of decorative cast iron, granite, and brick rose on building lots originally devoted to residential and mixed residential-commercial activities. The regularization of the iron frame permitted enlarged commercial building heights and presented a new awesome image in Washington to match that in other American cities.

EXCELLENCE IN BUILDING DESIGN

The rise of outstanding school buildings marked not only the expanding population, but a concern for an improved physical environment and the high quality of public education in Washington. Most indicative of educational excellence were the prizewinning school designs provided by Adolph Cluss for the Wallach School in 1864 and the Franklin School in 1865. These buildings represented both a social and a structural departure from the flimsy frame buildings or rented facilities in church basements that had been utilized for schools in Washington prior to the Civil War. The construction of the new "citadels of democracy" indicated, as Tanya Edwards Beauchamp points out, an "initial step in the modernization of the city . . . and a promise of better things to come." Cluss, abreast of the latest building materials on hand and conversant with innovative school design in America and Europe, provided the city's children with structures that embodied modern concern for safety, expanded teaching and learning facilities, climate control, healthy conditions, and adequate lighting. The success of these two pioneer schools in the city was remarkable. All subsequent designs furnished by Cluss in his capacity as architect of "virtually all the public buildings erected by the Washington City government" would be seen as much more modest in appearance. The school buildings constructed in the 1880s and 1890s

Franklin School Building As It Looks Today

were not intended to rival the celebrated Wallach and Franklin school buildings, but were nevertheless functional and economical while exhibiting the latest developments in building materials and techniques. The growth of the District of Columbia's school system, in terms of both sheer numbers of buildings constructed yearly and new residential populations which they were to serve, was a major barometer for the physical growth of the city.

Churches constructed in the post-Civil War era, like schools, reflected the cultural needs of the growing population. Second only to federal office buildings, Washington's churches were the chief public buildings, fronting on many of the principal sites L'Enfant had originally provided. The architectural design of church structures was assertive and in many instances hotly competitive. In the residential communities churches were the largest and most visible buildings, and thus contributed most to the community identity. The nineteenth century was not yet the time when Episcopalians, Roman Catholics, Mormons, Presbyterians, and others would erect in Washington symbolic edifices which associate their national institutional prestige with the national capital city. Yet the churches of the day in the central city did aspire as churches, and some as national shrines and religious centers; at Sixteenth Street and Columbia Road, half a dozen faiths scrutinized each other. Mammon had put his stamp on these buildings, dictating their highly visible location and fashionable appearance. In the future, this great interest in a prominent central location notwithstanding, the churches often unresist-ingly followed their wealthy parishioners to the higher ground of suburban Washington.

Residential Washington and the Growth of Suburbs

The designer of so much of the postbellum cityscape, Adolph Cluss, also participated in the remarkable growth of residential areas of the city. Himself a resident of the architecturally pleasing Judiciary Square neighborhood—centered on Hadfield's City Hall, and Meigs's Pension Building—Cluss developed close friendships with major speculators in his position as a member of Shepherd's Board of Public Works between 1872 and 1874. A result of these friendships was played out in Shepherd's investment activity not only in the "Row" that bore his name facing Farragut Square, but also in other blocks in the vicinity of rapidly developing Dupont Circle. Shepherd's own house had been designed by Cluss. So also in 1873 was "Stewart's Castle" designed by Cluss, on Dupont Circle at the intersection of

Connecticut Avenue, Looking toward Dupont Circle and Stewart's Castle, 1890s

Dupont Circle, 1900

Connecticut and Massachusetts Avenues. This structure acted like a magnet, attracting similar sumptuous dwellings to be constructed nearby on ground that had been, previous to the 1870s, an open stretch of commons characterized by swamps and shanties. The process of residential growth was abetted by two developments. Congressmen who now attended sessions of longer duration and therefore brought their families to Washington were interested in residences of greater permanency than the boarding houses on Capitol Hill or along Pennsylvania Avenue. Also, America as an emerging world power attracted a growing diplomatic corps which needed suitable accommodations.

Dupont Circle and Kalorama. The purchase of the building site at the northwest corner of Connecticut Avenue and N Street for the British Embassy further established this clustering around Dupont Circle of luxurious structures commissioned by wealthy and important clients. "In one fell swoop, wealth, political power

and diplomacy made this area highly desirable as a residential area" until the 1920s. It is interesting to note that although it lay within the walking city, the Dupont Circle area in its heyday was poorly served by public transportation; residents had to be of sufficient means, therefore, to provide their own.

As a neighborhood for those who had earned their wealth elsewhere in the country and had come to settle or even retire in a congenial but politically powerful milieu, Dupont Circle set the pattern for nearby residential development for many years to follow. Henry Adams could have set his novel *Democracy* here rather than on Lafayette Square. And the expansion continued. In the 1880s, a Philadelphia syndicate of speculators moved in the Northwest quadrant along Massachusetts and Connecticut Avenues onto the old Kalorama estate, considered to be of great natural beauty, chopping out blocks of subdivisions that were fortuitously shaped by the land a particular owner was willing to sell. Erasing the startling contrast between the "unimproved" Kalorama property and the handsome houses that studded Massachusetts Avenue near Rock Creek, the frantic pace of development between 1890 and World War I left the area with an irregular street plan. Some subdivisions followed the Washington grid adopted in 1888 and reinforced in 1893, while others were constrained by the contours of the former estate grounds.

For residents of more modest means, the vast majority of ordinary civil servants, Dupont Circle and Kalorama were beyond reach financially. But there were many alternative possibilities. The growing concentration of the city within the original city limits encouraged groups of speculators to settle the less desirable areas of Capitol Hill or more probably to look beyond the old city boundary into the highlands of the District of Columbia.

THE ROW HOUSE IN HISTORY

The row house, by no means original in the new residential enclaves carved out in the city, continued as the dwelling type suitable and affordable by the thousands of government employees. Washington's first multiple row-house dwelling had been Wheat Row, built as a speculation in 1793. In the same decade, clusters such as the Six Buildings and the Seven Buildings (1796) on Pennsylvania Avenue, NW, were built in other parts of the city. At the bottom of the income spectrum, cheap wooden houses in groups of three or four, often only a single story high, exploited the inherent economies of the type.

In Georgetown, the early Federal row house of red brick was represented by Cox's Row, built in 1817, and Smith Row, in 1815. On Capitol Hill, Philadelphia Row, constructed in 1856, showed a later version of the Federal row house. It was the popularization of this housing type and its mass production that met the housing needs of the lower income families. By the 1840s row housing for all income levels had become commonplace, and after the Civil War it became the rule. In the parts of the city planned by L'Enfant such developments have often disappeared from view. This occurred in the Southwest as a result of clearance and redevelopment, and along Massachusetts Avenue in the vicinity of Union Station.

The Row House and the Constituent City. Life in mid-nineteenth-century Washington was marked by a certain comfortable congestion reinforced by the increasing predominance of the row houses. The charac-

teristic type is illustrated by the Peterson House, where Lincoln died. Its origins were solidly planted in the eighteenth-century townhouses built in cities along the East Coast. Washington was at the southern end of this region, below which the more distinctively southern house types appeared. From the townhouse type evolved the commercial builder's row house, built in the southern parts of Washington in developments at the scale of a block or even larger areas. Thus, the row house enunciates the true urban vernacular that ultimately produced the constituent city, in contrast to the monumental, official city of Washington. As this city expanded to the north, especially after the coming of the streetcar, whole districts were covered by the characteristic row houses. Brookland, Park View, Petworth, Mount Pleasant and even Woodley Park were communities whose names were emblazoned on streetcars as destinations. The row-house type also appeared at larger scale on undeveloped lots and blocks at the fringe of the old river-bottom city.

The Front Porch and the Welsbach Mantle. The row house in its typical expression stood on a full basement. The house was entered from a porch, which as time went on evolved from a stoop or landing with

The Row House Vernacular: 1800 Block of Newton Street, NW, in Mount Pleasant, 1977

heavy iron railings into a fully developed living porch with room for furniture, swings, grass rugs, lamps, awnings, and other amenities. The earlier red brick was supplanted by lighter hues, and the porch took on Greek Revival overtones. Heating was initially provided by coal-burning stoves, the most popular type being called a latrobe (from its designer), semicircular in form with isinglass doors, and fitted into a fireplace. Illumination came from gas fixtures, in their prime from the Welsbach mantle. The first floor contained a parlor, dining room, pantry, and kitchen opening onto a back porch and yard surrounded by a six-foot board fence. The second and perhaps a third floor were typically given over to bedrooms, although it was not uncommon for larger houses to provide a library or den on the second floor, as a more secluded living or family room. Before the era of the automobile, the residential street was a public environment of continuing interest. The sidewalk offered space for children to play hopscotch, jump rope, tag, statues and other games, all supervised by the parental eye—from the porch. The row or the block had its distinctive life, its individual characters, its behavior, its morale. Such streets, with their gas lamps, their summertime life in the humid heat of the city, their local standards of removing snow and trash, were found throughout the constituent city of Washington.

Design Vernacular and the Builder's Art. As a design vernacular, the row house was the product of tradition. It was improved by the carpenters and masons, practical builders, and those who graduated from these skills to the entrepreneurial ranks. Progress in design was the result of piecemeal improvements to tradition in building materials, construction techniques, household services, and living habits. Many of the characteristics of the row house were the result of building regulations or codes. When central heating arrived, houses had to have basements for furnaces. The use of air shafts and "notches" provided air and light for interior rooms, especially the little-used "blind dining room." As gas and later electricity were provided, the use of candles and lamps declined. Many design changes were experimental, and some were short-lived fads. The popularity of the front porch was one of the more durable reforms in

row-house design. The vestibule, often paved and walled with ceramic tile, and the hallway itself was reinterpreted by successive generations of builders. And in Washington, as in London or nearby Baltimore, it was the large estates encircled by urbanization that provided the principal sites for row housing.

NEIGHBORHOOD LIFE IN WASHINGTON

The population was thus accommodated in a product of the builder's art which expressed the economies and technology of a highly competitive business. That Washington was predominantly a brick city, again like Balti-

Tenallytown Trolley Car, Early 1890s

more and Philadelphia, was ordained by its clay banks gradually being consumed now by brickyards reaching from the Anacostia around to Arlington. The row house possessed the inherent economies of the party wall. Using limited amounts of space with great efficiency, it was eminently suited to the requirements of the walking city and later the streetcar city. Many of the most desirable residential streets lay off some principal artery where the trolley car had spawned a commercial strip containing the essential shops and services, and frequently churches and schools. Consumer services were seasonally supplemented by the street peddlers who enlivened the residential streets and heralded the advent of strawberries and watermelons, Potomac shad and saltwater trout, with characteristic cries, and provided such essential services as mending umbrellas, sharpening knives and scissors, or collecting old clothes, bottles, rags, and papers. Along the street at appropriate times came the newsboy to hurl his product onto the porch, the garbage man with his horn, the iceman or baker's cart, the ice-cream vendor or the popcorn and peanut man, and the purveyor of bananas or flavored snowballs made to order of shaved ice.

The distinctive and durable neighborhood with its traditional form of housing was rocked and shaken by the advent of the automobile and the illusion that everyone could live in verdant villas in the suburbs. Enough of these neighborhoods survived, however, to respond to the demand for rejuvenated intown communities and neighborhood conservation, and the houses were flexible enough in plan to stand being reoriented from the street to the backyard, now become a garden. The row house also inspired the revived vogue for townhouses.

Washington in the latter half of the nineteenth century did not develop vast areas of low-income slums. Rather, the poor lived in communities with the rich and middle classes, occupying the characteristic dwellings in alleys that were generated by the large blocks and long lots of the city. These dwellings stood side by side with carriage houses, stables, woodsheds, privies, and commercial structures for services such as horseshoeing. Around the corner from the well-to-do families at Logan Circle or Massachusetts Avenue were the narrow-fronted little clapboard houses of the less prosperous. *Black and white, rich and poor were mingled in almost every block*, each housed according to his own circumstances. Only after 1900 did the separation of races and classes take the accentuated form known in most recent times—a reflection of the segregation in employment and in urban life, indeed, in the modern city itself.

Capitol Hill: Durability and Restraint. Representing the eastern extension of the row-house speculator's dream, Capitol Hill benefited little from Shepherd's or succeeding public improvements. Grand residences developed by Captain Albert Grant along A Street and East Capitol Street caused a faint flurry in anticipation of that section's becoming one of the finest residential neighborhoods in the city. In 1871, however, when the British legation considered securing two of Grant's

houses, the developer's unwillingness to remove the adjoining partitions sent the legation to look elsewhere, thus relegating Capitol Hill to clients of more modest means. These residents continued to rely on wells, springs, and an unpredictable supply from the city's waterworks. In fact, until the completion of the East Capitol Street water main, the route of the city's water supply originating in the west subjected the eastern half of the city to constant threats of a water shortage—and this actually occurred in 1889. Thus, while Capitol Hill lured a few residents of wealth, the area increasingly was staked out by people of modest means who could not afford to live in the more lavishly supplied and accommodated (and commensurately priced) western sections. The blocks of tidy brick row houses on Capitol Hill were constructed not only for transients but for the "stable middle class." Despite the physical isolation from the rest of the city, the Capitol Hill community that developed during the last quarter of the nineteenth century typified the values of a secure permanent population in houses of modest cost, durability, and restraint in detail.

Expansion of the City Northward: Mount Pleasant. The growing middle-class population of Washington gradually looked northward into the highlands in the District, to higher altitudes where one could escape the heat and congestion of the basin city. In 1865, Maine-born S. P. Brown divided his farmland along Fourteenth Street—with a commanding view of the city—into a subdivision which he called Mount Pleasant. This first subdivision to be created after the Civil War attracted a "large number of gentlemen, mainly clerks in the government employ" bonded together by a common New England heritage, who wanted homes in the suburbs of Washington. They were attracted to Mount Pleasant by the convenience of the site to a streetcar line, laid out in 1862 and stretching as far north on Fourteenth Street as Boundary Street (present Florida Avenue). Mount Pleasant also was within range of the walking city. Settlers there built their own detached frame homes around a village green on oddly tilting cross streets west of the major north-south street. Despite the subdivision's proximity to the downtown, the residents were far enough away from the urban orientation to form their own community with strong self-identity. A virtually separate suburban village, Mount Pleasant developed its own social institutions: Bible classes, parties, entertainment, and the inevitable citizens' association. This identity was physically revealed in Mount Pleasant's irregular business and residential street system, and was patriotically celebrated in a mini-history of its first decade written by its citizens' association on the occasion of the nation's Centennial.

Columbia Heights. Other suburban subdivisions followed, spreading according to the dictates of transportation lines along Fourteenth Street, Seventh Street, and the Baltimore & Ohio Railroad, with the Rock Creek Park gorge an effective western boundary to development until it was bridged for heavy traffic in the early 1890s. Columbia Heights developed in the 1880s along Fourteenth Street, taking advantage of its proximity to Meridian Hill Park and Columbian College, and was serviced by the streetcar line that had been extended north of Florida Avenue. In addition to the advantages of a higher altitude and lower summer temperatures, the physical arrangement initially offered much open space.

LeDroit Park and Brookland. LeDroit Park, developed along Seventh Street in the 1870s, offered the amenities of the "suburbs of the city." Here, moreover, the neighborhood identity was reinforced with its own street system and names and its own water and sewer mains. This exclusiveness was physically emphasized until 1890 by a fence built to keep out what LeDroit Park considered undesirable elements of the population. Over in the northeast sector of the city, the development in the late 1880s of the 134 acres of Brookland followed close on the heels of the founding of the Catholic University of America in 1885 and was serviced by the Baltimore & Ohio Railroad. Located on one of the highest points in the city, Brookland developed a characteristic pattern of single-family houses with deep lots, gardens, and trees in what had previously been an isolated and poorly serviced area. By the late 1880s, electric streetcars further engaged the residents to the central city, with additional public improvements to come in response to activity by the powerful citizens' association.

Petworth. Laid out in this critical street-planning era in the final decade of the century, and located east of Fourteenth Street in a landscape of short hills, Petworth reflected a strong reaction to privately designed street layouts. Like a piece of fabric cut out of the original city plan, Petworth's pattern embraced the strong diagonals of New Hampshire and Kansas Avenues.

Chevy Chase. The blossoming of the residential neighborhoods east of Rock Creek marked the major trend of development until the gorge was bridged—at Klingle Road in 1886 and at Calvert Street in 1891. Designated trustee to the vast land holdings of the late Senator Sharon along Connecticut Avenue, Senator Francis G. Newlands led the advance into the rural lands west of Rock Creek. Connecticut Avenue extended in perfect alignment beyond Calvert Street to the Maryland border. At the northern terminus of Connecticut Avenue, Newlands created Chevy Chase Village, a graceful haven of tranquility. He correctly envisioned the subsequent development by others along Connecticut Avenue, now graded and conveniently serviced by the street railroad.

Silver Spring and Takoma Park. The formerly rural Maryland villages of Silver Spring and Takoma Park were more accessible to city residents anxious to find a countrylike respite from their urban weariness. Silver Spring, serviced by the Baltimore & Ohio Railroad after 1873, developed into a middle-class community, increasingly tied by virtue of this popular train service to the fortunes of the District. Takoma Park, a true streetcar suburb, offered large frame houses to a dispersing population and commodious hotels to weekend and summer vacationers. The ads boasted clean spring waters.

Rosslyn and Alexandria. The expanding system of streetcars also radiated out into Virginia, linking the distant towns of Herndon, Vienna, Dunn Loring, and Falls Church to the central city and offering families a farmlike residential setting and the accessibility to a city job. Transportation lines such as the Southern Railroad that formerly brought farm produce and dairy products to the city could now be developed to accommodate civil servants as well. Rosslyn, a terminus of several transportation routes that crossed the Potomac at Aque-

Cabin John Hotel in Suburban Maryland, 1890s

duct Bridge, was laid out shortly after the Civil War, and its working-class character reflected the concentration of incoming supplies and light industry. Alexandria, once a proud, independent, and prosperous port city, was faced with a similar absorption into the fortunes of the capital city, especially as Peter Hains surveyed a route between Mount Vernon and Aqueduct Bridge.

Anacostia. Across the Anacostia River, Anacostia--often considered to be Washington's first suburb—was founded in 1854 as Uniontown. Established as a white working-class neighborhood close to the Navy Yard, Anacostia found its ties with the central city strengthened in 1875 by a horsecar line, and in 1895 by an electric streetcar. In the post–Civil War years, Anacostia witnessed the rise of several residential neighborhoods to augment its market gardening communities. Congress Heights above Bolling Airfield (now Bolling Anacostia Tract) was inhabited by employees of both Saint Elizabeths Hospital and the Navy Yard. The neglect of the eastern sections of the city was especially evident along and east of the Anacostia River. An area of commanding panoramic views and a hilly topography, it had not even been shown on L'Enfant's plan. Grading operations, essential city services, and street systems such as those provided in the western sections of the city were frequently denied to the eastern sections. Furthermore, Anacostia was dotted by many pockets of poverty, ripe for further enlargement and institutionalization in the twentieth century.

MULTIPLE-FAMILY DWELLINGS AND THE APARTMENT HOUSE

As residents began to move into newly subdivided areas, the homes they left were factors in the phenomenon of the succession of social classes. When the poor moved in on the heels of the rich, the houses, public facilities, parks, streets, and the local environment as a whole were adapted to the scarce means and life-style of the new occupants. Many families crowded into previous single-family dwellings or building lots; multiple-family dwellings were improvised or created, and people literally spilled out of the houses onto the streets and back alleys. The Octagon, two blocks from the White House, once the townhouse of the proud Tayloe family, was found by Charles McKim at the end of the century to be occupied by seventeen families.

Multiple-family dwellings did not necessarily imply undesirable living conditions. Apartment houses, desired by an increasingly cosmopolitan population with fond thoughts of Parisian flats, made possible the acceptance of similar dwellings in Washington. Adolph Cluss in 1883 designed at Thomas Circle the Portland

108

Apartments, considered to be the first notable apartment house in Washington. Luxury apartment houses in the Dupont Circle area became fashionable places of residence, especially as seasonal homes.

Highway Legislation in the 1890s

The Official Street Plan. As early as 1878, the Annual *Report of the Commissioners of the District of Columbia* had noted the continuing spread of subdivisions beyond Boundary Street (Florida Avenue), woven onto the formerly rural landscape in street plans that did not conform "to those of the city or to each other." Anticipating the need to condemn property within these subdivisions in order to provide for roads between city and country, the report urged a new topographical survey and an official street plan applied to the District, steps that would insure the orderly continuation of Washington's plan into the adjoining lands. In the language of the 1878 *Annual Report*, "The beauty of the city of Washington arises from the fact that it has not—like most other cities—grown up at haphazard, but in accordance with a well-matured plan framed in advance and uniformly adhered to for the general good without regard to particular interest."

EFFORTS TO REGULATE GROWTH AND
THE STREETS THAT GO NOWHERE

By the 1880s, sections of Washington outside the L'Enfant city were experiencing rapid growth and development. L'Enfant had laid out streets only within the area prescribed by President Washington, and thus far no provision had been made for orderly extension beyond that original area. Developers, particularly in the area bounded by Sixteenth Street, NW, what is today Florida Avenue, NW, North Capitol Street, and Spring Road, NW, subdivided their holdings and laid out streets at will, with total disregard for incompatibility of new streets with the planned extension of the L'Enfant streets. By 1887, the District commissioners' *Annual Report* was referring to the alarming number of streets which "go nowhere and connect with nothing."

The commissioners and most citizens recognized that there was little they could do about the nonconforming subdivisions that already existed, but they hoped that future development could be regulated. The first step in this direction was taken in August 1888, when Congress passed an act forbidding any plat or subdivision that did not conform with the "general plan of the city." What the commissioners produced was a list of directives which included provisions covering widths of alleys and minimum widths of lot subdivisions. More importantly, the commissioners ordered that streets and avenues of subdivisions be in exact alignment with and of equal width to those in the city of Washington. New circles and public squares would be laid out and dedicated when the commissioners felt them necessary "to make a subdivision conform to the general plan of the city of Washington." With future subdivisions more or less under control, the commissioners continued to hope that the worst of the deviations in existing subdivisions could eventually be corrected. The Washington Board of Trade, on the other hand, was vigorously opposed to all irregular subdivisions, existing or contemplated, and advocated the ratification of all subdivision streets with the general city plan.

THE 1893 HIGHWAY ACT

The stricter view of regulation prevailed and in March 1893, Congress passed an act "providing a permanent system of highways in that portion of the District of Columbia outside the cities of Washington and Georgetown." This act authorized the commissioners of the District of Columbia to prepare a plan for the extension of the L'Enfant streets, and required that all subdivisions—including those already extant—conform to this new plan.

A new map of the city was to be made showing the "boundaries and dimensions of and number of square feet in the streets, avenues, and roads," and providing that circles be drawn up at intersections of principal avenues and streets. Anticipating that many legal difficulties would arise between existing subdivisions and condemnations by the commissioners to enforce the lines of this new highway map, the statute provided for a process of hearings and damages to be paid to the landowners.

The Engineer Commissioner's office was, however, extremely slow in preparing the new plan provided for by the 1893 Highway Act. In the next four years, under the direction of Engineer Commissioner Charles J. Powell, the map was drawn up and issued in two sections, the first in 1895 and the second in 1897. For the years intervening, a great deal of uncertainty existed as to the exact location of the proposed streets. Real estate transfers in the potentially affected areas came to a virtual standstill: no one wanted to purchase property that might be condemned for a right of way.

Not surprisingly, the 1893 Highway Act was opposed by developers and private property owners alike, and the ensuing legal battles made it obvious that the new legislation was unworkable. By 1898, five years after the legislation had been enacted, only one section of the extension plan had been completed and not one of the condemnation cases had been decided by the courts. District officials were unhappy with the act's requirement that compensation funds were to come from the District only; the federal government, which they felt also would benefit from the orderly extension of streets, was not required to pay anything.

THE 1898 HIGHWAY ACT

Protest and opposition to the provisions of the 1893 act reached such a pitch by 1898 that a congressional committee was appointed. This committee recommended that the 1893 act be repealed and new legislation enacted. Congress did just that several months later. Like the 1893 act, the Highway Act of 1898 authorized preparation of a plan extending the L'Enfant streets, but it differed from the earlier act in that it specifically exempted subdivisions in existence before 1893. The new legislation made no mention of who was to provide funds for compensation when and if the need arose. Despite the failure of the 1893 and 1898 highway legislation to create a uniform District street and highway system, the city and its politicians at this time renewed their interest in Washington's original street plan and attempted to revive its aesthetics and efficiency—even if in the end they were to find that the full enforcement of such provisions was obstructed by public disinterest in the first place as well as the past decisions of private

land developers. Nevertheless, what was termed the "Permanent System of Highways Plan" is a major and deliberate extension of the city's plan. As a matter of long and continuous control of growth, the highway plan effort stands respectably above most American cities' suburban sprawl. It provided a coherent network for additional parkways, special sites, and other improvements that were to come under the McMillan plan and later on.

THE BUILT ENVIRONMENT: END OF THE CENTURY

At the end of the century, the physical outlines of L'Enfant's plan, still visible after the Civil War, had become strongly defined by public engineering and architectural efforts—and filled in with the artifacts of private investment. The public works of the durable Army Corps of Engineers and the short-lived Board of Public Works created early stirrings of the City Beautiful movement even before the 1893 World's Columbian Exposition in Chicago. The rising heights of both commercial and residential structures was nipped in 1899 by a Building Heights Act. Residents and visitors of all economic levels met on the common ground of the major business thoroughfares, dispersing at night, however, into their increasingly separate residential enclaves. Strong and socially isolated communities, voteless but represented by citizens' associations, spread the new city beyond the old pedestrian or walking city, temporarily enforcing their separateness, but at the same time heralding their ultimate physical merging in the following century. Topographical hindrances having been conquered by streetcars, railroads, grading operations, and reclamation, the form of the city would no longer be dictated by predominantly natural conditions. The full effect of man's imagination on the city and the creation of what would in the future be termed the built environment was now ascendant.

CHAPTER V   THE McMILLAN PLAN   1901–1902

The McMillan Plan 1901-1902

Turn of the Century: The Promise of American Cities

The conquest and victories of nineteenth-century science and politics persuaded Americans that man possessed the inventiveness to control and manipulate his own physical environment. The Eads Bridge at Saint Louis and the Brooklyn Bridge were early manifestations. One dramatic indication of man's accomplishments—at urban scale if not urban complexity—was the World's Columbian Exposition which itself celebrated conquest of a vast continent. The designers who produced this compelling spectacle in Chicago, the Great White City along the shores of Lake Michigan, revealed the ability of a small group of talented men to translate their concepts of architecture and civic design into the reality of plaster. At the opening of the new century, resounding memories of the 1893 Chicago triumph convinced Americans that their seemingly unplanned cities, including Washington, could embark upon a fresh course of order and grandeur. In the air was the promise of American cities sparkling new but equal to those of the Old World. In accepting the concept that buildings and parklands are interrelated—as had been exemplified at the Chicago Fair—designers in Washington at the turn of the century fulfilled the unsuccessful attempts of earlier architects to build on the work of L'Enfant and plan for areas larger than individual buildings. Modern urban considerations evolved out of this effort. In the city of L'Enfant, a small group of the country's best-known designers was given the task of developing a new design of the city, an early exercise in comprehensive planning—and indeed for teamwork and institutional aspects a forerunner of the city's later comprehensive planning.

The Centennial of the "removal of the government" to Washington provided the occasion for intensified interest in improvement of the capital city. Most fundamentally this sense of purpose came out of the post–Civil War decades of growth and piecemeal civic improvement, and the increasing conviction that although Washington had achieved excellence in its residential neighborhoods, its schools, and its parks, it had not orchestrated these gains into a comprehensive urban statement. In 1898, a group of civic-minded Washingtonians formed a committee to meet with President McKinley and discuss proposals for the Centennial celebration.

The committee's plans initially included a ceremony plus a more permanent memorial such as an appropriately commemorative edifice or the long-desired and much-discussed bridge connecting the District of Columbia with Arlington National Cemetery. McKinley responded favorably and asked Congress to authorize formation of a committee to oversee planning for the celebration. Congress took action and a joint committee made up of selected members of the House and Senate, governors of the states and territories, and Washington citizens held its first meeting on 21 February 1900.

A BEGINNING IS MADE: PROPOSALS AND PLANS

During the morning session a committee of five was appointed to sift through the various proposals made by the citizens' group. Senator James McMillan of Michigan, a wealthy and influential member of the Senate, was chairman, and well qualified. In Detroit he had been prime mover of Belle Isle Park. He had served as chairman of the Senate Committee on the District of Columbia since 1890. With the aid of his efficient secretary, Charles Moore, who served as clerk of the Senate Committee and was attuned to local sentiments, McMillan had initiated numerous improvements in the District. The water supply and filtration system had been improved and a comprehensive sewer system constructed, highways had been extended in a planned fashion beyond the area covered by the L'Enfant plan, the city's twelve streetcar companies had been consolidated into two, and a reorganization of the city's charitable institutions had been undertaken. The city was ready to move into the future—the twentieth century.

During the afternoon session McMillan reported back to the joint committee. His committee of five recommended that a Centennial celebration be held in December, and that the event be marked by both the greatly needed enlargement of the Executive Mansion and the construction of a tree-lined boulevard, to be known as Centennial Avenue. This avenue was projected to run through the Mall from the grounds of the Capitol to the Potomac River. The terminus of the avenue at the river might then become the site of the much-discussed bridge to Arlington; moreover, as McMillan rather ambiguously pointed out, "L'Enfant had

provided for just such an avenue." Unsure of the feasibility of his committee's proposals, McMillan also introduced an amendment to create a team of experts to study the proposals and report back to the president. The compromise bill that passed appropriated $6,000 toward the study—to be carried out, however, by the Chief of the Army Corps of Engineers, guardian of the city's parks since 1867. Thus began a series of studies and plans proposed between 1900 and 1902 for the Mall and its appendages as well as for the White House.

The Plans of Franklin W. Smith. The Corps's study had in fact been preceded by those of 1890 and 1900 by Bostonian Franklin W. Smith. A multitalented but eccentric individual, Smith suggested in his two plans that the land later associated with the Federal Triangle and the Northwest Rectangle be cleared and designated for public buildings and functions. At a time when municipal improvements and the Centennial of the city were joined in a reassessment of Washington as a capital city, McMillan had Smith's plans published as a Senate document for general information and comment. If Smith's diagrams appeared amateurish in their graphic standards, their grand conception for the cleared area nonetheless reflected national interest in the city's image. Far more than any plans of the decades past, Smith's work was comprehensive regarding architectural methods and effects, popular educational values, the combinations of landscape and other arts, and civic possibilities in parks, street frontages, and schools. By comparison, engineers' plans tended to be street or topographic plats with some incidental planting shown.

The Plans of Colonel Bingham and the Corps of Engineers. Theodore Bingham, in his continuing capacity as the Corps's officer responsible for public buildings and grounds, prepared two plans, in March and April of 1900, based on his interpretation of L'Enfant's original treatment of the Mall area. The plans featured a major boulevard from the Capitol to the Washington Monument area. In the first plan, the avenue terminated in a sculptural grouping just north of the monument; in the second, it terminated at the monument itself. Both plans suggested that the projected bridge across the Potomac to Arlington National Cemetery be built on the line of New York Avenue, and both retained Downing's park areas and the railroad track and sheds. In the second plan, Bingham showed the triangle created by Pennsylvania Avenue and B Street (now Constitution Avenue) between the White House and the Capitol as providing sites for future public buildings. Colonel Bingham's plans were notable for another reason: he included a treatment of the newly formed Potomac Park created to the south and west of the monument by his associates in the Corps of Engineers during the reclamation of the flats. By including this land in his projections, Bingham significantly enlarged the scope of the study area.

Bingham's plans received adverse publicity in the *Washington Post*, and the *Evening Star* spoke against putting a "mere street" on the Mall. Colonel Bingham, according to the *Post*, had shown his plans to President McKinley and to members of Congress, governors, and the citizens' committee. While his plans were technically competent, Bingham was an engineer, not an architect. For a city awakening to feelings of its new prominence as a capital of a world power and having visions of the Great White City on Lake Michigan, an army engineer's plan would not be enough.

The Parsons Plan. In May of 1900 Senator McMillan, presumably unhappy with Colonel Bingham's plans, introduced legislation authorizing the president to appoint an architect, a sculptor, and a landscape architect "each of conspicuous ability" to prepare plans for the enlargement of the White House, the treatment of the area between Pennsylvania Avenue and B Street, SW, and a connection between the Potomac River and the National Zoological Park. The House of Representatives drastically altered the proposal, however, and its final version called for the Chief of Engineers—Colonel Bingham—to make the study and authorized him to employ only one expert, a landscape architect. Bingham, despite the fact that he had just completed two such plans, asked landscape gardener Samuel Parsons, Jr., of New York, who had worked with Vaux and Olmsted on the plans for Central Park, to do the study.

Parsons, like Frederick Law Olmsted, Sr., viewed a park as a pleasure ground set apart from the sight and sound of the surrounding city. The desirability of a "people's park" and the efficacious influence of nature on urbanized human beings was a concept—epitomized in Central Park—not appropriate in some eyes for a park running from the nation's Capitol to its principal monument. Parsons's plan, which encompassed the entire kite-shaped area south of Pennsylvania Avenue and north of Maryland Avenue from the Capitol to the Washington Monument, featured a series of connecting oval drives running the length of the Mall and diminishing in size and dropping to lower grades as they approached the monument. Where transverse roads crossed the Mall they were to be depressed and carried under the linking strips of parkway connecting the oval drives. Charles Moore waspishly described the scheme as one of a series of "goose-egg Mall plans."

Parsons's design was submitted to Bingham in November, and to Congress just before the Centennial celebration planned for December 12. On that day Colonel Bingham would be one of the speakers at a reception at the White House where a model of his proposals for enlarging the White House was to be displayed. The day's festivities culminated in a banquet sponsored by the Washington Board of Trade, evidence of business interest in the city's future.

1900: The American Institute of Architects' Convention in Washington

While the joint congressional committee had been planning its celebration of the city's Centennial, the American Institute of Architects had been drafting its own commemoration of the event. Glenn Brown, an indigenous Washington architect then serving as secretary of the Institute, had long been interested in the artistic development of Washington. He had recently published an impressive book and portfolio on the history of the United States Capitol. Pursuing his historical interest, but with a reformer's zeal, he had vehemently attacked the federal government in the past for its failure to allow more private architects to design public buildings. Brown saw in the approaching city Centennial an ideal time to generate nationwide interest in the improvement of Washington as well as to emphasize the contribution of professional architects. He arranged to have the American Institute of Architects' convention, opening the day after the Centennial celebration, take as its major topic the future development of Washington.

The first session was held on the morning of December 13 at the new Arlington Hotel. Many of the convention's delegates had attended all or some of the Centennial programs of the previous day and joined with Glenn Brown in condemning both Bingham's and Parsons's plans, favoring instead a return to the L'Enfant plan for the Mall. H. B. F. McFarland, president of the Board of Commissioners of the District of Columbia and chairman of the joint committee on the Centennial celebration, welcomed the delegates and said: "We hope to receive, while you are here, further instruction as to how to make the city more beautiful than it is." The American Institute of Architects' president, Robert S. Peabody, spoke next: "One does not need a professional education to feel mortified at the sight of certain buildings that have been thrust upon these beautiful highways in comparatively recent times." Peabody vowed the architects' cooperation with the politicians in promoting the "improvement of architecture controlled by the national government."

PROFESSIONAL VIEWS

Papers dealing with the landscape, sculpture, and grouping of public buildings in Washington were scheduled that evening. Brown had worked strenuously to put forward the ideas of some of the best architects in the country. The speakers spoke of the need for a comprehensive study and plan for the capital; of the possible formation of a commission to advise the government on building sites, design, and models for public buildings and sculpture; of the positive attributes of the plan of the "founding fathers"; of the lessons of Chicago in terms of vistas, uniform scale, broad terraces, balustrades, and reflections in water basins; of various treatments for the Mall area; and of restoration of the axial relationships of the Capitol, the White House, and the Washington Monument. They also arrived with plans of their own.

Cass Gilbert, who later served on the Commission of Fine Arts, advocated monumental groups, preferably in the "so-called classic style," with buildings of prominence on axes of streets and a height limitation of three or four stories. He proposed a historical museum as the terminus to the White House axis, projected onto the reclaimed Potomac Park. Edgar Seeler echoed McMillan's committee and the joint committee in proposing that a Centennial Avenue be constructed through the Mall terminating not at the monument, but passing north of it. Drawing on the Chicago Fair and other expositions for inspiration, C. Howard Walker saw the Mall as a national court of honor, with monumental buildings bordering a stretch of park. Paul Pelz, a Washington architect and member of the Washington Board of Trade, said a strong movement was growing within the Board, with support from the press, for the purchase of that portion of the District of Columbia bounded by Pennsylvania Avenue, Fifteenth Street, B Street, and Seventh Street, an area—containing the notorious Murder Bay—which had deteriorated badly since the Civil War and was considered a civic disgrace. Pelz's plan recommended widening of the two B Streets (north and south of the Mall) and construction of public buildings along the perimeter of the Mall. He proposed a grouping of buildings around the Capitol, and located a "Hall of Records" on Pennsylvania Avenue at Eighth Street, where after thirty years and many vicissitudes it would eventually be constructed as the National Archives. Depicting a bird's-eye view of a restructured Mall, George Oakley Totten, Jr., regretted that the World's Columbian Exposition had not been held in Washington as it could have provided a trial run of temporary civic buildings in this study area.

Presenting the point of view founded in landscape architecture, Frederick Law Olmsted, Jr., stated that landscape design embraced more than romantic tracts set amid a bustling city. Landscapes, he pointed out, could be formal as well, and *should be designed* in concert with the buildings to which they were related. Prophetically for the outcome of the McMillan plan, Olmsted suggested that the Champs Elysées be the model for the Mall, a formal park lined with "several parallel rows of trees with several pavement and turf strips."

Glenn Brown himself had a plan for the capital. In an article in the *Architectural Review* he advocated a boulevard through the Mall, grander than the Champs Elysées, which served as a common source of comparison in reference to a Mall avenue. Brown also recommended the purchase by the government of the triangle between B Street and Pennsylvania Avenue, and urged clarification of the Mall plan before any more vistas were destroyed. The article was illustrated with photographs of formal compositions that Brown had collected at the Paris Exposition of 1900.

To the architects, and particularly the elite represented by the American Institute of Architects, there could be but one urban design model—Paris. It was in the city of light that the most articulate and influential members had won their professional spurs in the competitions of the Ecole des Beaux-Arts. When they spoke of the "classic" they meant the academicism of the Ecole. Theirs was the white architectural style of the "City Beautiful" and of future Washington, just emerging from gray Romanesque and utilitarian red brick models.

THE CITY OF WASHINGTON: DECEMBER 1900

The architects were generally unhappy with what had been happening in Washington in recent years. The city that presented itself to the Chicago, New York, and Boston designers was far different from that we see today. Its early neoclassicism, reinforced by the public buildings of Mills and his contemporaries, had been effectively obscured by the romanticism that stamped itself upon the landscape no less than upon the city's architecture. The Mall was chopped into winding carriage drives and bosky walks—"overgrown Downing," it was called, in allusion to the romantic landscape plan drawn up in 1851 by Andrew Jackson Downing. The principal new buildings echoed the eclecticism of the past generation; the Romanesque Post Office tower, the Italianate Pension Building, the florid Library of Congress, the cascading columns that formed the French Second Empire façade of the State Department were elements in the contemporary cityscape. The central

city was laced by railroad tracks and a conspicuously sited depot marked the Mall. The cast-iron shed of "Marsh Market" dominated Pennsylvania Avenue. And back of all this lay the residential city, the characteristic streetscape of tall, narrow row houses with gables, turrets, arched porches, and cast-iron window ornaments. This individualism in both residential and commercial areas was not greatly different from other American cities, but Washington's role as a national capital suggested a different standard—a "world standard," as Moore suggested, reflecting the dignity, order, and continuity of the national, even an imperial, state. It was to be "all executed by American artists trained in European schools to minister to the satisfaction of American needs." The city to be transformed was also smaller than the Boston or Chicago or New York from which the designers came; Washington in 1900 numbered 279,000 people and covered an area of seventy-six square miles, most of it still south of Florida Avenue.

At the close of the architects' convention, a special legislative committee was appointed to bring before Congress a resolution calling for a commission to consider certain improvements in the Capitol. William A. Boring of New York was designated chairman and W. S. Eames of Saint Louis, J. R. Coolidge, Jr., of Boston, George B. Post of New York, and Glenn Brown of Washington were chosen to serve on the committee.

Meanwhile, Charles Moore, a witness to the grumblings of the American Institute of Architects, brought their complaints to the attention of Senator McMillan. McMillan had been embarrassed at the outcome of the Parsons plan and now requested through Moore a conference with the American Institute of Architects' legislative committee. As a result of that meeting, McMillan introduced a joint resolution in the Senate on 17 December 1900. It urged "that the President of the United States be authorized to appoint two architects and one landscape architect, eminent in their professions, who shall consider the subject of the location and grouping of public buildings and monuments to be erected in the District of Columbia and the development of the entire park system of the District of Columbia and report to Congress in December of 1901."

1901: Senator McMillan and the Senate Park Commission

Realizing that opposition in the House would prevent passage of the resolution, McMillan decided to handle the subject in what Moore called a "somewhat different manner." On 8 March 1901, at an executive session of the Senate, Senator McMillan reported from his District Committee a resolution directing that committee to report to the Senate a plan for the improvement of the entire park system of the District of Columbia. The District Committee was to be authorized to employ experts, the necessary expense to be paid from the contingent fund of the Senate. The resolution was adopted and a subcommittee was named consisting of Senators McMillan, Jacob H. Gallinger, and Thomas S. Martin.

At an informal hearing before the subcommittee on March 19, with members of the American Institute of Architects' legislative committee in attendance, McMillan pointed out the difficulty of going beyond improvement of the park system to siting of future public buildings, a topic which would necessitate negotiations with the Senate and the House Committee on the Library and on Public Buildings and Grounds. It was finally agreed, however, that the subcommittee might make "suggestions" as to siting of buildings. This verbal formula solved the parliamentary dilemma, and it was agreed to appoint an architect and a landscape architect who would then choose their own third member. McMillan summed up the proceedings in the following carefully worded statement: "These gentlemen [the commission to be appointed] could study the question between now and next December and submit privately to this committee a plan which would practically cover the matter of parking [sic] of the city and incidentally suggest where the public buildings should be placed." Thus, the Park Improvement Commission of the District of Columbia, to be commonly known as the Senate Park Commission, or simply the McMillan Commission, was born out of an elaborate legislative maneuver, avoiding the necessity of the concurrence of the House or conferencing with other committees. An immediate solution, it contained the seeds of future difficulties.

Daniel Burnham was selected almost immediately by McMillan and Moore to be the architect member of the commission, as he had been the "mainspring of the Chicago Fair." Head of the well-known Chicago architectural firm of Burnham and Root, Burnham had been chief architect and director of works for the 1893 World's Columbian Exposition. He had already designed the Railroad Exchange and Marshall Field's buildings in Chicago, and—most importantly, as it turned out—had been chosen as the architect of the new station for the Pennsylvania Railroad in Washington. Burnham's executive ability and his talent for effecting cooperation among various artists were proven. He was confident and tireless, traveling almost constantly in relation to his work. He thought on a "grand scale" and was greatly productive, with some of his best work—such as his celebrated plan for the city of Chicago—still ahead.

Frederick Law Olmsted, Jr., who had made an earlier study of Washington, was selected primarily because of McMillan's experience with the elder Olmsted on the Belle Isle Park. As McMillan reasoned, "I guess the son is as good as the father." Olmsted junior, "Little Rick," had been his father's apprentice during the older man's last year of active work and in 1898 was himself admitted to the firm, which then underwent another of its frequent name changes, becoming Olmsted Brothers. The youngest of the McMillan Commission members, Olmsted brought to Washington the experience he had gained with his colleague, Charles Eliot II, in designing the comprehensive Metropolitan Park System in Boston.

Olmsted was already in Washington for the subcommittee hearings. Burnham arrived in Washington on March 21 and that evening met Charles Moore for the first time. Moore offered him chairmanship of the commission. When Burnham inquired about the third member, Moore said the choice was his and Olmsted's, but suggested Charles F. McKim. This suggestion Burnham apparently welcomed, for Moore quoted him as saying that McKim was "the man I had in mind. He was the one I most relied on in the Chicago Fair work."

Burnham left for New York two days later where he successfully sought McKim's acceptance of the appointment.

Charles McKim had studied at the Ecole des Beaux-Arts in Paris, and was the leading exponent of academic classicism in the United States. He headed his own firm of McKim, Mead and White in New York City. Having already designed the Boston Public Library, the Rhode Island State Capitol, and the new buildings and fence in the Yard at Harvard University, he would in the future, after his work on the McMillan Commission was concluded, be chosen to remodel the White House and design New York's Pennsylvania Station.

Charles Moore, who functioned closely with the commission as Senator McMillan's personal surrogate, had an intimate knowledge of how Washington worked. He had himself prepared the reports on the District that led to the improvements McMillan had initiated through the District Committee. Moore had a reputation on the Hill as a very efficient secretary, and Senator McMillan relied heavily on his judgment and knowledge. Moore had gone to Harvard (as had all of the Senate Park Commission members except Burnham) and studied with Charles Eliot Norton, who he said had shaped his views concerning art. Moore would later write biographies of both McKim and Burnham.

Not an artist himself, Moore had a profound respect for the elite professionalism these men represented. He shared both their Republican politics and their Brahmin outlook. He enjoyed their sociable dinners at the Century Association in New York, where projects could be discussed and decisions made. He found his relationship with these men a rewarding experience. Later on, Moore was appointed to the Commission of Fine Arts—where he served for twenty-seven years, twenty-two of them as chairman—and there became a formidable voice in realizing the intentions of the McMillan Commission plan.

THE BASIS OF A NEW DESIGN

Much is known of the working procedures as well as the designs of the McMillan Commission, more by far than is known of L'Enfant's work, even if still not enough to allow a fully detailed comparison of these two major planning efforts. The greatest distinction was that by 1901, planning for the capital city was already set in a context of continuing activity. Plans produced in the years preceding the formation of the McMillan Commission provided an archives of ideas on which commission members could draw. The beautiful natural setting of the city, the river and the hills, and the classic design imposed on it by L'Enfant formed the

The Optical Survey of the District of Columbia from the Top of the Washington Monument down the Mall to the Capitol, 1901

foundation on which they would build. The inspiration of the Chicago Fair made beautifying the capital as important as developing new land and providing for a park system. Above all, the time was ripe for a grand design, and the men with the talent and experience to produce it had been put in a position to do so. The power and personal wealth of Senator McMillan made the venture possible, and the political acumen of Charles Moore would be the guide "through the trying world of officialdom" on what Moore himself called a "quest of good order and beauty made incarnate in the National Capital."

The Optical Survey of the District. The first meeting of the McMillan Commission took place on 6 April 1901. The remaining days of April were filled with preliminary studies. The commission made what Burnham called "an optical survey" of the District, going through it in every direction, touring the outskirts, encircling the city on hills, going as far as Great Falls, source of the city's water supply, taking a boat ride to see the city from the river, visiting Alexandria and Georgetown. But a ground-level view was not enough. Burnham climbed to high points in the city in order to get a larger view—from the heights of Arlington, Meridian Hill, Anacostia.

Seeking those American precedents and inspiration on which Washington, Jefferson, and L'Enfant had drawn, the McMillan Commission members also toured notable colonial houses. Taking the lightship Holly (made available to them by Secretary of the Treasury Lyman J. Gage) down the Potomac to the James and York Rivers, they visited Stratford Hall, Carter's Grove, Upper and Lower Brandon, and Shirley. They also stopped at two colonial capitals, noting the circles and radial streets of Annapolis and the axial relationships of Williamsburg.

"Then," Burnham said, "we examined the documents," the L'Enfant plan and the available maps and surveys. The Senate Press Gallery was commandeered for a drafting room, and J. G. Langdon from Olmsted Brothers was put in charge. Here they studied the fine maps of the outlying areas already prepared by the Coast and Geodetic Survey, and drew new and more nearly accurate maps of the older parks and central areas, all "with the aim of making throughout the entire District a well-articulated park system extending as far as Great Falls and Mount Vernon."

Work continued through May with McMillan Commission members commuting between their offices and Washington. Early in June McKim wrote to Burnham that Augustus Saint-Gaudens, the noted sculptor, had been visiting him and taken an interest in the work of the commission. McKim suggested that Saint-Gaudens be made a full member, noting that "the question of sites refers to sculpture as well as architecture." Burnham, in turn, wrote to Senator McMillan saying they wanted Saint-Gaudens made a member of the commission, and then made the appointment simply by placing Saint-Gaudens's name on their letterhead.

The Grand Tour and the City of the Future

On June 11 the McMillan Commission sailed for Europe in search of Old World inspiration. The purpose of the trip, Burnham had explained at their first meeting, was to "see and discuss together parks in relation to public buildings. That is our problem here in Washington and we must have weeks when we are thinking of nothing else." They were also there to track down the European influences reflected in the L'Enfant plan and thus to add substance to the skeleton of L'Enfant's original intentions. But they were also looking further, toward the city of the future, and intended to "make a closer study of the practice of landscape architecture as applied to parks and public buildings . . . what arrangement of park areas best adapts them to the uses of the people, and what are the elements that give pleasure from generation to generation, and even from century to century."

Charles Moore was a member of the party but not Saint-Gaudens, whose health would not allow him to take the strenuous seven-week trip. The itinerary, drawn up by Olmsted, was based on viewing the works of Lenôtre that L'Enfant had experienced as a young man and used as inspiration for the original Washington plan. Olmsted brought with him maps of the District of Columbia and a camera; of this he made good use, many of his photographs being included in the commission's report.

Often inspiration came directly. Moore later wrote that while standing on the steps of the little temple at the Villa Borghese, the commission members decided that the projected "Memorial Bridge should be a low structure on a line from the site of the Lincoln Memorial to the Arlington Mansion—a monumental rather than a traffic bridge, but a significant element in an extensive park scheme." Admiring the vista from the terraces of the chateau of Vaux-le-Vicomte with the *tapis vert* and lines of tall trees, the Americans thought of the Mall in Washington. In England they measured the green carpet between rows of trees at Hatfield House, to find proper width for the Mall. Olmsted's objections to a central driveway down the Mall were strengthened by seeing a similar scheme in Windsor Great Park.

In London Burnham found the opportunity to visit Alexander J. Cassatt, president of the Pennsylvania Railroad, and learned that the railroad was willing to abandon its site on the Mall and join with the Baltimore & Ohio Railroad in building a new "Union Station" at their site at New Jersey Avenue and C Street providing Congress would pay part of the added expense of tunneling under Capitol Hill. Having viewed the tracks on the Mall as a major obstacle to their plans, the commission was now ecstatic. Their plan was already in motion. They telegraphed Senator McMillan and celebrated the good news at dinner.

DOWN TO THE DRAWING BOARD

Returning to the United States in August, the commission set up an office in New York to prepare the necessary designs, with a young man from McKim's firm, William T. Partridge, placed in charge of the drawings. Partridge a quarter century later would serve as consultant to the National Capital Park and Planning Commission.

The McMillan Commission members had early divided up the work. Burnham's assignment on the design of Union Station proved very demanding, calling for a second change in location and hence a new design for the new site near the Capitol where the station would serve as a "vestibule" to the city. A design treatment was needed also for the Grand Court in front of the depot. Burnham's time was consumed in numerous conferences with railroad officials and legislators. As for the McMillan Commission, therefore, Burnham's primary responsibility was to oversee the plan as a whole. The outlying regional parks and their connections was to be the responsibility of Frederick Law Olmsted, Jr. The central composition was to be handled by Charles McKim. Saint-Gaudens was to advise in matters of scale and the location of monuments and statues. Burnham's commitments allowed McKim, who devoted almost all of his time to the work of the commission, to act, as Moore described it, as the "refiner" of Burnham's ideas.

The commission was painstaking in its planning, especially where details of a major element like the Mall was concerned. They had decided the Mall should have a formal treatment, as earlier suggested by Olmsted at the American Institute of Architects' convention, wiping out Downing's romantic winding paths but preserving the Mall as an appropriate landscape setting for the related public buildings. The commission members envisioned the Mall as similar to Lenôtre's formal compositions at Versailles and Vaux-le-Vicomte: a wide, open vista with a green carpet down the center, bordered by narrow roadways flanked by rows of elm trees. They had measured similar spaces in Europe, but now in order to find precisely the right width for the grass-covered panel down the center of the Mall, they had the Supervising Architect of the Treasury erect flagpoles that could be viewed on the Mall from the Capitol steps and the Washington Monument. Trials were made with the flagpoles 250, 300, and 400 feet apart. Three hundred feet was chosen as the ideal distance. (According to Moore, McKim later said in regard to narrowing the Mall, "rather would I lie down on the floor of this court and die first.") Great care was exercised also in deciding how many elms should form the rows on either side of the green panel. Burnham said, "having examined every notable avenue in Europe, we found that not less than four trees constituted an avenue and three produced a bad effect. . . . The American elm was chosen not only because of the architectural character of its columnar trunk and the delicate traceries formed by its widespreading branches, but also because in the District of Columbia this tree is at its best, notable examples being found in the city parks and in the grounds of the Capitol."

Even before the commission members had gone to Europe, they with McMillan and Moore had understood the need to win allies to their work. For the Senate Committee on the District of Columbia, Moore gathered and published background data, and more importantly, a significant number of hearings, thus recording and disseminating the views of community and civic groups regarding parks. At the commission's inception, Senator McMillan had given a party at which he introduced the members to prominent Washington figures, giving the gentlemen of the commission what Moore called their "social credit." Soon after, McKim sought out Secretary of War Elihu Root for advice—and other cabinet members, as well as influential senators and representatives, were kept well informed about commission activity. Frequent meetings were arranged with the commissioners of the District of Columbia.

Selling the plan was an important aspect of the McMillan Commission's work and would prove immeasurably important in the plan's reception. Moore, who had been a journalist earlier in his career, released just enough stories to the newspapers to keep the interest of the press and public whetted. McKim's concern about the layman's ability to appreciate plans and drawings led him to ask leading illustrators of the nation's magazines to do renderings of the designs and landscaping for public buildings and monuments in relation to the over-all scheme. McMillan gave his approval for this project as he had for others, saying, "if the government will not pay for it, I will." This allowed the freewheeling Park Commission members to move ahead, avoiding penny-pinching and bureaucratic delays. Most of the money was advanced by McMillan through Moore, who paid the bills. Vouchers were then submitted to the Senate, and if they were approved, McMillan would be reimbursed. The commission members

themselves advanced money—as, for example, for the scale models of Washington—and at least once Moore sent them money from his own account.

1902: The Commission's Report and the Models of Washington

The McMillan Commission's report, written by Moore and Olmsted, incorporated photographs of proposed treatments of Washington, analogous compositions in Europe, and examples of parks in Boston and Hartford. Maps were also included, one series comparing present and proposed park areas in Washington to those in the large cities of Boston, New York, London, and Paris. The report was a masterful piece of work. It was meant to stir imaginations, and it did. It was readable and "its essentials were easily grasped even by laymen," a point important in Burnham's view of planning efforts, as Hines has noted. Burnham wanted the plan to "appeal to the ordinary citizen" and thus dressed the text of the report to "inspire enthusiasm among a broad constituency."

On 15 January 1902, the commission's official report was submitted to the Senate Committee on the District of Columbia. This submission was followed by the opening of an exhibition in the hemicycle of the still-new Corcoran Gallery of Art. McKim had worked for three days—staying up almost the entire night before the opening—hanging and rehanging the photographs and illustrations and adjusting the lighting.

The place of honor was held by two models: one of the city as it existed in 1901 and the other showing proposed changes. The models included an area of about two miles from the Library of Congress to the Lincoln Memorial. George C. Curtis, a geographic sculptor, had made the models in Boston. Every public building was exactly shown in miniature, every private building outlined. The grades of streets and kinds of trees lining them were exact; over 5,000 photographs had been taken of buildings, streets, and city blocks to insure accuracy. A third model, produced in McKim's New York office, exhibited a proposed treatment of the Washington Monument featuring terraces, a sunken

Three-Dimensional Scale Models of Washington Prepared for the McMillan Senate Park Commission, Showing (left) Existing Conditions and (right) Proposals, 1901–1902

Washington's Topographic Heights: View of the City from Cardozo High School on Thirteenth Street, NW

garden, broad marble steps, and a long decorative canal symbolically connecting the monument with the proposed Lincoln Memorial.

Despite snowy weather, the planned reception was held at the Corcoran Gallery of Art in Washington. Theodore Roosevelt and his party arrived first. President Roosevelt thought the Washington Monument model "too fussy," but when he viewed the entire treatment of the Mall he began to realize the "greatness of the conception itself." Secretary of State John Hay pronounced himself satisfied, although he noted that the location of executive buildings around Lafayette Square would destroy his house. Secretary of War Elihu Root, already an enthusiastic ally of the plan, was even further enthralled by the exhibit. Members of the Senate Committee on the District of Columbia received the guests, among them senators and congressmen. The exhibition was then opened to the public.

THE PARK SYSTEM AND THE CENTRAL CORE

In the commission's report to the Senate, McMillan called the plan the "most comprehensive ever provided an American city." Actually the plan, as directed by its authorizing resolution, concerned itself with two main problems: the building of a park system and the grouping of public buildings. By connecting existing parkland and carrying the park system to the outlying areas of the District and across the river as far as Mount Vernon and Great Falls, it addressed the regional character of the city. By grouping public buildings in formal compositions, the McMillan plan created a highly concentrated central core. It gave the city an "official" architecture as well as a plan. Nor did the plan for the monumental city neglect its people.

Frederick Law Olmsted, Jr., drew heavily on the Boston Metropolitan Park System in his recommendations for Washington parks. In the published version of the plan he included photographs of a Boston beach, showing a recreational bridge, bathing house, outdoor gymnasium, and children's sandpiles. In his proposals, Olmsted provided for neighborhood parks where they were lacking, especially in that portion of the District lying outside the L'Enfant city. He suggested additions to Rock Creek Park, and outlined individual treatments

for important parks. In transforming parks from the promenading and reposeful variety to those of more intensive recreational use, Olmsted tied parks to the planning process. Park needs thus became an integrated part of a functional program to acquire land. Parks also were now more democratic; they would serve the popular needs in their recreational purpose, and form an important element in humanizing the city.

BOULEVARDS, DRIVES, AND PARK CONNECTIONS

Along with the provision of connections between parks, to be related to the area's topography, scenic boulevards were suggested—on the Virginia lands through an as yet undetermined route south to Mount Vernon, and on the Washington and Maryland sides along the Potomac Palisades as far north as Great Falls. Another road was planned to follow the Potomac from the Lincoln Memorial to Rock Creek Park, to trace the winding crevice to the zoo, and then connect the old Civil War sites into a Fort Drive. A second riverside drive emanating from the Lincoln Memorial was planned to lead down the river, paralleling an embanked quay, to a recreational area on the reclaimed land of Potomac Park. Landscaping in the newly reclaimed Potomac Park, according to the commission's report, was to be modeled after "the landscape of natural river bottoms—great open meadows, fringed by trees along the water side," and would mirror across the Washington Channel an improved commercial waterfront of the Southwest quadrant. Olmsted urged the government to reclaim and frame with raised quays the Anacostia mud flats, on the brink of industrial use, in order to bring recreation space to the eastern residential neighborhoods. As the planned park connections encircled the city, enveloping the heights of the topography, they also crossed outlying residential areas. Between Rock Creek Park and the Soldier's Home, the much widened and tree-lined Savannah Street (now Varnum Street) would, according to the plan, set a formal tone to the neighborhood and provide a park façade to an otherwise familiar street of row houses. On the surrounding heights of the city's topographic bowl, moreover, the plan suggested sites for memorials. Where the radials met the crests of distant encircling hills, it was thought that a "simple white shelter will prove the most effective treatment," whereas closer to the city, such sites for memorials would call for treatment on a "more comprehensive scale."

The Grand Plan for the Mall

The grouping of public buildings and development of the Mall represent the best-known portions of the McMillan Commission's report. Executive functions were to expand into new office buildings surrounding Lafayette Square. Buildings relating to the legislative and judicial functions of government were to be constructed around the Capitol in a relationship already established by the Library of Congress. The Botanic

Garden at the foot of Capitol Hill and the east end of the Mall were to give way to a Union Square with statues of Generals Grant, Sherman, and Sheridan. Fountains, terraces, and statuary would complete the treatment of the proposed square, an American equivalent of the Place de la Concorde in Paris.

The Mall, patterned in part after the Champs Elysées, was proposed to be a green panel bordered by narrow roadways and rows of elms; it was planned to tilt slightly south, forming a new axis with the Washington Monument. According to the plan, it would then follow a vestigial canal, or reflecting pool, recalling the buried waters of the Tiber Creek—as well as the decorative canals at Versailles, Fontainebleau, and Hampton Court—and terminating on a site then still a "marshy backwater," but later to be the site for the

Detail of the Mall Design in the McMillan Commission Plan of Washington, 1901–1902

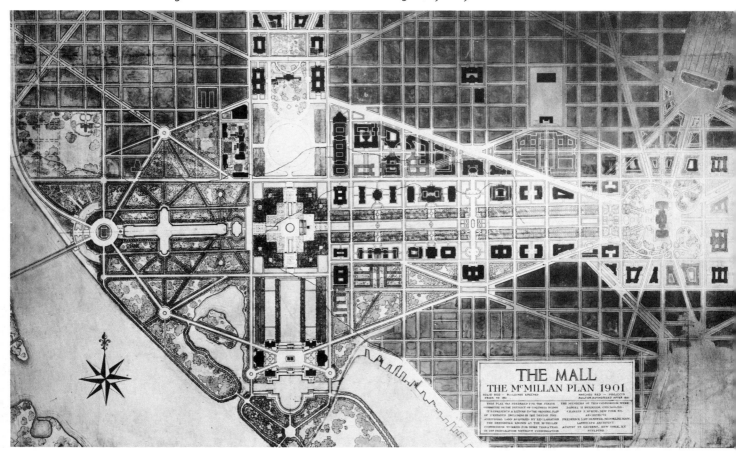

126

Lincoln Memorial. The new memorial, recommended in the plan as having a "character essentially distinct from that of any monument either now existing in the District or hereafter to be erected," was proposed to be set in a *rond-point* or circle in the same way that the "Arc de Triomphe crowns the Place de l'Etoile at Paris." From this proposed circle, avenues were to radiate out into connections with Potomac Park to the south, along the riverside drive to Rock Creek to the north, and across the Potomac to Arlington House on the Virginia hills. This arrangement was similar in form to the avenues radiating out from the Place de l'Etoile into the Bois de Boulogne and several other axial points in Paris.

THE WHITE HOUSE CROSS AXIS

The north-south cross axis extending from the White House to the Potomac River was, according to the plan, to be recreated by the location of a great sunken garden and a round pool of ornamental water at the base of the monument. The axial line would then terminate at the Potomac where a future memorial, perhaps a pantheon to honor the Constitution's writers, was to be located. Critical to this realignment of axial relationships was the design of the Washington Monument grounds. As the commission's report stated, of all the elements in the McMillan plan, "no portion of the task set before the Commission . . . required more study and extended consideration than has the solution of the problem of devising an appropriate setting for the Monument; and the treatment here proposed is the one

Rendering of the McMillan Commission Plan of the Mall, 1901–1902

Rendering of the McMillan Commission Plan for a Pantheon and Washington Common, 1901–1902

which seems best adapted to enhance the value of the Monument itself."

The design for the monument terrace and gardens required a 300-foot-wide marble stairway fronting the west and descending 40 feet from the monument platform. This feature, surrounded by terraces, paths, trees, and fountains, would have necessitated removal of the high ground that supported the obelisk. The monument's reflection in the round pool was to provide the illusion of the monument's realignment with the north-south axis. Thus, the design would have accomplished the desired geometric aspirations. From an engineering standpoint, however, removal of the hill on which the monument was secured would critically weaken its foundations. In the end, what the commission hoped would become the "gem of the Mall system" was abandoned. Nonetheless, this emphasis on the problem of the incorrectly aligned monument most clearly illustrates the axial design concern of the architect-planners trained in the French tradition at the Ecole des Beaux-Arts; few aspects of their work better express the effort that produced their concept of the grand design.

As compared with the majestic respite offered in the monument gardens design, active sports were designated in the area just to the south. A "Washington Common" was planned with a stadium, ballpark, open-air gymnasium, and playgrounds. A realigned Tidal Basin would have facilities for water sports. According to other portions of the plan, in the area south of Pennsylvania Avenue—which it was suggested the government buy—would be municipal buildings, a modern market, and a national "Hall of Records." Public or semipublic buildings such as museums were to front on the Mall.

DEFINING THE WIDTH OF THE MALL

The commission members did not propose demolition of buildings (such as the Treasury, the State, War and Navy Building, or the Library of Congress) blocking original vistas of the L'Enfant plan. They did, however, advocate moving the Smithsonian Institution back from where it projected onto the Mall. While the commission members did not mention this in their report, knowing the furor it would create, their models

128

and illustrations of the Mall did not show the Smithsonian infringing on it. In addition, Burnham—during his testimony before a hearing of the Senate District Committee on Senator Francis Newlands's resolution to define the width of the Mall—shed some light on the thinking of the McMillan Commission members. "We frankly confess that our scheme would result in moving back the Smithsonian Institution so far as it now projects into the composition; in that scheme involving many millions of dollars if one object already in position can not be made to harmonize with the composition, we frankly confess that in our opinion it ought not to stand in the way of a grand improvement."

THE URBAN AMBIENCE

The static models of the city, largely devoid of human reference, gave credence to the notion that McMillanism spelled vacant streets and oppressive architecture.

But while Burnham and his associates by no means forged a new architecture of democracy in their limited terms of reference, they were oriented to settings and architectural designs that would please visitors and residents of Washington. The entire discussion of parks referred to appropriate activities to be ascribed to the various park areas—action sports in the Washington Common, the Tidal Basin, and along the Anacostia; riding and hiking in Rock Creek Park; pleasurable walks along the formal parts of the Mall. If the traffic along the Mall between the proposed Union Square and the Lincoln Memorial did not resemble the commercial life along the Champs Elysées between the Place de la Concorde and the Place de l'Etoile, it was because in Washington, the walk was lined only with museums—and flanked by grand office buildings—rather than that mixture of shops, restaurants, and residential functions that give the Parisian street its lively charac-

Rendering of the McMillan Commission Plan for the Lincoln Memorial, 1901–1902

teristic. Pedestrian traffic might have been generated by retention south of Pennsylvania Avenue of the market functions (moved slightly to the west and under a new roof in the plan). This pattern was precluded by removal of the Victorian market sheds to make room for the construction of the National Archives Building as part of the Federal Triangle in the 1930s.

While the piecemeal projects (associated with the plan) that were ultimately executed did not in themselves create the urban ambience the designers had intended, the aspirations of these men—especially as to the District parks outside the river-bottom L'Enfant city—gradually found expression in the planning activities of succeeding generations of designers.

For all of its suggestions of imperial glory the plan was an amalgam of various foreign and domestic influences. While the commission members may have stated their indebtedness to Rome, Roman influences were evident primarily in the architectural styles and in the water displays. The Mall itself was derived from French and British sources. Suggestions for river treatment, especially the raised quays, could have been derived from a number of European cities. Nonetheless, the commission members had wanted to understand the motivations of Washington and Jefferson, and had also sought examples of urban design and landscaping the American colonies could provide. In the commission's recommendations for parks, Olmsted drew on more recent American models and also reflected his long experience and that of his father in Boston, Hartford, and Brookline. The final product of all these influences was a plan that was a uniquely American creation.

Selling the Plan: The Task of Enlightenment

By and large, those who viewed the models, illustrations, and photographs were pleased. The job of selling the plan to the public was, however, still ahead. It was one of the strengths of the 1901–1902 plan that the commission that created it did not neglect it, even after its official function as a commission had ceased. Much of the early opposition to the plan was based on the cost, which bothered the economically minded members of Congress. To money objections the commission members answered by arguing that the plan was intended to guide building projects that were already in the pipeline or were clearly necessary and were to be appropri-

View of Union Station Terminal, ca. 1915

ated in future. Opponents also attacked the plan because of the genesis of the McMillan Commission; it had been authorized without concurrence of the House, which was not in session during the commission's formation and early work. McMillan regretted having to work without House participation, but he had judged that a comprehensive body of studies or proposals would be a good starting point for the next Congress.

Most of the response from official sources was positive, but Speaker of the House Joseph Cannon of Illinois played the role of a chief obstacle to the plan just as he had earlier in forcing compromises in McMillan's original amendments to create a team of experts. Cannon voiced vigorous opposition to the existence of the McMillan Commission and to the various elements of the plan as individual building projects arose. Not inclined to debate the merits of the plan on an equal basis Cannon was moved more by issues of prerogative and opposing political philosophies. It was Cannon who made the famous remark that he would "never let a monument to Abraham Lincoln be erected in that God-damned swamp."

In order to move Congress, members of the McMillan Commission and supporters of its plan conducted an intensive campaign to make the details of the plan familiar to the public. Burnham in Chicago, McKim in New York, Olmsted in Boston "set about," says Moore, "the task of enlightenment." The American Institute of Architects gave its support, and Glenn Brown made a speaking tour as far west as Saint Louis. Charles Moore talked to school children in all parts of the country. Well-illustrated articles appeared in newspapers and magazines, and the report of the commission complete with photographs, maps, and illustrations was published and made available to the public.

The first part of the plan to be tested before Congress was the legislation to clear the railway tracks from the Mall. Burnham also wanted the location of the new Union Station terminal changed to north of Massachusetts Avenue to avoid having to carry that major avenue through a long tunnel under the tracks. The bill changing the location of the terminal was passed, with McMillan's guidance, on 15 May 1902. After McMillan's death in August, progress on the remaining legis-

lation slowed. The toughest fight, involving a large government expenditure to reimburse the Pennsylvania Railroad for part of the extra expense of moving its tracks and terminal, had to be fought without McMillan's influence—and over the opposition of Representative Joseph Cannon. Although Cannon opposed legislation authorizing any part of the plan, the reimbursement measure finally passed in February, 1903.

THE FUROR OVER THE DEPARTMENT OF AGRICULTURE BUILDING

There being no specific endorsement or approval by Congress of the McMillan plan as a whole, supporters of the plan were summoned to defend its recommendations each and every time they were threatened by opportunistic decisions. One such threat appeared in 1904 in the proposed siting of a new Department of Agriculture Building that would have projected beyond the proposed building line defining the Mall. Secretary of Agriculture James Wilson defied the prescription of the plan and ordered his architects to observe a 300-foot setback. This brought the controversy to the desk of President Roosevelt, who was embarrassed to learn that he had earlier given his approval to the building without knowledge of the Mall design issue. To express the concern of the members of the McMillan Commission and the American Institute of Architects, Senator Francis G. Newlands sponsored a Senate resolution providing that no building should be erected on the Mall within 400 feet of its center line (a reduction from the 450 feet proposed in the original Senate Park Commission plan). The hearings on the Newlands bill disclosed a rather thin constituency for the plan, but the arguments advanced by its proponents were persuasive and compelling. The result of the hearings on the Newlands resolution was substantial Senate support for the 800-foot-wide Mall, providing the basis for a presidential directive in support of this provision of the plan. Subsequently an equally important decision was made to maintain the gradients of the flattened Mall as proposed in the plan. Thus, in piecemeal decisions on closely fought issues a national commitment to the key provisions of the McMillan plan was built up over the years. It was not until more than a quarter century after the plan had been drafted that Congress provided general approval for the plan.

The McMillan Commission members maintained a role as unofficial advisory board and arbiter of design. They were often asked to comment on building plans or to serve as jurors for competitions, as they did in the case of the Grant and McClellan memorials and the District Building (as Washington's City Hall is known). In the case of the Grant Memorial, they were able to choose a design most appropriate for their proposed Union Square site at the head of the Mall and to urge successfully that the memorial be located there.

THE NEED FOR PERMANENT REGULATION . . .
AND A MORAL FORCE

After the furor over the Agriculture Building, it was clear that a permanent regulatory body was necessary. President Theodore Roosevelt appointed the members of the McMillan Commission along with Bernard R. Green, Superintendent of the Library of Congress, to an unofficial Consultative Board. This arrangement did not prove satisfactory. In 1907, the placement of the Grant Memorial caused another battle when it was learned that some historic trees would have to be cut to make room for the sculpture in the Botanic Garden. This time the newspapers attacked both the plan and the McMillan Commission for wanting to "substitute a pantalooned statue for the living sculpture of God." The plan was again upheld, but Burnham was disgusted by having to fight brushfires over and over. He wrote to Moore: "What we need in Washington is a system. . . . When work affecting our plan is afoot it should be someone's business to know about it and to promptly post all of us."

With the formation of the Commission of Fine Arts in 1910, Burnham would have his "system," a watchdog for the national capital. In 1932, Ulysses S. Grant III wrote that "not unnaturally the Commission of Fine Arts becomes the guardian of the plan of 1901; and has not only helped materially in getting various of its projects adopted, but has also deserved the gratitude of the nation for the bad things it has prevented." The Commission of Fine Arts would see that the Lincoln Memorial be located according to the plan and that it

be designed by a disciple of McKim's. It would lead the fight for locating the Arlington Memorial Bridge by the Lincoln Memorial and enforcing the low and monumental character that the designers of the plan had intended. Saint-Gaudens, McKim, and Burnham would all be dead by 1912, but Moore and Olmsted remained active for another two decades.

Congress did not adopt the McMillan Commission plan in a single action. As the years passed, the plan gained authority in proportion to the diminution in opposition, especially with the electoral defeat of Representative Cannon in 1913. (As a sidelight on history, when Cannon returned to the House two years later and viewed the site of the Lincoln Memorial, he admitted his protests had been a mistake.) The plan achieved additional official sanction as a body of policy by two other routes. One was a series of individual plan-conforming project approvals ranging from the Freer Gallery of Art to the Lincoln Memorial. The second route involved more direct congressional actions. On 30 April 1926, by Public Law 69-159, the National Capital Park and Planning Commission was established and instructed to implement almost all of the McMillan plan's park proposals—as was implied in the description of parkland to be included in the development of a "comprehensive, systematic, and continuous development of park, parkway, and playground systems of the National Capital and its environs." Then Public Law 1036, an act passed on 4 March 1929, in addition to its basic purpose of enlarging the Capitol grounds, "authorized and directed . . . development of that part of the public grounds in the District of Columbia connecting the Capitol grounds with the Washington Monument and known as the Mall parkway in accordance with the plans of Major L'Enfant and the so-called McMillan Commission, with such modifications thereof as may be recommended by the National Capital Park and Planning Commission and approved by the Commission for the Enlarging of the Capitol Grounds." A third direct action was passage in 1930 of the Capper-Cramton park program which was based on an assessment of those McMillan plan features not already rendered—by time and development—irretrievable.

Seeking legislation for one project at a time made, however, for inadequate progress. This was especially true in the acquisition of parkland. From 1901 to 1925, parkland area in the District increased 24 percent while population increased 70 percent, and assessed land values in the District of Columbia increased 240 percent. In the area of public buildings, however, the McMillan plan did become, as Glenn Brown called it, "a moral force." When Washington prepared for the public buildings program in the 1920s, Moore had the 1901 Curtis models set up on the first floor of the National Museum where the public could see them and refresh their memories.

The 1901–1902 Plan: Reaction and Response

Just as L'Enfant established the basic design of the federal capital city, the plans of the Senate Park Commission gave Washington its modern aspect. Together they define the capital city known to its inhabitants, to the nation, and the world. The L'Enfant plan, translated into Ellicott's survey and then staked out on the ground, became an eternal factor in the physical development of the city. When the McMillan Commission members first looked at the city, they saw both its enhanced natural features in the Potomac basin setting and its physical character as derived from L'Enfant. This framework they had to accept as the basis for their new design. For all the continuity this represented, their 1901–1902 plan addressed the present and foreseeable future problems of the capital city. The city they designed was for all purposes a new creation: new in its nineteenth-century sense of space and grandeur, new in its metropolitan regional concept, new in its appreciation of natural parks and environment, new in its splendid architecture, new in its cosmopolitanism. Perhaps most of all, the capital city was new in a political sense, designed as it was to provide a unified vision for the city as a whole, where earlier efforts had been limited to single buildings or monuments, or remained programmatic ideals without significant physical expression.

The plan gathered forces to power the great forward leap in urban development, to support the growth of the city, its metropolitan spread, its increasing complexity, and its new cultural institutions and apparatus. In its handling of the railroad, firmly thrust underground as it passed through the monumental core of the city, the plan exhibited a humanistic command of technology. In its development plan for the flood plain of the Anacostia, the plan offered new quality to urban life and leisure. In its provisions for architectural beauty that extended to bridges and fountains as well as buildings, the plan satisfied a nation's yearning for order and urban significance. In its image, the city was given a symbolic character it would never lose.

THE CITY BEAUTIFUL MOVEMENT

The L'Enfant plan—the plan of the founding fathers, of Washington and Jefferson—was recognized as a source of legitimacy for the plan offered in January 1902. In reflecting past urban design, reference was made now to the L'Enfant plan "restored, developed and supplemented." L'Enfant's Mall was broadened to Victorian scale, and lengthened by half to reach the new banks of the reclaimed Potomac flats. L'Enfant's Federal architecture evolved into the academicism of the Ecole with its Roman overtones. These changes in scale would be overtaken, in time, as the small buildings proposed around Capitol Square, the Mall, and Lafayette Square turned into the huge if relatively low structures seen today. L'Enfant's eighteenth-century city of pedestrians, horseback riders, and carriages—promenades, arcades, and urban squares—evolved into the metropolis of railroads, asphalt, elevators, and other products of modern building technology. "Restored, developed and supplemented," indeed, what Burnham, McKim, Olmsted, and Saint-Gaudens offered with such confidence and panache was precisely what the nation wanted at the turn of the century, and for which it soon found a name: "the City Beautiful." Under this banner the new style would be taken to other aspiring cities from coast to coast.

Given its urbanistic expression by the McMillan Commission, the design philosophy of the Chicago World's

Fair of 1893 was brought to bear on the immediate problems of an emerging urban America. The Great White City of plaster was reconceived in marble, but its dazzling nighttime character, its landscape setting of space, fountains, and greenery, and its sense of order were continued at even larger scale than in Chicago. As the plan unfolded and materialized, a style of urban design, the City Beautiful style, was born. Cleveland, Saint Louis, Denver, and San Francisco produced new civic centers whose design had been born in Washington, and whose art of mobilizing architecture, landscape design, sculpture, lighting, and other special characteristics became a new technology.

The City Beautiful became a visible expression of the urban reform movement that flowered in the early years of the twentieth century, a movement and a cause. It was voiced most significantly by the planner-publicist Charles Mulford Robinson, who popularized the new unity of parks, plazas, and boulevards and re-lated it to the business progressivism of the age. Robinson's popularizing talents stemmed from the then-new realm of advertising, and were first exhibited in his book *Modern Civic Art, or The City Made Beautiful.* It was a comprehensive gathering of urban experiences, but no city more than Washington convincingly illustrated the virtues as well as the authority of the new style. The capital city became an urban model, one that gathered strength from the past and projected it nationwide into the future. Robinson deftly cited the presidential inauguration of 1901, celebrated from roofed stands and pavilions that for the first time had been designed by architects and were, moreover, "painted white and decorated with vines" to complement the design of Capitol and White House. This joining of the new architecture to the urban design of the city's great processional route was formidable evidence that the City Beautiful was more than another style in the panorama of nineteenth-century architectural eclecticism.

Illustration of the Court of Honor at the Inauguration of President William McKinley, 1901

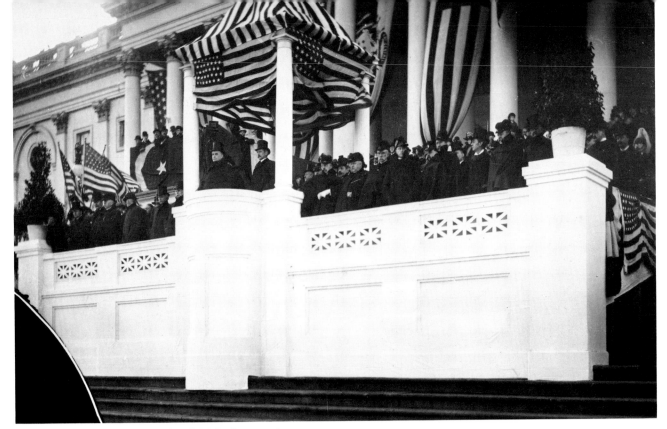

Presidential Reviewing Stand at the McKinley Inauguration, 1901

It would endure, like the laws of the nation. Or, it could be said, like these monumental structures would the laws of the nation endure.

WASHINGTON AS THE CITY BEAUTIFUL

Whatever its reflection of the national temper or its artistic influence—even the street lighting standards of the national capital city were adopted in other cities— the greatest accomplishment of the McMillan plan was its ability to perpetuate itself, to expand and develop, and achieve its goals in the city of Washington. From the moment of the plan's inception to the completion of the Federal Triangle, no public building was erected in the capital city that did not conform to the ideals of the plan and, in most cases, to specific sites and locations. A long generation of artistic dominance extended to the building of the Jefferson Memorial and the National Gallery of Art in the mid-thirties. By then only buildings of acknowledged monumental character were designed in the styles of academic classicism and those that fell short of that standard became the victims of architectural controversy and shifting standards.

The City Beautiful movement in Washington was not limited, as was the McMillan plan, by its original parks and public building sites, but was swept along to include city entrances, parkways, boulevards, monumental bridges, and entire streets. The McMillan plan, reflecting the vast scope of L'Enfant's creation, became the basis for later comprehensive and specialized planning activity. It spread beyond the monumental core of the official city to the whole of the federal district and far into the countryside beyond. It reestablished the Classical Revival style, pushing aside the architecture of ambiguity that had characterized the later nineteenth century. The new city illustrated in the 1901–1902 plan created the image that the public came to associate with the nation's capital in popular magazines, picture postcards, movies, and newsreels. Thus projected across the country, and increasingly reinforced by the experiences of tourism, the renewed city served as a unifying force, a national image with which the country could associate its role as a world power. When implemented, this idealized city would look like the capital of a new kind of America—clean, efficient, orderly and, above all, powerful.

The McMillan plan spawned its own adherents.

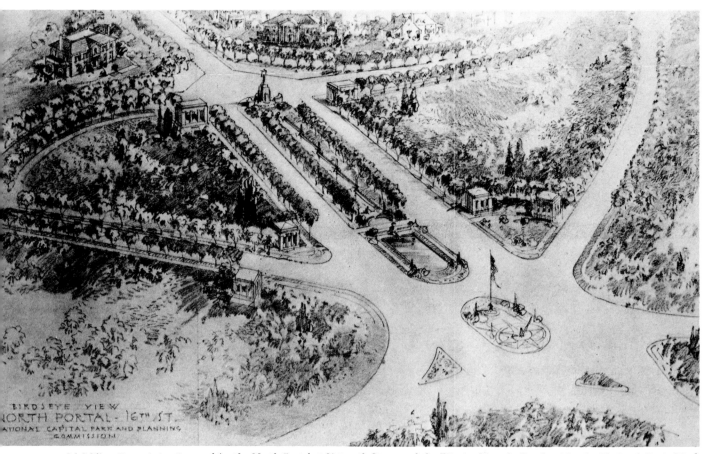

McMillan Commission Proposal for the North Portal at Sixteenth Street and the District Line, As Rendered by the National Capital Park and Planning Commission, 1930

Thirty years later figures like Charles Moore and Frederick Law Olmsted, Jr., still held power in Washington and dictated the fulfillment of the 1901–1902 intentions. New generations had been indoctrinated with these ideals. But what was in fact built? The Federal Triangle filled the space between Pennsylvania Avenue and Constitution Avenue west to Fifteenth Street with enormous office buildings never contemplated in the McMillan plan, which had in fact designated the area for a rebuilt public market and municipal buildings of modest size. In a different fashion, the realization of the 1901–1902 plan did not extend to the building of the Washington Common sports center south of the Washington Monument, the Executive Group surrounding Lafayette Square, or the Capitol Group. On one hand, advancing demands of federal office space and new building technology outpaced the more modest earlier proposals. On the other hand, changed city planning priorities and objectives generated projects unknown to the turn-of-the-century planners.

CHAPTER VI TOWARD METROPOLIS 1902–1926

Toward Metropolis 1902-1926

The Plausible Pattern and a Quest for New Planning

By the turn of the century, increasing urbanization of the capital city forced its planners to grasp an area much larger than the original L'Enfant city. This recognition of space needs for the physical future of the city had already been expressed in the nineteenth century's official highway plan and in improvements to the surrounding countryside. Although the McMillan Commission looked to L'Enfant's original plan for guidance and inspiration, it also made several recommendations that parkland be acquired outside the original L'Enfant city boundaries as well as on land reclaimed from the river flats.

As the physical city spread north from Florida Avenue toward the larger boundaries of the ten-mile square and then into the suburban counties, municipal and federal decisions continued to rearrange planning and development priorities in the monumental core, but now these policy decisions gradually incorporated the whole of the District and provided the basis for extend-ing the radius of planning policy formulation and development activity into the suburbs. Thus, while the metropolitan scale of the capital city had been acknowledged before the Civil War and had gained military recognition during the war, it actually took form in the postwar era. Streetcars and commuter rail lines transformed the former countryside, spawned commuter towns, and eventually generated lineal extensions of the central city. According to contemporary urbanists, the spokes of settlement pinned to the commercial hub represented an idealized city; the rural areas of open space separating the spokes were inaccessible to commuter traffic and, besides offering recreational opportunities, also served as reminders to town residents of the landscape's former appearance.

THE AUTOMOBILE AND NEW PLANNING CONCERNS

This plausible pattern of spokes of development and open spaces was altered drastically by the automobile. As early as 1911, the Army Corps of Engineers suggested that Conduit Road (now MacArthur Boulevard) be resurfaced for benefit of the "increasing use of the road by automobiles." By 1925, the automotive mode of

Construction on Massachusetts Avenue, Looking West, 1911

transportation had been irreversibly adopted by the average Washingtonian. The automobile thus projected a host of new planning concerns: what would the impact of the automobile be on the congested central city and the sprawling suburbs and what new housing patterns would emerge? Transportation routes were now planned for the motorist. As evidence of this change, the United States Geological Survey in 1924 issued its first "automobile edition" map of the Washington area, labeling in red the all-year through and connecting roads. The rush-hour traffic jam appeared. The problem of parking proved insistent, and inspired the construction of parking garages interspersed among office buildings. In the suburbs, the rural areas of open space became accessible to the commuter, freed now from the exigencies of train or streetcar schedules and restrained only by road improvements. With the scattering of residential settlements, a similar spreading out of employment followed. Then began what would become a continuing battle of philosophies between the concentrated government employment and corridor development concept *versus* proposals for dispersal of such facilities throughout the region.

THE ARMY CORPS OF ENGINEERS AND THE PLANNING FUNCTION

In concert with the plans of the McMillan Commission, the Army Corps of Engineers continued to work on physical improvements in the city, cooperating with the new federal planning bodies (such as the Commission of Fine Arts, established in 1910), or being represented there as a member (of the Public Buildings Commission, established in 1916, and the National Capital Park Commission, 1924). Thus the planning function continued until 1925 when responsibility for public buildings and grounds in the District—save for river improvements—was transferred to the new independent office of Public Buildings and Public Parks of the National Capital. Important projects of the Corps's sunset years in molding the city were reclamation of the Anacostia flats, provision of parks to fulfill new functions, and supervision of the construction of several new public buildings. By the 1920s, the Corps's Office of Public Buildings and Grounds had become the repository for a wide and diverse range of duties, from the care of statues and monuments to the role of military and social aide to the president. And in the piecemeal proce-

Anacostia River Scene, Early Twentieth Century

dure of having new structures authorized, an officer of the Corps served as executive and disbursing officer for the Commission of Fine Arts (until 1922), the Lincoln Memorial Commission, and many other bodies.

Urban Park Development: Theory and Practice in Washington

The fortunes of the twenty-mile-long Anacostia River, tidal but not saline, resembled those of the Potomac prior to 1881. The wide and extensive flats from its mouth to far north of the District line were caused by widespread deforestation and erosion of cultivated coastal plain lands upriver. In planning for the river's improvement, the Army Corps of Engineers was chiefly concerned with the "navigable" lower six and one-third miles encompassed by the District, although for all practical purposes, the Navy Yard represented the extent of navigable waters. By the beginning of the twentieth century, these flats were covered by a dense growth of grasses. Sewage and other wastes in the river accumulated in this vegetation, and were popularly believed to

have created (in the words of the 1908 *Annual Report of the Chief of Engineers*) the "prevalence of malarial diseases in the portions of the city and District of Columbia which border the Anacostia." In 1898, a congressional act directed that the river be dredged and reclaimed material placed on the flats with the objectives of land reclamation, sanitation, and promotion of navigation and commerce.

ANACOSTIA RIVER IMPROVEMENTS

Not until 1902, however, did work begin in earnest. It commenced in the portion closest to the Navy Yard, described in the 1903 *Annual Report* as "one of the finest gun shops in the world," and the dredged material was deposited on the flats below the Government Hospital for the Insane (now Saint Elizabeths). Hydraulic dredges worked continually until the early 1920s when the project was largely completed. In order to provide suitable enclosure for the deposited material, a trench was dug and filled with riprap stone, and then a sea wall was constructed to hold in the dredged material conveyed from the river by discharge pipes. By 1914, Major Charles W. Kutz (in that year's *Annual Report*

141

of the Chief of Engineers) questioned the objective of the commercial and navigation interests, as "the flats are not now needed for commercial purposes. . . . Until there is a commercial need for this reclaimed area, it is believed that it should be developed as a public park, as was done in the case of Potomac Park, which is made up of land similarly reclaimed." The McMillan Commission had reached the same conclusion in 1901, and the National Capital Park and Planning Commission confirmed the concept as public policy in its 1928 Potomac River Parks Plan.

Thus, what the Commission of Fine Arts in its 1914 *Annual Report* called the "Anacostia Water Park," an important element in restoring the "balance in development that has tended toward the northwest," was formally declared in 1919 as Anacostia Park. The proposed park treatment was to embrace an open fifteen-foot channel from the Anacostia Bridge upstream to Massa-

chusetts Avenue and a nine-foot channel continuing north to the District line. The river's edges in the northern portion, according to the 1921 *Annual Report of the Chief of Engineers*, were to be "created by a dam on the line of Massachusetts Avenue, forming a lake of sufficient area to permit pleasure boating . . . and also affording navigation to the District line." Instead, a lateral lake (Kingman Lake) was created along the west shore of the river. Measuring six feet in depth, this lake allowed for the juxtaposition of recreational and commercial activities. The parallel open channel on the east permitted the free movement of silt from upriver, acknowledging that the problem was larger than the District's borders. By 1921, the improvements sustained the modest $5 million worth of trade then transacted in the area between the Anacostia and Pennsylvania Avenue Bridges, relieving what the 1921 *Annual Report* termed the "crowded condition in the Washington

Aerial View of the Army War College (Now Fort McNair) on *Greenleaf Point, ca.* 1909

Channel," whose trade was estimated in that year to be worth $16,206,554. The improved channel also supported activities at the Navy Yard and Buzzard Point. A yacht harbor and allotment gardens—continuing the popular wartime garden activity—characterized noncommercial uses.

The stretch of improved river was given added importance in several ways: by the retention of Bolling Airfield (now called Bolling Anacostia Tract) after World War I as a permanent aviation facility; by new efforts of the Commission of Fine Arts to devise a park connection between the Anacostia and Rock Creek Parks; by completion, in 1907, of the Army War College on Greenleaf Point; and, in 1927, by beginning construction of the massive National Arboretum between Mount Hamilton, Hickey Hill, and Anacostia Park. By 1925, the parks in the Northeast quadrant of the city inspired the Commission of Fine Arts to suggest that in a cooperative agreement with Maryland, a parkway (to be designed by the versatile Horace Peaslee) should be constructed to connect busy Bladensburg Road with the upper end of Anacostia Park.

DEVELOPMENT OF WASHINGTON'S PARKS

The success of the reclaimed Potomac Park, setting an example for the Anacostia Park system, was subject to many more modern notions about social functions of parks, beyond the winding walks of the nineteenth century. While some talk lingered in the early years of the century about the creation of a "rural park" along the Potomac, the influence of Frederick Law Olmsted, Jr., and the precedent of the Boston Metropolitan Park System argued for a more varied and distinctively urban scheme for Washington's parks. The move toward more actively used parks stemmed from the belief, expressed in successive annual reports of the Corps of Engineers, that "street play is in a large measure an evil and that the space between curbs is altogether too narrow and confined for the physical development of child life." As early as 1890, a congressional statute provided for the temporary construction by the Corps of children's playgrounds on the Washington Monument grounds and the park south of the White House. In 1903, this authorization, as quoted in the 1903 *Annual Report of*

the Chief of Engineers, extended to "all other reservations in the District of Columbia." In the full spirit of what the *Annual Report* called "progressive city improvements and especially modern park creations," playgrounds were designed to mitigate undesirable residential conditions. Here "children and young people can take exercise and find innocent recreation, and [realize] the great value thereof in developing health of body and mind in the citizens of the future. . . . A suitable playground draws children by the hundreds . . . under the care and control of suitable persons." By the new combination of open spaces and playgrounds, the city gained in the adornment of its landscapes and in the "desirable and healthful resorts for outpourings of [its] surcharged population." Thus, old and new parks were outfitted with tennis courts, baseball diamonds, swimming pools, sandboxes, croquet grounds, and golf courses. Washington was, in fact, in process of pioneering urban recreation. Moreover, the reclaimed Potomac Park system offered the most elaborate experiment in recreational park functions with construction in 1917 of a sloping sandy beach on the shores of the Tidal Basin.

THE PARK MOVEMENT AND MODERN PARK DESIGN

In the interplay of theory and practice, Washington was propelled into the front rank of urban park leadership among American cities. In this, it reflected the remarkable assets of its natural setting, the basic city plan designed by L'Enfant, and the opportunity provided by the thousands of acres of newly acquired parkland, especially land reclaimed from the Potomac. Still more, it reflected the aspiration to build a model city that would exhibit the highest urban ideals of the period, the progressive social awareness of parks in building ideal environments, the talents of Olmsted and other urban designers, and the technological contributions of the Army Corps of Engineers. The park movement also generated its own forward movement as recreational leadership developed, associated with the community role of the public school and a new appreciation of neighborhood life. While much derived from Chicago and Boston, Washington contributed its share to this distinctive movement so characteristic of the twentieth century.

A "Riverside Drive" around the Tidal Basin toward the Washington Monument, 1905

The nineteenth-century public garden had by no means been eclipsed by the modern enthusiasms for park recreation. Potomac Park exhibited another artifact of modern park design—developed in New York and in later parkway design—in the winding "riverside drive" from the Tidal Basin's inlet to the foot of Twenty-sixth Street. In the words of the 1903 Annual Report of the Chief of Engineers, "the soft roadway, or speedway . . . will be greatly appreciated by all owners and drivers of fine horses. . . . Nearly every important city in the country has built and maintains such a driveway somewhere within its borders, and whenever one has been built it has contributed so much to the pleasure and profit of the people that it is now regarded as an essential."

The aesthetic park system in Washington was further buttressed by the modest Logan Park in Anacostia (specifically, in the Uniontown section), constructed in 1913 and outlined by an elongated brick terrace; by the balustraded stair that carried Twenty-second Street, NW, in Kalorama to higher levels; and by other grace notes of urban design.

On a highly formal scale, Meridian Hill Park, com-menced in 1910, was designed by the architect and landscapist Horace Peaslee as an Italian garden to be built on the "last height along Sixteenth Street." Patron-ized by Mrs. John B. Henderson, this monumental park, embellished by a handsome cascade, was envisioned—apparently after a conception of Cass Gilbert—by the Commission of Fine Arts (in its Annual Report for 1921-25) to serve as a "monumental entrance to Wash-ington" and "to develop there a great circle command-ing a view of the White House, the Washington Monu-ment, the Potomac River, and the Virginia Hills," and thus arguing for a grand street extending into Maryland —and connecting with Baltimore and Gettysburg.

EARLY PARKLAND ACQUISITION IN WASHINGTON

As in the case of the proposed Bladensburg-Anacostia parkway, the aggrandized Sixteenth Street entrance to the city, and the suggested Fort Drive embracing the old Civil War sites, so improvements to Rock Creek Park responded to the same impulse to provide a screen of parkland between the suburbs and the monumental core. From 1917 on, when the Olmsted Brothers were

144

contracted with by the Chief of Engineers, to 1926, many additions in parkland were made to Washington's great reserve of natural beauty. The Olmsted Brothers' plan for Rock Creek Park (as described in the 1921 *Annual Report of the Chief of Engineers*) recommended that the "moving principle [be] to preserve the natural beauty of the park while making it available for the use of the public, riding, driving, and walking. For this purpose the area of the park is divided into 'use' areas and 'growth' areas, depending on the location and character of soil and present growth." In the implementation of this plan, land was graded to allow for new footpaths, roads, and bridges, and the old Pierce Mill was used as a teahouse. In the final definition of the park, as given in the 1922 *Annual Report*, it was stated that additional lands needed to be protected even if by easement to "prevent destruction of the watershed of Rock Creek." By 1923, this requirement had stretched into broader metropolitan implications. In that year, the

Corps recommended that the remaining unimproved land along Broad Branch from its northernmost point be acquired, because "protection for the park can only be afforded by acquiring control of strips of land at least about 400 feet wide on each side of all tributaries of Rock Creek in the undeveloped sections of the District and Montgomery County."

The urgency of parkland acquisition was prompted not only by the need to protect vulnerable natural and historic resources in the city and to devise a system of connecting and "grand entrance" parkways, but also to correct the potential impact of the complete development of the city according to the highway plan initiated by the 1893 congressional statute. In 1918, the Commission of Fine Arts suggested that the permanent system of highways be revised to allow for the new park schemes. The relentless grid, designed to run over the city regardless of the natural features of the original landscape, did not allow for the development of new

Plan of Meridian Hill Park, 1910

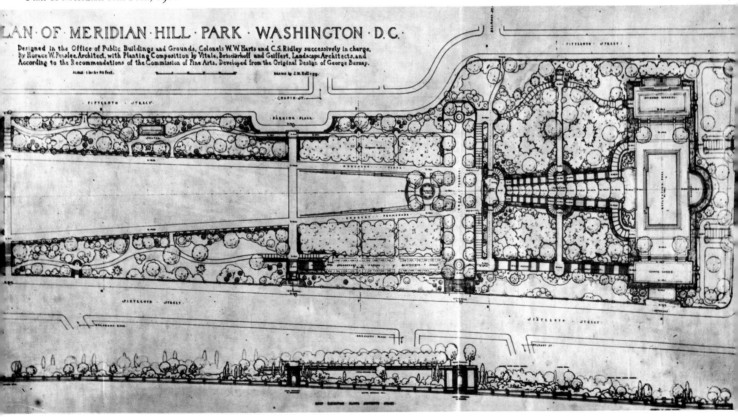

145

park areas. A revised plan "with a view of adapting the suburban highways to the topography" would, in the view of the commission, reverse the tendency to "tear down the hills and to fill up the valleys, thereby destroying the charm of large portions of the District. . . . Especially it is desirable to retain the country roads as park entrances and park connections." As it was, the complete connection between Rock Creek and Anacostia, as would have been accomplished by the proposed Fort Drive, could never be fulfilled because of steady development within the grid.

Public Architecture: Constituent Buildings and Orchestrated Urban Form

Construction of public buildings and identifying headquarters buildings for national organizations formed important elements of a strengthened monumental core and set its visual character. The McMillan Commission had favored classical styles patterned after aesthetic ideals taught at the Ecole des Beaux-Arts. This form of eclecticism reached its peak of popularity in the opening decades of the twentieth century. Beaux-Arts architecture found outstanding expression in the United States,

and some of the best examples of it are in Washington. The revered New York architect, William Adams Delano, correctly said that the modern image of the capital city was created by Charles F. McKim, Cass Gilbert, Henry Bacon, and John Russell Pope. The Lincoln Memorial and the Memorial Bridge, the Supreme Court, the National Archives Building and the National Gallery of Art, the modernized White House, the Jefferson Memorial—these are some of the key buildings contributed by these four leaders of the New York architectural establishment. There were other architects, like Charles Platt and Ernest Flagg, but Delano's selection was not arbitrary. The taste of this group was nationalized, particularly by Daniel Burnham, Edward Bennett, Paul Cret, and the architects of the Federal Triangle (and it can be said that, on the whole, the Supervising Architect, Louis Simon, was a force toward this nationalization of an architectural style)—but the creative center of this style rested in New York City and probably, as has been claimed by Delano, in the Century Association. This style reflected the presidency of Theodore Roosevelt, the taste inculcated at Yale and Harvard, the European influence institutionalized in alumni of the Ecole and of the American Academy at Rome, but most powerfully it reflected the influence of great wealth, particularly in the banking community.

Beaux-Arts Architecture: Central Public Library (Carnegie Library), Mount Vernon Square, Completed 1902

The nationalized style has been characterized as imperial, and certainly its flowering coincided with the emergence of the United States as a world power. Too much can be made of that coincidence, however, and architectural history can stand correction from the history of planning by reference to the idealism and reform elements of the City Beautiful movement as well as to the influence of more romantic elements of American architecture. This influence was best expressed in the tradition of Henry Hobson Richardson, Louis Henri Sullivan, and Frank Lloyd Wright, the tradition that found its stylistic peak in the American version of art nouveau and the Craftsman movement in the first decade of the century. From the first essays toward a modern concept of the city, spread before the architectural profession at the American Institute of Architects' meeting of 1900, through to the exhaustion of the Classical Revival in the early Depression years, these alternatives were constantly present, and if they never prevailed in the endless quest for a public architecture, they were nonetheless influential.

Washington's select residential streets were filled with Richardsonian Romanesque mansions no less than with copies of the Petit Trianon. The proposed plan of George Oakley Totten, Jr., for the capital's monumental core can be regarded as an art nouveau exercise in urban design. Throughout a long generation and down to Eliel and Eero Saarinen's competition design for the aborted Smithsonian Gallery of Art on the Mall, and John Carl Warnecke's red brick complex flanking Lafayette Square, this influence was never absent. It was most strongly felt, however, through building designs never realized and in the work of architects never represented in Washington—a continuing challenge. The selective process of preservation and destruction by which cities grow and renew themselves is, like the writing of history, a reinterpretation of the past, correcting its taste by present standards. The critical examination of Washington's architectural history that has now hardly begun will set these factors in perspective and thus trace the beginnings of modern architectural design not in the establishment traditions fostered by the Commission of Fine Arts and its chairman, Charles Moore, but in the broader currents of American art.

In this first quarter of the century, the Classical Revival in Washington architecture appeared and received the encouragement of the Commission of Fine Arts that produced both its official acceptance and its orchestrated urban form: the architecture not of buildings but of a city. Yet in the early years, and indeed throughout the period, other ideas and dissenting voices were heard, and the steady growth of the constituent building types —office buildings, factorylike structures, museums that were warehouses as well as monuments—was the fertile ground for their expression. If the essence of eclecticism was the association of building types with certain historical styles of building design, these unclaimed building types proved the opportunity for architectural deviation and advance.

The Government Printing Office and the Smithsonian's Natural History Building. In 1904, two architectural events in the city reflected this design duality. Commissioned in 1899, the new railroad-oriented Government Printing Office was commenced, just northeast of the Capitol, after designs of former Supervising Architect of the Treasury, James G. Hill. Nearly complete in 1904, Hill's new red brick government building followed the Romanesque tendencies of his earlier Bureau of Engraving and Printing on Fourteenth Street. Also in that year, the new National Museum (later the Smithsonian's National Museum of Natural History) was inaugurated on the Mall. This new classical-styled structure emphasized a horizontal mass crowned by a dome. Beneath the masonry skin, however, was a steel skeleton, the functional building of the museum director, George Brown Goode. The key to the design was the module of a museum storage case. The museum was described by the Commission of Fine Arts as the first building to be located and erected according to the McMillan plan. Noting that the building was aligned to the new Mall axis, hopeful sympathizers with the American translation of Beaux-Arts expected this new museum to replace the utilitarian red brick National Museum (now happily surviving as the Smithsonian's Arts and Industries Building) on the other side of the Mall.

Government Printing Office Building, 1906

The Lincoln Memorial, Freer Gallery of Art, and Department of Interior. Other public buildings and monuments on the Mall followed, including the Lincoln Memorial designed by Henry Bacon and the Freer Gallery by Charles A. Platt, both structures consistent with McMillan plan concepts. Contrary to the neat and coherent clusters devised by the plan, however, the new Interior Department Building (now occupied by the General Services Administration) was located between E and F Streets and Eighteenth and Nineteenth Streets, and represented a technological advance in office building design. Posing a possible threat to the McMillan Commission's plans to unite the White House and the Capitol by stretches of public buildings along the Mall and Pennsylvania Avenue, the Interior Building's massive size as well as its location to the west of the White House were interpreted by the Commission of Fine Arts as shifting the center of departmental activity to the west, adding to the isolation of the Capitol. As a reaction to the Interior Department's apparent desertion of the McMillan plan's specifications, the Commission of Fine Arts suggested in 1918 that any further office space for the department should follow the example of the Bureau of Standards which was then located on sixteen acres far out on Connecticut Avenue where the climate was cooler and "urban pollution and vibrations" were remote. The commission recommended that "in the case of the Interior Department, as demand for additional clerical room arises, the quarters now assigned to the Geological Survey and the Bureau of Mines be utilized for strictly office purposes and that these two bureaus either jointly or separately secure suburban locations and there construct buildings of separate character on sites adequate in size for anticipated future requirements."

Lafayette Square and the Executive Group. The acute need for increased office space for the executive departments found possible resolution in the new public buildings to be constructed according to the McMillan Commission configurations: buildings around Lafayette Square facing the White House, to be referred to as the Executive Group, and buildings in the triangle of land formed by Pennsylvania Avenue, Fifteenth Street, and the Mall, to be known as the Federal Triangle. In 1913, a Public Buildings Act instructed a Public Buildings

Contemporary View of Lafayette Park near Pennsylvania Avenue and Jackson Place

Commission to devise standards for new public buildings. This commission's successor bodies, most notably the commission created by the act of 1916, set up a fifteen-member body to "investigate and ascertain what public buildings are needed in the District of Columbia." In the following year, the Treasury Annex Building, facing both the old Treasury Building and Lafayette Square, was constructed according to designs by Cass Gilbert, to remain as the sole contribution of the federal government to the proposed Executive Group.

Lafayette Square: Courtyard in Rear of Restored Houses on Jackson Place

Civic Design:
First Quarter of the Century

In the absence of any new comprehensive plan for public buildings, the Commission of Fine Arts as one of its first recommendations had reminded the lawmakers about the McMillan Commission's scheme, suggesting that buildings for the Departments of State, Justice, Commerce, and Labor be located south of Pennsylvania Avenue, facing Fifteenth Street. The possible location of an Archives building south of the avenue would aid in restoring greater physical balance in the city and allow executive departments to be more convenient to the Congress.

World War I Tempos on the Mall. With the advent of World War I, rapid expansion of the executive departments and the creation of new bureaus demanded that new office space, if only temporary, be constructed immediately. Long rows of reinforced concrete "tempos" lined the Mall and East and West Potomac Park. Luckily for the future of the Mall, Colonel W. W.

Harts of the Corps's Office of Public Buildings and Grounds arranged with the Washington architect Horace Peaslee to design the tempos so that "upon their removal," as the *Annual Report of the Commission of Fine Arts* for 1921–25 stated, "the roads, walks, and open spaces would be identical with those shown on the [McMillan Commission's] Mall plan. Moreover, the Monument vista was preserved, and the axis was marked by placing the two smokestacks in such manner that from the Capitol terrace the Monument is seen between the round brick columns." This was an architectural whimsy. By 1929, the seemingly indestructible character of the concrete tempos plus the proliferation of automobiles over the roads and open spaces caused Charles Moore to complain (in the *Annual Report of the Commission of Fine Arts* for 1926–29) that the "entire Mall Park has become an open-air garage."

NATIONAL HEADQUARTERS IN THE NATIONAL CAPITAL

The filling in of the outlines in location and architectural style of the McMillan plan was abetted by the interest of national organizations in maintaining head-

World War I Tempos along Constitution Avenue Southwest of the White House, ca. 1920

Government Dormitories and "Hotels" for War Workers, Union Station Grounds, 1919

quarters in the national capital. Completion in 1897 of the new Corcoran Gallery of Art on Seventeenth Street south of New York Avenue, after designs by Ernest Flagg, provided the first element in a new monumental grouping to be constructed on what was known as the White Lot. In 1908, the stately Pan American Union Building, designed by Paul Cret and Albert Kelsey, was located at the northwest corner of Seventeenth and B Streets, anchoring the southernmost boundary of the grouping, but predicting its extension westward along B Street (now Constitution Avenue) toward the river. Construction between 1914 and 1917 of the building intended to house the American Red Cross, the Memorial Building to the Women of the Civil War, facing Seventeenth Street, acted as a filler in this line-up of impeccable Beaux-Arts creations. Designed by the New York firm of Trowbridge and Livingston, the Corinthian-styled white marble memorial not only served as a powerful reminder of women's good works but also provided administrative space. Meticulously detailed with Tiffany stained-glass windows and furniture from Edwin F. Caldwell & Co. of New York City, the building, along with its significant garden and sculpture, was a fitting step in creating a secondary ceremonial way. In the late 1920s, John Russell Pope's Memorial Continental Hall for the Daughters of the American Revolution

completed this lateral façade. To the west of the Pan American Union Building, a less convincing but similar grouping and façade of monumental buildings connected Seventeenth Street with the Lincoln Memorial: the National Academy of Sciences Building by Bertram Goodhue completed in 1921, the American Pharmaceutical Association Building by John Russell Pope in 1929, the Public Health Department Building by J. H. de Sibour in 1933, and the Federal Reserve Building by Paul Cret in 1937.

Indicative of the emphases of the City Beautiful movement on monumental groupings and extensions, homogeneous styles, and the balancing of architectural masses (as intended in the Executive Group to the north of the White House), the proposed grouping of government buildings along Fifteenth Street was envisioned to mirror that of Seventeenth Street and in effect to create a more balanced grouping south of the White House. It was not until the 1930s and completion of the Commerce Department Building that this Fifteenth Street façade was achieved, although the two façades certainly were never balanced in scale. Similar in form to the Seventeenth Street grouping, monumental buildings of the Federal Triangle lined Constitution Avenue from the Commerce Department eastward toward the Capitol.

Aerial View of the Central City from the Washington Monument, 1908

THE COMMISSION OF FINE ARTS: CONTINUITY AND THE CONTINUING PLAN

Custodian of the McMillan plan, the Commission of Fine Arts, established in 1910, was its executor as well by the institutionalization of informal recommendations made by former members of the 1901–1902 commission to the government on artistic matters. During the century's first decade, the American Institute of Architects appealed to the president for the establishment of a bureau and later a council of fine arts. Created by executive order in 1909, the Council of Fine Arts met to discuss the site of the Lincoln Memorial. In the following year, the Senate Committee on the Library happened to be faced with the question of acquiring a painting but did not feel "competent" to make such a decision. Senator Elihu Root recorded that then "we recalled . . . the advantage received from the report of park development of the informal commission selected by the McMillan Committee."

Sponsored by Congressman Samuel W. McCall of Massachusetts, a bill creating a permanent Commission of Fine Arts passed both houses in May. The original legislation outlined the duties of the new commission to "advise on the location of statues, fountains, and monuments in the public squares, streets, and parks in the District of Columbia." Later that year, President Taft extended this scope of duties to include public buildings.

The membership of the commission expressed continuity with the McMillan Commission, with the Beaux-Arts triumphs, and with the combination of varied artistic talents: architect Daniel Burnham, landscape architect Frederick Law Olmsted, Jr., architect Thomas Hastings, sculptor Daniel Chester French, painter Francis Davis Millet, architect Cass Gilbert. And most important for the long perpetuation of the "Plan of 1901," as he termed it, was commission member and later chairman, Charles Moore. In the early years of the commission, a close relationship was maintained with the Army Corps of Engineers' Office of Public Buildings and Grounds, occupying adjoining offices on the fourth floor of the Lemon Building at 1729 New York Avenue, NW.

Armed with congressional support, the commission

reviewed plans for all public buildings and parks projects in the city. Architectural styles of successive public buildings were molded to conform with the Beaux-Arts sympathies of the commission's members. This pattern was seriously challenged in the 1930s by practitioners of the modern style, who found support in the growing receptiveness of the architectural profession to design requirements of utilitarian buildings such as incinerators and sewage treatment plants. City planning—especially as applied to the monumental core—was motivated by the aesthetic arrangements of public buildings and spaces seen as offering civic lessons.

THE NATIONAL CAPITAL PARK AND PLANNING COMMISSION

Before creation of the National Capital Park and Planning Commission in 1926, when the first opportunity was provided for the new planning profession to address the problems of planning a national capital city, a self-confident Commission of Fine Arts had supervised through nearly a quarter century an architecturally dominant work of civic design. So the initial program of the planning commission strongly addressed elements of the city that had previously been disregarded: Washington's alley dwellings and housing reform; the rising tide of automobile traffic, its congestion and parking; the social issues of employment and poverty; the city's commercial and industrial elements, and tourism; the growth of suburbia; and natural resources. The heritage of the first quarter of the century, nevertheless, was indelible, to be seen in key buildings and monuments, in whole street scenes and groups of buildings at unprecedented scale.

The significant administrative change of 1926 added up to a great continuity and established complementary roles for the two agencies. Where certain conflicts arose they were over the increasingly irrelevant interpretations of a plan that was now more than twenty-five years old. Elihu Root's recognition of the "informality" of the McMillan Commission acknowledged that the 1901–1902 report was the product of a congressional committee but had never been adopted by the Congress in a single action. In the Commission of Fine Arts' constant reference to the McMillan plan, however, the status of the plan both as a mirror of the L'Enfant plan

and as an act of national will was created and perpetuated. Often an effective obstacle to designs contrary to the McMillan proposals, the Commission of Fine Arts justified its stance in the belief that it was "by unanimous consent rather than by specific legislation [that] this Commission is charged with the maintenance of the plan of 1901, subject to such modifications as possibly may be found necessary owing to changing conditions."

Residential Development: Homes and Houses in City and Suburb

Extensions to the park system into the District and the suburban counties followed the paths blazed by residential development. The spread of development responded to the rapid rise in the District's population, especially between 1910 and 1920 when the city grew by nearly a third. Economy, profit, and technology dictated the perpetuation of the row house. A reinforcement of the rectangular grid as drawn by the highway engineers, the seemingly endless vistas of row houses moving northward through the District were deplored by the Commission of Fine Arts as presenting a "monotonous . . . shape of blocks of houses instead of isolated residences."

The Row House: Building Type and Block Development. The row house stemmed from a long tradition in the city and echoed the predominance of this house type in Baltimore and Philadelphia. The origins of the row-house type in building technology, standardization, and mass production allowed for the separation of housing units by party walls. Economy was achieved in the intensive use of the lot and the lack of a fourth independent free-standing wall. In the row-house mode of living, the front porch or stoop as well as the backyard was a platform for neighborhood social life. On Capitol Hill and in the Southwest quadrant, the row house had long served the needs of the thousands of middle-class white-collar civil servants. The continuing influx of these employees argued for more of the same block development, following streetcar lines, and blanketing the rest of the city—almost regardless of topography.

Foxhall Village As It Looks Today

giving each adjoining dwelling a unique identity and differentiating the entire complex from surrounding neighborhoods.

Foxhall Village. In the same decade, between 1925 and 1930, Foxhall Village, exemplary of this community design concept, was constructed west of Georgetown University on Reservoir Road. Foxhall's developer, Waverly Taylor, described the "group houses" designed in the half-timbered English style as harking back to the old English village: "While adjoining, [they] are absolutely distinctive from so-called 'rowhouses' which are simply a number of houses all identical and adjoining one another. These houses are of an absolutely distinctive character and grouped together in such a way that the total mass makes a pleasing and harmonious composition." As in Burleith, here too were echoes of Baltimore's Roland Park. The Foxhall Village development, promising "city convenience with suburban atmosphere," incorporated the amenities of a verdant background in the form of Foundry Branch Valley Park (later part of Glover-Archbold Parkway) with memorable historical associations of the Foxhall Foundry and antebellum country residences. Unlike the row-house developments east of Rock Creek Park, Foxhall Village's network of streets was adapted to the hilly terrain by roadway layout within straight rights-of-way. To some extent this "Garden City" of row houses as outlined in the Village was made possible by retention of the natural topography of varying grades. Whereas in the city earlier dependent horse-drawn vehicles necessitated the leveling of a formal grade, the automobile was able to conquer with less effort wide changes in the natural grade.

Wesley Heights and Spring Valley. Development of the land west of Rock Creek Park continued unabated into the twentieth century despite the best intentions of the Army Corps of Engineers and the McMillan Commission. Large tracts of rugged land previously inaccessible were now with the automobile made available to more intensive occupation. Developer William C. Miller studied prizewinning suburbs nationwide and hired John H. Small, III, a landscape architect, to lay out the affluent suburbs of Wesley Heights and Spring Valley

Development of Burleith. To the west of Rock Creek Park, new interest was expressed in the development and design of entire architectural complexes or communities rather than single blocks. The development of Burleith between 1922 and 1927 represented an initial departure from the standard row-house design. A creation of the real estate skills of Shannon and Luchs, the five hundred homes were designed by architect Arthur Heaton with varied roof and façade treatments, thereby

south of the extended Massachusetts Avenue. These subdivisions exhibited aspects of the most sensitive street geometry in the 1893 Highway Plan and were further defined by retention of the natural contours of the land marked in careful planting of trees and creation of rolling landscapes. Miller's developments also exemplifies the cooperative spirit set to work between real estate interests and the National Capital Park and Planning Commission as the latter adapted street plans both to hilly terrain and to the new park frontages. The completion in 1900 of the electric railroad up the Potomac to Glen Echo and the later popularity of the automobile allowed developers to take advantage of the "hilly, long-dormant lands" of the Palisades to create "showplaces of suburban beauty."

Massachusetts Avenue: The Fifth Avenue of Washington. Within the boundaries of the old city, and especially along Massachusetts Avenue, urban living on a grand scale clothed itself in eclectic classical garb. These grand private residences, a Washington equivalent of those on New York's Fifth Avenue, were gradually converted into embassies with the multiplication of new foreign delegations in Washington. From Dupont Circle and northwest toward Rock Creek Park, these large urban mansions were constructed in the century's first two decades, clear evidence of the political and economic power of their clients. The mansion built for oil baron Senator Richard H. Townsend was constructed between 1899 and 1901 by the firm of Carrère and Hastings. On a powerful corner site, the Townsend residence—now the Cosmos Club—resembles the Petit Trianon at Versailles. Across the street, the Boston firm of Little and Browne created the sumptuous mansion for American diplomat Larz Anderson. The building now serves as headquarters for the Society of the Cincinnati. Described in *Massachusetts Avenue Architecture* as "one of the largest and costliest homes in the city," the structure exhibits the fusing of classical elements into an over-all design reminiscent of a grand-style English country house. Several architects of the Beaux-Arts responsible for the monumental public and institutional buildings in the post-McMillan-plan era contributed as well to the residential growth of Kalorama and Massachusetts Avenue. Stanford White designed the elegant Patterson mansion on Dupont Circle. J. H. de Sibour was responsible for at least four structures on Massachusetts Avenue, including the luxury apartment building near Eighteenth Street designed for Stanley McCormick, son of reaper inventor Cyrus McCormick. Other

An Urban Mansion at Massachusetts Avenue: the Cosmos Club (Originally the Townsend Residence), Built 1899–1901

An Apartment Building at Connecticut Avenue and L Street: Stoneleigh Court, ca. 1905

apartment buildings and cultural institutions filled in the interstices, especially along Connecticut Avenue south of Rock Creek Park.

Beside the predominantly New York architects was the Virginian Waddy B. Wood, designer of more than thirty mansions in the Kalorama and Massachusetts Avenue district, and architect of the present Interior Department Building. Without compromising the panache of the Beaux-Arts school, Wood's greater attention to interior design and domestic detail allowed him to reflect in a more intimate fashion the characteristic lifestyle of the native Washingtonian.

FROM THE FAIRFAX COURTHOUSE TO ROCKVILLE

Less affluent residential areas had traditionally spread east of Rock Creek Park, reaching to both sides of the Anacostia River. The deteriorated or inadequate physical condition of housing in these areas inspired Charles Moore to respond to the housing emergency of 1919 by proposing, as the *Annual Report of the Commission of Fine Arts* for 1926–29 reported, the "establishment of garden suburbs about the city of Washington, either within or without the District of Columbia, as residence places for Government workers of the intermediate and lower grades, both men and women."

Moore's vision of the large metropolitan areas as a resource available to resolve the District's environmental problems was significant because it reflected gradual realization of the city not only as the monumental core but as the historically defined ten-mile square plus the four adjoining counties in Maryland and Virginia. As early as 1918, as we have seen, the commission suggested "suburban locations" for bureaus of the Interior Department. In the following year, the commission stated that cooperation with Maryland and Virginia beyond the District line was necessary, especially if the commission was to influence the creation of Great Falls Park in its picturesque form as well as Mount Vernon Parkway, both recommended earlier by the McMillan Commission. Just six years later, in 1925, the automobile's impact on the metropolitan landscape forced the commission to acknowledge (in its *Annual Report* for 1921–25) that the regional city measured forty miles in diameter, extending from the Fairfax Courthouse to Rockville. "The use of the automobile has resulted in the expansion of the city into the surrounding country. The city [of Washington] itself has become the business nucleus."

CHAPTER VII THE YEAR OF DECISION 1926

The Year of Decision 1926

Legitimization of Planning: Metropolitan City, National Capital

1926 was a landmark year for planning for the metropolitan city. In that year, the National Capital Park and Planning Commission was established and the Public Buildings Act was passed authorizing construction of the massive Federal Triangle.

In placing major federal commitment behind planning for the monumental core and the city's ever-expanding edges, these congressional acts also responded to City Beautiful ideals. The elements of this abstract conception of the City Beautiful included carefully landscaped, architecturally designed approaches to the city, by both land and water; an administrative center or "civic center"; business districts whose visibility and access were reinforced by cutting in great diagonal boulevards; residential developments planned around focal points spinning out from the center of the city in a spiderweb configuration; open spaces emphasizing hills, waterfronts, and highlights of the city's topography; and winding parkways connecting open spaces and residential areas with the central city. Promoters of the plan-

ning legislation saw these ideals—as translated and enunciated in 1902 by the McMillan Commission—imperiled by the relentless process of haphazard, piecemeal development. The legislation creating the planning commission laid the foundation for an agency that would be affected by changing expectations of planning and by a rapidly changing city. By contrast, the Federal Triangle stands in style and plan as an artifact of Classical Revival impulses subject but not responsive to intrusions of the modern city.

BATTLE CRIES FOR PLANNING

Unlike all other American cities, Washington had no body of local constituents that could persuade elected officials of the needs for a planning commission. How was planning legitimatized? National as well as local organizations seized the cause of planning in the nation's capital, congratulating themselves after passage of the 1924 act that created the National Capital Park Commission and then the 1926 act that created the National Capital Park and Planning Commission. A planned capital city would be an inspirational symbol for the nation's cities. To progressives, it would serve as an expression of municipal reform. To businessmen, moreover, a planned city held the promise of an improved urban appearance, magnet for commercial activity.

The notions of what a planning commission should do were by no means clear. Some thought the city should relate to L'Enfant and the precedents set by Washington and Jefferson. Others, like Charles Moore, thought that the 1901–1902 plan should serve as the controlling design for the city's future. Still others wanted for Washington a metropolitan park system commensurate with the urban systems designed for Boston and Chicago. Observers cognizant of comprehensive planning as already established in many American cities recognized the need for park planning but were concerned also with other comprehensive considerations, such as traffic, housing, water, and the siting of public buildings. In the push for a planning commission in the capital city, the City Beautiful proponents and business-minded progressive reformers prevailed.

The McMillan plan of 1901–1902 had been the first major achievement in raising the planning consciousness of Washington residents and the nation alike. Drawing on planning experience in other cities, much discussion flowed about the City Beautiful agenda—parks, public building siting, the monumental core, and extension of physical amenities into the surrounding counties. Although in its time considered a "comprehensive plan," the McMillan plan was soon overshadowed in nationwide terms by Burnham's Chicago plan of 1908. Burnham, an architectural superstar, was not regarded as part of the embryonic planning establishment. Burnham's name and promotional abilities, however, as well as the vastness of the plan (covering a sixty-mile radius around the central city) and the ardent support of the Chicago business interests magnetized the aspirations of other cities. These aspirations began to be realized when Hartford, Connecticut, established a planning commission in 1907, followed by Milwaukee, Wisconsin, in 1911. But in Washington, with its urban design tradition, it was the parks issue that inspired the initial battle cries for planning rather than the examples of the Chicago plan and newly established planning commissions.

Emphasis on the acquisition of what was left of the city's open space was a product of the city's natural landscape and the historical forces that molded the monumental core. Parks—as in lower Rock Creek valley—were also a means of urban rehabilitation. By the early twentieth century, the city embodied a strong landscape identity; as John Nolen, Sr., said, in an interview with Harland Bartholomew, Washington was "a city set in a framework of open space . . . a city proud and aware of its setting and place."

These features were capitalized on by the landscape emphasis Olmsted had given the McMillan plan. Green open space served as the monumental core's basic cloth in which the public buildings were woven. This emphasis was sustained somewhat by the dreamy illustrations of Burnham's Chicago plan as drawn by artist Jules Guerin, although that plan also dealt with many other concerns of physical planning. The Boston Metropolitan Park System offered compelling illustrations of continuous and comprehensive strips of greenery. Emphasis on parks was also an element of lingering interest to romantics in picturesque landscapes and to reformers in the presumed social benefits of playgrounds and recreational facilities.

THE 1920 ZONING ORDINANCE

The adoption in 1920 of a zoning ordinance for Washington signaled the importance of planning for the nonpark areas of the city. Some controls on Washington's growth had earlier been exercised by regulation of building heights and separation of business activities from residential areas. In order to draw up the zoning ordinance, planner Harland Bartholomew worked closely with District of Columbia Commissioners Louis Brownlow and Colonel Charles W. Kutz. Borrowing staff from the Army Corps of Engineers, Bartholomew studied land-use data and made recommendations for the separation of residential, commercial, and industrial use, each with specific regulations for "height, use, and area of buildings to be erected." Bartholomew described Washington's zoning as a compromise between the three categories drawn up in the 1916 New York ordinance and the several subcategories he designed for Saint Louis in 1918. Upon completion of the Washing-

Aerial View of the Sixteenth Street and Columbia Road Area, Showing "Typical Results of Failure to Plan Land Use," Early 1920s

ton work, Bartholomew recommended the creation of a planning commission to coordinate zoning with future growth of the city—and avoid typical results of the failure to plan land use.

THE AMERICAN PLANNING AND CIVIC ASSOCIATION

Local citizens' efforts were effective in mustering support for planning in their cities and working with planning bodies once they were established. In 1924, John Nolen, Sr., of Cambridge, Massachusetts, summarized the work of citizens' groups working for planning in ten American cities, ranging from the metropolis of Chicago to cities more modest in size, such as Johnstown, Pennsylvania. As for promoting planning in the national capital as well as throughout the nation, the American Planning and Civic Association (known as the American Civic Association until 1935) played a key role. It was primarily a civic association aimed at numerous and diverse city improvements across the nation. In the 1920s, planning for cities, national parks, and civic centers had been assigned a higher priority than many other municipal activities.

Frederic Delano and Harlean James. Frederic Delano, president of the American Planning and Civic Association until 1935, worked for the creation of a planning commission in the nation's capital and served as chairman of the National Capital Park and Planning Commission after its founding in 1926. Born in Hong Kong in 1863, Delano followed an illustrious career in American railroads, in both engineering and executive capacities. A longtime resident of Washington, he was deeply committed to its future. As uncle and father-figure to President Franklin Roosevelt, he urged his nephew to make major decisions affecting the city, as, for example, to commit presidential influence in support of Edward Bennett's proposed Apex Building in the Federal Triangle.

Delano "discovered" the future secretary of the American Planning and Civic Association, Harlean James. Delano had brought James to Washington during World War I as manager of the wartime women's residence halls sited between Union Station and the Capitol. James, born in Mattoon, Illinois, in 1871, was graduated from Stanford University in 1898, the class also of the future Mrs. Herbert Hoover. Moving to Honolulu in 1901, James worked as a court reporter and as an executive secretary to various island corporations. Returning to the mainland in 1911, she launched her planning and civic career in Baltimore where she worked as executive secretary of the Women's Civic League between 1911 and 1916. After her national defense and housing appointments in Washington during the war years, she became executive secretary of the American Planning and Civic Association in 1921 and editor of its yearly publication, the *American Civic and Planning Annual*, serving in these capacities until 1948. Harlean James also achieved professional recognition as author of *Land Planning in City, State and Nation*, an important early study in land economics.

The clout exercised by the American Planning and Civic Association was attributable to the executive talents of James. Grafting association members' expertise onto the congressional process, the association worked with congressmen and their staffs, wrote speeches and drafted legislation, presented testimony, and acted as an effective lobbying organization. Working through the old-boy network of West Point and Harvard graduates and other elitist connections, the American Planning and Civic Association was able to influence congressional action, appointments, and policies in all government agencies concerned with parks and planning. Through the process of holding meetings, passing timely resolutions, and writing effective letters, the organization exercised remarkable power, particularly in defending parklands from incompatible intrusions.

The Grassroots Committees. Important to the development of planning in the national capital, the American Planning and Civic Association also created "Federal City" committees in various states, seventy-five committees by 1924. The popularity of these grassroots committees was explained by a new national awareness of the rapid expansion Washington had experienced during World War I. The city had become a "suddenly enlarged metropolis." These field committees voiced a common cry for the coordination of zoning, park development, and city planning in the nation's capital. They were as weary as were other civic and trade organizations of the failure of annual legislation and appropriations to cope with the rapidly disappearing forests and mementos of the National Capital Region's rural past.

Thus, while the voteless city of Washington had no local constituency, it did have national voter concern, as expressed in the appeal of the American Planning and Civic Association and other organizations to "citizens of the entire nation." This sentiment was epitomized by Colonel C. O. Sherrill, officer in charge of public buildings and grounds in the District, in a 1923 address to the Association of City Planners in Baltimore: "If we are ever to have a great national capital, worthy of the greatest nation on earth, we must arouse a deep personal interest among the people of the whole country in the development of the nation's capital. A splendid start has been made in this direction by the American Civic Association."

Besides marshaling support throughout the nation for the planning of the federal city, the American Planning and Civic Association fostered an alliance of the professional societies of architects, landscape architects, city planners, and progressive real estate interests. This alliance was formalized as the Joint Committee on the National Capital and for it Harlean James provided the secretarial and executive function. Not only did the nation's citizens look upon the capital city with great affection, second only to their own home towns, but they moreover viewed the success of planning the capital city as the inspirational model for planning in other American cities.

In Washington itself, the Committee of 100 served, for all practical purposes, as the local branch of the American Planning and Civic Association and in many respects an extended arm of the Washington Board of Trade. Initially composed of the city's leading businessmen, especially owners of the Washington newspapers, the Committee of 100 served as a powerful local voice in the push toward a national planning commission. Frederic Delano was also a leader in this organization.

HERBERT HOOVER AND AMERICAN INDIVIDUALISM

Organized governmental and business initiative paralleled the rising civic demand for planning in the nation's capital. Ideas expressed by these organizations found fertile ground in the person of Herbert Hoover. An embodiment of the interests of the businessman and government, Hoover followed a notable career as a financially successful mining engineer and as a relief administrator during and after World War I. The tools of technology and the politics of a society's renewal prepared him for his key role in planning. As an engineer, Hoover was concerned with efficiency and overcoming waste, both objectives achieved by sound management and standardization. As an administrator of food and recovery programs in war-torn Europe, Hoover had witnessed at first hand the effects on an entire society, especially the children, of war brought on by deep-seated ideologies. After nearly four years of European work, Hoover returned to America, grateful for his country's relative detachment from extreme politics. He found, however, an America unsettled by the war experience of rapid industrialization to provide army materiel and the attendant urban congestion created by settlements close to strategic manufacturing centers. Throughout the 1920s, generally stereotyped as an era of prosperity, large pockets of poverty persisted, ripe for exploitation by what Hoover viewed as un-American economic philosophies. Fearing the "infection of America" by the socialist and communist movements raging in Europe, Hoover wrote *American Individualism*. In this treatise, he attempted to formulate an orderly definition of the American system of capitalism, democracy, and the foundation for the system, family life.

THE FIGHT FOR BETTER HOUSING

Appointed by President Harding as secretary of commerce, Hoover settled in Washington and commenced to "reconstruct the American economy." Beginning at the society's roots, he saw the supply of more and better housing as critical to America's ability to recuperate from the war. In 1922, he created within the Commerce Department the Division of Building and Housing of the Bureau of Standards, headed by Harvard economist John M. Gries. During Gries's tenure, the division pursued research and published results on housing construction and maintenance, as well as zoning and credit. Applying efficiency procedures of the engineering profession, the division sought to standardize building

methods and regulations, a concern of the construction industry. Convinced of businessmen's obligation to lead the nation toward better cities, Hoover sought their blessing for government projects and goals. Among several gestures of cooperation, the United States Chamber of Commerce also endorsed greater efficiency, lower costs, and the development of resources in the sphere of housing as outlined by Hoover.

The other side of the problem in housing construction was slum clearance. Hoover looked proudly at the decade's major public building projects in Washington, the Federal Triangle and the expansion of the Legislative Group around the Capitol, as significant examples of slum clearance. In promoting housing, Hoover recognized the larger issues of city planning, municipal activities, and land use as affected by zoning, often drawing on Washington for examples of excellence in appearance and management.

In his advocacy position as secretary of commerce, Hoover spread the housing theme into the civic sector, creating a volunteer organization called "Better Homes in America." Spurred on by Mrs. William Brown Meloney, a talented publicist, the organization served to support the Commerce Department's ideas. Throughout his presidency, Hoover served as president of Better Homes in America.

THE 1931 CONFERENCE ON HOME BUILDING

Hoover's pursuit of the housing cause for more than a decade climaxed in December 1931 with the President's Conference on Home Building and Home Ownership. Organized by Gries and his former Harvard colleague, James Ford, the conference brought together thousands of the country's major figures in planning, housing, and business. Symbolic of this coalition, the sessions were held at the Willard and Washington Hotels, the United States Chamber of Commerce, an office building occupied by the Commerce Department, and the D.A.R. Constitution Hall. The entire proceedings were carried to the public by nationwide network radio. The conference commenced with a speech by President Hoover in which he crystallized the deep American sentiment for home ownership and the "sweetness of family life." Underlying this basic philosophy of housing was Hoover's belief that "there can be no fear for a democracy or self-government or for liberty or freedom from home owners no matter how humble they may be." Hoover exhorted the conference participants to take advantage of tools offered them by science and technology, to correlate their experiences, to establish standards, and to push for legislative action. Summaries of the conference were published, and in addition ten bound volumes outlining the work of thirty-one committees.

Reflecting to this conference Washington's experience and aspirations, Charles Eliot, director of planning at the National Capital Park and Planning Commission, recorded the virtues of the planned neighborhood unit. Former president of the Chamber of Commerce, Harry A. Wheeler, chaired the committee on "Slums, Large-Scale Housing, and Decentralization," and presented illustrations of the alley dwellings in the national capital. These alleys were described as "small, hidden communities in centers of large blocks." John Ihlder, former executive director of both the Massachusetts Housing Association and the Pittsburgh Housing Association and in 1931 a housing consultant to the National Capital Park and Planning Commission, outlined his study of census data, describing housing and family-life patterns deduced from the information. Throughout the published records of the conference, the city of Washington—then at its apogee of middle-class occupancy—was referred to repeatedly, both for examples of desirable housing types and arrangements and for illustrations of the "problem."

BUSINESS SUPPORT FOR THE PLANNING ISSUE

Reliable support for city planning as indicated by Herbert Hoover and Harry Wheeler emerged from strong business traditions exemplified in Chicago as much in the recovery after the 1871 fire as in the successful 1893 World's Columbian Exposition. Business interests in other cities followed suit, bearing the responsibility of influencing creation of local planning commissions and enactment of zoning laws. And it was, in fact, enlightened and progressive businessmen who promoted the planning issue in the national capital city.

Initially, a sector of business had responded coolly to Harland Bartholomew's 1920 zoning design on the as-

sumption that row housing would be threatened by the imposition of zoning. Washington was in some respects a bad place for real estate investment as residency was often only temporary and the future of government operations concentrated in the monumental core uncertain. Thus a distinctive pattern of tenancy, mortgage lending, real estate and housing ownership developed, characteristics that when translated into physical form amounted to rental housing and low-cost row-house building. Bartholomew's detailed land-use study in 1920 had revealed only 190 apartment buildings in the city but showed that sufficient land existed for additional housing of this increasingly popular type. The study also showed that while of the city's population, 71 percent occupied row houses, only 14 percent lived in detached houses, and ample additional sites were provided for both categories. In the end, the city's progressive business interests voiced heartiest support for the regulation of land use in the city in hopes of stabilizing real estate values and improving the appearance of the city. There was support also for the creation of a planning commission to match zoning with urban growth as recommended by Bartholomew.

THE UNITED STATES CHAMBER OF COMMERCE:
NATIONAL PLANNING CAUSES

The responsibility of the businessman was further registered in the activities of the United States Chamber of Commerce. Founded in 1912 to represent trade and civic associations, the Chamber of Commerce was housed in a number of office buildings close to the financial district along Fifteenth Street. During World War I, the chamber worked closely with the government through its War Services Committee so that war materiel could be supplied efficiently. This government–business community relationship, strained under the trust-busting of the Theodore Roosevelt era, became harmonious in the interest of national defense. At the chamber's annual meeting in 1919, President Harry A. Wheeler suggested that the chamber construct a headquarters building of its own. Such a building would secure the identity of the Chamber of Commerce, state its permanency, and "commemorate the patriotic part which American business had played in the World

View of Lafayette Square, Showing the Hay–Adams House and behind It the Site Being Cleared for the Chamber of Commerce Building, 1922

War." The building was to mark a climax in business prestige in the capital city. Symbolic of the chamber's sympathies with the planning goals in Washington, the new Chamber of Commerce building was located on the site of the old Corcoran residence at Connecticut and H Streets. As the 1925 *Annual Report of the United States Chamber of Commerce* noted, the site "opposite Lafayette Park places it in a position close to many of the executive departments of government" and "in

conformity with the general plan of the Federal Fine Arts Commission for the development of Lafayette Square as an Executive Center." At the time the chamber's building was being planned for the Lafayette Square site, it was reported that a new State Department Building was also to be sited on the square, just to the west, between Jackson Place and Seventeenth Street, although this proposal was never implemented. Thus, when its building was occupied in 1924, the chamber

Chamber of Commerce of the United States of America, 1924

had expected that most of the square would be completed according to the outlines of the McMillan Commission report and the plans of the Commission of Fine Arts. In the building's architectural style, the chamber building was equally harmonious. Designed by Cass Gilbert, architect also of the Treasury Annex on Lafayette Square, the Chamber of Commerce building displayed a classic Corinthian exterior which enclosed an arcaded court, an important environmental amenity before air conditioning. Having in mind more than just an office building, Gilbert designed several meeting rooms, a library, and a memorial hall on the first floor. It was in these rooms that many significant meetings and conferences promoting improvements in Washington were held.

THE ROLE OF JOHN IHLDER

Reflecting Hoover's and the chamber's common belief that the future of cities' business communities would be "largely determined by their housing accommodations," the chamber's Civic Development Department was established in late 1920. This department, important in expressing the businessman's interest in housing, was headed by John Ihlder between 1920 and 1928. Best known in Washington history for his later work as director of the National Capital Housing Authority, Ihlder was born in Baltimore in 1876. He began his career as a writer for newspapers and magazines. In 1908, he moved to Grand Rapids, Michigan, where he worked for its Chamber of Commerce. Branching into the housing field in 1910, he worked for a number of social and housing organizations until 1920 when he joined the United States Chamber of Commerce. Under Ihlder, the Civic Development Department echoed Hoover's prescription for a recovered America: maximum use of resources and minimum wastage. The Civic Development Department's Bureau of Housing and City Planning offered member trade associations instructions on zoning and planning, responding to the view that planning was a "modern method of ensuring the use of every natural advantage and preventing waste in city building." Whereas in the past the direction of city growth had been unregulated, the Civic Development Department stated that with zoning, businessmen and residents

could expect stabilized property values, more building construction and thus prosperity, and prevention of "great losses due to the blighting of neighborhoods in unwise developments." A tool of "order and economy," zoning appealed to the scientific and statistical persuasions of Hoover and Ihlder, and thus the effort to standardize zoning in the Bureau of Standards.

THE METROPOLITAN WASHINGTON BOARD OF TRADE: LOCAL PLANNING CAUSES

While the Chamber of Commerce espoused national planning causes that reflected heavily the capital city's experiences, it was the Washington Board of Trade that took up the banner of purely local improvements. Founded in 1889, the board is the city's major business and trade association. Its membership has been composed of businessmen, artists, civil servants, and architects like Horace Peaslee, Louis Justement, T. A. Mullett, and George Oakley Totten, Jr. In the absence of a constituency to which the Congress and the president might be responsive, the board saw itself as representative of "all sectors and interests of the city." A strong influence on the affairs of Washington was exerted by the Board of Trade, especially in cooperation with such nationally recognized associations as the American Institute of Architects and the American Planning and Civic Association. The board saw the voluntary nature of its work as a strength: "Only through their civic organizations and popular bodies whose standing is entirely unofficial can Washingtonians express their needs and wishes for the general welfare, in such concerted manner as to command the respect and attention of the national legislators who are charged with the duty of maintaining the District government." The board's motives were not entirely altruistic. Its members' prosperity rode, in fact, on the city's growth and appearance. For several years, the board published *The Book of Washington*, an impressive collection of articles, illustrations, and advertisements reminiscent of nineteenth-century city "booster" publications. Unabashedly, the 1927 issue stated, "our one aim is to make Washington . . . the most beautiful and the more desirable community in which to live and transact business." Toward this goal, the board established among its committees several that gave special attention to the promotion of public improvements: the Committee on Bridges, on Municipal Art, on Parks and Reservations, on Public and Private Buildings, on Sewerage, and on Streets and Avenues.

COMMENDED . . . DISAPPROVED: COMMITTEE REVIEW

The Committee on Municipal Art and on Public and Private Buildings followed ideals of the McMillan Commission and the Commission of Fine Arts. Taking comfort that the Commission of Fine Arts oversaw the appearance of public buildings, the committees, in an unofficial way, sought to set standards for private architecture and art works. The Committee on Municipal Art issued annual awards for outstanding examples of architecture as judged by two Baltimore architects. Appleton P. Clark, Jr., architect and chairman of the committee for much of the 1920s, suggested that in improving Pennsylvania Avenue the "Chicago example" be followed, and thus, through voluntary efforts by building clients, a control of façades was exercised. In order to stimulate such cooperation—as seen, for example, in the widely admired addition to the Evening Star Building, designed by the firm of Marsh and Peter—tax incentives were proposed although never adopted. As the 1921–22 *Annual Report of the Washington Board of Trade* stated, "the only feasible method . . . [of] encouraging a certain standard of improvement [is] with subsidies in the shape of remissions of taxes for a period of possibly twenty years." The board's Committee on Public and Private Buildings attempted to persuade the clients and architects of private buildings by opinions generated by the Architects' Advisory Council. Working through a panel of five "elders of the profession," the committee reviewed all plans filed in the municipal building permit office, and rated them by one of four classifications: Commended, Approved, Not Approved, Disapproved. In 1924, the committee stated, "The most frequent suggestion is for simplification of design." Despite the noncompulsory nature of the Advisory Council's assessments, "with such assistance, freely given, it is inexcusable that any man would put up a building which is a reflection of his own [individual or personal] good taste or a blot upon his city." Architectural design was to be arrived at through a consensus.

EXTENSION INTO VIRGINIA AND MARYLAND

In committees such as those on Bridges, on Streets and Avenues, and on Sewerage, the Washington Board of Trade favored extension of the city into Virginia and Maryland via bridge connections. Virginia was an attractive area in residential and real estate terms, especially when the historic and bucolic charms of Old Virginia were evoked. Keenly aware of the effect of modern transportation on the tourist business, the board in its 1924 *Annual Report* recommended the improvement of Chain Bridge to connect with the hard surface road to Berryville (under construction by the State of Virginia) in order "to permit tourists to take advantage of a trip to Washington in going to and from this popular tourist section." A similar improvement of the Pennsylvania Avenue Bridge over the Anacostia River was to link the city of Washington to Maryland roads leading to the Chesapeake Bay beaches, Leonardtown, and Annapolis. The Committee on Streets and Avenues endorsed congressional bills extending Fourteenth Street, New York Avenue, and New Hampshire Avenue to the District line, strengthening the city's impact in Maryland. Yet, growth brought its own hazards, as studied by the Board of Trade's Committee on Sewerage. In the board's 1923 *Annual Report*, this committee stated that "healthful growth is throttled and imperiled here by a failure to develop the suburban sewerage system of the national capital sufficiently to keep step with the home building." Already the area's rich natural and recreational resources were being defiled: polluted waters entering the Tidal Basin's bathing beach caused eye and ear infections. According to the 1921–22 *Annual Report*, raw sewage flowing into the Potomac had "menace[d] the oyster beds of the lower river." In listing the sources of pollution, the Committee on Sewerage had recommended an Upper Potomac Interceptor to remove sewage between the mouth of Rock Creek and Little Falls, the completion of the interceptor in Rock Creek and the Anacostia to "carry off sewage from Maryland towns," and the construction of purification works at Shepherd's Point on the Potomac to purify the river.

The Overwhelming Speed of Development: Row Houses Constructed in Petworth on Land West of Soldiers' Home, 1920s

THE COMMITTEE ON PARKS AND RESERVATIONS

Among the Washington Board of Trade's many contributions to planning and parks acquisitions in the city, the achievements of the Committee on Parks and Reservations, chaired by Fred Coldren, stands as the most substantial. Like other civic groups and individuals, the committee decried the loss of open country to the hand of the developer. Citing the words of Lord Bryce, the former British ambassador—a glorious description of Washington as transcending any European counterpart—the committee suggested that "this address of Lord Bryce should be made a textbook in our public and private schools." In the same *Annual Report* for 1924, the committee claimed that as early as 1900, the Washington Board of Trade had adopted a resolution recommending that "Congress pass an act authorizing the appointing of a Commission to devise and report a plan for development of the Capital City." There had been no official response toward a general plan and for the twenty-four years that ensued, the Board of Trade watched the McMillan Commission's recommendations for parks dwindle away under the exigencies of piecemeal congressional appropriations for individual tracts of land and the overwhelming speed of development. In 1922, as the board's *Annual Report* for 1921–22 reported, the Committee on Parks and Reservations drew up a draft bill to create a National Capital Park Commission, stating that the "forests and valleys are being destroyed far more rapidly than they can possibly be preserved under the present system." Aided by en-

dorsements by the United States Chamber of Commerce, the chief of the Army Corps of Engineers, the Committee of 100, and the American Planning and Civic Association, the bill passed "with very slight amendments from the draft as originally framed." Most of the changes in the final bill were in the provisions for membership of the new commission.

Legislation for Comprehensive Planning: The Acts of 1924 and 1926

Although the McMillan Commission's work was not specifically mentioned in the 1924 and 1926 acts, the work of that commission was constantly referred to in annual reports and in maps prepared by the National Capital Park and Planning Commission. Strongly promoted by the Planning Commission, the McMillan plan finally received congressional endorsement in 1929. The acts of 1924 and 1926 would thus achieve one of the major objectives—to include basic concepts of the McMillan plan in all new comprehensive planning for the city and region.

THE NATIONAL CAPITAL PARK COMMISSION AND COMPREHENSIVE PLANNING

The act creating the National Capital Park Commission was signed into law on 6 June 1924. The membership was composed of the chief of the Army Corps of Engineers, the Engineer Commissioner of the District of Columbia, the director of the National Park Service, the officer of the Corps in charge of public buildings and grounds (who also served as executive and disbursing officer), and the chairmen of the Senate and House committees on the District of Columbia. In outlining the general areas of park and playground acquisition, this act authorized the commission to acquire lands in the District, Virginia, and Maryland, with the advice of the Commission of Fine Arts. To carry out these acquisitions, the act provided $1,100,000 on an annual basis. Both the Boston Metropolitan Park System and the McMillan plan were invoked in the recommendation that the commission turn its attention to "Rock Creek and the Potomac and Anacostia Rivers . . . and to provide for the comprehensive, systematic, and continuous

development of park, parkway, and playground systems of the National Capital."

The Board of Trade and other civic and government groups had won the battle but not the war. To be sure, the Park Commission was created—but Congress still had to appropriate annual funds for parkland acquisition. In Coldren's 1924 annual report of the Committee on Parks and Reservations to the board, he complained that the Bureau of the Budget had assigned only $600,000 to cover the 1924 and 1925 fiscal years. His study of possible park areas revealed the alarming situation that many of these tracts were "now imminently threatened with destruction or . . . irreparable injury," a situation

Aerial View of Glover-Archbold Parkway Site Located West of Georgetown University on Land Donated in 1923

not likely to be reversed by the meager appropriations. One means for limiting development on the picturesque tracts sought by the Park Commission was to enlist the aid of the Chamber of Commerce and Board of Trade to "informally arrange for individuals to secure critical areas and hold them for later consideration for purchase by the [Park Commission] at the same prices which they paid for the tract." This plan of relying on the beneficence of wealthy citizens to provide a sort of revolving fund seemed feasible in light of the sources of support for the 1924 act. The 1923 gifts by Charles C. Glover and Anne Archbold of the land in the valley of Foundry Branch—later known as the Glover-Archbold Parkway—stood as proof positive of the potential importance of private grants.

Not only were the annual appropriations a severe hindrance to carrying out the expectations of visitors and city residents for the amenities of parklands, but even more the commission found itself powerless to influence the city's plan except for structuring growth within the configurations created by the protected parklands. In March 1925, the National Capital Park Commission asked the executive secretary, Lieutenant Colonel C. O. Sherrill, to hire the park planner, James G. Langdon, and to create a City Planning Committee to operate under the Park Commission. Drawing on the Park Commission's longtime supporters, this committee was to be composed of a representative of the Committee of 100, "preferably Mr. [Frederic] Delano," and members of the various district engineering and parks offices. Clearly the Park Commission was functioning in a position of weakness. By October and November of 1925, the commission was discussing broadening its functions to include comprehensive planning.

THE NATIONAL CAPITAL PARK AND PLANNING
COMMISSION: THE COMPREHENSIVE PLAN

Planning powers were finally granted in April 1926 as an amendment to the 1924 act. Renaming the body the National Capital Park and Planning Commission, the 1926 act outlined a host of new duties in "preparing, developing, and maintaining a comprehensive, consistent and coordinated plan for the National Capital and its environs," embracing transportation, subdivisions, pub-

lic building sites, sewerage, zoning, commerce and industry, and "other proper elements of city and regional planning." Charged with coordinating the plans of federal and district departments, the National Capital Park and Planning Commission was empowered to exercise influence, although not force compliance, in the planning of the massive building projects inaugurated by the Federal Triangle project, also funded in 1926. Members of the National Capital Park and Planning Commission responded to the professionalization of planning. In addition to the ex officio members who were members of the Park Commission (except that the Director of Public Buildings and Public Parks of the National Capital now replaced the officer of the Army Corps of Engineers in charge of public buildings and grounds) four "eminent citizens well qualified and experienced in city planning, one of whom shall be a bona fide resident of the District of Columbia, [shall] be appointed for the term of six years by the President of the United States." The National Capital Park and Planning Commission was also authorized to employ a professional staff and consultants. Answering the long-heard pleas of the Commission of Fine Arts and the Washington Board of Trade, the 1895 Highway Commission was abolished and its powers transferred to the National Capital Park and Planning Commission.

The establishment of a planning commission for the capital city can be said to have long postdated the experience of many other cities where planning commissions had been created in the early years of the twentieth century. Yet even prior to the 1926 act, in fact since the postbellum era when the Corps of Engineers exercised de facto planning powers, the city had experienced specialized functions of planning such as the platting of extended transportation routes, the regulating of height limitations, and zoning. The city had also been affected by broader conceptions about *groupings* of public buildings and monuments, and the comprehensive parks system plan enunciated by the McMillan Commission and supported by the Commission of Fine Arts. In this context, then, Washington was in 1926 by no means lagging behind planning activities elsewhere in the nation.

The 1926 act vested powers in the National Capital Park and Planning Commission to prepare a compre-

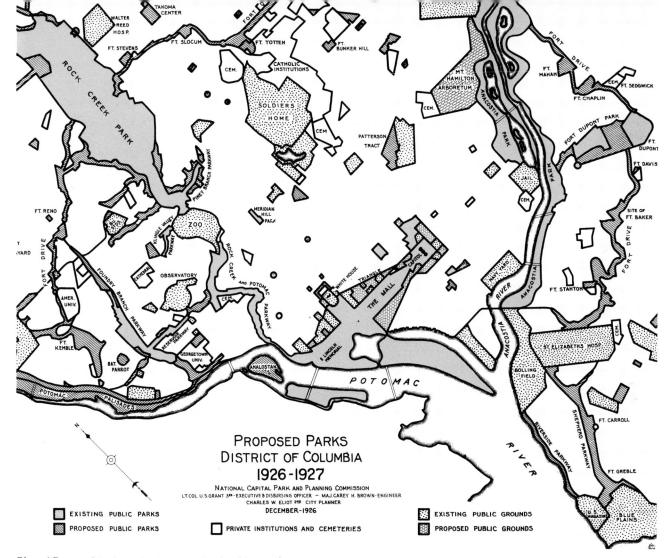

Plan of Proposed Parks in the District of Columbia, 1926–27

hensive plan, but parkways to and through the city remained the dominant themes in the agency's work program. These landscaped ribands were basic elements of City Beautiful planning and as such were the foundation stones of a movement nearing the end of its sway. While some promoters of planning might have rested content with the motto of the Municipal Art Society of New York, "To make us love our city, we must make our city lovely," others were looking toward newer goals. For Washington, the 1926 act marked the beginning of newer goals in planning. These were partly expressed in the fact that the business community and government agencies had already voiced concern for housing, traffic, the effects of land use, health issues, and neighborhoods —social issues that would envelop planning in the following decades.

Renewal of large sections of the historic city would produce a strengthened central focus for the metropolitan city. It was this monumental core that would give the larger area its unique character, with which both residents and visitors could identify. Representative of the federal establishment, this core would now demand the attention of lawmakers. New public buildings would, on the functional level, house the expanded bureaus of government but on the symbolic plane would serve as indicators of the nation's cultural achievements. In Washington, the settings and arrangements for these buildings would help determine future planning constraints in the L'Enfant city. At the same time, these powerful images of the federal presence would fuel the mounting forces toward dispersal into the metropolitan city.

The lack of a comprehensive plan for the siting and building of public facilities resulted in a piecemeal decision-making process which appropriated funds for each building project as it was individually deemed necessary. Thus, prior to the McMillan Commission which provided the first large-scale plan since L'Enfant, the city had illustrated many rapidly evolving notions about "good" public architecture. Building sites chosen were often determined by structural feasibility rather than by grand design. Today, this dispersed and variegated pattern speaks of design evolution over historical time. In the early twentieth century, however, these artifacts of a less organized planning process were deplored.

As long as the federal establishment continued to expand, the government was faced with securing new spaces to house its employees. The leisurely pace of public building construction prior to World War I was hastened dramatically during the war by construction of the seemingly permanent "tempos." After the war, the federal establishment did not shrink back to its pre-war numbers but reflected new and enlarged services demanded by postwar conditions. Executive department employees were accommodated in rented spaces secured in private office buildings; thus, the extent of the government's presence in the city was somewhat obscured. In 1925, however, the Department of Commerce alone reported that it was housed in seventeen separate buildings. As the *Annual Report of the Public Buildings Commission* for 1924 had pointed out, the variously housed government departments suffered from a "feeling of separateness, even of isolation, on the part of remoter units, that is harmful." Often these private quarters were deemed to be on the brink of condemnation, posing serious fire risks.

The Public Buildings Act of 1926: The Federal Triangle Project

Actively supported by Secretary of Commerce Herbert Hoover, the Public Buildings Act of 1926 provided $50 million for the construction of public buildings in the District of Columbia. Half the amount was to be spent on building south of Pennsylvania and New York Avenues and west of Maryland Avenue, the site later known as the Federal Triangle. The other half of the appropriation was to be spent on sites for the Supreme Court and extension of the Government Printing Office. The triangle area was the large squalid slice of land that had accumulated an infamous reputation in the nineteenth century as a haven for the city's criminal element, and included the area known as Murder Bay. Prior to the Potomac flats reclamation, frequent threats of flooding in the area had discouraged the siting of public buildings in this uncertain lowland. The Center Market stalls were surrounded by a busy and noisy atmosphere, but the importance of the triangular area was diminished by removal of much of the residential population beyond comfortable walking distance and introduction of light industry. Viewed thus as a blighted area, the triangle was set for marked change. In this direction, completion in 1899 of the Romanesque Post Office on Twelfth Street provided a false start but one that nonetheless provided an indicator of the government's interest in the area. In 1910, the long strip along Fifteenth Street—facing the White House and grounds—was acquired for executive department buildings intended to mirror the developing monumental line-up of Beaux-Arts creations opposite, along Seventeenth Street. Had Congress appropriated funds for public buildings at that site and the 1910 plans been carried out, the Federal Triangle might never have been realized as a single composition.

Planning for the Project: Initiatives and Responsibility. Responsibility for the Federal Triangle project fell to the Treasury Department, traditional home of the Office of the Supervising Architect. At this time the office was held by Louis Simon, a talented design administrator. Since the project was of unprecedented scale and involved the skills of architect, landscape architect, and planner, coordination called for designers representing the widest national experience. The Federal Triangle project was launched before the newly organized National Capital Park and Planning Commission had a chance to come to grips with the project's design. Thus, the new commission was unable to influence planning for the Triangle until after the essential

Aerial View of the Federal Triangle Area Prior to Development by the Federal Government, with the Then-Existent Louisiana Avenue Diagonal Shown (right of center), 1912

View of Center Market Stalls (foreground) from the National Museum of Natural History of the Smithsonian Institution at Constitution Avenue and Tenth Street, ca. 1915–20

form had been agreed upon. As for the Treasury Department, never had it exercised its wide-ranging powers over public buildings to such advantage. Most significant, for the first time since the McMillan plan had been formulated a quarter century earlier, there was strong federal commitment to achieving its goals.

The Mellon-Bennett Relationship. Key to the project's success as a work of art was Secretary of the Treasury Andrew W. Mellon. Born in Pittsburgh in 1855, Mellon had had experience almost wholly in financial and industrial corporations, and in local public affairs in Pittsburgh, until 1921 when he became Treasury secretary in President Harding's cabinet. Mellon gathered the nation's brightest professionals into his daily circles. Later on, in 1933, in face of mounting but unsubstantiated accusations of tax irregularities, Mellon resigned from the Treasury to assume the post of ambassador to Great Britain. Although his public image was thus shadowed, Mellon won the affection of friends and associates by his enthusiasm for sharing his art collection which later became the nucleus of the National Gallery of Art.

When the Treasury Department was faced with the large-scale Federal Triangle building project, representing an expansion far beyond any earlier dreams for a Fifteenth Street classical façade, Assistant Secretary of the Treasury Charles S. Dewey suggested to Mellon that Edward H. Bennett of Chicago advise him. Dewey had earlier consulted with his friend Bennett on the initial building plans and suggested that Bennett serve as chairman of a new Board of Architectural Consultants. Bennett, born in Cheltenham, England, in 1874, had worked for Daniel Burnham as a planning assistant on the 1905 San Francisco and 1908 Chicago plans. Prepared with an education at the Ecole des Beaux-Arts, and several years experience in the New York office of George B. Post, Bennett worked with Burnham before launching his independent planning career in 1909. In 1924, he formed an architectural and planning partnership known as Bennett, Parsons, and Frost. Much of Bennett's midwestern work, especially in Chicago, was derivative of Burnham's far-reaching Chicago regional plan, and Bennett also followed Burnham's footsteps in

Manila and other cities. Thus, it was a man of considerable and specialized experience that Dewey called upon in September 1926 to advise Mellon on public buildings. Mellon's instructions were broad: he wished Bennett, as the latter recorded in his diaries, to be his "personal architectural advisor." In the six years of the Mellon-Bennett relationship, the architect so advised the secretary on the Federal Triangle, the Mall, the site for the intended art gallery, the Legislative Group, the site for the Supreme Court Building, and proposed memorials.

THE 1929 CONFERENCE ON THE CAPITAL'S DEVELOPMENT

With the legislation passed and the designers chosen, President Hoover and other key Federal Triangle supporters realized that the project needed to demonstrate public support if congressional appropriations were to be made on schedule and the entire program accomplished within a few years' time. On 25–26 April 1929, a significant conference entitled "The Development of the United States Capital" was held at the recently completed United States Chamber of Commerce Building. The illustrious program of speakers included Hoover, Mellon, Bennett, Charles Moore, Milton Medary, and Congressman Richard M. Elliott, one of the sponsors of the 1926 bill. Attention focused on the Federal Triangle, its expected effect not just on the face of the physical city but in the minds of patriotic Americans. A star-studded conference such as this drew the nation's attention to important events in planning for the city.

The Board of Architectural Consultants. The Board of Architectural Consultants was composed of the nation's leading architects: Louis Ayers of the New York firm of York and Sawyer; Arthur Brown, Jr., of San Francisco; William Adams Delano of New York City; Milton Medary of Philadelphia; John Russell Pope of New York City. Bennett himself was at the helm. While Mellon could not reimburse members of the board for more than expenses, he promised each of the architects the opportunity to design one building in the complex. The efforts of the board were coordinated with the newly established National Capital Park and Planning Commission; with the Commission of Fine Arts; and with

Louis Simon, Supervising Architect of the Treasury, whose office was also assigned the design and construction of one of the buildings. The progress of the Federal Triangle project was recorded in the annual reports of the Public Buildings Commission.

Architecture, Design, and Style. In selecting the dominant architectural style, Mellon was much influenced by the McMillan Commission report. As a government official, he felt a responsibility to translate the plan's mandates into reality, agreeing that any "deviation in any important detail might mar great developments to which general approval has been given." One of these "important details" was the classical style, set by the two major public buildings, the White House and the Capitol, as well as by the buildings occupying other critical sites identified in the L'Enfant plan: the Treasury, Patent Office, City Hall, and the antebellum Post Office Building. Although the Federal Triangle was to be built of twentieth-century building elements, that is, of steel frame construction with limestone facing, Bennett noted in his diary that "modern 'blunt' architecture [was] not acceptable to Mr. Mellon for Department Buildings in Washington." President Hoover reminded the Board of Architectural Consultants to address itself to intangible values: "It is our primary duty to do more than erect offices. We must fit that program into the tradition and the symbolism of the Capital." The over-all stylistic character of the buildings was to be an "adaptation of the eighteenth century classic," but within this framework, eclecticism would reign: from the Italian Renaissance–styled Commerce Department, to the Corinthian–styled Archives Building, to the Ionic-order Post Office Building. The mixing of classical orders, rusticated façades, and sculpted pediments with Art Deco–styled metal doors and grilles was typical of the wide variation in the seemingly monolithic Beaux-Arts creations. According to the 1931 *Annual Report of the Public Buildings Commission,* the Federal Triangle represented a "distinctive product of the early twentieth century, depicting the revival of classic architecture for the use of modern business demands."

Design Alternatives. By defining the design parameters for Bennett, Mellon expressed his alliance with the prerogatives and precedents that had been offered by the McMillan Commission. Had he been given a free rein, Bennett might have dictated a more uniform Roman style, less eclectic and less Renaissance. He would have argued for a more unified scheme with enriched open spaces and would have given the ensemble greater amenities of fountains, squares, and wide public access. As one who had planned civic centers for other cities and thus had a large view of planning capabilities, Bennett might also have expanded his reach to the entire Pennsylvania Avenue façade, a more comprehensive vision than Congress and others could have accepted. But Bennett's final product probably would not have conflicted greatly with the over-all architectural traditions in Washington public buildings.

The modern European design alternatives were certainly visible in the 1920s, but they were little understood by the American public or by the architectural profession, some of whose members translated the Bauhaus ideas into stern factorylike buildings worthy of the clichés of "brutal" or "blunt." Because of his own inclinations, Bennett would not have espoused the more modern or romantic style that characterized the work of Philadelphia architect George Howe or the holistic and highly individualized work of Frank Lloyd Wright.

In 1926, there were few challenges to the Federal Triangle design. Never had there been such unanimity among architectural leaders as to the course that should be followed. Never had there been such a powerful commitment from the president and the principal cabinet-level secretary responsible for this work. These mutually reinforcing influences turned Washington toward its characteristic concentration of government buildings in the central area, particularly in the Triangle and the Mall, and dictated their architectural style, with its roots in Paris and Rome. Whitehall provided the model for the concentration of government departments, as Mellon viewed the capital city. Mellon also suggested to Bennett that the Federal Triangle buildings, "while having each a separate treatment, shall be of harmonious design and grouped around two large interior courts or plazas somewhat after the arrangement of the Louvre in Paris."

As a specific undertaking, the Federal Triangle expressed in Washington the civic center ideal. In more general terms, the civic center ideal had been a chief element in plans of American designers for several decades. It may have had earlier origins, but after the triumphs of the 1893 Chicago Fair, the City Beautiful movement—of which the civic center was the characteristic expression—had dominated the thinking of designers. It was expected that benefits of the civic center concept would be in the order of civic pride, moral reform, and an integrating device for the nation's diversity of ethnic origins. The aesthetic values communicated by the harmonious groupings would serve to inspire the common man.

The principles of such civic centers had been effectively outlined in 1903 by Charles Mulford Robinson in *Modern Civic Art* and repeated in the reports of the Public Buildings Commission. Land values and individual real estate interests argued for the massing of departmental buildings. In the concentration of public business in one area, efficiency in communication was attained, and a heightened sense of the dignity and importance of the individual buildings. To municipal reformers, as Robinson pointed out, this architecture en masse promised the "cooperation of departments rather than individual sufficiency which separate buildings recommended and which is at the root of so much administrative evil."

In 1922, Werner Hegemann and Elbert Peets published *The American Vitruvius: An Architect's Handbook of Civic Art*, an analysis of the civic center principles. Synthesizing the American experience as illustrated by world fairs and development of college campuses and other institutional groupings, the authors outlined from the perspective of the new art of urban design the elements of civic centers. These elements emphasized the "essential relation between a building and its setting, the necessity of protecting the aspect of the approaches, the desirability of grouping buildings into harmonious ensembles, of securing dominance of some buildings over others."

The Federal Triangle expressed more than the civic center ideal; in the Triangle planning, other City Beautiful principles also ruled. The land was defined by the right triangle formed by the city's two major axes, the Mall and Pennsylvania Avenue, with the short leg defined by the White House–Washington Monument axis. It is around this basic geometric form that the rest of the original L'Enfant plan is based. The architectural massing in this area provided a clearer definition to the constitutive triangle and thus to the monumental core of the city. The seventy acres of land were sliced into sites for seven major structures: Ayers designed the long Commerce Department Building between Fourteenth and Fifteenth Streets; Brown, the Labor Department Building, the Interstate Commerce Commission Building, and the Departmental Auditorium; Delano, the Post Office with its hemicycle; the Supervising Architect of the Treasury, the Internal Revenue Building; Medary, the Justice Department Building; Pope, the National Archives Building; and Bennett, the Apex Building, the final structure that later would house the Federal Trade Commission. All the buildings were of the same height and limestone façade. While each was of a unique design, all corresponded to the limitations of classical forms. The grouping was subordinate to the monumental core's major foci, the White House and the Capitol, and great pains were taken to improve the complex's immediate environs. The Federal Triangle enhanced the edges of the Mall and White House parkland and they, in turn, served as appropriately formal settings to the Triangle's structures. The complex was designed around two plazas: the Grand Plaza, which drew the Post Office hemicycle laterally toward Fourteenth Street, and the Twelfth Street Circle, seen as the pivot of the architectural assemblage and marked by a commemorative column. In Bennett's view, the "vital element binding the entire group is the connection between the two large plazas."

The Competition between Automobiles and Architecture. In designing this large complex, the board was faced with problems larger than those of architectural

Architect's Presentation Model of the Federal Triangle, Looking East down Pennsylvania Avenue toward the Capitol, 1929

Architect's Presentation Model of the Federal Triangle's Grand Plaza, 1929

Aerial View of the Federal Triangle, Showing the Grand Plaza's Actual Use as Parking for Government Employees, 1977

design. The concerns now embraced traffic flow and parking. The street system of the triangle area prior to 1926 was based on the original layout by L'Enfant: a grid cut by two diagonals, Ohio and Louisiana Avenues. To insure maximum usage of the land for the Federal Triangle complex, the existing street system was disregarded and a new street system drawn up emphasizing the north-south thoroughfares and relying on the peripheral avenues for east-west circulation. The new street design, however, was not solely oriented to traffic; it provided for generous sidewalks and landscaping, as well as broad roadways, in order to produce a more open character for the new public precincts. The grand façade facing the Mall allowed for the aggrandizement of Constitution Avenue as a "great, new artery." To improve traffic conditions in the area, the National Capital Park and Planning Commission suggested that the north-south thoroughfares underpass the Mall, that a streetcar line form a loop within the Triangle, and that the Triangle be "self-contained as to parking." When land values and building costs were assessed, the Planning Commission viewed parking provided on open ground to be more expensive than parking space within the building network.

The impact of automobiles, especially in the Federal Triangle–Mall area, has been a nagging problem from the conception of the Triangle up to the present time. Because the McMillan plan predated the automotive age, no provisions were made in the plan for accommodating cars. Later City Beautiful plans for other cities also did not provide for parking either under or above ground. Thus, the plaza spaces shown as formal design elements on many city plans have in fact been turned into parking lots. This has been the fate of the Federal Triangle's Grand Plaza. It was not that Bennett and the Board of Architectural Consultants never recognized the problem but that parking was considered only after the architectural and landscape outlines had been agreed upon—and the board's response to the problem was by no means unanimous. Speaking for the Commission of Fine Arts, Charles Moore in an annual report termed the parking situation a "nuisance that could well nigh destroy the beauty of the National Capital." Bennett and Brown recognized that parking was one of the unpleasant realities that had to be incorporated into a static building arrangement.

Seeking a solution, the Board of Architectural Consultants commissioned the advice of traffic experts, Na-

178

tional Garages, Inc. For the projected 7,415 automobiles, the firm suggested that provisions be allowed in spaces under the Ellipse (the park area located between the White House and the Washington Monument), under the Triangle, under the Mall, and in two spaces north of Pennsylvania Avenue. In response to the firm's suggestion that 1,300 spaces be designed under the Great Plaza, John Russell Pope objected, urging that the "point of view of the Board should not be lost sight of, namely, its efforts to conserve the beauty of the public park and the beauty of the buildings." Representing the National Capital Park and Planning Commission, and sympathetic with most of Bennett's views, Frederick Delano suggested that a parking lot, enclosed by an eight-foot wall and planted with shrubbery and trees, be allowed at the base of the Washington Monument. Additional parking was proposed by Delano in low garages on the north side of Pennsylvania Avenue and under the Ellipse if four to five ventilating stacks could be constructed. Pope objected to Delano's schemes as too conspicuous and destructive to the 1901–1902 plan and detrimental to the foliage of the monumental core. Less satisfactory suggestions included parking north of Pennsylvania Avenue as far as G or H

Street and on sites south of the Mall.

In the last analysis, parking was incorporated into the Federal Triangle building scheme only on a highly restricted basis (as in the Apex Building basement). Contributing factors were difficulty in justifying additional costs during the Depression and openly expressed fear of dangerous ramps and underground driving. Solutions to the traffic problem were also severely limited by poor soil and drainage conditions in the area. Realistic long-term solutions were further thwarted by the assumption that 65 percent of the nearly 30,000 employees then to be located in the Federal Triangle would use mass transportation or walk to work. Taking solace in this assumption, the board in its disarrayed response to the parking problem allowed for saturation of the area with auto parking in every available large open space within the Triangle, a result that no member of the board foresaw or desired.

The Final Days. Edward Bennett remained with the project until its virtual completion in 1937 but the first six years, from 1926 to 1933, would stand as the most satisfying. In those halcyon days, as he recorded in his diaries, he enjoyed the confidence and support of Presi-

179

dent Hoover, Secretary of the Treasury Andrew Mellon, Assistant Secretary Charles Dewey, and Frederic Delano of the National Capital Park and Planning Commission, all of whom might accompany him on site visits and to hearings before congressional committees. A realist in terms of what could be accomplished, given the cooperation of these important figures, Bennett worked to incorporate their views into more contemporary terms, especially in the matter of parking facilities. After Mellon's resignation, Bennett was suddenly faced with the prospect of dealing with a new secretary of the Treasury—and a rash of conflicts between himself, members of the Board of Architectural Consultants, and Charles Moore. With his original sources of support—except for Delano—now gone, Bennett saw his own Apex Building almost expunged from the project because of fears on the part of some that the Apex would screen the Pope-designed Archives Building and because of the hope exhibited by others for possible use of the Apex site as the location for a Thomas Jefferson memorial. By the end of his service, Bennett designed and —through the efforts of President Franklin Roosevelt— saw his Apex Building realized, although in finished form it was stripped of original ornate detail as well as plans for a terraced fountain where the Federal Triangle met Sixth Street.

Crisis and Critique: Evaluations and Second Thoughts

In the heady days of affluence, the emphasis on inspirational and patriotic symbols appeared justification enough for the large expenditures on the Federal Triangle project. The terminology of the 1926 Public Buildings Act underscored aesthetic concerns: the secretary of the Treasury was to provide "suitable approaches" to the buildings, and beautify and embellish their surroundings "as nearly in harmony with the plan of Pierre Charles L'Enfant as may be practicable." In proposing that the several buildings of the Triangle be designed as a harmonious whole, supporters of the bill desired that the Triangle look as if the elements had been designed and constructed at the same time, present

a monumental image, and preclude any chance of further additions of "incongruous new buildings." Charles Moore reflected satisfaction with the Federal Triangle plans as of 1929 in that they conformed to the 1901–1902 McMillan plan, the Lincoln Memorial and the siting of new Mall buildings serving to fasten that plan on the city for the ages. Taking the Federal Triangle project together with other public building projects in the city, Congressman Louis C. Cramton, chairman of the House District Committee, saw the nation's capital city "on the threshold of glorious things."

Functional Concerns and Shortcomings. Functional concerns had been voiced in early discussions by members of the Public Buildings Commission who were torn, as the commission's annual reports from 1922 on reveal, between a "modern office building" type constructed with an "appropriate but simple finish" as against what some viewed as "Greek temples" that were "foolish and unnecessary . . . exceedingly expensive and wasteful of space." Nonetheless, it was recognized that the clustering of buildings for many agencies remedied the legislative confusion of "various departments and bureaus [submitting] plans for individual needs to Congress" and the past unsatisfactory experience with piecemeal planning. Efficiency was also served in that formerly scattered bureau offices were now in close proximity to one another, to the policy makers of the legislative branch, and to the executors in the White House.

The larger perspectives of city planning showed the environmental shortcomings of the Federal Triangle plan, especially its parking deficiencies and the congestion associated with the daily ebb and flow of government workers. Few benefits of the plan touched the adjoining parts of the city; the north side of Pennsylvania Avenue, for instance, with its wealth of commercial buildings evoking the historic urban past, was to remain under shadow of speculative blight and uncertainty for at least another half century. Shortcomings of the Triangle plan were sufficient to vitiate efforts through successive administrations to complete it (that is, to replace the Post Office and the Southern Railroad Building, and build the Great Plaza facing the Commerce Department Building) and contributed to the air of disenchantment that surrounded the Pennsylvania Avenue redevelopment efforts. It was estimated that in the area surrounding the Federal Triangle 60 percent of the same buildings had been standing in 1880 and, until the beginning of the 1950s, in the old market spaces and along Indiana Avenue there were still hay and feed merchants, blacksmith shops, horse watering-troughs, brick sidewalks, and other evidences of this as a market-linked precinct.

Economic Realities. After the stockmarket crash, the Federal Triangle project was interpreted less as an aesthetic symbol than a sign of governmental efficiency. In the expanding role of the government in dealing with the economic crisis, the Public Buildings Commission suggested in its 1930 *Annual Report* that "the impression of well-ordered and properly designed Government buildings insures popular respect for the Government." The discordant conditions in the nation would be overcome by heavy injections of planning as symbolized by the Triangle's "example of good taste

and intelligent planning." In 1932, Karl K. Hardy, secretary of the Public Buildings Commission, labeled the project as "one of true conservative economy," in contrast to the earlier and limited view of planning that had stressed beautification. The Federal Triangle offered a solution to the problem of unsafe working conditions in private buildings. Moreover, the building program was held out as now "concerned primarily with the utilitarian problem of housing adequately the Federal activities in order that they might function efficiently and economically."

Aesthetic and Functional Success. The Federal Triangle complex offered remarkable potential attraction to visitor and resident alike. Each building offered numerous lobby displays and exhibitions depicting the department's primary activities, mirroring the interaction with the public that took place in the cultural institutions flanking the Mall. Lobbies and auditoriums were handsomely adorned, offering a warm welcome to

Proposed Municipal Center for the Eastern End of Pennsylvania Avenue, Showing (upper right) Judiciary Square, 1929

visitors. The Department of Commerce Building even boasted a large aquarium, and in the Department of Justice Building the FBI museum offered a shooting demonstration straight out of "Gangbusters."

In the federal perspective the Triangle helped define the tourist's Washington and the focus on the monumental core of the city. It gave a clearer definition to the northern boundary of the Mall and in the process cleared the vista for a new ceremonial route along Constitution Avenue. Such a street had already been foreshadowed by the monumental frontage along Seventeenth Street and westward on Constitution Avenue toward the Lincoln Memorial. To the north along Pennsylvania Avenue, the project could be incorporated into the promise of a proper ceremonial way, it was thought, if private development along the north side of the Avenue would conform in height, architectural flavor, and cornice line with the Triangle. Reflecting national interest in the future of the capital city, Alfred Granger, representing the Chicago chapter of the American Institute of Architects, submitted plans for proposed buildings on the north side of the Avenue. His plans fused new office buildings with compatible existing elements, cornice lines of the Washington Hotel, the Willard Hotel, and the Evening Star Building. At the far eastern end of Pennsylvania Avenue, the proposed Municipal Center to be constructed around Hadfield's much-admired City Hall would initiate public improvements along that side of the street. The aesthetic and functional success of the proposed development also encouraged future plans for a Northwest Rectangle west of the White House as far as Rock Creek Park, thereby vindicating the "mistaken" siting of the old Interior Department Building (now the General Services Administration Building); a Southwest Triangle south of the Mall; and the unimplemented plans for similar clusters along East Capitol Street and in the Southeast quadrant surrounding the Navy Yard. Of these proposals, the largest realization was the extensive massing of federal departments south of the Mall, where nearly three times the population of the Federal Triangle would ultimately be concentrated.

The replacement—by the Federal Triangle complex—of a large section of the decayed mid-nineteenth-century business district did not fulfill all the expectations of a redeveloped area. While it may have satisfied some critics in that architectural quality of the area had been improved, the office buildings filled with a large mass of workers did not generate business activities, or even life after working hours. Instead, when night fell, the complex illustrated the fate of many downtown areas of cities: empty office caverns through which by night only the brave would walk.

The Expanded Federal Presence. By 1937, the design decisions and most of the construction of the Federal Triangle were virtually complete. Most notable for hampering full realization of the project was the Internal Revenue Service Building under construction near the Old Post Office. In the comprehensive view, the Federal Triangle project and proliferation of similar groupings and large land acquisition programs throughout the city were indicators of a substantial realization over time of the broad concepts of the McMillan plan. Although many of the 1901–1902 proposals faded with changing conditions, the federal presence and investment in the city forced a remarkably comprehensive realization of its City Beautiful plan, a result totally unlike the fragmented development of many other American cities.

CHAPTER VIII THE EARLY NATIONAL CAPITAL PARK AND PLANNING COMMISSION 1926–1933

The Early National Capital Park and Planning Commission 1926-1933

Planning in the Nation's Capital

The early years of the National Capital Park and Planning Commission saw a unique combination of comprehensive planning and project planning that captured the attention of Washington's political leaders and of citizens throughout the nation. Not since the grand days of the McMillan Commission had so many illustrious political figures sought to associate their names with the appearance of the capital city. The personnel of the commission, both full-time staff members and consultants, were professionals at the forefront of the still-young planning movement. With the city extending into the far reaches of the historic ten-mile square District and beyond, into the adjoining counties, the commission looked not only backward to the turn-of-the-century McMillan Commission recommendations and the even earlier L'Enfant plan, but also forward to the emerging regional city with its characteristic social problems and range of modern concerns.

In devoting daily energies to inspecting, recording, and planning the city, the commission stretched its comprehension of the city into the unexplored questions of slums, pollution, urban sprawl, and waste of resources, problems unrecognized in the tourist's view of the static, serene, monumental city. Studies and recommendations made early on by the commission, revealing both the magnificence of the monumental core and the heretofore obscured constituent city beyond, would serve as the basis for planning in Washington for at least the next twenty-five years. This vision of the city, present and future, strongly established it as a national city expressive of the federal interest and aware of its identity as the capital.

MEMBERSHIP OF THE PLANNING COMMISSION

In 1929, Representative Louis C. Cramton described the members of the Planning Commission and staff as "men of the widest experience and greatest ability of any planning commission in the country." In general, the six ex officio members came and went according to changes in the agencies and congressional committees. It was in the four presidentially appointed members that the Planning Commission secured its professional status and its continuity. These members often volunteered to carry out special planning or design studies for the commission, or became professionally engaged in

rial View of a Portion of the
st Capitol Street Corridor and the Mall,
owing the Library of Congress (left)
d the Supreme Court (right)

work related to the commission, as was Olmsted in his continuing work on various projects in the city.

In the early years the leading figures were commission members Frederic A. Delano and Frederick Law Olmsted, Jr., and staff member Charles W. Eliot II. Delano and Olmsted were longtime activists in planning in Washington. Frederic Delano, an uncle of Franklin Delano Roosevelt, contributed his name and his family's prestige to the cause of planning, often urging decisions on his nephew, Roosevelt, when the latter was in the White House. With no specific professional training in planning, Delano was primarily a political and administrative figure and an indubitable business and political leader. He had, moreover, been the leader of the outstanding city planning program in Chicago and was a prime organizer of the Regional Plan of New York and Its Environs. By 1926, Olmsted had established his own reputation distinct from that of his famous father. As a figure of long professional experience nationwide, having secure lines of communication with influential people, Olmsted made substantive contributions to the Planning Commission in its early years, taking on much of the work himself. His wisdom mesmerized people like Delano and they trusted him implicitly.

Charles Eliot was nephew and namesake of the famed landscape architect who with Sylvester Baxter had in 1893 drawn up the Boston Metropolitan Park System, a model which many Washingtonians admired. He was born in Cambridge, Massachusetts, in 1899. Like Delano and Olmsted, Eliot was a graduate of Harvard University. In 1923, he enrolled in Harvard's Graduate School of Landscape Architecture, where professional training in city planning was then offered. Prior to his employment by the National Capital Park and Planning Commission, he had worked for Olmsted on plans for several Massachusetts towns. There he gained a "strong sense of the popular interest in historic shrines, landmarks, and scientific features of the landscape." Eliot's appointment as the commission's "city planner" at the age of twenty-seven startled many activists in Washington, chief among them Harlean James, who on first meeting viewed Eliot as "that kid." Nonetheless, Eliot's educational background, his sturdy historical orientation, his familial roots in the New England landscape

tradition, and especially the decisive experience under Olmsted allowed him to deal effectively with Washington as a vast metropolitan area, especially in the matter of parks. Eliot saw his job as the function of "allowing for necessary municipal growth, yet preserving as much as . . . I can of the flavor of the past."

THE COMMISSION'S WORK PROGRAM

At the outset, the commission outlined a work plan. When questioned later about this first work program, Eliot recalled, "Olmsted dictated it; I wrote it down." First, basic data would be collected to guide comprehensive planning. Second, coordinating the more immediate plans of other federal and local agencies would make up the administrative core of the work. Third, a Comprehensive Plan would be formulated to provide for long-range guidelines in controlling physical growth. The second and third activities were broken down by geographical districts and then by functional subheadings: highways, transportation, water supply, parks, neighborhood centers, and zoning. A timetable was imposed for development of the Comprehensive Plan to guard against its postponement under pressure of more expedient piecemeal planning decisions.

The Coordinating Committee. The City Planning Committee created under the old Park Commission was reborn in the Coordinating Committee empowered to recommend for or against the actions of federal agencies. By 1933, the Coordinating Committee met every two weeks and consisted of thirteen members representing the several government agencies that comprised commission membership. From the start, the original Coordinating Committee was directed to deal with the major federal agencies and to reconcile their physical plans for the city. Later, other committees were created within the Planning Commission to deal with specific subjects, such as federal and municipal projects, school and recreational plans, and the broad question of water supply for the region.

Work Agenda for Members, Staff, and Consultants. Work was allocated according to the experience of the members, staff, and consultants. Olmsted volunteered to supervise planning for parkways, parks, and neighbor-

186

hood centers, with the work actually carried out by Eliot, who was designated staff director in 1930. Harland Bartholomew, author of the city's 1920 zoning ordinance, was contracted to work on highways, with many of his ideas translated at the staff level by staff engineer, Major Carey Brown. Commission member J. C. Nichols brought his experience with the phenomenal residential growth of Kansas City and its distinguished Country Club District to bear on the molding of new residential sections of the city; here attractiveness would be defined by parks and transportation planning. Nichols was particularly valuable as a practical, money-making type who supported planning as economical and was able to communicate this conviction to real estate people.

In the area of housing for low-income families, John Ihlder, valuable for his experience as executive director of the Pittsburgh Housing Association, was engaged as a consultant. Member of the commission and executive officer until 1933, and chairman of the commission from 1942 to 1949, Colonel and later Major General Ulysses S. Grant III served also as director of the independent Office of Public Buildings and Public Parks of the National Capital. (This office accounted for one of the ex officio memberships on the Planning Commission until the office was absorbed by the National Park Service in 1933.) Grant's contacts with President Hoover prompted Eliot later to credit Executive Officer Grant with "managing the White House" on policies affecting planning in the city. Presidential appointee to the commission Milton B. Medary, the architect, represented the City Beautiful tradition, concerning himself with the aesthetic values of the city in the monumental core and in naturally landscaped parkways.

The Automobile

Washington could be seen now as a metropolitan city verging on a regional city, and underlying any view of this city was the automobile. Other functional issues—housing, parks, highways, siting of public buildings—were now hinged onto the spatial dimensions afforded by this most private mode of transportation.

J. C. NICHOLS AND THE PROTECTION OF RESIDENTIAL SUBDIVISIONS

As early as 1928, Planning Commission member J. C. Nichols correctly predicted the automobile's effects on the city. He observed that, contrary to public notions about city planning's ornamental results, "the growing acuteness of automobile congestion in all our population centers . . . is forcing upon the public . . . the dire need of better planning to meet the rapidly changing conditions in the size and number of our transportation units." This enlarged physical dimension of the city was fed by the automobile, increasing the "tendency of business to move from downtown districts to suburban neighborhood shopping centers, accentuated by the building of outlying apartments and kitchenettes, neighborhood picture shows, filling stations and chain stores." These massive intrusions into formerly rural lands intended as settings for new residential groupings had "thrust city planning problems—particularly zoning—into the residential areas of nearly all urban communities." Nichols's primary interest was in the development and protection of residential subdivisions, the focus also of his earlier work in Kansas City. He defined the ideal subdivision in both economic and aesthetic terms. The expense of street maintenance would be lessened, Nichols pointed out, by the "fact that the automobile has annihilated distances and that blocks may be greatly lengthened." As opposed to the common grid cross street pattern found in many central city areas, the platting of subdivisions in suburban areas was adapted to the topography of the land and was not dictated by some arbitrary street scheme. Highways constructed to handle automobile traffic, while facilitating economy in movement of people and goods, were found detrimental to the value of property facing such highways.

Nichols blamed the street plan ordered by the 1893 Highway Act for the wasteful "checkerboard plan of streets with short blocks" forced "throughout all these beautiful hills and valleys." In order to execute the 1893 Highway Plan, expensive grading operations had ripped out forest trees in the far reaches of the District, "resulting in large sections of our capital city becoming characterless and unattractive." Nichols suggested that the National Capital Park and Planning Commission restudy "these street plans, and their better adaptation to the peculiar contours of the land, and the conservation of the valleys and brooks for park purposes."

HARLAND BARTHOLOMEW'S STUDY OF WASHINGTON STREETS

The highway was the focus for this increased concern about mobility expressed by Nichols and others. The planning act of 1926 placed responsibility for city high-way planning in the National Capital Park and Planning Commission program. Harland Bartholomew, employed by the commission to conduct highway studies, looked sharply at the ribbons of paving which by 1930 ac-counted for nearly 30 percent of the city's usable sur-face. Bartholomew's characterization of the evolution of the city's street system was a precise and skillful résumé. Development, as Bartholomew depicted it, be-gan with the narrow streets of Georgetown in the pre-capital-city era of the eighteenth century. While these old streets possessed charm, it was difficult to join them via major arteries to the rest of the city. For Bartholo-mew, the second stage of development was represented by the wide streets and avenues designed by L'Enfant, "proof of the value of proper planning." Then followed the third stage, which Bartholomew characterized as the "dark days of the capital city, as far as its circulation system is concerned," where streets beyond the bounda-ries of the old city were independently determined by the landowners and subdividers.

The drawing up of the 1893 Highway Plan repre-sented the fourth stage, which Bartholomew described as "belated but praiseworthy" in its effort to control land platting. Unfortunately for the natural landscape of the city, the extension of the grid and radials of the L'Enfant flat basin city over a more rugged terrain de-stroyed many of the city's distinctive features, especially east of Rock Creek Park. In the final stage of develop-ing the street system, the National Capital Park and Planning Commission was entrusted with altering the 1893 Highway Plan (as amended by the 1898 Highway Act and subsequent congressional acts). In March 1932, the commission reported that since 1926 it had made 107 changes in the plan. The commission was to be guided by what Bartholomew boldly diagrammed as three goals: differentiation of street functions, planning

for subdivisions according to the natural terrain, and "an attempt to restate the L'Enfant ideal in the terms of a motor age."

In planning for the circulation pattern of the future, Bartholomew designated several streets as major thor-oughfares to serve intown, crosstown, and streetcar traf-fic. He suggested that these thoroughfares be differenti-ated from the secondary streets by distinctive street lighting, traffic signals, paving, public service institu-tions, and tree-planting. He recognized that employ-ment centers were sprouting out beyond the monu-mental core and he planned for bypasses as well as cross-town and interchange routes. L'Enfant's radials had provided well for through traffic, but the 1893 highway system reflected the more restricted view of daily com-muting patterns as movement primarily between the suburbs and the monumental core. Bartholomew's plan sought to overcome this.

Outside the District's boundaries, Bartholomew stud-ied the commuting zone within Prince George's, Mont-gomery, Arlington, and Fairfax Counties. Because of the limited construction of county highways and heavy use of streetcar and railroad lines, the commuting zone re-sembled spokes about the hub of the L'Enfant federal city. Bartholomew recommended the strengthening of radial highways already largely defined by pre-automo-bile transportation routes. To adapt these radials to the automobile, the routes were to be dramatically widened. To connect these radials and fill in the spokes, Bartholo-mew drew up a series of bypass routes resembling many belt roads encircling the District. The intersection of the radials with the belt roads were intended to be lo-cated at extant county towns in order to maintain the already developed points of concentration. Thus, the configuration of highways outside the District would resemble a vast man-made spiderweb.

Planning for Natural and Cultural Landmarks. With the commission's interest in incorporating natural and cultural landmarks to enhance its utilitarian planning work, blank maps were sent out to knowledgeable individuals who were requested to locate important sites. Architects listed structures that should be pre-served—Pohick Church, Cabin John Bridge, the locks

188

at Great Falls. Historians pointed out battlefields, ornithologists charted bird sanctuaries, geologists defined important rocky formations, and botanists described stretches of woodlands. When these special interest maps were incorporated with other planning studies, the L'Enfant city—according to a July 1931 newspaper account—marked the center "with its abodes of past and current history setting the motif for the surrounding variations and repetitions of the design." It was reported that the commission anticipated there would extend outward from this nucleus "beautifully landscaped radiating parkways, with frequent connecting links, all of which [would] serve as approaches or settings for numberless exhibits in a vast outdoor museum."

Housing

New patterns for residential development came into being as a result of changes in the 1893 Highway Plan. More attention was paid to the natural contours of the land in outlying locations where little or no development had taken place. Within the District, more attention was likewise given to identification of various income groups and their housing needs. Rehabilitation of existing deteriorated housing stock was given higher priority.

Wesley Heights and Spring Valley. Many changes in the 1893 Highway Plan were made to conform new streets to the rugged topography west of Massachusetts Avenue in the Wesley Heights and Spring Valley sections of the District. Although Wesley Heights was planned as an upper-middle-class subdivision, Colonel Ulysses S. Grant III argued for the economy inherent in the "better layout of the streets and grades, which will alleviate the need for much grading." The actual layout of Wesley Heights was predominantly rectangular with fewer cross streets than in earlier District subdivisions. This subdivision, although recorded as early as 1890 by the firm of W. C. and A. N. Miller, was not actually developed until the 1920s. Surrounded by

Street Plan for Spring Valley, Showing Pattern of Superblocks, 1928

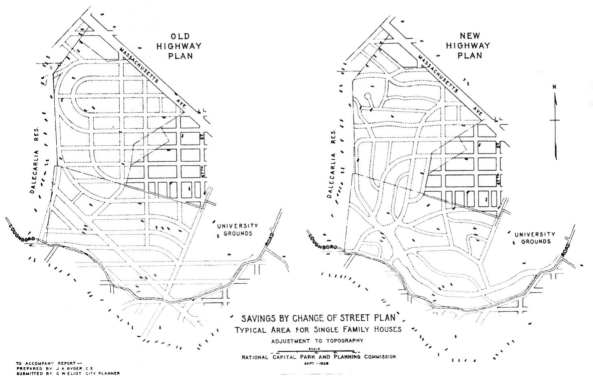

189

Wesley Heights
The Garden Spot of Washington

with its distinctively designed homes, carefully preserved trees and contours of the land, parallels the consistent growth in beauty of our National Capital

Truly a remarkable achievement in suburban development

Endowed by nature with wooded beauty, which the hand of man has not desecrated by destruction and which the protecting influences of development guard jealously — assuredly "The Garden Spot of Washington."

Every house Miller designed and Miller built

AWARDED HIGHEST HONORS

The home of Charles H. Pardoe at 4320 Cathedral Avenue N.W., Wesley Heights, was selected by the Municipal Art Committee of the Washington Board of Trade as the winner—in the Suburban Home Class—of the meritorious buildings constructed in the District of Columbia and surrounding territory for the period between January 1, 1924, and January 1, 1926. This house was designed and built by W. C. & A. N. Miller.

Three miles from the Mayflower Hotel, with Massachusetts Avenue, Washington's finest boulevard, as its approach.

CATHEDRAL AVENUE
One of the Picturesque approaches to
Wesley Heights
THE GARDEN SPOT OF WASHINGTON

Motor out Massachusetts Avenue, across Wisconsin Avenue, into Cathedral Avenue—or take Wesley Heights Bus at 20th and P Sts.

Builders — **W. C. and A. N. Miller** — **Realtors**
1119 – 17 St. — Main 1790

Advertisement for Wesley Heights, 1927

Glover-Archbold Parkway and its appendages as well as the American University campus, Wesley Heights with its single-family houses separated by wide expanses of natural woodland was informally known as the "Garden Spot of Washington."

The success of Wesley Heights inspired the Millers

to develop a still more expensive subdivision, Spring Valley, again below Massachusetts Avenue but west of American University. In this subdivision, the Millers carried the garden suburb further, planning what was described as the "first curvilinear development of any magnitude in the District." The street plan for Spring Valley submitted to the National Capital Park and Planning Commission for approval epitomized the commission's efforts to preserve the trees, hills and valleys, and streams—and to carve out fewer cross streets in future developments in the District. The large single-family homes in Spring Valley presented a wide variety of building materials: stone, brick, wood. In what was described as the "costly type" of residential development, the grounds surrounding each house provided space and "elbow room [to] avoid the mistake of overcrowding." Spring Valley was built over a period of more than a decade, from 1928 into the late 1930s, with its attractiveness enhanced by proximity to several country clubs, parks, and other recreational opportunities. The feasibility and attractiveness of Spring Valley's pattern of superblocks, curving streets, and single-family homes were held as the ideal for several decades to follow and in general configuration were replicated in more modest metropolitan subdivisions.

John Ihlder's Housing Program for the District. Housing for the vast middle class was provided in less dramatic proportions throughout the District and suburban counties. In 1930, housing consultant John Ihlder reported to the National Capital Park and Planning Commission on the local and national importance of residential development of the capital city. In his report to the commission, Ihlder argued: "The prestige and appeal of the Capital do not lie wholly in its governmental structure, but do lie largely in its dwellings." The automobile had changed the demands for housing in requiring parking and garage space and in opening to development new areas beyond the streetcar network. The ideal housing package would include accessibility, detached single-family dwellings, and open spaces. With spaciousness as the primary objective in housing, Ihlder decried the trend of housing toward more intense development. In order to plan for housing, Ihlder recom-

190

mended that the Planning Commission gather data on family incomes and sizes, and project each income group's housing needs based on economic considerations, rather than continuing to anticipate these needs on "the trial and error method," persisting in the trend toward providing first for the well-to-do.

In housing for the lower income groups, Ihlder predicted the study would reveal that such families were forced to accept unsuitable dwellings. He also predicted that the study would demonstrate that the "lowest income people are not self-supporting."

Alley Dwellings in Washington. Alley dwellings had long been regarded as the most blatant illustration of substandard housing in Washington. In 1930, Ihlder counted more than 250 inhabited alleys, some dating as far back as before the Civil War. These alleys were distributed throughout the old L'Enfant city and in nearby District blocks, especially in the Southwest quadrant and in the industrial area of Foggy Bottom. Alley dwellings began as quarters for servants employed in houses fronting on streets. Throughout the nineteenth and twentieth centuries, these hidden communities were the subject of much public discussion. A landmark bill was passed in 1914 providing for the phasing out of all alley dwellings within a period of ten years, with the inhabi-

tants to be relocated. Mrs. Archibald Hopkins, leading advocate of the 1914 act, organized a corporation to build new low-cost housing for evicted alley-dwellers. The problem of relocation of poor families would plague both private activists and public officials. To deal with what Ihlder termed this "difficult problem," new housing was to be sought in other blocks where blacks lived. As the alley population was relocated elsewhere, the next problem to be solved, according to Ihlder, was reuse of the property on which the dwellings were located. The 1914 act had not resolved this issue except to forbid the property's future use for dwellings. Alternative uses suggested by Ihlder included space for parking and loading or, in the tradition of Gramercy Park in New York, as "tea gardens or outdoor dining rooms appurtenant to hotels, semiprivate gardens or parks appurtenant to apartment houses or private dwellings."

Georgetown: An Example of the Historic and Distinctive Old Neighborhood. Rehabilitation and relocation were two sides of the housing picture in the old city. Before thoughts of demolition and rebuilding gripped housing officials as they would in the post–World War II era, interest was expressed in the distinctive historical and aesthetic qualities provided by old Washington neighborhoods, especially Georgetown.

View of a Georgetown Street, Late 1930s

This interest was expressed as social workers walked through old Georgetown photographing derelict housing and children's play areas in the narrow streets. The process of upgrading Georgetown houses had originally been initiated by the wives of junior officers and war workers during World War I and had continued afterwards. Although far from complete, by 1931 the process of transforming Georgetown was compared to that of Beacon Hill in Boston, where restoration had revealed the "original charm of the fine old houses, packed tightly together under the shade of ancient trees and as closely crammed with the memories of silk and top hats, capes, and creaking coaches, gay parties and political intrigue." This élan Georgetown would once again recapture by the late 1940s when the restored buildings attracted back the rich and powerful. But in the 1930s, Georgetown was viewed more as a potential laboratory for experimental social programs to combat the effects of the Depression and create a sense of community among its inhabitants rather than as an example of restoration efforts. For example, in 1933 Horace Peaslee (representing the Allied Architects) initiated studies of Georgetown architecture, primarily for the purpose of employment relief. This was a theme more of the mid-1930s than of the Planning Commission's earliest years, the Depression having forced many architects and draftsmen as well as carpenters and the building trades out of work. Restoration of Georgetown houses was viewed as a lever for renewing the construction industry locally.

Planning for Parks and Parkways

Park planning drew heavily on the Chicago experience. In 1928, at the behest of Frederick Law Olmsted, Jr., Frederick F. Stephen of the Community Research Council of the University of Chicago summed up the Chicago experience begun more than twenty years earlier. Olmsted senior had planned Chicago's first large parks in the 1870s, primarily as an introduction of nature's amenities into the booming prairie city. Like Washington's nineteenth-century parks of repose and moral uplift, many of Chicago's boulevards and large

parks were later converted in part to recreational uses at the end of the century. In a movement to limit the conversion of these Chicago parks and in recognition of the often-long distances between home and recreational facilities, the South Park Commission began creating small local recreational parks throughout the city. By 1928 there were 135 of these newly specialized parks, located according to the ethnic, social, and physical barriers already extant in the city. Chicago's immigrant groups tended to live among their own, thereby creating social barriers between one neighborhood and another. These well-defined neighborhoods were often further delineated by physical barriers: railroads, industrial centers, and business thoroughfares. The South Park Commission offered a variety of attractions: playgrounds, gyms, swimming pools, and buildings for indoor sports and craft activities. In addition, some of these parks were packaged together with libraries and school buildings.

NEIGHBORHOOD AND RECREATION CENTERS IN WASHINGTON

Local Washington parks had been generously provided in the L'Enfant plan but the 1893 Highway Plan had made few such allowances. In its 1927 *Annual Report*, the National Capital Park and Planning Commission predicted that the intensification of urbanization across the District—by both the automobile and residential development—would erase the "many vacant lots and unused open spaces in private ownership [which] provided amply for such physical exercise as was needed by the young people." Recreational facilities inaugurated by the Army Corps of Engineers were often in the monumental core and inconvenient to much of the expanding population. Taking a leaf from sociologist Philip Archibald Parsons, the report predicted that lack of properly supervised recreational facilities within neighborhoods might be expected to increase the tendencies of children toward delinquency. Therefore, the Planning Commission in 1927 recommended that between ten and twenty small residential parks be provided. Olmsted and Eliot changed the recreational center to a neighborhood center concept by insisting on the simultaneous location of library and school buildings in one place. With such a cluster, children and adults would be brought together and the family unit thus strengthened. Community life

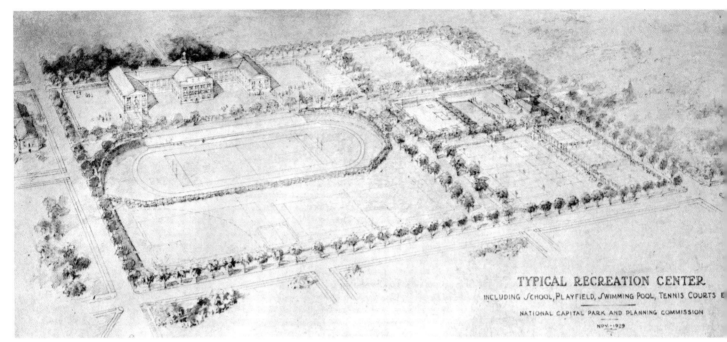

Plan for a Typical Recreation Center, 1929

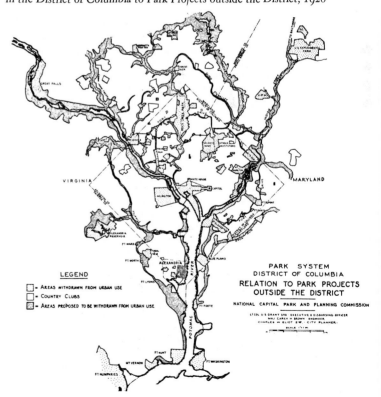

Plan of Regional Park Projects, Showing Relation of the Park System in the District of Columbia to Park Projects outside the District, 1926

would also be benefited by the attraction of entire families to a common focus. Olmsted saw the creation of "simple, carefully planned and systematically managed recreation units" as an efficient and economical way to obtain desirable physical planning and social results.

The Planning Commission proposed that the centers be situated so that residents of any neighborhood would not be more than a quarter of a mile from a center. As the physical city had already engulfed much of the land bordering the old L'Enfant city, the commission considered demolition of existing buildings to make way for the centers. In the following year, the commission drew up a map displaying natural and man-made boundaries and thus designated the physical and social neighborhoods that were to be served by neighborhood centers. In order to provide the combination of educational and recreational facilities, the plans of the commission were coordinated with those of the District for new public schools and branch libraries, as well as with the provision of public utilities. The Depression eclipsed this energetic planning for the constituent city, however, and only three centers were constructed: the Banneker Recreation Center near Howard University, the

Eckington Center, and the McKinley Center. Centers were later constructed at the Wilson, Coolidge, Taft, and Spingarn-Phelps schools, some in conjunction with the National Capital Parks System, as at Fort Reno. Still later, the combined educational/recreation center would become the mainstay of the 1960s comprehensive planning.

Washington's approach to neighborhood recreation showed more than flexibility in reinterpreting the city's notable park tradition. Washington planning clearly was in step with developments in other cities and in step also with the times. The most notable exposition of the neighborhood unit in city planning was just being put forward by Clarence Arthur Perry in his part of the Regional Plan of New York and Its Environs. While Washington had not embraced Perry's philosophy of housing, it articulated more clearly—and in advance of Perry's exposition—the underlying social theory and provided a concrete expression suited to the existing rather than the redeveloped city.

The Self-Contained Proposal for Georgetown. The emphasis on recreational and physical construction may have obscured the social goals intended by Olmsted and Eliot in the strengthened communities they anticipated. In fact, a neighborhood center alone could not spontaneously stimulate community consciousness. In epitomizing Georgetown as a potential self-contained community, Eliot stated that more was at stake than leisure-time activities. Both neighborhood residents and outsiders had to see the area as a community. The 1933 Allied Architects study made by Horace Peaslee had suggested that future plans focus on Georgetown's uniqueness, its distinctiveness from any other part of the city. Specifically, Georgetown enjoyed a distinctive architecture which by the 1930s coincided with the vogue for colonial and early Federal-style houses. The old port city was surrounded on all sides by open space and the Potomac River. In order to enforce this self-contained identity, the study recommended that principal traffic arteries and other barriers be confined to the outskirts of the community. Peaslee suggested that traffic from the north, from the newer developments of Burleith and Foxhall Village, should bypass Georgetown via R

Street. Traffic from the south should be funneled on a proposed road on the old Chesapeake & Ohio Canal bed or else connected with R Street by a road from Key Bridge. Not only would these proposed traffic routes help outsiders bypass Georgetown on their way to the monumental core but, when joined with natural barriers such as parkland and waterways, they would also symbolically bind the self-contained community to the "larger fabric of the whole city."

FUNDING THE PARKLAND SYSTEM PLANS FOR WASHINGTON

Development of the larger citywide and regional parks was still severely hampered by low funding for the intended vast acquisitions. The funding of $1,200,000 over two fiscal years was inadequate to preserve land being rapidly eaten away by development. Nevertheless, the Planning Commission continued to entertain hopes that private citizens would donate land or funds for these acquisitions. After all, national interest in the capital city's appearance had been important in creating the commission itself. In the acquisition of parkland as outlined in the 1926 act, especially additions to Rock Creek Park, the commission suggested that in the case of Piney Branch valley a group of private citizens raise the funds. The land could be bought and donated immediately to the city or else held until the commission received sufficient appropriations to purchase the protected land. In this way, the commission reasoned (as its Minutes for December 1926 reveal), the nation could participate in development of the national capital, as the citizens "are all interested in their Government in some way or other." In November 1926, Stephen T. Mather, director of the National Park Service and member of the National Capital Park and Planning Commission, offered to use his "connections with wealthy people" to urge them to purchase parklands. In favoring such arrangements, the commission resolved that it could not under the law bind itself to purchase the tracts, but that future acquisition by the commission would be considered.

FORT DRIVE: AN UNFULFILLED PASSION

The parkland system outlined by Olmsted and Eliot followed closely the 1901–1902 McMillan Commission plan, although neglect of the park proposals had wiped out chances for realizing the vast park schemes, especially within the District. The attention of the Planning Commission and lawmakers focused on the proposed park strip of Fort Drive and the George Washington Memorial Parkway from Great Falls to Mount Vernon. The projected program was progressive by comparison with the new parkways of the New York metropolitan area and Connecticut, and in design looked even further ahead. The concept of a parkway to link the ring of

Civil War forts into a pleasure drive of natural and historical interest—this a proposal of 1901—took on added importance in light of highway planner Harland Bartholomew's emphasis on bypass and belt roads to prevent congestion of the monumental core. In the commission's study of historical points of interest, the Civil War forts ranked high.

Throughout the early years of the National Capital Park and Planning Commission, requests for funds to realize Fort Drive as a "single and unified project"

General Plan for Fort Drive Parkway Connecting the Civil War Forts Encircling the City of Washington, 1930s

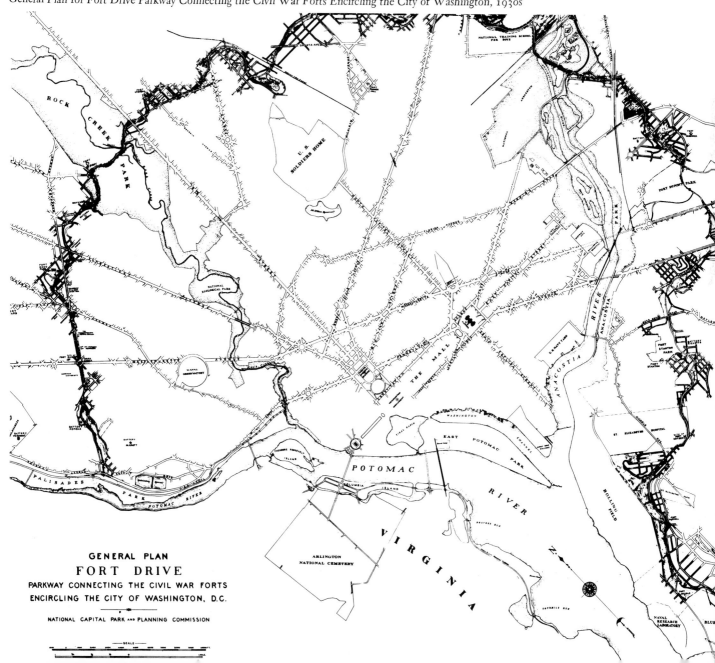

GENERAL PLAN
FORT DRIVE
PARKWAY CONNECTING THE CIVIL WAR FORTS
ENCIRCLING THE CITY OF WASHINGTON, D.C.

NATIONAL CAPITAL PARK AND PLANNING COMMISSION

never captured the imagination of Congress. By 1926, the land required for the drive lay too close to the built-up city, so that the cost of this land would be much inflated over possible parkland farther out. Additional inertia in realizing the Fort Drive dream may be attributed to the circular drive's being unique to Washington and not an element of City Beautiful prescriptions. In the next forty years of readjusting McMillan park proposals, planning issues related to the city's fort system gradually shifted away from circulation to open space and recreational uses extending through residential neighborhoods. The individual sites were fine enough, high, cool, airy, commanding impressive views, but they were also related visually and physically to each other and to the central city. To implement the proposal after 1926, however, most of the sites still had to be purchased. Although the forts themselves were already partially connected, in many cases by old military roads incorporated in the official street plan, it was suggested that a unifying drive would greatly increase accessibility. In addition to scenic and recreational value, the forts had historic associations reinforced in some cases by surviving earthworks, rifle pits, and other structures; as late as 1920, the forts were still fruitful locales for surface archaeology, yielding military buttons, buckles, and other wartime trophies. Above all, it was the topographical value of the forts that was most esteemed: that they ringed the city, defined its rim of surrounding hills, and (before trees had grown again over the cleared lines of fire) offered such superb views of the city itself, the broad and gleaming Potomac, and the surrounding metropolitan landscape. Yet, however reinterpreted, even as a circumferential highway, the Fort Drive failed to win sufficient support to be realized.

GRAND APPROACHES: MOUNT VERNON PARKWAY

Construction of a Mount Vernon Parkway also had been one of the recommendations of the 1901–1902 McMillan Commission. This entrance to the capital in the form of a parkway connection between George Washington's home and the city was intended as a combination of utilitarian highway between north and south and an aesthetic creation. In 1926, the Bureau of Public Roads had already surveyed the area and planned the landscape treatment. It was hoped that financial backing for the nearly fourteen miles of proposed road would come in part from private contributions for a memorial to commemorate the upcoming Washington Bicentennial in 1932. During congressional hearings in 1924, the celebration was viewed as a "world event," of enough importance to justify public expenditures. Chief of the Bureau of Public Roads Thomas H. MacDonald in 1926 voiced the disappointment many Americans probably felt upon leaving the capital city for Mount Vernon. MacDonald viewed it as a "disgrace to allow the large numbers of people who annually come here from all over the world to visit this national shrine to be dumped into the mud at the entrance gate [to Mount Vernon] in the way that they now are." In regard to the Washington terminus of the parkway, in 1928 Milton Medary, the architect and member of the Planning Commission, criticized the appearance of the southern approach to the city: "Those of you who came from the south passed four or five miles of railroad yards and rubbish heaps." Mount Vernon Parkway, to be constructed close to the river, would pass important historical sites and the historic city of Alexandria, an emotional experience that some congressmen argued would transform visitors into better Americans. Plantings for the entire stretch were to follow the same general plan used in Arlington National Cemetery near the parkway's Washington terminus and in Potomac Park across the river.

Extension of the landscaped parkway concept to other major land approaches was suggested in 1928 by Medary who admired the scenic views in the approach to the city "over the Virginia hills where you find at the brow of those hills, suddenly and dramatically at your feet, the whole city of Washington across the Potomac." Thus, he also spoke highly of the approach to Washington from Baltimore by way of the Anacostia valley, or from the north down Sixteenth Street or through Rock Creek Parkway, or from the west by Great Falls. Unfortunately, development of the proposed Mount Vernon Parkway—as well as other city parkway approaches—had to await future definitive congressional action.

THE POTOMAC PALISADES PARKWAY PROPOSAL

As early as 1926, Eliot had studied potential parkland in

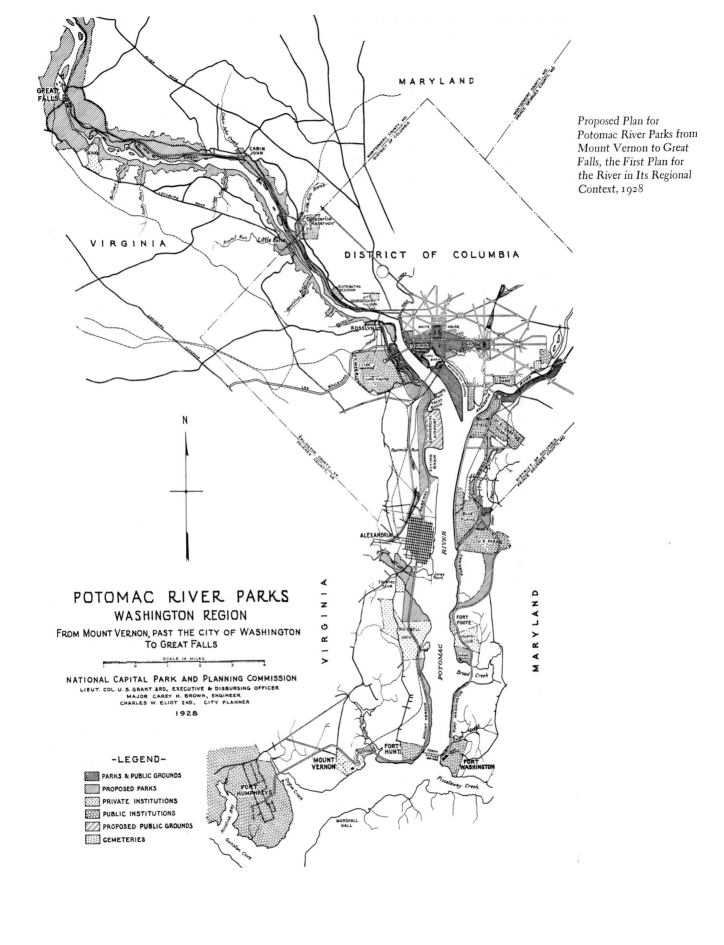

Proposed Plan for Potomac River Parks from Mount Vernon to Great Falls, the First Plan for the River in Its Regional Context, 1928

the rugged topography west of Rock Creek Park, and recommended a drive along the length of the Potomac Palisades. East of Rock Creek Park, he reviewed the new bridge proposed between South Capitol Street and the rural shore of Anacostia, predicting that the "route into Maryland through the now blighted area of the south-west would have an important influence toward rehabilitation and effectively utilizing an area very near the heart of the city." Looking over the river to Anacostia and its sweeping views of Washington, Eliot suggested a parkway along the ridge between Oxon Run and the Eastern Branch. One year later, Eliot spoke of the desirability of creating a riverside drive from Potomac Avenue in Georgetown extended out to the District line. To duplicate the proposed Mount Vernon Parkway on the Virginia shore, and serve as a southern extension through Prince George's County of the proposed Potomac Palisades Parkway, Eliot suggested that a similar parkway on the Maryland side "should someday extend to Fort Washington so as to form a circuit drive 29 miles in length down the Virginia shore to Mount Vernon, across the river by ferry to Fort Washington, and back to Washington on the Maryland side."

THE CAPPER-CRAMTON ACT OF 1930

The enlarged visions of regional parkways now espoused by the Planning Commission required a dramatic increase in funding. In 1930, a bill sponsored by House and Senate District Committee chairmen, Louis C. Cramton and Arthur Capper, was passed authorizing $16,000,000 in the District alone to be used for parkland acquisition. The Capper-Cramton Act, a legislative gesture of support for the Planning Commission, provided an opportunity for the commission to show concrete results of its work program. The act also served as model for similar grant programs later instituted in other parts of the country.

THE GEORGE WASHINGTON MEMORIAL PARKWAY

The Capper-Cramton Act (46 Stat. 482) provided land acquisition funds for the regional George Washington Memorial Parkway along both sides of the Potomac, on the Virginia side from Mount Vernon north to Great Falls and then south again on the Maryland side to Fort Washington. For the land in Virginia and Maryland required for the parkway, both states were required to commit one-half the cost, either directly or through eight-year no-interest federal loans. The route of the George Washington Memorial Parkway ran through many reservations already owned by the government; nevertheless, massive coordinating efforts with the several federal agencies with interests along the route were required. In addition, the state agencies needed to be consulted about acquiring rights of way and making direct purchases of land. Some of the land, however, was to remain in private hands with restrictions placed on development.

Commercial development along the route was discouraged, except in those areas of Alexandria traversed by the parkway. Passage of the Capper-Cramton Act had been accomplished despite impending development of a power plant at Great Falls and the option taken by the Sun Oil Company on land above Key Bridge for a pier and oil tank farm. In the late 1920s the Potomac Electric Power Company was in the process of negotiating with the local United States District Engineer, Major Brehon B. Somervell, to develop a power plant at Great Falls. All members of the Planning Commission, save Major General Edgar Jadwin of the Army Corps of Engineers, vigorously urged retention of Great Falls for a park, defending what had been proposed in the McMillan Commission report. Although the power company had presented a "combination park and power scheme," the Planning Commission (in its *Annual Report* for 1929) argued that incidental creation of a park on the margins of the public utility development "would be a totally different kind of park from the natural valley." Reminding its constituency of the unique scenic and historic qualities of the gorge, the Planning Commission concluded that it was "inadvisable to decide now upon the destruction for all time of the scenic and recreational and inspirational assets of such large prospective importance as those included in the Valley of the Potomac at the doors of the National Capital." The impending Sun Oil Company tank farm brought up the question of future use of the Rosslyn waterfront, now in its declining years. Although many Virginians favored creation of the landscaped parkway and aggran-

Construction along the Mount Vernon Parkway Section of the George Washington Memorial Parkway, 1931

dized bridgeheads as portals to the city in the automobile age, local Rosslyn businessmen protested against the park development.

On the other side, several national organizations supported commission proposals for the parkway. In addition to providing general support, the American Engineering Council offered to preserve the locks and other works of the Potomac Company at Great Falls as part of a "Washington engineer memorial parkway." The American Society of Landscape Architects proposed that a portion of the river park be dedicated to Frederick Law Olmsted, Sr. The Theodore Roosevelt Memorial Association purchased Analostan Island with the intention of retaining it in its sylvan state as a tribute to Roosevelt's interest in conservation. The George Washington Memorial Parkway's future was further secured by the organization of a George Washington Memorial Parkway fund for collecting monies to match federal grants

Rendering of the Proposed Hydroelectric Power Development at Great Falls, 1929

provided by the Capper-Cramton Act.

THE FOREST BETWEEN WASHINGTON AND BALTIMORE

The City Beautiful preoccupation with landscaped entrances extended to the main route between Washington and its regional urban neighbor, Baltimore. Such an entrance from the north to the capital city had long been an interest of various members of the Commission of Fine Arts and other residents and politicians. In 1931, the Planning Commission, with the cooperation of the American Planning and Civic Association, the National Council for Protection of Roadside Beauty, and the American Nature Association, surveyed the appearance of major entrances to the city. Along the notorious U.S. 1 highway connecting Washington and Baltimore, surveyors counted 1,099 signboards. Implementation of proposals for the entrance lagged over the years because, as the Planning Commission noted in its Min-

utes for June 1933, Maryland officials had "never been warm toward the idea of the Government buying land in the State." In that same year, however, the United States Department of Agriculture's Forest Service received an emergency fund of 20 million dollars to purchase forest lands. The Planning Commission suggested that a forest be established "adjoining the fall line" between Baltimore and Washington. Acquisition of forest lands in this important location was accomplished through use of these emergency funds. This strategic landscape connecting the Piedmont Plateau and the coastal plain would serve as a "sample plot at the door of the National Capital" to teach congressmen and the public about the Department of Agriculture's Forest Service activities. It was envisioned that such a forest would serve the recreational needs of a vast region and secure future sites for expanding Washington's water supply. The Planning Commission cited the beautiful municipal forests adjoining old German cities that "gave a marvelous setting for such cities compared with the usual unkempt surroundings of American cities. There is a large field for the development of the city forest idea in America, and the establishment of such a forest here at the gateway to Washington would dramatize the whole idea."

Public Buildings: Location, Design, and Concentration

In 1930, the Shipstead-Luce Act was passed providing for the Commission of Fine Arts to review building permits for new construction adjacent to or abutting existing or proposed public buildings and parks to insure that there would not be a negative effect on these public properties. The area defined for such review covered the whole of Rock Creek Park in the District; the Potomac Parkway; and the monumental core of Mall, White House, and Capitol. The scope of review embraced the new buildings' "height and appearance, color and texture of the materials of exterior construction." The act affected all residences constructed in view of Rock Creek Park. With later expansion of federal government facilities, the geographic boundaries of Shipstead-Luce Act

Entrances and Approaches to Washington, 1930

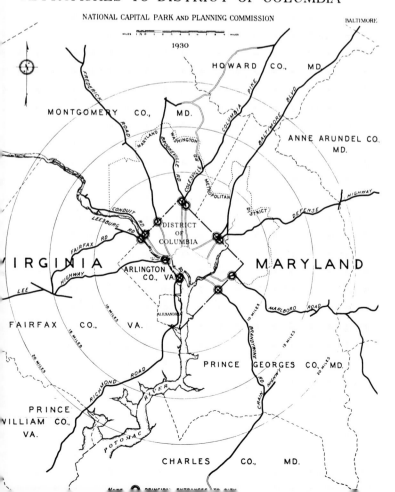

 APPROACHES TO DISTRICT OF COLUMBIA

NATIONAL CAPITAL PARK AND PLANNING COMMISSION

1930

jurisdiction were partially expanded, but were not adjusted to account for the location of all new government facilities developed during the next three decades.

THE HORIZONTAL CITY

Perpetuation of the horizontal city was supported by the conviction, expressed in the 1928 *Annual Report of the National Capital Park and Planning Commission*, that "the dominance of the Capitol, both real and apparent, over the Federal City should not be destroyed." Zoning provided for specified height limitations which were varied according to locations of buildings. In 1929, the Planning Commission acknowledged nationwide trends toward increased heights of buildings but rejected such an increase in Washington not only for aesthetic and symbolic reasons, but because of congestion problems anticipated as a result of more intensive use of land. The increasing trend toward dispersal of new low-rise public and private buildings throughout the District and the region was strengthened by building height limits, which tended to produce lower-density development. In addition, as the *Annual Report* pointed out, "before the telephone, the trolley, the autobus, and the automobile, when communication and transportation were slow and laborious, there may have been an economic advantage in bringing all kinds of business into a small area. This is no longer the case."

The Central Urban Core and Alternatives to Concentration. The location of public buildings in Washington involved a fundamental decision on the shape and functions of the central urban core. In the initial difficulties of moving and parking automobiles in the central area, and the conspicuous failure of the Federal Triangle to deal with such elements of congestion, the problems of concentrated federal buildings were clearly posed. The alternatives to concentration were either modest decentralization to the edges of the downtown federal core, or more drastic dispersal to the urban fringe. To those who saw the center of Washington as the Capitol, it was an attractive possibility that federal establishments could be encouraged to locate east and north of that point. To those who saw the center of the city as the White House, development had to be west and north. Between the two key points lay the Federal Tri-

angle and the congestion it had produced. For these reasons the struggle between opposing viewpoints on the location of federal buildings focused on the areas west of the White House and east of the Capitol.

ECHOES OF THE MC MILLAN PLAN: THE WASHINGTON AND JEFFERSON MEMORIALS

It is a paradox that while the McMillan Commission's recommendations for the location of public buildings and features such as bridges and parklands generally succeeded, its most painstaking and elaborate proposal—for the Washington Monument grounds—in the end failed. As described earlier, this design proposal was intended to reconcile the relocated Washington Monument with the geometry of L'Enfant by a series of terraced parks and ornamental bodies of water. Engineering technology and cost were the most commonly given reasons for failure of the proposal. It is likely, however, that changing architectural taste and altered convictions concerning design precision were contributing factors. But more significant is the subtle indication that the heart had gone out of the McMillan plan even as it had out of the City Beautiful movement. Echoes of the 1901–1902 plan were apparent in the approved 1938 plan for location and design of the Jefferson Memorial, but essentially the architectural elaboration of the McMillan designers was set aside—although the problems of axial relationships and sight lines which it hoped to resolve continued as a factor in subsequent building and park plans.

THE EAST CAPITOL STREET CORRIDOR

As a result of continuing concern for balance and sight lines, the Planning Commission envisioned a lineal development of public and semipublic buildings along East Capitol Street terminating in a sports center facing the Anacostia River. Also called the "Avenue of the States" because of plans for new structures to house exhibits and information centers for each sovereign state or groups of states, the East Capitol Street corridor was to relieve traffic congestion west of the Capitol, a problem heightened by construction of the Federal Triangle. The plan also physically strengthened the corridor which was designed by L'Enfant to be the major commercial strip of the city. By the late 1920s, when the

Planning Commission was first considering areas appropriate for possible public buildings sites, the Capitol Hill neighborhood, with row on row of Victorian houses, appeared deteriorated. Just as development of the Federal Triangle had served to eliminate another blighted urban area, so the planning for East Capitol Street aimed to replace the worst of the slums by modern office buildings, to start similar upgrading of the immediately adjacent neighborhood, and to develop new centers on the Anacostia. Over the next three decades, several design proposals were cast for East Capitol Street, since many of the new buildings proposed for location along this street required new studies and design proposals of the over-all route. These design proposals became more graphically detailed in 1941 with the Downer-Clarke Plan for the Federal Works Agency. In contrast to the tightly knit consistency of the Federal Triangle, however, the East Capitol Street "mall" always exhibited highly individual buildings surrounded by ample green spaces. Neither the mall's hoped for civic features nor the planned interaction with adjacent residential areas ever took hold. Many, indeed, felt the decades' long threat of land acquisition for development of new public facilities encouraged further deterioration of neighborhoods such as Capitol Hill.

CONCENTRATION VERSUS DISPERSAL

The conflict between concentration and dispersal of public buildings was not new. Dispersal already existed, as witness the far-flung military reservations, federal bureaus such as the Bureau of Standards and agricultural research stations in the suburbs, and the Walter Reed Army Medical Center. The logical location of these dispersed facilities served as magnets for development of other new public buildings. In 1931, the Planning Commission—as its *Annual Report* for that year shows—requested the Public Buildings Commission to study which federal bureaus could be located on sites other

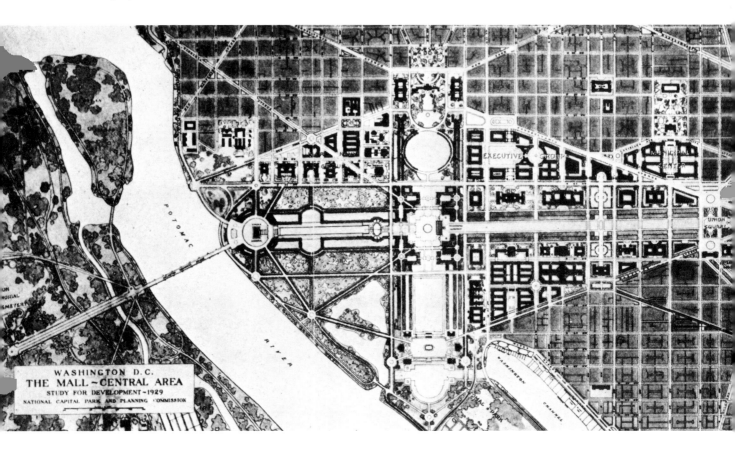

WASHINGTON D.C.
THE MALL ~ CENTRAL AREA
STUDY FOR DEVELOPMENT ~ 1929
NATIONAL CAPITAL PARK AND PLANNING COMMISSION

than in the central area, "without impairment of or with improvement in the efficiency of the Government work involved." The concentration of public buildings in the monumental core, as accomplished by construction of the Federal Triangle and the Legislative Group, met aesthetic standards for higher-density development and defined the federal presence for visitors and residents alike. Architects, planners, and politicians also argued that concentration promoted efficiency in cooperation, coordination, and communication; although the newly undergrounded telephone wires could tie bureaus together, much business still had to be conducted on a face-to-face basis. (But no one proposed as precedent that uniquely convenient facility, the Capitol subway.) It was argued, moreover, that visitors and businessmen would have difficulty enough in finding their way through different government agencies in proximity to one another, let alone between far-flung offices.

THE NORTHWEST RECTANGLE

Chief among the departments in need of new accommodations were the War and Navy Departments. The intended large massing of buildings for these agencies would have a significant impact on the monumental core. The Commission of Fine Arts favored the new buildings site to be along the ridge paralleling Pennsylvania Avenue west of the White House. Alternatively, the Treasury Department Board of Architectural Consultants headed by Edward Bennett suggested the Independence Avenue areas just southwest of the Capitol, facing across the Mall to the planned Municipal Center at Judiciary Square. As another possibility, the Northwest Rectangle—defined by the Mall on the south, E Street on the north, between Seventeenth Street and the Naval Hospital grounds facing Twenty-third Street —offered little-developed but distinctive sites overlooking Potomac Park and the new Lincoln Memorial. Seek-

sted Eastward Prolongation of the Mall and Development of East Capitol Street as the Avenue of the States with a Stadium at Anacostia Park, 1929

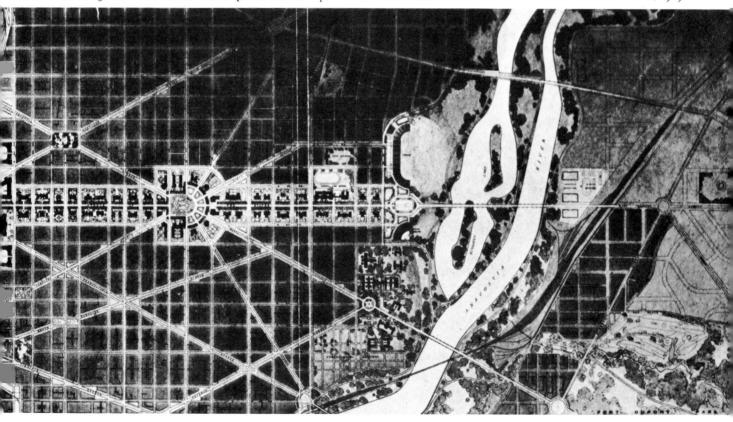

Model of the Building (Now Occupied by the State Department) Intended for the War Department, in the Northwest Rectangle, 1930s

Site Plan for the Proposed Northwest Rectangle Public Buildings Group, 1934

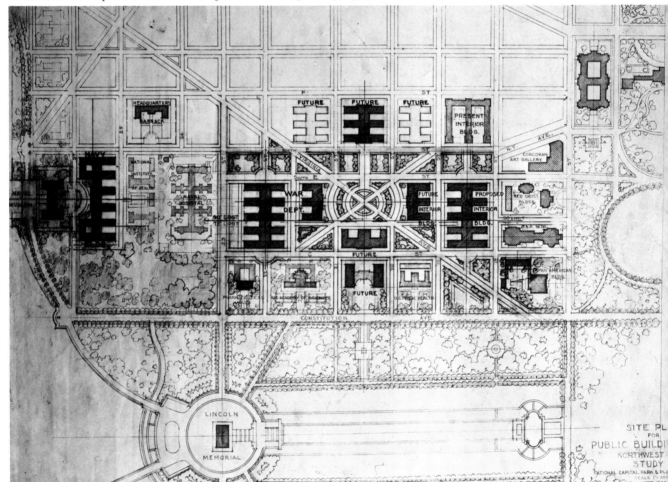

ing relocation from its massive concrete tempos along the reflecting pool, the Navy Department was interested in the historic site of old Observatory Hill (above the equally historic "Key of Keys") with its appropriate marine environment along the Potomac.

The 1901–1902 McMillan Commission report and the National Capital Park and Planning Commission in its *Annual Report* for 1928 had stressed the importance of the Mall and the White House as the foci of future public buildings. In 1931, the Planning Commission altered its earlier emphasis by agreeing with the Navy Department and recommending the Northwest Rectangle for the site of the War and Navy Departments. This break with the past reflected the commission's claim that it was "looking many years into the future" in planning for buildings of a permanent character that might well house different departments in generations ahead, an idea later embraced by public buildings officials. Duplicating the planning for the Federal Triangle, the Planning Commission, in its *Annual Report* for 1931, recommended that "all the permanent buildings existing and proposed in the northwest building area should be regarded as part of a single related group insofar as the varied character of the existing buildings to be retained will permit." These extant buildings included the semipublic buildings facing the Mall and the Interior Department Building (now the General Services Administration Building). The height and style of the new buildings close to the Mall were to be harmonious with the Lincoln Memorial, it was recommended. Now that the Planning Commission had the power under the Shipstead-Luce Act to influence planning in the Rectangle, it requested that the new group be "self-contained as to parking . . . and that parking be prohibited outside of buildings." In order to coordinate plans for the Northwest Rectangle, the Planning Commission organized a northwest building committee to agree on "basic principles governing the design of the area, including such items as building lines, heights, materials, and location of axes."

PROPOSED PUBLIC BUILDING SITES

In rejecting the Commission of Fine Arts' suggestion of Pennsylvania Avenue west of the White House as a public buildings site, the Planning Commission in its 1931 *Annual Report* stated that the Commission of Fine Arts, traditionally assigned the task of protecting the McMillan plan, was digressing "from and to some extent violat[ing] the principles of the L'Enfant and McMillan plans." Additional investment in the Northwest sector, beyond that proposed for the Northwest Rectangle, would reinforce the tendency toward unbalanced development of the city toward the northwest. "From the larger standpoint of regional and city planning any such stimulus would be hurtful rather than helpful to the development of a balanced, efficient, and well-coordinated national capital." The Planning Commission had already considered sites along East Capitol Street between the Capitol and the Anacostia River. Although accusing the Commission of Fine Arts of deviating from the McMillan plan, the Planning Commission nearly followed suit in questioning the need for the Executive Group around the White House, this an important recommendation of the McMillan plan. The Planning Commission noted that the Agriculture Department on the Mall appeared to function satisfactorily. Fearing that a White House Executive Group would again increase the northwest emphasis of the city, the Planning Commission wobbled on its commitment to concentrated clusters in stating in the same breath that the "commission sees a real menace to the future of the city if all Government activities are packed very closely together. It would be a great mistake to emphasize the trend to the northwest, ignoring the splendid possibilities to the east and northeast."

THE WORK OF REPRESENTATIVE LOUIS C. CRAMTON

When forced to reconcile differences in the public architecture persuasions of various individuals and agencies, some planners of the city may have agreed with Representative Louis Cramton that "artificial beauties such as monuments, boulevards, and pretentious buildings, if they are not built this year, they can be built next year or twenty years from now." Cramton was more interested in the natural beauties of Washington, beauties that "if not now [in 1929] preserved . . . cannot be restored later." An ideal ex officio member of the National Capital Park and Planning Commission, Cramton displayed an unusual interest in the city, owning a large library of Washington-related books, walking the streets and roads of the city, and faithfully attending Planning Commission meetings. With such a formidable knowledge of the city and its unique physical attributes, much beyond the scope of many residents, Representative Cramton, as chairman of the House Committee on the District of Columbia, was able to overcome the shortsighted opposition of power and energy development interests and secure passage of the Capper-Cramton Act. The act was jointly sponsored by Senator Arthur Capper, chairman of the Senate Committee on the District of Columbia, whose interest in Washington, however, was less pronounced than that of Cramton.

Regional Planning and Cooperation

The primary legacy of Cramton's legislative efforts on the city of Washington's behalf was the creation of the George Washington Memorial Parkway. The Capper-Cramton Act also provided $1,500,000 in funds for extension of Rock Creek Park into Maryland and extension of the Anacostia Park System further up the valley of the Anacostia River. In this act, Washington finally possessed the makings of a truly regional park system, and at the same time had an important opportunity for demonstrating cooperation among the National Capital Park and Planning Commission and the Virginia and Maryland planning agencies.

Since the National Capital Park and Planning Commission's approval authority did not extend beyond the District line, the future of commission plans for the regional city lay in its ability to influence through planning policy recommendations and by coordinating with planning agencies in Virginia and Maryland. The Planning Commission believed that its plans were appropriate guidelines for the surrounding counties because, as it stated in its 1931 *Annual Report,* the "region must be responsive to the influences of the dominant center."

EXPANSION INTO THE OLD DOMINION

The state of Virginia created the Virginia Park and Planning Commission, but its lack of authority through-

out the 1930s hampered any effective regional participation. It was in 1930 that the Virginia legislature set up a planning commission "with authority to make plans for a district including Alexandria, Arlington County, and all or parts of Fairfax County." The acceptance of the act hinged on the agreement by two of the three jurisdictions named, but as of 1932, no acceptance by any of them was actually at hand. In the absence of a concerted Virginia voice, therefore, the Planning Commission dealt with the jurisdictions separately, noting the zoning ordinances adopted by Arlington County and the City of Alexandria and the comprehensive city plan under consideration by the Alexandria City Council.

PLANNING FUNCTIONS IN MARYLAND

Some early planning powers in Maryland had been exercised by the Washington Suburban Sanitary Commission. Created in 1916, this commission controlled and operated the water and sewer system, approved plats of subdivisions, established street grades, and surveyed and platted future subdivisions. By the 1920s, the Washington Suburban Sanitary Commission was also considering preparing a highway and park plan. When rumblings of a suburban planning commission were heard, several members of the Sanitary Commission argued that their commission ought to be given the larger planning powers.

In 1927, however, the Maryland–National Capital Park and Planning Commission, representing portions of Montgomery and Prince George's Counties, was created. The local leadership in Montgomery County was well exercised by E. Brooke Lee, speaker of the Annapolis House of Delegates. Lee secured House support for the planning act through the "courtesy system" by which bills of a local nature could be passed if they had support of the local delegation. The movement for planning in the counties had been largely stimulated by the establishment in 1926 of the National Capital Park and Planning Commission, which in its organizing act was instructed to cooperate with local planning agencies. None of these existed at that time, but they soon appeared. Lee, a hereditary power and large landowner in Montgomery County, saw support for planning as stemming from educated people living on the edge of the national capital and from those who ran the national government downtown and wanted to improve county conditions. Lee worked to cement these interests at community meetings and at dinners at the old City Club on G Street, across from the Epiphany Church. Key members and staff of the Planning Commission attended these functions, explaining the work of the national commission to the suburbanites.

THE MARYLAND–NATIONAL CAPITAL PARK AND
PLANNING COMMISSION

It was in 1927, then, that the Maryland legislature passed legislation providing for a district containing the two counties contiguous to the District of Columbia. The Maryland–National Capital Park and Planning Commission was established with authority in this district to plan, to acquire land in the public interest, to levy taxes to pay for park acquisitions, and to draw up zoning ordinances. Important especially in the post–World War II dispersal of federal agencies, the Maryland–National Capital Park and Planning Commission was given an advisory role in the location of public buildings. The area initially covered by the Maryland commission consisted of 141 square miles in the southern portions of Prince George's and Montgomery Counties closest to the District of Columbia, and embraced twenty-seven incorporated towns and villages. With six appointed members, the commission included three from each county, appointed by the governor and approved by the respective boards of county commissioners. The chairman of the Washington Suburban Sanitary Commission was an ex officio member, providing continuity with the past and the possibility of over-all plan coordination with sewer and water plans.

Even though the Maryland–National Capital Park and Planning Commission was set up as a joint effort of two counties, in reality the past and present needs of the two counties were very different. Montgomery County was the more affluent of the two counties, with a topography of rolling hills and rich soils. Its location was conducive to high-value real estate developments. Montgomery County residents proved willing to be taxed to support a county park system. Prince George's County was characterized, especially along the highway between Wash-

ington and Baltimore, by old tobacco farms and new industrial development, functions unattractive to high-cost housing. As a less affluent county, it did not enact any park legislation or a tax for such amenities for many years.

The relationship between the National Capital Park and Planning Commission and the Maryland–National Capital Park and Planning Commission was one that saw suburban planners identifying with the aspirations set forth by the federal commission. This relationship between the suburbs and the city was characterized by the similarity in the name selected by the Maryland commission. Also symbolic of this identification with the regional goals set by the federal Planning Commission, the 1927 law directed the Maryland commission to maintain offices in the District of Columbia as well as in the two counties.

The Work of Irving R. Root. Attracted to the national capital, Harvard-educated Irving R. Root joined the Maryland–National Capital Park and Planning Commission as the commission's first planner and engineer. Root, a city planner of high caliber in the landscape architect tradition, was from Flint, Michigan. At the commission he was instructed to prepare a Comprehensive Plan for the two counties. Root maintained a close relationship with the National Capital Park and Planning Commission, and as Charles Eliot described the situation in 1928, "their engineer [Root] is in our office every week and is thoroughly conversant with [our] plans."

Later on, amendments to the 1927 act added more detailed transportation planning responsibilities to the Maryland commission. In drawing up a highway plan, Root retraced the major thoroughfares of radial and connecting highways outlined by Harland Bartholomew. Many of these highways were not built in the 1930s, but their location on the Maryland commission's plans insured their retention for future consideration. Progress was made in the construction of a highway connecting Bethesda and Silver Spring (East-West Highway). Plans were underway also for linking Silver Spring and Sixteenth Street, paving the Rockville–Potomac–Great Falls Road, and improving River Road to connect with

Massachusetts Avenue (later with Wisconsin Avenue as well). Highways planned and constructed provided visible signs of public improvements that assured residents of the counties that the Maryland commission was producing vital public works and thus justified its planning powers.

CAPPER-CRAMTON ACT BENEFITS TO MARYLAND

The Maryland commission, like the National Capital Park and Planning Commission, was strengthened by passage of the Capper-Cramton Act which provided for implementation of park plans. The tax base even in Montgomery County was very low, inadequate to purchase the massive park systems envisioned by the two planning commissions. Thus, financial aid provided by the Capper-Cramton Act was crucial. Chief among the benefits of the act was the extension of Rock Creek Park and its major stream valleys into Maryland "to

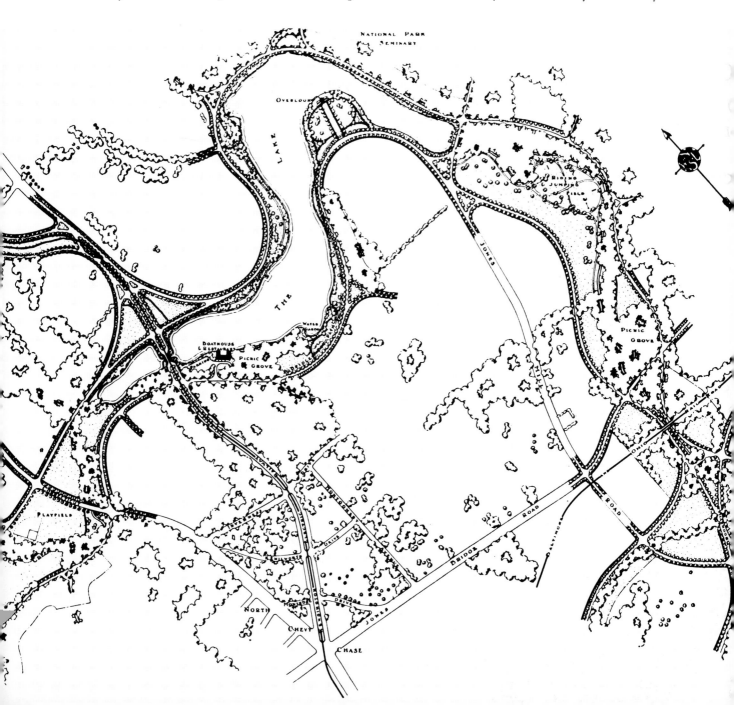

preserve the flow of water in Rock Creek." In 1929, Root and Roland W. Rogers, a landscape architect consultant at the Maryland commission, drew up a plan for Rock Creek Park in Maryland, in close consultation with the National Capital Park and Planning Commission. The thin ribbons of green commenced just southwest of the northern corner of the ten-mile square and followed the crooked route of Rock Creek northward, with some of the creek's tributaries encompassed as

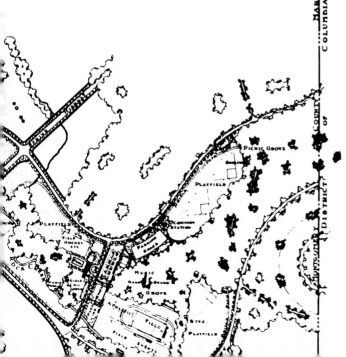

GENERAL DESIGN PLAN
CK CREEK PARK
ECTION FROM THE DISTRICT OF COLUMBIA
TO CONNECTICUT AVENUE
ONTGOMERY COUNTY-MARYLAND

SCALE OF FEET

0 100 250   500   750   1000   1250   1500   1750   2000

MARYLAND-NATIONAL CAPITAL
PARK AND PLANNING COMMISSION
IRVING C. ROOT   CHIEF ENGINEER
ROLAND W. ROGERS   LAND. ARCHT.
SILVER SPRING MARYLAND

1929

parklike appendages. Root's plan for Rock Creek provided a protected stream valley richly furnished with recreational facilities as well as dramatic overlooks, and a lake created in the broader stretches of the creek closest to the District line.

Plans for other regional parks in Maryland were implemented in the Capper-Cramton Act. Anacostia Park was extended northward, branching to the west in Sligo Creek Park. Other branches were extended to protect the minor stream valleys. To the east, Anacostia Park fed into what later became the massive Greenbelt Park and the Baltimore–Washington Parkway. The valleys of the Potomac River in Maryland were absorbed into Montgomery County's park system, including the valley of Cabin John Creek, which was an appendage of the George Washington Memorial Parkway. These thin slivers of protected parkland radiating from the District's parks followed the irregular routes determined by nature and provided a faint hint of the wedges of greenery that would be translated into the wedges and corridors plan of the 1960s.

The coordination of parks and highways between the District and the Maryland counties persuaded planning officials of the feasibility of regional planning. No official coordinating body existed. The success of cooperative public improvements depended instead on the willingness of the District and Maryland planning agencies to pay attention to each other's plans.

REGIONAL COOPERATION ON WATER SUPPLY AND SEWAGE PROBLEMS

Regional cooperation was also evidenced in 1929 with the creation of the Washington Region Water Supply Committee formed by representatives from the Maryland–National Capital Park and Planning Commission, other Maryland agencies, Virginia agencies, District representatives, and the National Capital Park and Planning Commission. The committee was requested to advise the National Capital Park and Planning Commission on the adequacy of the present water supply and make recommendations on future sources of water. The 1929 sources of water—from Great Falls, from the Northwest Branch of the Anacostia River, and from Holmes Run in Virginia—were reported by the committee to be "lagging considerably behind the urban development of new areas." The committee report commented that "like highways, parks, and other elements of planning, water service plays a part in determining the direction of urban growth." The increased demand for water by cities and towns north of Washington, such as Cumberland, Martinsburg, and Hagerstown, diverted water from the Potomac above Great Falls and affected the supply available to the District. The committee considered several joint or independent arrangements for the District, Maryland, and Virginia, simultaneously studying possible water sources to be found in the Patuxent River and Seneca Creek in Maryland and the Occoquan Creek in Virginia. Although no decisions were made about permanent regional cooperation or new construction, in general the Maryland and District representatives on the Water Supply Committee favored separate action by different authorities whereas the Virginia representatives were in favor of continuing to depend on cooperating with the federal government and the District. (Arlington County and even the town of Falls Church received aqueduct water.) Articulation of the inclinations of the tripartite region and the areas intended to be developed was viewed by the committee as "important" in anticipating "an ultimate plan of development [of the water supply], which will include all the work done in the immediate future."

A similar representative regional committee was established in 1929 to report on drainage and sewerage problems. No sewage treatment plant existed in the region except for small facilities to serve Gaithersburg and Washington Grove. Thus, whether by direct discharge or by interceptor sewers, all sewage was discharged into the Potomac River or other streams. District Commissioner J. B. Gordon reported that the District was contemplating construction of a treatment plant at Blue Plains and had already acquired the property. When built, the Blue Plains Treatment Plant could service both the District and Maryland, but in 1929, the Maryland authorities were inclined to favor separate treatment plants on all streams then serving as discharge points for sewage. Even if the sewer system—complete with trunk lines, interceptors, and treatment plants— were accomplished, the committee anticipated persisting

problems of pollution. "The condition of the river is a matter of great economic interest to the shellfish industry as well as to the people of the Washington region," the committee reported. Pollution of the Potomac stemmed largely from overloaded sanitary sewers flowing into storm drains at high water, especially along Rock Creek. Planning for sewage influenced other elements in planning since, as the committee noted, construction of treatment plants in the region "would affect the proposals for parks along the Potomac River and smaller streams." Planning for parks was also affected by the open valley treatment adopted in Maryland and Virginia whereby strips of land along streams were secured to absorb and channel high waters during flood conditions. In the treatment of these flood plains as park areas, the states thus obtained both recreational and drainage advantages. The committee concluded its work recommending that the representative regional committee continue meeting to discuss regional sewage and drainage needs.

REGIONAL AND PROJECT PLANNING

The farseeing, wide-ranging studies produced by such representative committees and by the regional planning commissions represented a significant body of data on which the future of the region could be projected. Those who had worked earnestly for fulfillment of the McMillan Commission's recommendations could find concrete satisfaction in the massive George Washington Memorial Parkway, the preservation of Great Falls in its natural state, and the overriding emphasis on concentrated groupings of public buildings in the monumental core. Planning for the constituent city and for the region as a whole was also in full gear, with interest expressed in Washington community life—and in cooperation on resources, cutting across jurisdictional lines. This work was carried out in an atmosphere of high professionalism enhanced by substantial staff work and the support of key political figures.

Yet, the circumstances of decision-making by the National Capital Park and Planning Commission were still far from ideal. In its 1928 *Annual Report*, the commission admitted: "The most striking shortcomings of the situation at Washington as it begins to be studied closely

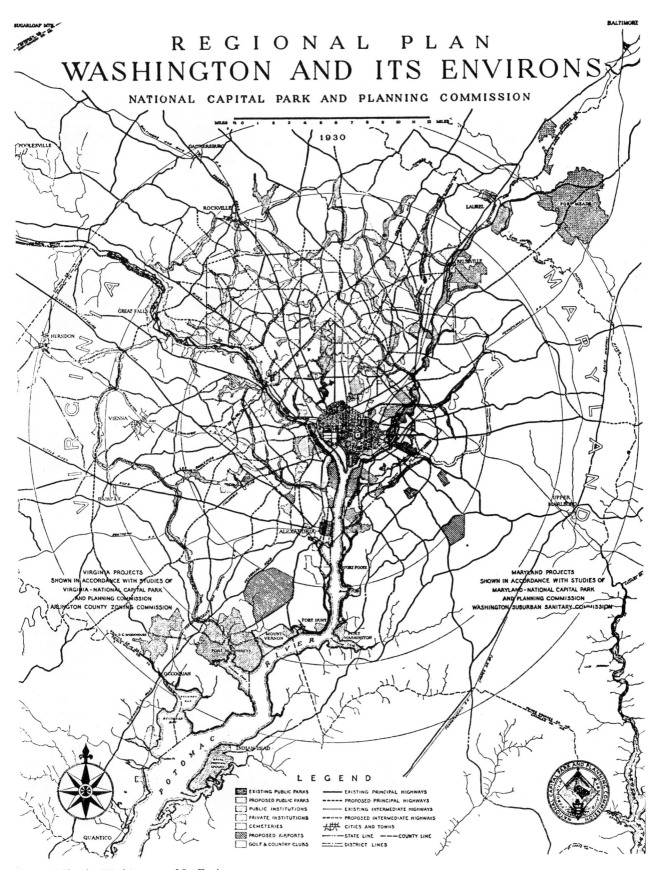

Regional Plan for Washington and Its Environs, 1930

Contemporary View of Fort Stevens Park at Thirteenth and Rittenhouse Streets, NW

are not in the quantity but in the quality of the planning that has been done in the past and is being done today." The tendency to make decisions of consequence based on brief studies was characteristic of "our hurried time." To be sure, the commission had produced many studies. The exigencies of project and specialized planning to deal with immediate problems, however, had forced the effort away from comprehensive and master planning and away from pursuing and updating basic studies. As for the cooperative committees representing agencies from the District, Maryland, and Virginia, this relationship was informal, not fixed by law, and not institutionalized in any single authority.

The buoyant early years of the National Capital Park and Planning Commission, strengthened by the land acquisition programs of the Capper-Cramton Act, were superseded by the Great Depression and its problems. Social issues such as unemployment had already brought Georgetown to the Planning Commission's agenda.

Planning for public improvements would now be abetted by public works programs rather than according to a Comprehensive Plan. Symbolic of this transition in the planning picture, Frederick Law Olmsted, Jr., retired from the commission in 1932, refusing a reappointment. Upon his leaving, the commission cited Olmsted for his "devoted and unselfish service to the cause of farsighted planning in Washington over more than 30 years, and [expressed the] hope that he will join the meetings of the Commission in the future as member 'emeritus.'" Olmsted was replaced by Harvard professor, and president of the American Society of Landscape Architects, Henry V. Hubbard. In the following year, 1933, Charles Eliot was appointed director of the newly created National Planning Resources Board, and therefore left the commission. Planning direction at the commission staff level was then taken over by John Nolen, Jr., who had joined the commission staff two years earlier.

CHAPTER IX THE NEW DEAL IN PLANNING 1933–1941

The New Deal in Planning 1933-1941

The Shift from Comprehensive Planning to Short-Term Goals

The New Deal transformed Washington and accelerated the city's growth. Suburbanization became the overwhelming form of growth, most particularly in the Virginia counties after construction of Key Bridge and Memorial Bridge. This suburban development was spurred on by new federal programs. Thus, to a noticeable extent, began the dispersal from the central city of not only residential functions but also commercial and governmental functions.

Despite concern with unemployment and recovery, and a liberal orientation to social problems, the New Deal in Washington, as in many metropolitan areas, was not innovative. Fundamental urban problems were largely ignored; unable to function in the vacuum, city planning became almost totally ineffective. Many federal programs, particularly the Federal Housing Administration mortgage insurance program and expanded federal-aid highway programs, directly subsidized suburbanization without comparably strengthening the planning arrangements that would have guided it into more compact forms.

The New Deal initiated public programs aimed at stimulating employment by providing funds for public works projects, many of them long overdue. There was a distinct tendency to build what had already been planned and was ready to go. Many administrators of these new agencies looked to the city of Washington as a case study of what could be accomplished nationwide —as, for example, in the model city of Greenbelt, in Prince George's County, Maryland.

Funds were channeled through agencies like the Works Progress Administration, the Public Roads Administration, and the Public Works Administration. New areas of public activity appeared in housing and other fields. In the rise of these new agencies to prominence, the National Capital Park and Planning Commission continued to provide local coordination and advice, but found increasing resistance to such planning guidance among federal agencies, intent upon short-term program goals. The drop in funding to the National Capital Park and Planning Commission, through both direct appropriation and the Capper-Cramton Act, cut the Planning Commission's ability to update or even sustain its Comprehensive Plan. Planning decisions were made independently by federal

Multicentered Regional City:
l View of Virginia and National Airport
s the Fourteenth Street Bridge

Aerial View of the Model City of Greenbelt in Prince George's County, Maryland, 1938

agencies. The drop in funding, and hence the commission's diminished influence on planning decisions, led to increased demands by the architectural and planning professionals—and even from members of the Planning Commission itself—that the commission's structure be reorganized. The Comprehensive Plan, project planning, and coordinating efforts that were among the accomplishments of the Planning Commission's early years were no longer adequate for a city rapidly spilling over into Virginia and Maryland in seemingly haphazard directions. And by 1941 a still more urgent historic factor was the domination of urban needs by overwhelming requirements of the defense establishment.

THE MALL DEVELOPMENT PLAN

In September 1933, Harold Ickes, secretary of the Department of Interior and administrator of the Public Works Administration, announced an allotment of $600,000 for the Mall Development Plan. It was estimated that the project would provide jobs for 350 men. This plan included the Mall proper and Union Square, the plot of land joining the Capitol grounds to the Mall, and provided for "roadway construction, general grading, landscaping, tree planting, and a water supply system." The Mall Development Plan had been authorized in 1929 by Congress but had never been funded.

Aerial View of the Monumental Core Prior to Implementation of the Mall Development Plan, 1932

The 1929 act instructed that modernization of the Mall be in accordance with the L'Enfant plan and the McMillan plan, "with such modifications thereof as may be recommended by the National Capital Park and Planning Commission and approved by the Commission for the Enlarging of the Capitol Grounds."

As early as 1927, Frederick Law Olmsted, Jr., Frederic A. Delano, and the other commissioners prepared—along with Charles Eliot—guidelines for the Mall development according to their interpretations of what L'Enfant would have done and what the McMillan Commission had recommended. Eliot interpreted L'Enfant's intentions for the Mall as an open vista between the Capitol and the Washington Monument. Eliot, in his 1927 memorandum, combined this aesthetic with the McMillan Commission's recommendation that the central vista be "enframed by rows of elms." Olmsted built on Eliot's proposal by stating that to accomplish this geometric stretch of greenery three major elements had to be coordinated: first, new public buildings had to be designed to insure the longitudinal boundaries and open vista; second, the "obstructive trees along the axis" had to be removed; and third, the entire Mall's length had to be graded and planted with formal rows of elms. Olmsted's 1927 memorandum recognized that many public officials and residents "jealously cherished" the Smithsonian grounds and Department of Agriculture grounds as artifacts of earlier romantic landscaping. Nevertheless, Olmsted justified his plan by the promise of "a very great permanent advantage" in the future clearance. Olmsted's and Eliot's plans were approved by the Commission of Fine Arts and served as the basis for later work on the Mall Development Plan.

Olmsted was also influential in the over-all design of Union Square. He conferred with W. L. Parsons of the Chicago firm of Bennett, Parsons, and Frost, the firm responsible for the new Botanic Garden at the foot of the Capitol as well as landscaping the extension of the Capitol grounds north of Constitution Avenue and toward Union Station. In planning Union Square, Olmsted had to design a connection between an essentially Beaux-Arts creation and the romantic Capitol grounds designed by his father years earlier.

PLANS FOR PUBLIC BUILDINGS SITES

The Mall development inspired new plans and studies for the adjacent urban environment. Accordingly, the Municipal Center, located at what is now called Judiciary Square, was reviewed, as were traffic arrangements through the Federal Triangle. It was proposed that the south side of Constitution Avenue should mirror the style and grandeur of the Federal Triangle buildings. Still, the ability of the federal government alone to effect extensive rehabilitation of the central area was limited, especially in the area north of Pennsylvania Avenue. As Henry V. Hubbard, successor to Olmsted on the Planning Commission (but of a different philosophy of design) stated, "it is evident that the Government has neither the funds, intention nor desire to spend public money for actual construction of buildings on the north side of Pennsylvania Avenue. . . . The actual construction must be a matter of private initiative." Hubbard suggested that local architects make tentative sketches for that side of Pennsylvania Avenue "as suggestion and an inspiration" to architects actually commissioned to design the separate private buildings. John Nolen, Jr., Planning Commission director, anticipated that the Mall Development Plan would spur interest in several long-term projects such as the Northwest Rectangle and the Southwest Triangle as sites for future public buildings. The Northwest Rectangle was defined by E Street, NW, Seventeenth Street, Constitution Avenue, and Twenty-Third Street. Boundaries of the Southwest Triangle were B Street, SW (now Constitution Avenue), Maryland Avenue, and Fifteenth Street. Both sites had been studied as potential locations for public buildings and were deemed compatible with McMillan Commission plans inasmuch as this planning, according to Nolen, "recognized the Mall and the cross axis of the White House as the basis for the central composition of the city." Nolen also envisioned that the Mall Development Plan would inspire the "moving of [the] old Smithsonian Building," and construction of the Twelfth and Fourteenth Street underpasses to facilitate traffic in the monumental core.

Members and Staff of the National Capital Park and Planning Commission, 1935. From left to right in front row: T. S. Settle, John Nolen, Jr., Colonel Daniel Sultan, William A. Delano, Frederic A. Delano, J. C. Nichols, Arno Cammerer, an unidentified man, Henry V. Hubbard (partially hidden), and T. C. Jeffers

THE JEFFERSON MEMORIAL

Later the monumental core was further strengthened by the location of the Jefferson Memorial on the south axis of the White House. This site had initially been proposed by the McMillan Commission for a national pantheon of monumental character, with a sight line projecting through the intended reflecting pool south to the banks of the Tidal Basin. This sight line was to realign the Washington Monument on its true axis. In the 1901–1902 plan, the idea for the pantheon assumed massive regrading and landscaping of the Washington Monument grounds as a prelude to the highly formal Washington Commons setting for the pantheon. It also assumed that the pantheon would be located at the meeting point of two major radial streets, one emanating from the Capitol and the other from a radial reflected off the Lincoln Memorial's axis.

In later years, the Thomas Jefferson Memorial Commission represented by the Jefferson scholar, Fiske Kimball, favored this Tidal Basin site for the project because of its proximity to the Lincoln Memorial and the Washington Monument. This site thus would give the memorial to the third president an equivalent national character. Kimball was further attracted to the site because it had been recommended by the McMillan Commission as a memorial site. Olmsted, himself a member of the McMillan Commission, studied the Tidal Basin site for the Jefferson Memorial Commission, but was skeptical. Without any foreseeable improvement of the Washington Monument grounds or grading of the low hills that ringed the monument to the south, the Memorial Commission's plans, in Olmsted's view, "involved far too great a risk of leaving the Jefferson Memorial stranded in an isolated location in Potomac Park, forever shut off from the central congestion of the Washington Plan by the 'cold shoulder' of the slanting wooded ridge which now intervenes." The National Capital Park and Planning Commission, represented by Arno B. Cammerer, favored a Jefferson Memorial location in Lincoln Park in order to stimulate improvements east of the Capitol.

219

The Commission of Fine Arts, led by Chairman Gilmore D. Clarke, considered the Apex site of the Federal Triangle and a site south of the Mall facing the National Archives Building, but concluded that the Tidal Basin site was the most favorable as it completed "the framework of the 'Central Area' as laid down by the McMillan Commission" and was not any more isolated than the Lincoln Memorial had been. Many of these plans for the memorial had been made by the Jefferson Memorial Commission and its architect, John Russell Pope, before the National Capital Park and Planning Commission had a chance to review them. The commission later acquiesced to the Tidal Basin site, fearing all the while that the government was being committed, in Olmsted's words, to "complete a major development of the surrounding for the Memorial area." The design for the Jefferson Memorial—in form a durable favorite of the architect—was justified by Kimball as embodied in Jefferson's rotunda at the University of Virginia. It was also said to be a form not yet evoked in any Washington memorial, though the dome was employed by Pope earlier in his Broad Street Railroad Station in Richmond, Virginia, and later in the National Gallery of Art in Washington.

THE MODERN MOVEMENT IN AMERICAN ARCHITECTURE

The urban planning contribution of the National Capital Park and Planning Commission introduced more comprehensive elements than had been considered by the architects of the McMillan Commission or the Commission of Fine Arts, factors of modern urban transportation, bridges over the Potomac River, and even matters of the riverfront, the landscape, and the environment. Of the many considerations it brought into view, the most important was location. Yet, the location of the Jefferson Memorial was only half the battle that was waged against the project. The persistence of Beaux-Arts sympathies in Washington public architecture in the 1930s was now confronted by a body of planning and architectural professionals conversant in the modern design alternative.

The important 1933 exhibition on the International Style at the Museum of Modern Art in New York City, and the exhibition catalog by Henry-Russell Hitchcock

and Philip Johnson, had crystallized the challenge of the modern movement in America. New York establishment architects *versus* New York modernists was replayed in Washington, and the Jefferson Memorial project was the first of successive design conflicts in the capital. The millions of visitors saw little in the Washington skyline to indicate the rising tide of modernism, unless by accident or by astute observation they discovered William Dewey Foster's streamlined Central Heating Plant in Georgetown. Foster's beige triumph was the first federal building of this era to knock aside the Classical Revival forms. This was followed by the more obvious Jefferson Memorial, a project that inspired a vocal uprising of letters, speeches, and testimonials by the modernists against the Pope design. The modernists did not provide a design alternative (they advocated a competition) but the strength they exhibited forced Pope and the Memorial Commission to compromise by relocating, reducing, and simplifying the original scheme.

Influence of the Planning Commission

The undercutting of effectiveness of the National Capital Park and Planning Commission in influencing planning decisions, as with the Jefferson Memorial Commission, was symptomatic of the Planning Commission's increasingly weakened financial and political standing. Demands of Depression spending reduced funding to the Planning Commission through the District's appropriations. From the high of $1,000,000 exclusive of Capper-Cramton funds in both 1929 and 1930, there was a sharp decrease; by 1932 Congress appropriated only $47,185 to the Planning Commission through the District of Columbia budget.

New programs set up by the New Deal, as for example employment programs, further reduced the Planning Commission's influence as a shaper of policy; at the worst its role among the new agencies was that of an observer. The National Industrial Recovery Act funded highway improvement schemes intended to create employment opportunities, the plans for which followed largely, but not entirely, the Planning Commission's earlier major thoroughfare system. The Public Works Administration's Housing Division provided for demonstration housing projects in the District of Columbia, issuing its own policies covering location, construction method, and financing arrangements.

HOUSING AND THE NEW MOBILITY

Private housing developments mushroomed in the suburbs, often oblivious to any regional plan. In observing that new homes and apartment buildings were being located in both Maryland and Virginia without consultation with the planning agencies, the Planning Commission deplored private decisions made without study of water and sewage facilities and other necessities of residential living.

Mobility in the vast metropolitan area was abetted by the popularity of the automobile with Washingtonians, a taste indulged not only by L'Enfant's wide streets and boulevards and but also by generous modern highways. A traffic study performed in 1934 by planner Charles Herrick for the Planning Commission revealed that the "proportion of people in Washington who use private automobiles or taxicabs is over twice the average reported from six other cities," a larger proportion even than in Los Angeles. Herrick discussed the possibility of imposing economic disadvantages on the automobile driver and encouraging greater use of public transportation. Without such incentives to change the riding habits of the city's population, Herrick—in 1934—predicted no end in sight to the "prohibitively expensive projects that may be necessary if the proportion of automobile drivers continues to increase." Chief among these "expensive projects" were parking facilities and improved highways to handle rush-hour traffic. The Planning Commission considered recommending staggered office hours but did not possess the necessary resources to draw up a new traffic plan to update the Bartholomew guidelines from the commission's early years. The result now was the day-by-day increase of parked cars on every street and green space around every federal building.

NATIONAL AIRPORT AT GRAVELLY POINT

In contrast to dispersal activities unrelated to any Com-

prehensive Plan, National Airport was carefully sited in 1940 at Gravelly Point—between the Fourteenth Street Bridge and Alexandria—after a number of sites in the metropolitan area had been studied. Washington had seen aviation history in the making since the days of the Wright brothers and Samuel Langley's unhappy termination of his flight in the waters of the Potomac. Washington's small flying fields like that at College Park, Maryland, had many vivid associations with aviation's infancy. Dirigibles had flown from Hybla Park, Virginia, and the earliest commercial passenger services operated from Washington Municipal Airport. This airport, originally improvised from a merger of two privately owned airports, Hoover Airport and what was called Washington Airport, eventually became impossibly constricted. Under the spur of wartime exigencies, at that only after presidential intervention, the decision was made to build a new federal airport to serve the capital city's expanding air traffic.

The most likely alternative location for this facility, other than Gravelly Point, was Camp Springs, Maryland, where the Andrews Air Force Base would one day be built. Camp Springs in the early days, however, posed major access problems that could not be resolved fully until completion of the Capital Beltway. Gravelly Point, on the other hand, was wonderfully accessible to the central city via the Mount Vernon Parkway and U.S. Route 1, the main highway south. By continuing the extensive fill of the Potomac river-bottom meadows, moreover, the need for large-scale acquisition of developed areas was avoided. Nor was the air traffic of the early years much of an environmental nuisance, save in the Old Town of Alexandria (where it was regarded as third in order of importance as a nuisance, after the sootfall from the Potomac Yards and the odors of the riverfront fertilizer factory). As finally built, the airport terminal itself became a work of architectural distinction. Nominally designed by Howard Cheney of Chicago, but more largely the work of Charles M. Goodman, the design was ultimately inspired, as was that of so many public buildings, by a sketchpad drawing headed "Stolen from the desk of Franklin D. Roosevelt."

Thus National Airport, a work of lasting urban signifi-

National Airport at Gravelly Point Shown from Washington, Looking down the Potomac toward Mount Vernon, 1940

cance, materialized—and became the capital city gateway for millions of travelers in the burgeoning era of air traffic. The image of the capital city from the air approach and via the riverside access parkway, an image seen during the day but even more spectacularly by night, strongly recaptured the formalism of the monumental city. The airport's location also recaptured that sense of a national city on the Potomac, largely lost in the days of rail and highway travel. Finally, National Airport's notably convenient location to central city destinations was to embed it in the fabric of the city

despite the deafening noise, vibrations, and atmospheric pollution that came with expanded aviation services and the jet planes.

THE GRAB-BAG METHOD OF DEVELOPMENT

The low funding and lack of a Comprehensive Plan that could be implemented led to the location of new public buildings almost at random. In 1941, Harold Ickes described the process of locating new public facilities as the "grab-bag method of putting a road or a building on any bit of vacant land that can be discovered." The influence of both Frederic Delano and Frederick Law Olmsted, Jr., the latter a continuing Planning Commission consultant, was still formidable in the planning field although both leaders of an earlier generation were now elderly. New figures at the National Capital Park and Planning Commission seemed unable to inspire confidence or the attention of federal officials responsible for agency plans. Such a situation could only invite criticism.

A TIME TO RECONSIDER

The diminished effectiveness of the Planning Commission was reflected in Frederic Delano's letter of resignation in April 1942 to his nephew, President Franklin Roosevelt, addressing him as "his Excellency, the President of the United States." Describing the original National Capital Park and Planning Commission as the "best that could have been worked out fifteen or more years ago," Delano reminded Roosevelt that the commission's only administrative duty was the purchase of parks and playgrounds. "Otherwise it was solely a planning and coordinating committee." Many of the ex officio members had come to give little if any time to the work of the commission and rarely attended meetings. There was no compulsory relationship of the commission with important agencies such as the Bureau of the Budget. Delano concluded that "now is an appropriate time to reconsider the set up [of the commission] on a sounder basis."

This concern with the effectiveness of the commission was reflected by the ever-vigilant Committee of 100 and the faithful American Planning and Civic Association in their suggested new philosophy for Washington planning: "No longer should we regard planning as a method of setting up restrictions to prevent officials and citizens from free action; but rather as a means of positive determination of the pattern of the future, under which sound plans are devised and practical projects outlined on an economic schedule." The two organizations recommended a mandated, integrated set of relationships among agencies most responsible for the appearance and functioning of the city. Most important, they recommended that sufficient funds be appropriated

to the Planning Commission to draw up and keep current regional plans.

Multicentered Regional City

Effectiveness of the National Capital Park and Planning Commission was significantly reduced by the shifting of the War Department installation from a long-intended building site in the Northwest Rectangle to the Arlington site adjacent to the National Cemetery. Many tugs on the city's neat central core and surrounding area had already dispersed public buildings into the District and beyond. As these public installations became large office buildings filled with armies of employees, the buildings themselves became subcenters in what was rapidly becoming the multicentered regional city. New building in dispersed locations necessitated provisions not only for access and parking but for other facilities such as water, power, sewage disposal, and housing for employees—and housing entailed more complex relationships with schools, stores, and recreation accommodations.

BUILDING THE PENTAGON

In the 1930s and early forties, historic lands associated with the Washington, Custis, and Lee families became a battleground between the National Capital Park and Planning Commission and the War Department. As part of the dénouement, early in 1940 the War Department conceived of a vast structure to contain its consolidated activities, accommodated from World War I days largely in the concrete so-called temporary buildings along the Mall. The Planning Commission had expected that the War Department's needs in replacing these tempos could be met by the officially designated Federal Office Building No. 2, planned to be located in the Northwest Rectangle. As the pace of national defense activity quickened and the scale of war involvement became evident, however, the War Department put aside earlier building plans and began to search for a site on the Virginia side of the Potomac River.

The Arlington Site: Background and Battleground. First to be considered by the War Department was the Arlington Experimental Farm, a tract of two hundred acres located west of the railroad. Part of the former Custis estate, the tract had long been used by the Department of Agriculture and was now scheduled to be turned over to Arlington National Cemetery. Possible use of this site by the War Department met with objections—from the Planning Commission and the Commission of Fine Arts—that such use would conflict with the setting of the Lincoln Memorial. The two commissions won this skirmish, but not their original objective to locate the War Department Building in the Northwest Rectangle as planned.

The entire river lowland area of Arlington between the Fourteenth Street Bridge and the National Cemetery was under intensive development pressure at this time. This pressure had been created by recently constructed bridges and highways and by freeing up of the old Washington Municipal Airport land. This lowland area as a whole was to accommodate several major projects, including a proposed facility for the Navy. The area had been surveyed by the Chief of the Army Corps of Engineers, who identified the major subcenters. These subcenters were Fort Myer, Arlington National Cemetery, Arlington Experimental Farm, the projected federal airport at Gravelly Point, and now, of course, the projected War Department site. The entire area thus was heavily shadowed by the military presence. Because of its location in Virginia, however, the area lay outside the jurisdiction of the National Capital Park and Planning Commission, although certainly not beyond its regional sphere of interest. From October 1933 on, when John Nolen, Jr., had reported to the Planning Commission that the Department of Agriculture was about to abandon its Arlington Experimental Farm and move to new facilities at Beltsville, Maryland, the general site had been very much within the Planning Commission's range of vision.

Once the decision had been made to abandon the old Washington Municipal Airport, there was speculation as to how the land would be reused. The Park and Planning Commission saw the best reuse of the old airport land as accommodating expansion of Arlington National Cemetery beyond what was to be provided for in the acquisition of Arlington Experimental Farm. Planning details for this expansion and land reuse had been put forward. The Planning Commission was alerted that these plans were in jeopardy, however, when John Nolen, Jr., reported in July 1939 that a detachment of troops from Fort Washington had occupied the Arlington land "with a view to developing permanent quarters at this site." And this was the beginning of the critical phase of the long engagement.

War Department Moves in Virginia. In the following months, the Planning Commission lost its bid for use of the Arlington Experimental Farm site for park activities, especially as the Bureau of the Budget wrote bills transferring the entire lowland site to the War Department. A compromise plan was reached—by the War Department, the Bureau of the Budget, and the president of the United States on one hand, and the National Capital Park and Planning Commission on the other—providing for the land to be divided between the Departments of Interior and War. The needs of Interior's nursery, greenhouses, and camp site were to be met first, with the rest of the land to be allocated to the War Department. The War Department agreed with the Planning Commission's over-all plan, provided that the commission would cooperate in getting the proposed compromise plan through Congress. In fact, the resulting bill as processed by Congress eliminated all mention of the Department of Interior and the Planning Commission, except that a right of way was given to Interior for an approach to the Arlington Memorial Bridge.

Design of the Pentagon. Once the War Department owned its large and commanding piece of Virginia land, as established now by congressional act, the Planning Commission and others waited anxiously to see what the department planned to build. For several months, there were announcements that only temporary buildings would be constructed on the site. Then, with sounds of war becoming louder, Congress appropriated $35 million for construction of the War Department Building—the five-sided structure later called the Pentagon—to occupy sixty-eight acres of land immediately north of U.S. Route 1 on a portion of the old airport land and a portion of the Arlington Experimental Farm site. The structure was to house approximately 30,000 office workers at its peak occupancy. What was in the works was a virtually self-contained city served by railroad and bus lines, shops, churches, health and recreation facilities, restaurants, and much more. Most visibly, it was to be surrounded by vast parking lots and an extensive network of highway interchanges. It was even to be connected by commuter launch to the Naval Air Station at the juncture of the Anacostia and the Potomac Rivers.

Objections and Outrage. With the full ramifications of this behemoth of a building now beginning to clarify, the Commission of Fine Arts issued an anguished press release on the first day of August 1941. Referring to the illustrious history of the Commission of Fine Arts, the article reminded readers that the McMillan Commission had requested that the land now destined to receive the Pentagon be kept open and free of permanent buildings, a sacred haven of repose for the National Cemetery, certainly in the category of a "great park," and an appropriate foreground to the capital city. The Commission of Fine Arts concluded by evoking arguments in favor of dispersal to spin out federal buildings into a vast regional city in the post–World War II era. And as for the needs of the War Department, "we are sure that there are other and better solutions to this particular problem which, incidentally, might result in decentralizing the offices of the Army to prevent that remote possibility of wiping out the whole establishment incident to the dropping of two or three bombs."

As powerful as the outrage of the Commission of Fine Arts was Harold Ickes's warning "against further encroachment upon the parks and playgrounds of the National Capital." As secretary of the Interior, Ickes deplored not just the independent action of the War Department, but even more the irreparable damage to the orderly development of the city. He accused the War Department of single-handedly creating "upsetting influences involving shifting population, traffic congestion, and a general disturbance of the whole city pattern. Ickes objected that at the rate we are going, the parks in Washington will soon be nothing but glorified boulevards."

Several months before Pearl Harbor, Washington had already begun to draw up its battle lines. Tempos and especially transitory defense housing began to rise again —a repeat performance of World War I. Now, however, defense construction reached far into the suburbs: tempos in Suitland, Maryland, and defense housing in Falls Church and on the farmlands of Saint Elizabeths Hospital. Barracks were everywhere. Perhaps spurred on by the warnings of the Commission of Fine Arts that only a few bombs were needed to immobilize the government, the Bureau of the Budget made studies regarding relocation of federal employees outside the National Capital Region. Access by roads and bridges from the city and suburbs to the War Department's Pentagon city and widely dispersed tempos had to be constructed, superimposing wide ribbons of highway on the once bucolic landscape. The head of the Public Roads Administration, provider of this new mobility, planned to move testing facilities from the National Airport area to far away and undeveloped Langley, Virginia, in order to avoid future agency moves that would be necessitated by encroachment of development on these facilities. The War Department Building itself attracted smaller auxiliary buildings. The National Capital Park and Planning Commission and the Washington Chapter of the American Institute of Architects discussed air raid protection in the area, suggesting studies be performed to determine the "location of wooded areas in the region suitable for evacuation in relation to access and transportation, such as the Catoctin Mountains of Maryland and Chopawamsic recreation area in Virginia."

A few days before the nation went to war, T. S. Settle, secretary of the Planning Commission, delivered a patriotic radio message entitled "Our National Capital." Settle recalled the many instances of tourists who, on looking over the monumental core, became better citizens with a heightened sense of patriotism. During the war emergency, Settle saw among the nation's problems the need for protection both from the enemy outside and from those who would disrupt and destroy from

The Wide Ribbon of Highway on the South Side of the Pentagon, 1946

within. He cited a list of insensitive public officials who for the sake of expediency would destroy the carefully planned city of public buildings and parkland. He stated that destruction of open spaces in the city would cripple the efficiency of employees. Settle blamed the tension in the city on the unwillingness of governmental agencies and Congress to look ahead and work with the National Capital Park and Planning Commission in planning for the future. In coupling war emergency with the protection of Washington as the patriotic national shrine, Settle defined the Planning Commission's work as an important element in the nation's morale and thus a contribution to winning of the war.

CHAPTER X WORLD WAR II AND POSTWAR YEARS 1941–1952

World War II and Postwar Years 1941-1952

Statistics of Growth

Washington had always grown with war, economic crises, and national emergencies. The years of World War II and of postwar readjustment were no exception. An analysis of Washington's growth showed that 67 percent of the city's growth had occurred in five of its thirteen decades of history. The analysis also showed that while population growth associated with the New Deal in the 1930s was largely in the District of Columbia, the wartime increase in the 1940s was a suburban metropolitan phenomenon. The District's population had grown from 486,869 in 1930 to 663,091 in 1940, and the metropolitan area population increased from 967,985 in 1940 to 1,464,089 in 1950. Growth in the Virginia counties came from construction of bridges, and even more from location of the Pentagon and other federal establishments on the south bank of the Potomac.

POPULATION AND HOUSING

The settlement pattern that earlier had followed main transportation corridors, especially those defined by the streetcar system, grew more diffuse as the automobile became the primary mode of commutation and the city decentralized its employment and retail trade. Lower population densities were also reflected in the pattern of sprawl, a new and specific condition of urban settlement, defined at the time as development at densities too low to enable the economical provision of full municipal services. Along with the building of wartime temporary office buildings came wartime temporary housing, much of it in the form of prefabs or mobile homes. The temporary type of construction was dictated equally by shortages of copper, iron, lumber, and other critical building materials, by scarcity of skilled building labor, and by fear that the local economy would collapse with a postwar glut of housing. Even conventional wartime and postwar housing reflected the qualitative decline. Under all these expectations lay two assumptions that were to prove spectacularly wrong: that the nation would enter a postwar recession on the model of the years following World War I, and that national population growth would decline. To these mistaken premises, Washington's experience was to add a third. The expectation that the end of the war would see a return to prewar conditions was blasted by the postwar obligations of the national government to its international responsibilities, to the Cold War, and to a new agenda of domestic programs, especially those that affected cities.

The Finger City. Growth to the south and west was shown on a 1947 development map in the form of a "finger city," like the more famous plan of Copenhagen, centered here on Alexandria, with the wrist and thumbs in Virginia, and the four fingers more clearly delineated than ever before. The barrier of the Anacostia—both the river and the heights—was clearly defined as limiting development towards the south and east, in spite of the new Indian Head Highway that had been built as a wartime measure. Between the fingers lay great spreads of public property, by no means all of it in the form of

The Finger City: Silhouette Showing Development in the Metropolitan Washington Area, 1947

parks, but comprising a distinctive body of open space to be reckoned with in future development as well as in the present.

Like the Civil War and World War I, World War II brought massive changes to the city. Open spaces in the monumental core and in many outlying areas were covered by temporary structures. Although some of the outlying buildings were later removed, the land seldom returned to its former open condition. Rather, this development of land and transportation connections predicted permanent development and extensions to the city's edges. The automobile had allowed for larger and more remote pieces of fringe areas to be enveloped into the wartime city. Whereas the city during the Civil War and World War I had spilled into the open lands that lay within the District's boundaries and were heavily defined by routes of public transportation, the city of the 1940s spread far into the surrounding counties. The magnified scale was abetted by the growth in numbers of federal government civilian employees, reaching a wartime peak in 1943 of 284,665 employees, whereas the city during World War I employed a maximum of just over 120,835 civilian employees in 1918. Lasting more than twice as long as World War I, World War II caused permanent development in the city. The wartime population endured after the second war, especially in terms of government employees. In contrast to the post–World War I city where the number of employees showed a steady decrease up until the Depression years, the post–World War II city maintained a largely consistent number of employees, hovering at about the 225,000 mark until 1951 when the Korean Military Action again created an expansion in federal employment. The World War II city grew in response to the dictates of the War Department and the Bureau of the Budget. The most planners could hope for was either a return of the city to its prewar order or an opportunity to draw up a new Comprehensive Plan for the postwar era.

Wartime Residences and Office Centers. The sudden need for wartime office and housing space involved more than buildings alone. Residences needed to be supplied

from the Top of the Washington Monument toward the Lincoln Memorial, Showing Temporary Federal Office Buildings Paralleling the Reflecting Pool, 194

in convenient—or at least expedient—locations for workers, and this need in turn entailed planning for water, sewerage, schools, shopping, parking, and recreation. Facilities in the central core were already taxed to their personnel limit (40,000 at the Naval Weapons Plant on the Anacostia River; 30,000–40,000 at West Potomac Park in tempos; 25,000 at the old Navy Munition Buildings on Constitution Avenue). Thus, new office centers, generally of contemporary style, began to be constructed in the District and suburban counties upon the once-open spaces that had been part of the regional park system. For such developments, the Planning Commission recommended that "additional temporary Federal office buildings should be constructed in outlying locations so distributed that concentration shall normally not exceed 2,500 employees in any one location, with a possible maximum of 5,000 employees." Even with the development of these low-density office centers, the commission saw limits to continuing to pack

Washington Row Houses Converted to Boarding House Use to Accommodate the Influx of Civil Servants, 1943

the defense needs into the Washington area and therefore proposed decentralization of some government offices to other cities.

McLean Gardens. Among housing sites on once-open space was the project undertaken on the McLean estate on upper Wisconsin Avenue, NW. Construction of this large concentration of garden apartments pointed up the tendency to build first and plan later. In the early stages, considerable opposition to the architecture was expressed, as the neighborhood was one of high property values, of single-family dwellings rather than housing projects. A highly concentrated population in blunted Georgian-styled boxes on a shaven landscape was inimical to the neighborhood of individual lawns and trees, well-defined architectural details, and generous proportions. Moreover, residents of the housing project would add to the already congested streetcar lines and major thoroughfares. Planned to include a complex of apartments plus a shopping strip, McLean Gardens was sited before the boundaries of the northern extension of the Glover-Archbold Parkway were defined. In addition to congestion, McLean Gardens also generated transportation problems. In 1942, the Defense Homes Corporation, which constructed McLean

Corner of N and Union Streets in the Southwest Quadrant of Washington, 1942

Gardens, was unwilling to design a streetcar loop at the intersection of Wisconsin and Idaho Avenues, as recommended by the National Capital Park and Planning Commission. This modest incident typified in capsule form a nationwide failure to integrate planning for mass transportation facilities with comprehensive planning, a shortcoming later illustrated manifold in urban renewal and large-scale suburban development.

The housing picture in Washington was further clouded by differences in facilities for war workers, white workers and black workers, and the displacement of a "small village" of indigenous black families in Arlington from the site of the Pentagon. Washington differed little from other cities responding to nationwide demographic changes. For the most part, the Planning Commission and the National Capital Housing Authority supported the development of housing for black families east of the Anacostia River, closer to the Navy Yard, Union Station, and other employment centers.

REHABILITATION OF SOUTHWEST WASHINGTON

Despite the rapid construction of new residential units in the Washington region, the housing supply was still severely limited by shortage of construction materials. Also in short supply were materials for automobiles. Arthur Goodwillie, director of the Conservation Service of the Home Owners' Loan Corporation, saw the blossoming of housing at the urban rim as creating additional problems in terms of time and cost for transportation. In line with the government's emphasis on conservation of critical resources, Goodwillie suggested that extant housing in old neighborhoods also be viewed as resources. In 1942, he presented a report, *The Rehabilitation of Southwest Washington as a War Housing Measure*, to the Planning Commission. In the report, Goodwillie delineated the nine-block area closest to Capitol Hill and produced assessments showing that rehabilitation of the old buildings would be cheaper than razing them and building anew. Not only would the government incur considerable savings by this plan, but the residents themselves would be within walking distance of employment in many government office buildings, Union Station, and the commercial water-

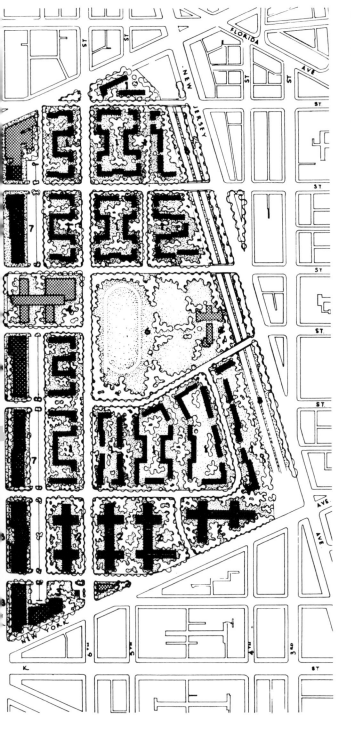

Illustrative Site Development Plan for the Redevelopment of a Portion of the Seventh Street Corridor, 1940s

front. The report also showed that additional densities could be achieved by constructing apartment houses in some of the interiors of city blocks where notorious alley dwellings had once stood. Although the Planning Commission approved of the Goodwillie rehabilitation plan in principle, it was never executed.

The 1942 Goodwillie plan was less an outline for neighborhood conservation than it was an economical design for housing in the face of severe material shortages. His survey of conditions in the quadrant did remind the city's planners that conspicuous and notorious slums existed within eyeshot of the Capitol. Significantly—and contrary to later conceptions of the Southwest's social situation—this 1942 plan recognized that the population of the quadrant was almost evenly divided between white and black residents, with the overwhelming majority of white residents desiring to continue living there. Goodwillie described the area's verdant atmosphere, with wide and well-shaded streets and large interior blocks available for green commons and play spaces. As an area physically and psychologically isolated from the rest of the city, first by the City Canal and later by the railroad, the Southwest had developed a homogeneous physical environment: small brick or wooden row houses, decorated with picturesque ironwork and gingerbread, and surrounded by front and back yards often richly planted with the characteristic landscape materials of the urban poor, ailanthus and pink rose of Sharon.

Postwar Planning and Legislation

As World War II drew to a close, the National Capital Park and Planning Commission discussed the shape of postwar planning, especially for housing, in view now of the increasing rather than decreasing population projections. Alfred Bettman, a national planning authority and specialist in municipal corporation law who would later serve as consultant to the Planning Commission on redevelopment legislation, first attracted attention of the commission when he reported that as a planning body it had "been criticized by architects and others from time to time with having done most of its planning for the central area and done nothing about the redevelopment of the older parts of the city." Thereupon, Chairman Ulysses S. Grant III invited Bettman to submit more recommendations. Much of the zeal in providing housing for war workers had obscured the continuing problem of housing for the poor so that the problem now surfaced anew in the postwar era.

Planning for the new city had generally been based on new construction in open land. Yet the old city had a well-recognized example of older city revival in Georgetown where, as has been mentioned, during World War I the wives of war workers who simply needed convenient housing had pioneered in what was later termed "unslumming." The Goodwillie plan for the Southwest offered similar advantages. Neighborhood conservation, however, as a means for meeting postwar housing needs was not in the forefront of federal planning philosophy in the late 1940s and early 1950s.

REDEVELOPMENT

Redevelopment synonymous with demolition and building anew had already given the city its dramatic Federal Triangle, an early example in Washington of the phoenix rising out of the ashes.

Redevelopment offered what Washington architect Louis Justement called "an opportunity to exercise a degree of control never before attained." Yet the definition of redevelopment differed among those who sought control of the land to be cleared of slums. John Ihlder, proponent of housing for the poor, drafted a bill for federal funding of housing on the cleared sites. During World War II, his National Capital Housing Authority had been crippled by the diversion of monies away from its program to wartime needs, and Ihlder now hoped discussions of redevelopment in the District would find an outlet in his housing agency. Business interests, most notably the National Association of Home Builders, and real estate boards alike fought off efforts like those of Ihlder out of concern that public housing would compete with private building interests. Battle lines over the impending Redevelopment Act were further complicated as some supporters of public housing did not admire the Housing Authority's past performance and sought to disassociate themselves from Ihlder.

To a country now emerging as the undisputed leader in the free world, it was an embarrassment that scruffy vestiges of nineteenth-century slums marred its major cities. In April 1943, Alfred Bettman offered a broad interpretation of postwar redevelopment: "It should include the replanning and rebuilding of the built up and subdivided areas of cities and metropolitan regions." Thus, the settled areas of cities were no longer to be regarded as static entities around which planners could insert parks, housing, and public buildings. Instead, these settled areas were now available to the planner's alterations so as to fit into new urban ideologies.

A Legislative Program for the District and the Nation. Discussions in Washington and in other American cities crystallized in local legislation, the District of Columbia Redevelopment Act of 1945, and in national legislation, seen first in the 1949 Housing Act. This legislation was a creature of its time; the ideas of the time were those of Frank Lloyd Wright as expressed in *Disappearing City* and of Eliel Saarinen in *The City—Its Growth, Its Decay, Its Future.* There were also the other prophets of decentralization who had translated into architectural terms both the suburban future and the potentialities of reconstructing central cities like Detroit, Chicago, and Washington. To hard-pressed mayors and city councils, the issue was frequently seen in fiscal terms and a search for an improved tax base. In areas where taxing authority was restricted largely to the real property tax, redevelopment took the form of high apartment buildings and high office buildings that reflected high property values and high densities. Washington's traditional character as a horizontal city—and restrictions placed on development by the 1910 Height of Buildings Act (Public Law 87-281)—prevented the worst excesses of the trend toward high-density development, and its role as the national capital allowed it to escape some of the pressures that other cities faced. Nonetheless, to some extent Washington redevelopment in the early years responded not only to urban economic and ideological considerations, but to fashions in urban planning that were seen in other cities.

Advanced City Planning for Washington. Exemplary

of what was later termed the "creative builder searching for the ideal community on the local scene," Louis Justement was influential during the early years of redevelopment in Washington. Even before his views were detailed in his 1946 book, *New Cities for Old*, Justement infused these redevelopment theories into the National Capital Park and Planning Commission's programs. In 1944, Justement appeared before the commission with "advanced city planning for Washington." Anticipating a rapid rise in the national income, Justement suggested that the long-delayed municipal and private improvements to American cities could now be addressed. New construction in cities would be a prime opportunity for "putting people to work and preserving our economic system." As long as cities faced radical physical changes, planners were offered, for the first time, the chance to start all over again, to rebuild cities according to sound economics and standards of efficiency. This would be the chance also to combat tendencies toward removal of vital urban activities to the city's outskirts, tendencies that threatened to bankrupt the municipal structure. Redevelopment in Washington would ideally be advantageous to the private developer and be focused on attracting business to the central city, thereby enlarging the tax base.

THE REDEVELOPMENT ACT OF 1945 AND THE REDEVELOPMENT LAND AGENCY

The passage in 1946 of what was known as the District of Columbia Redevelopment Act of 1945—largely based on Alfred Bettman's draft bill—paved the way for the process of redevelopment. The National Capital Park and Planning Commission was authorized to designate redevelopment areas and boundaries and to prepare and adopt plans in accordance with the existing Comprehensive Plan. In a bicameral action, the Commissioners of the District of Columbia were authorized to approve plans adopted by the Planning Commission. The five-member Redevelopment Land Agency was created and empowered with the unique public authority to acquire property designated for redevelopment. The land would then be prepared for transfer to public and private developers. In order to attract private developers, on whose participation the program depended, the cost

of the land to developers could be reduced as much as two-thirds of the original price. If no private developers were willing to take on a particular project, then the National Capital Housing Authority could step in and receive public funds for developing the property. A $20 million revolving trust fund was authorized, but no appropriations were ever made by the District commissioners.

In the language of the 1945 act, the limits of redevelopment were defined as "replanning, clearance, redesign, and rebuilding of projects." It was required that these projects be located in slums or blighted areas or "be redeveloped for this housing purpose," although some of the cleared land could be transferred to commercial and public purposes. Despite these definitions, various public bodies had in mind different priorities and different results from development. These divergent views set redevelopment in Washington on an uncertain course as the various interests argued their positions.

Although passage of the 1945 act served as battleground for housing *versus* business interests, little actually happened in the way of redevelopment for the next three years. The Redevelopment Land Agency existed—but only by the beneficence of a public-spirited member, department store executive Mark Lansburgh, who financed the agency's administrative costs. The Planning Commission was appropriated $75,000 to prepare plans and select sites. Till the commission actually issued a new Comprehensive Plan, however, no redevelopment sites could be designated. The commission therefore expanded its staff by engaging Harland Bartholomew, a link with the commission's golden years of the early 1930s, to supervise development of such a plan.

THE HOUSING ACT OF 1949

Before Bartholomew could complete his work, the National Housing Act of 1949 was passed, enabling the Redevelopment Land Agency under Title I to receive funds for slum clearance and redevelopment from the Housing and Home Finance Administration (later the Department of Housing and Urban Development), and also enabling John Ihlder's National Capital Housing Authority under Title III to receive funds to construct low-rent public housing as an "essential part of the redevelopment program." In order to harmonize the agencies and procedures involved, the Planning Commission set up a coordinating committee on housing and redevelopment, made up of representatives of the commission itself, the District commissioners, the Redevelopment Land Agency, and the National Capital Housing Authority.

The Redevelopment Land Agency actually began its statutory functions in 1951 when John R. Searles, Jr., was brought in as the first director. Princeton-educated Searles injected a high degree of administrative ability into the agency as well as a commitment to the health of the District's business community. Guiding the agency for ten years through what was for all practical purposes a new national experiment in rebuilding cities, Searles steered a middle course between the short-term vision of developers and the long-range vision of planners.

THE BARRY FARMS PROJECT IN ANACOSTIA

Several years before actual passage of the 1949 legislation, attention had been focused on Barry Farms and Marshall Heights as sites poised for redevelopment. Barry Farms was a community with deep roots in the nineteenth century since it had origins as an area designated by the Freedmen's Bureau for housing for former slaves. It was located on the east side of the Anacostia River, north of Saint Elizabeths Hospital (founded in 1855) and at the foot of the hill on which Fort Stanton is located, one of the highest points in the District. Defined by the higher elevations to the east and the Anacostia River to the west, the isolation of Barry Farms was reinforced by several nearby public reservations. Barry Farms' street system, which developed independently of any District plan, followed either the ridges or the valleys of the site. Housing was scattered (70 percent of the land was vacant), primitive, and primarily of

Barry Farms Area of Anacostia, 1947

wooden construction. The neighborhood's maturity, however, had brought well-developed streets, neighborhood services, churches, and two civic associations.

Barry Farms first came to the attention of the National Capital Park and Planning Commission when in 1942 a new temporary school building was proposed to occupy land already devoted to the neighborhood playground. The Planning Commission pointed out that the playground was a "war necessity" and that it was actually essential since the neighborhood's Fairlawn Recreation Center was occupied by the Navy Department. This temporary school facility was approved, however, with the recommendation that adjacent lands be acquired to compensate for the loss of playground space.

As part of the Planning Commission's "desire to study, analyze, and understand blighted areas and their causes and effects," the commission in cooperation with the National Capital Housing Authority made a major study of the Barry Farms area in 1944. When land values and costs of public services provided by the District were compared, the study found that the area did not pay its way. In fact, the District was subsidizing Barry Farms by at least $600 per family. "Rural blight" was largely a function of the layout of the area, which was difficult to police and provide with other essential services. Convinced that as things were, the most the neighborhood could expect in the future was piecemeal, sporadic, and unprofitable development, the study report suggested that Barry Farms "offers one of the best opportunities in the District of Columbia for the development de novo of a complete and integrated neighborhood unit." The area's advantages could be realized only when it was developed as a whole, the report suggested, especially if development were aimed at establishing a self-contained neighborhood providing for a wide range of economic groups. Thus, the commission defined its initial concept of redevelopment and urban renewal in keeping with broader national and professional concepts.

THE MARSHALL HEIGHTS PROJECT IN ANACOSTIA

Marshall Heights was also considered a redevelopment area, similar to yet different from Barry Farms. Also located east of the Anacostia, the triangular piece of land known as Marshall Heights was defined by Benning Road, Central Avenue, and the District line. Its physical appearance clearly revealed the narrow rectangular street grid drawn up in 1886 and imposed on steep slopes. The area was dotted by frame buildings. Many public improvements, such as grading and paving, provided by the District prior to 1945 were of temporary materials "anticipating the necessity of complete redevelopment of the area at an early date." Unlike Barry Farms, however, Marshall Heights had no long community past—as late as 1927 it contained only two houses. In 1945, Marshall Heights was characterized as a shanty town.

The commission's study of the area found that, like Barry Farms, Marshall Heights' tax base did not cover its costs in public services. This kind of evaluation, however, had not been fully applied to all other areas of the city. The commission saw the Heights as ripe for redevelopment as a self-contained neighborhood unit of low enough density then to predict only limited dislocation for current population. In the mid-1940s, the cost of acquiring both the Barry Farms and Marshall Heights areas was not prohibitive.

Decisions needed to be made quickly on designating Barry Farms and Marshall Heights as redevelopment areas and presenting plans to Congress for funding. In 1945, citizens of Marshall Heights were requesting the District to install sewer and water lines according to the old street plan, a proposal that the Planning Commission rejected as obstructing future redevelopment by strengthening the obsolete street pattern. Also, the postwar housing shortage had spurred speculative activities in Marshall Heights; developers were pressing for introduction of the related public services anticipated following the old grid. Wishing to avoid further complications to its redevelopment plans, the Planning Commission by withholding its approval placed a freeze on further improvements in Marshall Heights, an action that sparked fierce opposition from both residents and developers. The freeze lasted from 1946 to 1950 while the Planning Commission drew up plans for the area, attempting during these intervening years to answer charges that such specialized plans could not be drawn without the more Comprehensive Plan to be developed

Hopkins Place Housing Project in the Southwest Quadrant of Washington, 1941

for the entire city. Another change was that few of the present residents of Marshall Heights could afford to live in the new housing to be provided by redevelopment.

Opposition to the inclusion of Barry Farms in the Planning Commission's redevelopment plans surfaced and gained strength in 1947. Ulysses J. Banks of the Barry Farms Citizens Association stated that the community had grown during the war and was providing new homes of high standards. He argued that many building permits were pending and that these should not be held up while the Planning Commission, the District commissioners, and Congress made up their minds about redevelopment policy in the District of Columbia.

In 1948, the Planning Commission presented its plans for Marshall Heights to Congress for funding, but the residents of Marshall Heights blocked appropriations for both their neighborhood and Barry Farms. The final blow to the two projects was dealt in the passage of Title I of the 1949 National Housing Act that provided federal funding to the Redevelopment Land Agency except for those projects that had been presented to and rejected by Congress. The District commissioners

had already cited the "great hardships on legitimate private activities" in Marshall Heights and its instructions from the House Appropriations Committee that the project be abandoned and that the District government "furnish utilities and other municipal improvements on the basis of the 1886 narrow gridiron street plan." In 1950, the Planning Commission—as its Minutes for April 1950 show—formally dropped plans for the projects and recommended that the Redevelopment Land Agency turn its attention to the "inlying areas."

MOBILITY

Postwar planning was also concerned with mobility and its effects on the traditional structure of the city. This matter was taken up by the Washington Board of Trade. In October 1946, the Board of Trade created a City Planning Committee, with four subcommittees— on the Comprehensive Plan, coordination, research, and public relations. Fischer Black, chairman of the City Planning Committee, suggested that some regional authority be created to scrutinize planning within the several jurisdictions. As the official city chamber of commerce, the Board of Trade was also acutely aware that the increasing dispersal of population and employment centers would radically affect business operations.

The Highway Improvement Plan of 1944 and the Greiner-DeLeuw Report of 1946. Planning studies were also generated by the District of Columbia Highway Department headed by Captain H. C. Whitehurst. The Highway Improvement Plan of 1944 recommended widening major roads and transforming thoroughfares such as Rock Creek Parkway into major expressways. Canal Road, Fourth Street, and Arizona Avenue were also suggested for widening. Two years later, the Greiner-DeLeuw report was issued, differing from the 1944 plan in its emphasis on increased mileage and elevated highways rather than simple widening of existing thoroughfares. The Planning Commission judged the Greiner-DeLeuw proposals to be more realistic but questioned whether the new routes would serve primarily suburban territory or intermediate residential areas within the District. Commission member J. C. Nichols (as reported in the commission's Minutes for June 1947) dismissed the simplistic notion that highways alone would determine the health of the region. "Downtown and central business values will not be saved by the simple expediency of making it more easy to reach the downtown area." As with the impending plans for redevelopment, the Planning Commission postponed final approval also of highway plans until completion of the Comprehensive Plan.

The Committee of 100 added to the growing chorus of planning proposals. While objecting to the proposed expressway through Rock Creek Park, the committee agreed with the current attitude of opposition to a rapid transit system. The committee believed that ideally, transportation modes should be kept flexible, open to alteration. Large investments in what was seen as a rigid routing system were interpreted as not serving the future dispersed city.

Inviolate Elements of the L'Enfant Plan. Disturbed by the alteration of the old fabric of the city through proposed redevelopment and highway construction, Commission of Fine Arts Chairman David Finley expressed concern to preserve the features of the L'Enfant plan that had influenced so much of the city's development. Finley, as the Minutes of the National Capital Park and Planning Commission for June 1952 show, suggested that his commission supply the Planning Commission with a plan outlining the essential elements of the L'Enfant plan: "the streets, plazas, parks and structures that should be considered inviolate to any but the most necessary and generally approved changes."

Commercial Rezoning. The traditional downtown area along F and G Streets was now moving out like an octopus, embracing Farragut Square and Connecticut Avenue in a new commercial pattern. The Planning Commission considered the effects of commercial rezoning on Sixteenth Street from H Street to Scott Circle on the traditional commercial streets. The spread of commercial zoning beyond the traditional strips previewed eventual commercialization of most of the central city south of M Street. Other commercial patterns were indicated when Planning Commission member J. C. Nichols reported that major commercial and business concerns were "following the dollar" and establishing branch offices and stores in outlying areas, negating some of the need to travel to the central city.

THE NEW GEORGETOWN

For this section of the central city, the Planning Commission received suggestions in 1946 from Colonel Byron Bird of the District Engineer's Office that the declining waterfront be surveyed for new uses, a proposal that reflected his examination of the changing functions of the entire Washington river frontage. Construction in 1949 of the elevated Whitehurst Freeway siphoned traffic off the old town's congested narrow cross streets. The realization of a new Georgetown, a maturing of Georgetown as a distinctive community, had produced a strong concerted voice among residents and supporters against allowing the area north of M Street to be altered at will. Responding to these interests, Congress in 1950 declared all of Georgetown a historic district, and placed under judgment of the Commission of Fine Arts the design of all future construction in Georgetown. As the city's first official historic district, residential Georgetown served as an index of comparison with other historic neighborhoods. It also typified a life-style that would attract high-income residents to the District.

Aerial View of the Georgetown Waterfront, Showing the Whitehurst Freeway Paralleling the River, Early 1950s

The 1950 Comprehensive Plan

Rebuilding of obsolete areas of the city became the primary focus of the 1950 Comprehensive Plan, since a comprehensive basis was required for funding of renewal projects under new national programs and policies. Other requirements also contributed to the plan's form; parks and community facilities, population and land studies, transportation and housing were included. In preparing the plan, Harland Bartholomew, employed by the Planning Commission to direct preparation of such a plan, looked back to the McMillan Commission plan —and through it to the L'Enfant plan—especially in the area of parks, and to plans from the early years of the National Capital Park and Planning Commission on which he had been so much an influence, primarily in the area of recreation and neighborhood identity.

Almost a quarter of a century had passed since those early days. The postwar city offered new challenges and opportunities. Chief among these were questions of the increasing dispersal effects created by the automobile, ideas about security from atomic attack, congestion, and the environment. In response to these concerns, the 1950 plan recognized the need for a healthy and expanded employment center, and therefore proposed the East Mall, the Northwest Rectangle, and the Southwest Rectangle as suitable settings for government office building development. It also proposed the transportation facilities that would be required if those areas were developed.

RINGS AND RADIALS: PLANNING FOR THE BELTWAY
AND RAPID TRANSIT

The 1950 plan modified Bartholomew's circumferential road scheme proposed in the Planning Commission's early years and applied the same circumferential idea to the center of the city where inner rings and crosstown routes were ideographed. The inner loop of three circumferential or ring routes would be located one mile from the White House to carry traffic around parts of the central congested area. The second loop was planned for three to five miles from the White House, tracing the route of the McMillan Commission–inspired Fort Drive which connected the two riverside drive systems. The third loop was to be a new beltway completely around the city between six and ten miles from zero center. Strengthened radial roads would provide access between circumferential roads and allow access between dispersed employment centers.

As illustrated in the plan, however, none of these thoroughfare proposals approached the scale of later freeway programs, either in extent as a system or in size as individual roads. Bartholomew rejected plans proposing development of mass transportation facilities beyond the extant bus and streetcar system, pointing to the large proportion of Washingtonians traditionally tied to their automobiles, the low population density that could not efficiently support a rapid transit system, and the assumption by transit planners that the commuting pattern could be concentrated along a few radial lines. In short, Bartholomew viewed rapid transit as incompatible with the horizontal, dispersed, low-density capital city. As the plan itself stated, "Neither the existing nor the probable future population pattern contains

sufficiently high population densities over a large enough area to warrant the extremely high cost involved in the development of a rapid transit system," a view the Planning Commission was later to disavow in the Year 2000 Policies Plan.

The Constituent City and the Federal Presence. Central to all of these 1950 proposals was the constituent city, the city of homes and residents, and the services they demanded. The plan pictured in vivid graphic form the problem areas of the District, characterized by slums, overcrowding, alleys, and disease. The Washington mosaic of the three categories of "obsolete, blighted, and satisfactory" areas was compared to those of other cities. While specifically discussing Marshall Heights and the Northwest and Southwest quadrants of the L'Enfant city, the plan outlined new physical arrangements for only the Southwest quadrant by reproducing the Goodwillie wartime plans and then comparing them with suggested treatments.

Beyond recommendations the plan made for the constituent city, in the *General Summary*, the important employment role of the federal government in molding the metropolitan city was defined. "The Federal establishment itself, as the major economic base of the community, can make or break the future of the city by its policy—or lack of policy—on geographic arrangement of its operations." In conclusion, the plan suggested that in order to effect regional planning on the scale outlined in its transportation recommendations, a formal association of planning agencies in the area be created.

THE GUIDE FOR FUTURE PLANNING

The 1950 plan broke considerable new ground and it gained strength from the city plans that had preceded it. But such a stance did not guarantee its ability to generate action and compliance. In the *General Summary* of the plan, the commission acknowledged the provenance and clouded expectations of the 1950 recommendations. "The plan here published evolved out of a series of earlier plans, on which the Commission has been working since its start. . . . Its broad goals will not change. . . . To the extent that it is known and approved by the community at large, it will also be an effective

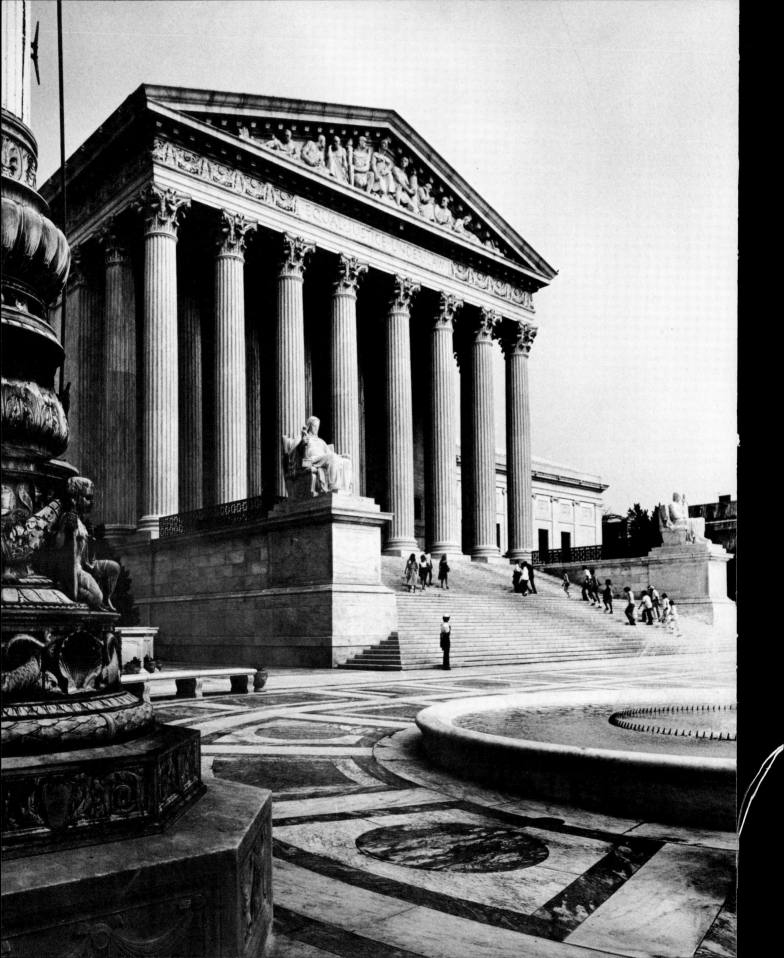

guide for the whole metropolitan area." The reception of the 1950 plan was weakened, however, by its issuance at a time when the composition of the commission was significantly altered by a change in chairmanship. Moreover, a bill to restructure the National Capital Park and Planning Commission was pending.

The all-important Comprehensive Plan, the expected foundation for all future planning, was presented to the public in 1950 by the new commission chairman, William C. Wurster. He had succeeded Major General Ulysses S. Grant III, whose career had been associated with the Planning Commission from the beginning. Grant was a symbol of the continuity of commission policies which were strongly oriented to conventional planning approaches traditionally supported by groups such as the American Planning and Civic Association. In marked contrast, Wurster's appointment reflected President Truman's express concern with the newly identified urban minorities. Wurster's professional qualifications were impressive, beginning with his chairmanship of the Massachusetts Institute of Technology's departments of architecture and planning; he was also married to one of the great leaders in public housing, Catherine K. Bauer. Certainly the appointment broke decisively with the past, and had Wurster not decided to return to the University of California after a year of service on the commission as chairman, his leadership would probably have left a more permanent mark. Upon Wurster's resignation, Harland Bartholomew, a long-time Truman associate originally from Saint Louis, was appointed commission chairman—and began immediately to show that association with the commission and the city since 1920 did not prevent him from reaching independent judgments. Bartholomew's most immediate past service to the commission was in directing the development of the 1950 Comprehensive Plan, and this, too, he was willing to jettison in tune with the times.

Metropolitan City at Mid-Century

The metropolitan city of the mid-twentieth century was actually defined by factors other than public decree. As a capital city Washington derived from the federal presence, but this was expressed variously at different historical periods. During most of the nineteenth century, the federal establishment was of direct importance; it was concentrated, but it was relatively small. By contrast, after World War II, between 1946 and 1950, the federal establishment had grown to what seemed a plateau of about 225,000 civilian employees; it was relatively decentralized throughout the city and the region; and it represented a diminishing share of the total employment of the area. What happened was, in a word, there had been growth of a large private sector, separate from the federal establishment if not independent of it.

SERVICES AND TRADE IN THE NATIONAL COMMUNITY

Service employment had always formed part of the Washington economy. This took the form of a large building industry, printing and lithography, transportation and communications, and other distinctive activities. There were also large numbers engaged in retail trade, in hotels and restaurants and a wide variety of health, legal, and other services. With the postwar era there came, in addition, a host of new activities reflecting Washington's attraction as a national center. Business and professional associations brought to Washington their important national conventions, lobbying, and communications activities. Headquarters or branch offices of many firms with contractual relations to the federal departments located here, as did a booming television industry and an enormous establishment devoted to higher education and academic research. Here also was the apparatus related to federal administrative decisions and appeals, of licensing and regulation, lawyers, expert witnesses, and influence peddlers.

By the 1960s, this national community, dispersed throughout the city and in office building concentrations such as Crystal City, Rosslyn, and around the beltway in Virginia and Maryland, grew at an unprecedented rate. This national community was to be largely independent of the zoning, budget, and other direct controls that could be exercised, however falteringly, over location and development. Many office buildings and other facilities were erected under the

National Community and the Judicial Branch:
Contemporary View of the Supreme Court Building
First and East Capitol Streets, NE, Completed 1935

A Suburban Arlington Subdivision, Showing Newly Constructed Single-Family Homes, 1942

lease-build policies of the Eisenhower administration to accommodate a wide variety of public agencies with a minimal amount of public supervision over physical character. There also appeared, with the promise of still greater growth, significant private industry concentrated mainly in the electronics field. Although not unrelated to federal agencies, the electronics industry was more independent of them than were the more than a thousand national associations and societies in Washington.

Development in Suburban Virginia

The rapid tempo of physical change forced regional planning agencies to respond quickly. In January 1942, the Arlington County Board reported that changes were made in the zoning map at almost every meeting. Major commercial areas were created at Clarendon, Rosslyn, and along Columbia Pike, with smaller centers established to serve more local needs.

A new zoning plan proposed in 1942 by the National Capital Park and Planning Commission called for apartment buildings visible from Washington to be restricted to sixty feet with a few allowances made for buildings of ninety feet. Special treatment was to be accorded the "Vista of Washington Line" that followed the ridge on which the Civil War forts were located. John Nolen, Jr., stated his opposition to the ninety-foot limit as blighting the low-rise buildings surrounding them. No action was taken on the proposal of the commission.

The Arlington County Board suggested, however, that such apartments, "scattered here and there, would tend to break up the monotony of the skyline." In 1945, the Commission of Fine Arts warned the National Capital Park and Planning Commission that private developers owning land in northern Virginia contiguous to Arlington National Cemetery proposed to construct apartment buildings that would be visible within the limits of the Mall. Such a discordant view from the ceremonial core would be a "threat to the integrity of the central composition of the Capital." Eventually, through the efforts of the Planning Commission, enough land—such as the Nevius tract addition to the

Arlington National Cemetery—was acquired along the length of the river in order to push back future high-rise development. In this way, a minimal landscaped foreground was provided to offset the mushrooming Virginia high-rises visible from many sections of the Mall.

Aesthetic problems posed by high-rise apartments and office buildings close to the Virginia waterfront must have caused Planning Commission members to regret that the Virginia lands within the original ten-mile square had been ceded back to the Commonwealth a century earlier. Now, faced with uncontrolled development, the commission began to consider the entire skyline identity of the national capital and its possibilities for coherent design. Pressures for loosely controlled development on what was once the backdrop to the Potomac intensified in the postwar era as the demand for permanent housing steadily increased. Entire portions of Planning Commission meetings were devoted to reviewing development plans in Virginia—and protesting their impact on the view from the District. In the search for leverage to mitigate these effects, the Planning Commission recognized as one offsetting item

the fact that the development was also subject to financing regulations of the Federal Housing Administration.

Arlington Towers. In 1949, the Planning Commission was faced with the proposed thirteen-story Arlington Towers project designed by architect Donald H. Drayer. The Arlington County Board had approved a "relaxation" in the zoning regulations to allow for the unusual height and density of the proposed building. The Planning Commission vigorously opposed the generation of more traffic in the area of Key Bridge, the creation of an "unsightly background for the Mall" in the special spot zoning, and the light color of the building that would compete with the Washington Monument, the Capitol, and other monumental structures. Eventually constructed in spite of commission opposition, Arlington Towers correctly predicted the height of future construction, as in the high-rise office cluster at Rosslyn. Even today the Towers remains a major element in the Virginia landscape.

George Washington Memorial Parkway. Other new developments sprang up along the extant access roads

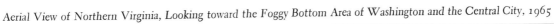

Aerial View of Northern Virginia, Looking toward the Foggy Bottom Area of Washington and the Central City, 1965

to Washington. For example, the memorial character of the George Washington Parkway, originally conceived of—and approved by the Planinng Commission—as a picturesque parkway, was threatened by the flood of new demands made on the land. These problems facing the commission Harland Bartholomew saw as symptomatic of large areas of disagreement among federal, state, and city planning officials. Threats to the special character of the George Washington Memorial Parkway included National Airport; commercial zone changes along Washington Street in Alexandria; Bellhaven, just south of Alexandria, on the brink of apartment construction, most notably in the form of the massive Hunting Creek Apartment development; and the Woodland Manor subdivision where the sponsors proposed a recreation and commercial area fronting on Mount Vernon Parkway. In all cases, until the relationship between the National Capital Park and Planning Commission and suburban planning agencies could be formalized, preservation of the scenic qualities of these extensions of the national capital depended on the individual resolution of each individual case.

Springfield. Extending the sight lines into Virginia, the Planning Commission could effect little influence beyond suggestions as to how proposed developments should be coordinated with federal, District, and metropolitan area needs. In the summer of 1947, John Nolen, Jr., then executive director of the Planning Commission, reported on a major development about to occur in Springfield, then "nothing . . . but a cross road" at Shirley Highway and Franconia Road. Six thousand acres along Shirley Highway had been assembled by developers to provide a residential community for over 45,000 residents. In the process of development, large tracts of agricultural land had been rezoned to residential, business, and industrial uses. Although this virtual city lay beyond the limits of Planning Commission purview, the commission suggested that new residents of Springfield could not funnel themselves entirely into Washington. "The development should not be planned solely as a tributary of Washington, but should be more of a self-contained community. . . . Consideration [ought to] be given to the development

of employment centers in the vicinity."

TALL BUILDINGS AT THE URBAN RIM

By 1950, tall buildings, often considered evidence of a commercial society, began to rise along the rim of the metropolitan city. The horizontal city within the boundaries of the District of Columbia was one of the features that distinguished Washington from any other city. Thus, pressures to build upwards had pushed high-rise construction to the very rim of the metropolis, on land in the Maryland and Virginia counties not subject to the capital city's height controls. Tall buildings were not just those built by private interests; the government was also a creator of these artifacts inimical to the city's traditions. Between 1947 and 1948, Commissioner of Public Buildings W. E. Reynolds brought new building plans for the National Institutes of Health in Bethesda for consideration by the Planning Commission. The National Institutes of Health research hospital as proposed was to rise thirteen stories and be located on the highest ground, with subordinate buildings grouped around the main building in a relationship reminiscent of the City Beautiful civic center formula. An epitome of the management-oriented civil servant whose philosophies influenced the spartan public buildings of the early postwar years, Reynolds justified the building's height from the "standpoint of economy and efficiency of operation." In January 1948, the Planning Commission approved the building plans.

Planning for Growth in the Maryland Counties

Growth was being generated in Maryland in such volume that M. Bond Smith, general counsel to the Maryland–National Capital Park and Planning Commission, characterized the situation as a "unique federal problem arising solely because this region is part and parcel of the Nation's Capital." In 1948, Prince George's County, Maryland, was the fastest growing section in the Washington metropolitan area, forcing the boundaries covered by the Maryland commission to be extended ever outward. Urban sprawl threatened the comprehensive stream valley park program authorized but never entirely funded by the Capper-Cramton Act. Director of the Maryland commission, Fred Tuemmler, stated that Prince George's County parks were being acutely affected by "both federal and private development of employment centers and the expansion of Maryland University." These much-threatened stream valley parks were more than decorative; they conserved natural resources, assisted flood control efforts, framed the metropolitan city, and added to the value of adjacent residential developments.

The 1948 Home Rule Charter. With the end of World War II, the pent-up demand for land pushed home construction and its related needs for schools, shopping facilities, and recreation into the forefront for the suburban counties. The population of both Prince George's and Montgomery Counties had nearly doubled in the ten years between 1940 and 1950. (Montgomery County increased from 89,490 in 1940 to 194,182 in 1950. Prince George's County rose from 83,912 in 1940 to 164,401 in 1950.) Pressures for developing land to its maximum density—and thus for developers to reap huge profits from the radical increase in value of the land— led to rumblings against the planning powers of the independent Maryland–National Capital Park and Planning Commission. In what was billed as a fight for home rule, forces in favor of the counties' controlling development of their own land succeeded in passing a home rule charter in 1948. The charter failed, however, to extract the planning powers from the Maryland commission. Antagonism over who would benefit from development dominated the activities of the counties' political and planning bodies for at least two decades. It was not until environmental and no-growth policies came to the fore in the late 1960s that these unchecked tendencies toward development for profit's sake were questioned.

Parks and Highways. The Maryland–National Capital Park and Planning Commission's most effective tools in channeling and directing growth were its park acquisitions and highway plans, both areas in which the commission achieved considerable distinction. Purchased jointly by the National Capital Park and Planning Commission and the Maryland–National Capital Park and Planning Commission, stream valley parkland acquired previous to World War II with Capper-Cramton funding, and that acquired by the same funding in the postwar era, funneled residential development in between thin wedges of open space and were usually close to major highways radiating out from the District. Following the lead taken in the National Capital Park and Planning Commission's 1950 Comprehensive Plan, the Maryland commission unveiled its highway plan two years later. The proposed spiderweb of radials and circumferential dual highways provided a basis for public discussions. The proposed new radials included the relocated Interstate 270 to Frederick and the Annapolis Freeway (U.S. Route 50), both under construction in 1952. The proposed circumferential roads were named the Intercounty Belt Freeway and the Outer Belt Freeway. Both provided for bypassing the District and linking suburban population centers. The Intercounty Belt Freeway anticipated the route later followed by the Maryland portion of the Capital Beltway. The Outer Belt Freeway, proposed to be located even further from the population center established by the District boundaries, was never constructed.

THE REGIONAL VIEW: REDEVELOPMENT, MOBILITY, AND FUTURE GROWTH

The ability of the Maryland commission to retain its planning powers throughout the postwar era of expansion did not necessarily reflect great effectiveness in structuring the urbanizing counties. The full effects of uncontrolled and uncoordinated growth had yet to shock development-minded officials into an appreciation of the waste in resources and large public costs incurred. Yet, the Maryland commission needed less to be reconstituted than it needed to express a regional point of view rather than the more parochial bicounty point of view that reflected the different traditions and outlooks of Prince George's and Montgomery Counties. The ability to develop this larger view of the interrelationships with each other and with the District of Columbia would portend the ability of all the national capital's jurisdictions to reach common goals and to put aside immediate gains in favor of long-term regional benefits.

Although the growth of the postwar capital city often appeared directionless, several themes that emerged in the decade following World War II were important in recharting the metropolitan city's future. The most important of these themes were *redevelopment* by both public and private efforts, *mobility*, and the need for future growth to be guided by *comprehensive and specialized planning*, based on the strengths of previous plans and continuity between the historic and modern city. Public redevelopment was transforming the appearance and functions of large sections of the inner city, perhaps an urban reflection of the heady postwar era of world leadership and unprecedented national wealth. Private redevelopment was finding new and profitable uses for older, settled areas in the region; new development was changing towns into employment subcenters, farm property into housing subdivisions with appropriately historical names, and rows of townhouses into commercial strips. On a less disruptive level, old areas of the city were undergoing renewal by self-regeneration, by discovery of the values of historic buildings and neighborhoods, and by growth of a strong community consciousness, as exemplified in Georgetown. Tying together concepts of residence and work, new platforms of mobility were planned, making the city accessible and siphoning traffic from sensitive areas—but at the same time creating their own environmental hazards. The 1950 Comprehensive Plan, while rooted in policies dating from the National Capital Park and Planning Commission's early years and reflecting the dispersal trends of its time, did reestablish the need for such comprehensive planning and for project and functional studies. The postwar city, suffering from the effects of planning by many and independent agencies, had already inaugurated the tools of its restructured future.

Mobility: Telephoto View along New York Avenue, NE

The Great Falls of the Potomac, a Major Topographic Feature of the National Capital Region

A Typical Suburban Vista
Just Ten Miles from
Washington: Telephoto
View of Shirley Highway
at Springfield, Virginia

Dulles International Airport, Serving the National Capital Region

CHAPTER XI THE TURNAROUND 1952–1960

The Turnaround 1952-1960

Regional Planning and the National Capital Planning Commission

Suburban growth had produced metropolitan Washington, embracing the four contiguous counties surrounding the city in Maryland and Virginia. In common with many of the nation's metropolitan areas, Washington witnessed the outward migration of families, the growth of outlying shopping centers, the emergence of large employment concentrations in the suburbs, and related evidences of the city's sprawling dispersal. Entire weekend sections of the *Washington Star* and *Washington Post* reported suburban homebuilders' activity. The characteristic low densities and sprawling nature of development had led to a huge demand for transportation, water and sewer lines, and other services provided by local government—all difficult to satisfy because all were at a predictably higher per family cost. Reality soon outstripped the initial illusions of suburban economy.

THE SUBURBAN BOOM: NO FREE LUNCH

There was to be no such thing as a free lunch, it turned out. The mystique of a parklike environment, the appeal of newness in housing and schools, the apparently more manageable scale of the small local community, and the feeling that one had escaped the problems of the central city added to the postwar suburban boom. Besides, that was where the houses were.

At the bottom of it all was the automobile, which had made possible this escape to the suburbs and was itself a fascinating adult toy. The car was an emancipating device for greatly magnifying the mobility of entire families, with access to new forms of leisure as well as more fundamental opportunities in specialized employment, education, and social experience. In most cities, the central core was filled with obsolescent industry, a deteriorating commercial downtown, and housing that was rejested by all but the most needy. People abandoned this scene with little regret. In Washington the central city was filled with federal establishments, offering by far the most significant concentration of employment and providing a viable metropolitan center.

As a metropolitan center Washington served a nation of citizens increasingly oriented to their national government and obliged to visit the capital for business as well as tourist reasons. Such coming and going did not benefit the retail shopping center. Instead, older settlements

e Residential City and a Positive
ban Choice: The Corner
R and Thirty-first Streets, NW

255

Evidence of the City's Sprawling Dispersal: Aerial View of Fairfax Village, 1947

within the metropolitan area were subject to renewal in the form of new office complexes and employment sub-centers, as along K and L Streets. This possibility was accentuated when it became clear that the temporary wartime boom would be extended by national growth, increasing industrial and social complexity, and unavoidable worldwide responsibilities.

The Need to Act. Demands for new growth of the capital city produced the movement in 1950 toward regional planning. What resulted was the 1952 legislation reorganizing the National Capital Park and Planning

Commission as the National Capital Planning Commission and creating the National Capital Regional Planning Council. By 1956, the need to act was also recognized in good part by the work of the new planning agencies, especially the description of metropolitan aims implicit in the Mass Transportation Survey. Finally, in 1957, came the creation of the Metropolitan Washington Council of Governments, the area's first voluntary but formal organization of local governments on a regional scale.

The major development over-all in this period was this move to facilitate regional planning, the scope of which had been recognized in the McMillan Commission's proposals and in the work of the National Capital Park and Planning Commission's early years. Regional powers were implicit in the Capper-Cramton program which had assisted the National Capital Park and Planning Commission in planning for and acquiring regional parklands. The Planning Commission had also assisted in the creation of suburban Maryland and Virginia county planning commissions. Activity of the National Capital Park and Planning Commission in the region had diminished in the Depression and wartime years, however, and the dispersal of new development had with so little warning flooded the countryside that regional plans now assumed new urgency. There was a need to formulate planning policies for acquiring additional open space, for building a mass transportation system, and for restructuring and developing a metropolitan employment and commercial center to offer conveniences superior to dispersed office clusters and suburban shopping centers.

EFFORTS TO REORGANIZE THE COMMISSION

Some of the same groups that had actively supported the creation of the National Capital Park Commission in 1924 and the National Capital Park and Planning Commission in 1926 now—as in the early 1940s—were urging the creation of a new planning commission but, like the American Planning and Civic Association, these groups had lost their political clout. The Capper-Cramton program was completed, and the settlement of the entire District precluded major new park acquisitions. At the same time the Planning Commission entered a transition period; its park planning and acquisition function was phased out and its city planning function gained importance. From 1947 to 1952 there was much community talk, especially in the suburbs, but little formal legislative discussion. The most influential congressional figures, particularly Representative Howard W. Smith of Virginia—who was also the formidably powerful chairman of the House Rules Committee—believed that the region was not sufficiently united in its views to permit successful action by the Congress, and that it was better to let local opinion mature. Smith's district had been redrawn in response to growth in the Virginia suburbs. Because Northern Virginia was rapidly urbanizing and becoming less "southern," the redrawing of the congressional district split off Arlington and Fairfax as a separate congressional district (represented by Joel Broyhill). Representative Smith retained a constituency — outside Broyhill's district — with conservative views to match his own and was therefore able to maintain his political power in Congress and in the committees of which he was a member. In the end, however, Smith and other members of the House District Committee were persuaded by Virginia planning bodies to act, and the 1952 National Capital Planning Act (*Public Law 82-592*) was passed.

THE 1952 NATIONAL CAPITAL PLANNING ACT

The National Capital Planning Act of 1952 (66 Stat. 781) gave more authority to the National Capital Planning Commission, significantly shorn of the word "Park" in its title. The National Capital Planning Commission was now recognized as a national government agency receiving its annual funding directly by congressional appropriation rather than as an element in the District government budget. Commission membership was also changed. In view of the importance of highway planning, the director of the Bureau of Public Roads was added as an ex officio member. The director of the Forest Service was dropped. The presidential appointments were expanded to five members, two of whom were to be residents of the District of Columbia or the metropolitan area.

Recognizing that the National Capital Planning Commission's planning powers were now focused both on the National Capital Region and on the settled city within the ten-mile square District, the 1952 act specified that the commission plan for the "appropriate and orderly development and redevelopment of the National Capital and the conservation of the important natural and historical features thereof." Like its predecessor commission, the new commission was empowered to establish coordinating committees to "correlate the efforts among the various agencies." The National Capital Planning Commission was instructed to prepare and adopt a Comprehensive Plan, and as a critical area a thoroughfare plan was suggested. When matters of new

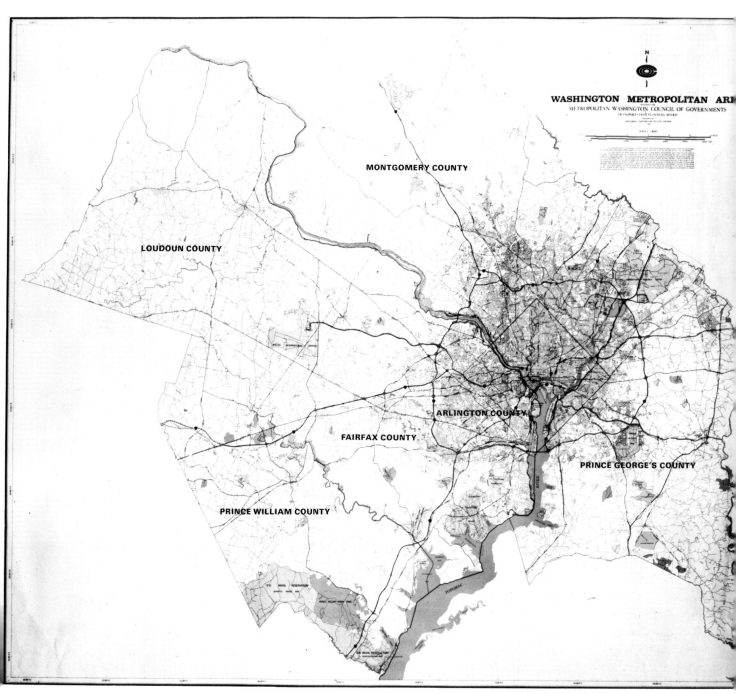

WASHINGTON METROPOLITAN ARE

METROPOLITAN WASHINGTON COUNCIL OF GOVERNMENTS

TRANSPORTATION PLANNING BOARD

MONTGOMERY COUNTY

LOUDOUN COUNTY

ARLINGTON COUNTY

FAIRFAX COUNTY

PRINCE GEORGE'S COUNTY

PRINCE WILLIAM COUNTY

Map of the National Capital Region, Showing the Area under the Jurisdiction of the National Capital Planning Commission, 1968

development or construction were proposed, the agencies involved were supposed to consult with the National Capital Planning Commission as to the effect on the Comprehensive Plan: "After such consultation and suitable consideration of the view of the Commission, the agency may proceed to take action in accordance with its legal responsibilities and authority." This provision of mandatory review was built on the earlier experience of the National Capital Park and Planning Commission and the Commission of Fine Arts.

THE NATIONAL CAPITAL REGIONAL PLANNING COUNCIL

Regional cooperation had deep roots in the voluntary regional committees of the National Capital Park and Planning Commission's early years. Regional planning was institutionalized on a formal basis by the 1952 National Capital Planning Act's Section 3, which established the National Capital Regional Planning Council. Membership of this council was composed of appointees from each of the jurisdictions, and staffing was provided by the Planning Commission itself. The important work of the National Capital Regional Planning Council was the regional studies it produced; especially significant was the Mass Transportation Survey conducted jointly with the Planning Commission. (On the Mass Transportation Survey, see further Chapter XII; on the Regional Planning Council, see Chapter XV.)

Redevelopment and the Turnaround Trend

Redevelopment theory contained the hope that a turnaround trend could be stimulated, bringing people back from the suburbs to the city. The assumption was that through redevelopment, or urban renewal, vital new communities could be created within the central city to provide homeowners a realistic alternative to suburban living, a positive urban choice. Redevelopment was seen, in part, as an opportunity to turn around the outward-bound movement to the suburbs and at the same time revitalize the central city. Thus, along with regional planning efforts, redevelopment plans moved ahead. Rebuilding the old city had been authorized by the District of Columbia Redevelopment Act of 1945, as amended, and institutionalized in the Redevelopment Land Agency (RLA) but was not funded until the passage of the 1949 Housing Act. The National Capital Park and Planning Commission had been authorized to designate the land and prepare the plans. The Redevelopment Land Agency possessed the novel authority to assemble land and prepare it for the developers. The Redevelopment Land Agency also had unique access to federal loans and subsidies for redevelopment.

In support of redevelopment efforts was the 1955–56 study conducted by consultant Harold M. Lewis for the Washington Zoning Revision Office. Designed to make more specific the zoning recommendations of the 1950 Comprehensive Plan, to coordinate zoning with the plan, and thus to resolve conflicts between the Zoning Commission and the Planning Commission, Lewis's report, *Rezoning Study of the District of Columbia*, was prepared. The report's basic thrust and only real success was to update the zoning regulations. The report also updated the neighborhood concept as it had been developed in the early years of the Planning Commission. Lewis studied 137 neighborhoods which he defined by major traffic arteries, parks, and institutional lands as well as by population densities sufficient to support one public school. Data collected for each neighborhood included information on playgrounds, parks, and business needs, with the community center focused on the employment and business centers. This involved a redefinition of the neighborhood center concept of the 1920s and 1930s where recreation and education facilities were the key indicators of neighborhood identity. Lewis identified 40 "problem neighborhoods"—most of them bordering the monumental core, south and east of the Capitol and north of Massachusetts Avenue—judged deficient in several of the criteria for an ideal neighborhood package. To improve these problem neighborhoods, Lewis recommended their designation as redevelopment areas, and thus gave further support to the 1950 Comprehensive Plan recommendation that the Shaw area and portions of the Northwest and Northeast quadrants be redeveloped. (For detailed discussion of Redevelopment, see Chapter XIV.)

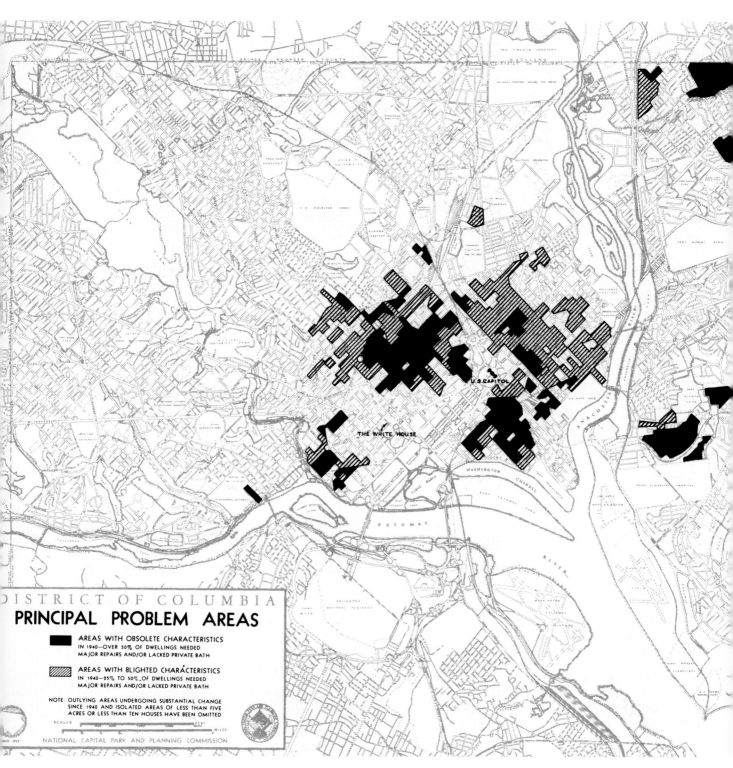

Map Showing Principal Problem Areas of the District of Columbia, 1950

Capitol Park, the First of the New Projects in the Redeveloped Southwest, 1960s

Transportation

An integral part of planning activities in Washington at mid-century, preparation of a mass transportation plan was called for in a provision of the 1952 reorganization act. Congress implemented this provision by designating funds in the National Capital Planning Commission's 1955 and 1957 budgets for the Planning Commission and the National Capital Regional Planning Council to jointly conduct the Mass Transportation Survey.

THE MASS TRANSPORTATION SURVEY

This became the first such study to be based on an integrated approach in which land-use implications of transportation were fully examined—and the first such study by a planning agency rather than an ad hoc committee or a highway group. While over-all policy direction was

exercised by the Planning Commission, the daily work of conducting the Mass Transportation Survey was supervised by a Joint Steering Committee established by the National Capital Planning Commission and the National Capital Regional Planning Council with representatives from both Maryland and Virginia agencies. The $400,000, two-year-long study was set up to survey both highway needs and mass transit needs so that a unified mass transportation plan resulted. Kenneth M. Hoover, Project Director of the Mass Transportation Survey, forecast that if the emphasis on the automobile and highways continued, by 1980 the region theoretically would need radial and circumferential expressways with capacities ranging from four to twenty-six lanes. The capacities of thoroughfares would need to be increased and widened not only in the outlying areas, but through the central city as well. With this startling picture of financial and environmental disaster, the study recommended a balanced transportation system made up of a new rapid transit system, the improvement and extension of existing highways, and a system of parking facilities at mass transit station sites. Supported by the area's planning bodies and local governments, and the federal government as well, the National Capital Planning Commission and the Regional Planning Council presented the recommendations of the survey to Congress. (On the Mass Transportation Survey, see the detailed discussion in Chapter XII.)

(On the Mass Transportation Survey, see the detailed discussion in Chapter XII.)

THE JOINT COMMITTEE ON WASHINGTON METROPOLITAN PROBLEMS

Metropolitan development planning had long been limited by categorical federal grant-in-aid programs and federal planning for the central city that included many of the metropolitan service networks. To look more closely at how federal interests and responsibilities beyond the ten-mile square city described in the Constitution were being affected by metropolitan growth, Congress in 1957 established the Joint Committee on Washington Metropolitan Problems. The committee—popularly called the Bible Committee, after its chairman—held hearings, submitted reports, and drafted legislation over the next three years. The Joint Committee urged Congress to enact—in the form of a joint resolution—an important policy declaration of federal interest in the proper development of the metropolitan area (Public Law 86-527); it published and gave widespread distribution to its research and more general recommendations; it supported enactment of legislation creating a Potomac Interceptor Sewer (Public Law 86-515). By far the most important activity of the Joint Committee was related to mass transportation. In the course of hearings on mass transportation, findings of the Mass Transportation Survey being conducted by the National Capital Planning Commission and the Regional Planning Council were presented. Along with the National Capital Planning Commission and others, it supported a mass transportation program (Public Law 86-669), which created the National Capital Transportation Agency.

THE NATIONAL CAPITAL TRANSPORTATION ACT

The outcome of the studies and hearings was enactment of the National Capital Transportation Act. This law directed the National Capital Transportation Agency, a federal corporation, to plan in detail for the construction of a mass transportation system to service the entire area, and to set such plans within the more comprehensive provisions for the region as a whole and the unified treatment of highways as well. It further provided for the negotiation of an interstate compact between the states of Maryland and Virginia and the federal government (including the District of Columbia) to create an effective body to take over what the National Capital Transportation Agency had commenced—although the interstate compact as ultimately created did not include federal representation. Nonetheless, the compact provided for the first metropolitan areawide operating agency. Thus, the definition of a working relationship between it and the planning activities of the region was cast.

Metropolitan Washington: City, Suburb, and Region

The city that the National Capital Planning Commission staff studied in order to have a basis for formulation of the Year 2000 Policies Plan (the commission's 1961 comprehensive guide to future growth) was like other cities in its expansion at the edges and its rebuilding of older portions. The rebuilding process was recognized at the public level—and seen in the inner city—by redevelopment activities. In the private sector, older portions in the various jurisdictions underwent change, most notably in the giant office subcenter of Rosslyn. Although constructed by private enterprise, these office buildings, like so many of those in the District, provided offices for federal employees when demands for space spilled beyond the capacity of existing public buildings. Witnessing creation of these office clusters, highly visible and making new demands on essential services, the capital city needed to redefine its image: did it represent the ceremonial capital city or would it become, like other

The Virginia Skyline, Early 1960s

American cities, bespangled by glass office towers and beribboned by connecting highways?

The Implications of Rosslyn. A settlement with firm commercial and industrial roots, Rosslyn's future role as a high-density commercial and office-building center had been predicted by construction of the Key Bridge in 1923. After World War II, Rosslyn was no longer a terminus of land and water routes but an important portal to the city from the Virginia side of the George Washington Memorial Parkway. A complex of over a dozen high-rise office buildings, luxury apartment buildings, hotels, and other commercial enterprises, Rosslyn was developed in the late 1950s along a multitiered arrangement of movement. The ground-level streets were devoted almost entirely to the automobiles, with upper-level footbridges and elevated sidewalks provided for pedestrian traffic. Below grade, pedestrian concourses, bus interchanges, and automobile parking were to be found

—below that, the Metro subway station. The crowding in of high-value construction at Rosslyn exhibited, as the *Christian Science Monitor* noted, the "partnership between business and local government [that] also reaped benefits for the Arlington taxpayer," since the investment added to the county's tax base. Despite the cluster's financial success, helped by large amounts of federally leased space and new rivalry with the skylines of other Virginia cities, its proximity brought "something of a Manhattan look to the Washington area."

The Ranch House and the Curtain Wall. Suburbanization, new transportation technology, the 1952 act that redefined the federal role in the city and the metropolitan area, and a more powerful thrust for planning were all generated by the confirmed growth of the postwar capital city. Never would there be a return to the simpler days of the New Deal or the even earlier period still fresh in the recollection of some Washingtonians.

New Suburbs, New Cities: Aerial View of Lake Anne Center at Reston, Virginia, 1977

The ranch house and the curtain wall were the architectural language of the period, but the outstanding determinant of urban design was the sprawling character dictated by the expressways—more important now than in their time had been the canals, railroads, or paved roads.

Regional shopping centers, industrial parks, office building complexes, and apartment house developments were some of the important building types to appear in the new suburbs, heralding the future character of the metropolitan fringes. Moreover, new federal establishments on the model of the Bureau of Standards were moving to outlying locations, while other agencies were relocating less visibly perhaps as tenants in the new office-building centers. Local government itself responded to the movement with big consolidated educational plants, including new community colleges, and Montgomery County attempted to prime the pump of expressway industrial development by erecting a series of public buildings along such a highly visible right of way. Such development was geographically defined in corridors, and the corridor and the cluster soon became important elements in metropolitan-scale planning. The most important of these corridors were located toward

Baltimore and toward Richmond, the Baltimore corridor containing not only the ancient post road, now called U.S. Route 1, and the two principal railroad lines, but also the Baltimore-Washington Parkway and a greatly improved U.S. Route 29. Much of the change had commenced earlier, but in the eight-year period from 1952 to 1960, the Washington area—certainly in terms of its metropolitan structure—turned decisively toward its regional future.

For by the decade of the 1950s everyone could see what William Finley (executive director of the Planning Commission from 1958 to 1962) and the new breed of city planners saw, the contrast between the central city and the mushrooming suburban belt. What was more acutely felt by the planners, however, was the lack of coordination between the two planning efforts, city and suburb, and so far as the Maryland side of the Potomac was concerned, a positive decline in the close working relationships that had characterized central city and Maryland suburban planning in the quarter century before World War II. The basic lack of coordination between planning efforts was most visibly stated in the accelerated construction of tall apartment buildings along the Arlington ridge and of the dense office-build-

Telephoto View of the Arlington Ridge and Rosslyn As It Looks Today

ing clusters at Rosslyn. And only a short distance away, similar developments were soon to rise in the direction of Alexandria, and in Silver Spring and Bethesda.

THE WASHINGTON IMAGE AND URBAN BALANCE

During the decade of the fifties the dichotomy was sharpened between the public federal buildings of the monumental core and the privately owned structures of the suburban communities; between the buildings mainly of the first half of the twentieth century and those of the quarter century immediately following World War II; between the carefully planned, architecturally articulated central city and the jumbled anarchy of laissez-faire; and—perhaps of greatest consequence for Washington—between the deliberate concept of an exceptional city, a *national capital city*, and a city that could have been built anywhere in the continental expanse of the United States. What was at stake was the image of Washington, the entire metropolitan city regarded as a whole: its urban planning tradition of nearly two centuries, its careful regard for

the natural setting and the continuity of its built environment, its specially designed entrances and carefully contrived vistas, its concept of parks and open spaces. Only exceptional measures of regionwide planning could express this image and its underlying philosophy of urban design.

From a practical point of view, sound decisions on the future of the central city were impossible without some assumptions and controls that would guide the future of the suburban subcenters. These understandings of the metropolitan city had to calculate the balance between office and other types of space in the central city as against that in outlying sites—and the question had become one of importance to the federal establishment, nearly one-third of which was located outside the District of Columbia by mid-century. Another assumption had to be made, moreover, on the balance between the federal establishment and private enterprise. On such assumptions would rest calculations of transportation and other urban services. And these understandings would determine, in the end, the critical elements of the future city and its growth.

Contemporary Urban Im
Aerial View from Washington C
down Pennsylvania Ave

CHAPTER XII MOBILITY 1920 – 1976

hoto View of the Capital Beltway
Tyson's Corner and
Dulles Airport Access Road

Mobility 1920-1976

Vehicles of Change

To a designer in the City Beautiful tradition, the urban experience was to be realized on foot. The scale figure in his drawings was not a Piranesian idler but a business-like stroller, traversing the malls, riverside promenades, or sidewalks of the city, as purposeful as a traveler or tourist. The period was one in which the man on horse-back, carriage traffic, and the omnibus had waned; the automobile had scarcely arrived. While planners hardly can be said to have embraced the trolley car—although the McMillan Commission report contained a memorable sentence, undoubtedly written by Frederick Law Olmsted, Jr., that referred to the "play of light and shade where the streets break through the columns of trees, and the passage of streetcars and teams give needed life to the Mall"—they did succeed in Washington in getting its characteristic wirescape suppressed and put underground.

Transition from Streetcar to Auto and Bus. Washington had fought World War I on foot. City residents used trolley cars, which were never altogether absent from the imagination of the city's planners. The annual reports of the Planning Commission contained references that could have been aggregated into a comprehensive trolley-car system—but American society was bound elsewhere. By the mid-1920s, the automobile and the bus had erupted in a city larger, of greater extent, and with greater need for mobility. Vast social changes in urban living commenced, extending beyond the separation of homes from work places—or the emancipation of suburban wives—to the reverberations caused by continuous waves of dispersal from the city's center. The great transition had begun. Miles of hard-surfaced streets lengthened. Some streetcar routes were abandoned and some streets were widened. By 1924, a gasoline tax of two cents per gallon assured highway builders of funds earmarked for highway use.

PLANNING FOR AUTOMOBILES, BOTH PARKED AND MOVING

As congestion of cars increased steadily during the 1930s and early forties, programs of additional street widening and various structural changes were undertaken. Later on, Washington's circles considered to be bottlenecks in L'Enfant's generous street system were refashioned.

Trolley Car and Other Vehicles on Dupont Circle, Late 1930s

Aerial View of the Southwest Waterfront, Showing
(left) a Portion of the Fourteenth Street Bridge and (right) the
Southeast/Southwest Freeway Bridge, Late 1960s

Tunnels and underpasses were provided to carry street-cars underground in the most congested stretches, as at Dupont Circle. Grade separations were followed by expressways on the model of the Whitehurst Freeway, over the Georgetown waterfront.

In the 1920s, the city grew toward the northwest across Rock Creek as major arterial roads were provided with bridges. In the following years, the Potomac was bridged at Georgetown and above, at Chain Bridge; historic Long Bridge at Fourteenth Street was doubled. The priority earlier given to crossings of the upper Anacostia to carry Baltimore-bound traffic was followed by bridges across the lower Anacostia. Thus, the early river-bottom city burst the natural bounds imposed by its rivers.

Between 1920 and 1930, automobile registrations in the District of Columbia quadrupled. Consequences of this growth and change in travel habits were felt in every sector of city life. Meetings of the Planning Commission had to deal directly with street widenings, new road-planning proposals, bridge construction, parking ar-

rangements, and more fundamentally with regulatory and zoning changes. Regulations were needed both to provide direct accommodation, as in the form of parking, and to recognize the pervasive shifts in population location and density that were primarily motivated by adjustments to the automobile. Not the least of these shifts occurred in residential neighborhoods, as pressure for higher densities stimulated the building of apartment houses and as streets were preempted by cars, both parked and moving. The decline of the small-scaled neighborhood commercial districts followed as business concentrated in larger-sized units at shopping centers where parking was provided.

Highway and Expressway Planning: The Comprehensive View

In ongoing change, which planners had little authority to control, there were opportunities to advance as well as to adjust, but the prevailing response was one of accommodation. By the time of World War II, it was becoming clear that the planning resources of the highway program in both city and region were producing a body of experience, data, and skilled personnel that, intent upon accomplishing its own objectives and probing ever more deeply into travel behavior, threatened to distort the balance of more comprehensive planning. More than simply formal adherence to some kind of master planning was involved. Creative interaction was needed between the two planning programs, with interpretation and application at regional scale. That this came about, with the influential support of the agency then called the Public Roads Administration (now the Federal Highway Administration), was a substantial accomplishment of the Planning Commission. And because of this accomplishment, Washington avoided many of the excesses and disasters of the urban expressway programs in other cities.

The Capital Beltway and the Interstate System. Construction of the Capital Beltway, the nation's first such circumferential expressway, was well coordinated with regional and local planning, and its impact was generally anticipated and approved. The over-all re-

gional effects that were later widely deplored reflected changing values rather than ignorance or error. Yet, for all its venturing into the interstate highway system, Washington did not become the international showcase of expressway extravagance that Los Angeles did. The congressional freeze on construction of the city's northwest expressway, and the protracted controversy over the routing of Interstate 66 and the bridge it would require above Georgetown, stimulated energetic community participation and established a basis for widely approved decisions. Such massive engineering features as a north segment of the proposed Inner Loop freeway system, and the proposed North Central Freeways and associated interchanges, were maturely appraised and rejected because of their social effect as well as economic impact. In all these decisions the Planning Commission led the debate as well as provided a forum for community views. Any summation of the postwar years would have to acknowledge that public emphasis—indeed, fascination—was with the new freeways.

The 1939 Highway Planning Survey. Launched by the Federal Aid Highway Act of 1938, continuous road planning in the District of Columbia commenced with the 1939 Highway Planning Survey. For the first time, the District had been treated "as a state" in the distribution of the federal road funds. The first highway plan for the city (replacing the earlier periodic road programs) was drafted in 1941. It was a more specialized and strong-minded highway planning effort than had been the street extensions offered in the 1893 Highway Plan or the more rounded and comprehensive Thoroughfare Plan of 1930 developed by the young Planning Commission. The 1941 planning efforts were succeeded by new ventures that would confirm the city's planning for the motor age.

Through Streets and Expressways. In 1946, the first comprehensive transportation report tentatively sketched the needs of the region. Within the District, a system of arterial highways emerged from this effort. The central area was defined by a box formed by K Street and Constitution Avenue, Fourth and Twentieth Streets, NW. At a distance of five or six miles, a cir-

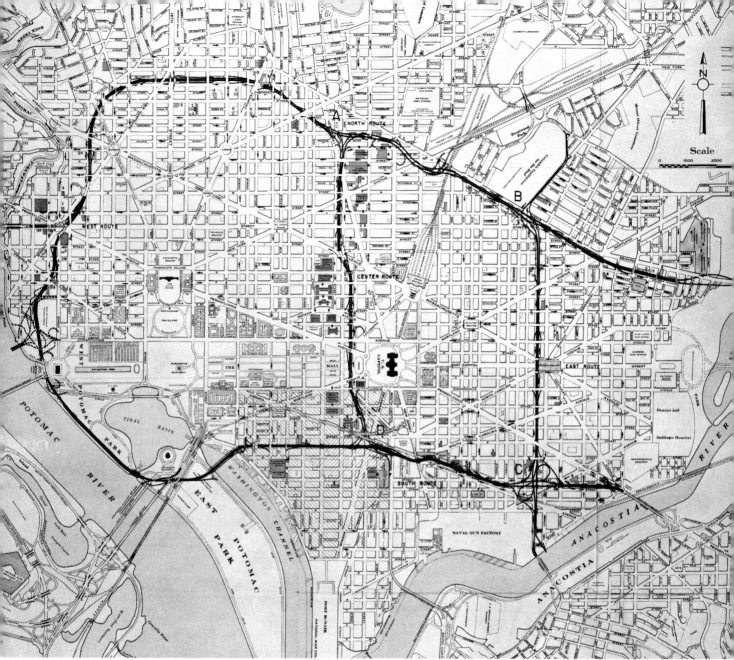

Proposed Inner Loop Freeway System, 1955

cumferential route defined by Nebraska Avenue, Military Road, Missouri Avenue, South Dakota Avenue, Bladensburg Road, and Benning Road carried traffic around the central city. This system was continued on the south side by roads paralleling the Potomac, and across Independence Avenue to South Capitol Street. By 1948, a further detailed network of through streets was described. The major forward thrust was a modest system of expressways, hopefully to be of limited access, but their design features had hardly been examined.

Under construction was the first of the expressways, the Whitehurst Freeway, an elevated highway above the Georgetown waterfront, which in conception was to connect with a high-capacity treatment of K Street never, in fact, undertaken. Except for the considerable improvements to the south where five bridges carried the arterials across the Potomac and the Anacostia, little was done to improve access to the central city. And the day of vast expressways and the interstate system had not yet dawned.

274

Regional Planning: Devices of Coordination

Creation of a regional highway system was a notable development of the late 1930s, although its fruition was not evident until 1947. The focus at the Planning Commission was on the immediate pressure points of coordination, the interjurisdictional Potomac bridges. The planners also succeeded in developing a comprehensive view of the city's future, and in this way raised the essential question of highway improvements in terms of land use. Generally, the desire was for the efficiencies of a balanced, rounded pattern in the evolving metropolis. The commission emphasized the importance of overcoming the city's historically persistent tendency to expand toward the northwest, of maintaining consistency throughout the network, and of realizing approximately uniform standards. This view of the city was reinforced in many zoning recommendations. The concern of planners with the future region tended to obscure the steady worsening of the central city's physical condition to the point—after World War II—where it appeared that only drastic measures of clearance and urban renewal would be able to deal with the rot situation. Uncertainty was also caused by creation of the Redevelopment Land Agency.

Fueled by the programs of the Federal Housing Administration, federal-aid highways, and nationally assisted public works, postwar suburban development surged forward and was welcomed heartily by real estate interests, home builders, and such professional organizations as the Urban Land Institute. Few gave an appropriate measure of critical evaluation or, indeed, recognized suburban development for the momentous change it was.

DEVELOPMENT IN MARYLAND

Development beyond the District line had largely erased this boundary in popular usage, but its jurisdictional significance had been reemphasized by the separate plans for highways that had been drawn up in Maryland, Virginia, and the District of Columbia. A notable illustration of the need for coordination was the Northwest Freeway proposed by the Maryland–National Capital Park and Planning Commission. This route was proposed to collect traffic from Gaithersburg along a line parallel to U.S. Route 240 (the historic road to Pittsburgh and the West since the days of General Braddock's ill-fated expedition) and to unload it at MacArthur Boulevard just outside the District line or possibly at Cabin John. In either case, the remainder of this route lay conveniently beyond the jurisdiction of the Maryland commission—and into Washington. The route from MacArthur Boulevard or Cabin John to downtown destinations was difficult and costly through the natural obstacle of the Potomac Palisades and the man-made obstacle of the Washington aqueduct from Great Falls, and existing narrow streets and roads. In this particular case, the Planning Commission's Regional Highway Committee and the Coordinating Committee in the 1950s showed their strength by elaborating the alternative route possibilities both in Maryland and the District before exploding the simplistic Northwest Freeway scheme. This experience showed the dangers inherent in the piecemeal approach to highway planning.

THE REGIONAL HIGHWAY COMMITTEE

The initial machinery with which the Planning Commission attempted coordination was a staff device, an outgrowth of the largely successful experience of the Coordinating Committee, but limited to the single function of highways. The Regional Highway Committee allowed the commission to use the steadily augmented strength of the Public Roads Administration, which under Commissioner Thomas MacDonald viewed Washington as a testing ground and showcase for its increasingly bold treatment of metropolitan highway problems. Sophisticated planning of this kind here and elsewhere culminated in the vast programs of urban expressways, bypasses, grade separations, and circumferentials that homogenized American cities, structured future growth, and everywhere changed life-styles into an approximation of Los Angeles or northern New Jersey. In Washington, to be sure, what had begun as a regional expressway system born of wartime transportation needs and experience was distorted into a system whose largest costs were incurred in metropolitan areas.

Proposed Regional Thoroughfare Plan for the National Capital Region As Shown in the Comprehensive Plan, 1950

Thus, it was no accident that Washington's Capital Beltway was the first major circumferential route to be planned, completed, and evaluated in any American city.

Insofar as transportation is the major influence in shaping urban structure, the Capital Beltway and later on the regional Metro system became the two principal elements that shaped the future of Washington and its metropolitan area. These facilities were altogether new. They grasped the essentials of the new urban mobility. They were regional in scale. And most significantly, they were dictated by comprehensive planning. At each step of development the National Capital Planning Commission led the way, and its broader interest in the rapidly developing region shaped final decisions. In this way a crucial link was forged connecting the efforts of city planning to those of transportation planning.

THE COMPREHENSIVE TRANSPORTATION PLAN

In facing the postwar period, the District of Columbia Department of Highways had taken the initiative with several successively bolder plans, culminating in the 1946 Greiner-DeLeuw report, which also spoke for the District commissioners and the Public Roads Administration. The plan was spectacular and sweeping. It interpreted the doctrine of continuous flow in a system of below-level highways and subways. In contrast to this plan, the Planning Commission wanted more gradual, incremental improvements. The March 1947 report of the Planning Commission pointed to the unsubstantiated cost-benefit aspects of the Greiner-DeLeuw report, and criticized the expensive highway tunneling proposals in particular. In short, the Planning Commission argued that first there were a number of remedial measures that were needed and should be undertaken for the existing highway system before embarking upon costly, sweeping, and generally unproved programs of new construction. The Planning Commission restated its 1945 recommendation to the District commissioners that they adopt a thoroughfare plan (a system of through streets) as the first step now before starting any program of below-level or other grade-separated highways. These recommendations, effective and moderating, further expressed the conviction that highway planning was no longer a spasmodic affair of individual project proposals to be dealt with piecemeal, but rather had become a continuous process requiring specialized attention. The Planning Commission thus acted to form a continuing committee on the Comprehensive Transportation Plan. This action recognized the exceptional significance and influence of transportation planning and its steadfast presence on the planning agenda.

The Mass Transportation Survey

Built upon a foundation of nearly a decade of interagency cooperation and continuity in highway planning, the Washington Metropolitan Area Transportation Survey was created by congressional action. In the 1952 reorganization of planning, Congress had authorized a mass transportation plan, but no action was taken toward funding or implementation. Three years later the Mass Transportation Survey finally was initiated through a supplemental appropriation of $200,000 to the National Capital Planning Commission's 1955 budget—and thus the process was started that ultimately has led to construction of the Washington Metro system. A second appropriation of $200,000 earmarked for the Mass Transportation Survey was written into the Planning Commission's 1957 budget. While this allowed the project to be completed, it was a far from adequate sum. The survey's basic data had come from a 1948 origins and destinations survey. In the fast-changing Washington metropolitan region, a dozen years was too long an interval between original data collection and the ultimate action by Congress. In 1960 Congress passed the National Capital Transportation Act (74 Stat. 537) which created the National Capital Transportation Agency to initiate planning for the recommended subway and highway program. Because of the lapse of time between the original survey and the enabling legislation, however, it may be said that congressional action was almost too late.

Riding to Work: Congestion and Projections. It had been the transportation problem that first drew the

Rush Hour, 1977

attention of planners to modern suburbia and the need for metropolitan integration. Of the many perceptions that emerged now from the Mass Transportation Survey, attention focused most upon the journey to work from the suburbs to downtown, the heavy reliance on private cars, and the related problem of peak-hour movement. The survey specifically pointed to the growing suburban structure that was generating major centers of congestion around highway interchanges, suburban shopping centers, large educational complexes, and even office-building concentrations, a congestion hitherto experienced only in the downtown heart of the city.

The 1980 projections of the Mass Transportation Survey, after making the maximum allowance for the automobile—including an extensive street widening program and construction of an outer circumferential beyond the Capital Beltway—demonstrated that major problems of traffic congestion would still plague the metropolitan area. The dispersed location of employment centers that lay predominantly in a north-south align-

ment from Bethesda to Bolling Air Force Base created an angry suburban pattern of trips "between districts other than sector zero." A similar outlying pattern, less intensively developed, was described in the Virginia counties from National Airport north to Tyson's Corner, with a possible extension on the Maryland side of the Potomac.

A City in Motion. In the Mass Transportation Survey a new pattern of metropolitan mobility had been detected, but more significant than its geographical configuration was the concept of a city in motion which it described. The dramatic revelation of the new data was the increased number of trips that would be made by the average person each day. The earlier life-style that could be fulfilled by weekly marketing, by walking to work, and by neighborhood-based leisure pursuits was being replaced by one that demanded such extensive transportation resources that even in a family in which every person had his own car, something like perpetual

278

motion was demanded to take advantage of the specialized employment opportunities, the regionwide recreational resources, or the programs of a dozen universities. And these were only a sampling of resources of the region, strewn with prodigal liberality throughout, wherein each part looked to the entire metropolitan population for its constituency. In the metropolitan capital city there already was richness, and access would soon be provided. It was the cost and time required for travel that had still to be reckoned with, while the social and cultural implications were not known.

The Regional Metro System

The fundamental advance in the Washington Mass Transportation Survey and plans for the Metro rail system was the appreciation of the interrelationship of transit and land use. In the survey itself, projections of travel demand had been based on a carefully regulated changing use of the land, and this suggested the appro-

priate way to pay for the system. When it came to the enabling legislation it was accepted that farebox revenues would not be enough to pay for the system. Therefore new proposed powers were advanced that would provide additional revenues out of the rents from parking structures, shopping centers, and other forms of development to be built by the mass transportation agency at station plazas throughout the system. It was also recognized, on the basis of the survey, that peak-hour service alone would not produce an economic operation, and incentives were therefore suggested to use the service for trips other than to work and at times other than peak commuting hours. Finally, selective higher densities (not necessarily in the form of buildings taller than presently permitted or in conflict with the basic concept of a horizontal city) were projected to overcome the handicap imposed upon the transit system by Washington's characteristic low densities. Aggressive promotion of the system, especially in these innovative uses, was expected over the course of time to change the city and its travel and social habits, to reorient it to downtown activities and institutions, and to build new

The Washington Metro Rail System in Operation at the Rhode Island Avenue Station, 1976

Washington Metro Rail System's Metro Center Station, 1976

patterns of leisure-time behavior. This had been done in Stockholm and other cities, and it seemed a reasonable objective for Washington.

To express this strategy it was further assumed by the survey that the system should be built in stages, with a nucleus to serve the downtown area and its principal federal establishments between the Capitol and the Pentagon. The area delineated, roughly comparable to that of the 1948 Highway Plan, was defined by K Street and Independence Avenue, Fourth and Twentieth Streets.

In subsequent stages, the system was to be extended to the District line and to commuter destinations beyond in the suburban counties. As the system expanded, so would the administrative structure that was creating the system and also would operate it. The downtown area system was to be built first. This area, the old L'Enfant city, is characterized by the federal presence and federal employment concentration. The practical impossibility of anything other than a subway in this downtown area was evident. For all these reasons it was logical that the transit system in the downtown area should be built as a federal operation. Thus, the National Capital Transportation Agency, a federal corporation, was specified in the implementing legislation for Metro.

These were the planning and implementing guidelines. What actually happened was a different story. The suburban counties and the states helped bring about premature creation of the regional transportation agency compact, and caused effective control of the system's planning to be transferred from the federal government to the states. There were several results: strong commuter interests subsequently caused priority to be given to current demands for commuter services rather than to unification of the city; Metro gave up its role as provider of station plazas with parking and off-peak uses— and the critically needed rental revenues that had been projected. As for the downtown area, proposals to connect directly to the Kennedy Center and other off-peak destinations that might have balanced the transit load were eliminated. In short, the system was based on current and projected demand rather than on a long-range plan for establishing new transportation patterns.

The Capital Beltway

Innovative and spectacular, the Metro system has been viewed popularly as a separate project rather than an integral part of the comprehensive and regional transportation network in which highways and expressways continue to carry the principal burden of cars, buses, and trucks. In terms of the proliferation of transportation origins and destinations outside the L'Enfant city, the significance of the Capital Beltway is obvious.

Encircling the District, at a distance of a dozen miles from the center, the beltway was completed in 1964. When built the beltway bridged the linear routes provided by highways and by the impending Metro. The impact of the beltway was described in two notable studies, the *Maryland Capital Beltway Study* and *The*

The Capital Beltway around Washington, Shown on the Major Thoroughfare Plan Element of the Comprehensive Plan for the National Capital, 1974

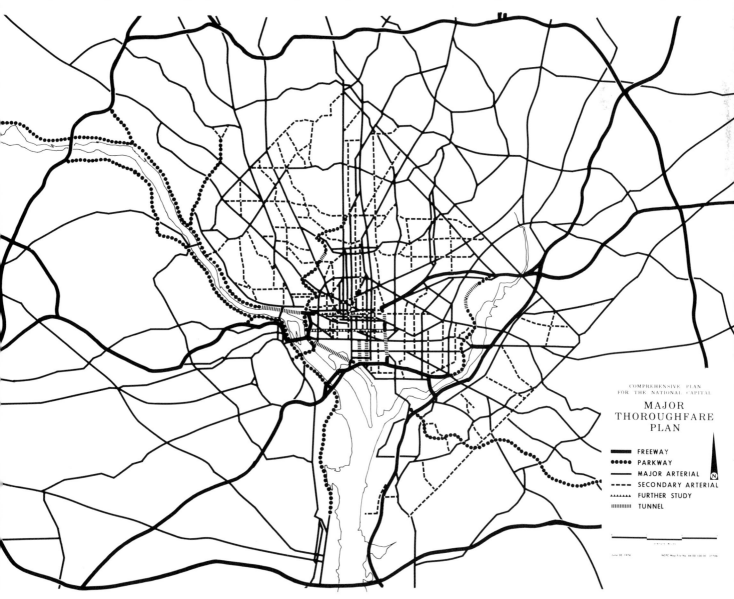

Socio-Economic Impact of the Capital Beltway on Northern Virginia. Published in 1968, these early analyses could not perhaps fully appreciate the impact of the new facility, but they easily established its revolutionary importance as it changed travel behavior and the configuration of land use throughout the region. The beltway actually redefined the position—within the metropolitan complex—of the older District of Columbia, not to mention the city of L'Enfant or nineteenth-century Washington. Much of the long-term effect of the beltway was caused by its construction at a time and in a location of extremely rapid urban growth, causing the emerging city to form itself around the new expressways and their major design opportunities at interchanges with the principal radial routes.

THE CENTRALIZED FEDERAL CITY

The interaction between powerful transportation forces, in the form of both expressways and mass transporta-tion facilities, and the forces of the rapidly growing city could be expected to reach a mutual accommodation over some undetermined period of time. But Washington as a capital city had a trump card to play in this game—the location of key federal employment centers. This factor influenced not only the number of federal jobs in the area but the location of a crucial part of Washington's constituent economy that was oriented to federal agencies and their work. Apart from the exceptional and, as it turned out, transitory program for strategic dispersal, Washington's planners tended toward a highly structured, if not a fully centralized, city. In Washington, therefore, it seemed likely that transportation would reflect and implement decisions about the nature of the city rather than simply accommodate current needs. Like the decision to limit the height of buildings, or to provide parks and open spaces according to a generous standard, Washington's mobility reflects its nature as a federal capital city.

Contemporary View of the Southeast/Southwest Freeway during an Off-Peak Period

282

In the Northeast Quadrant of Washington: Contemporary Telephoto View of the Railroad Yard and Residential Area Beyond

In the Northeast Quadrant of Washington: The National Arboretum

In the Southeast Quadrant of Washington: View of the Museum Area in the Navy Yard As It Looks Today

CHAPTER XIII NEW AGENDAS IN POLICIES AND COMPREHENSIVE PLANS 1960–1968

New Agendas in Policies and Comprehensive Plans 1960-1968

The Picture Window and Other Symbols of Growth

To the mid-twentieth-century visitor concentrating on the monumental core, Washington seemed still the "sleepy southern town" it has often been called. With the exception of redevelopment in the Southwest, much of the action seemed to be occurring at the city's edges. By contrast, a decade later—in the early 1960s—national observers saw in Washington a "city reborn," propelled out of its "blighted" condition and into major change. In 1962, *Time* magazine applauded the new public buildings "sprouting like marble mushrooms" south of Independence Avenue. The magazine article also described the new Southwest and an extravaganza of proposed solutions to the city's traffic congestion, including eight new Potomac River bridges planned or underway, and the new sports stadium at the terminus of East Capitol Street at the Anacostia River.

Although this exhilaration was genuine, the early 1960s nonetheless marked the threshold between admiration for physical symbols of growth and the resurgence of environmental concerns. The negative costs of laissez-

faire growth had long been described by humanists. Now their concerns gained increasing support among planners and became institutionalized in new growth policies during the 1960s. This awareness of the effects of uncontrolled growth in the nation's capital was described in 1962 by Allan Temko in a long article in the *Washington Post*. Temko saw the city as "out of control" despite the "majestic harmonies of the Federal design." He viewed the characteristic spread of settlement over once-rural landscapes, in Washington as in all American metropolitan centers, as dramatically altering urban civilization itself.

Disillusionment with suburban sprawl and the life-styles generated by mobility was already seeping into the philosophies of planners. Executive Director of the National Capital Planning Commission William Finley surprised the Washington Building Congress early in 1958 when he advocated abandoning the dispersal theme of the 1950 Comprehensive Plan and attacked the "crack in the picture-window vision of suburbia": He spoke darkly of suburban sterility, the lack of human interaction, and depicted suburban mothers bound to their stationwagon carpools. Finley argued for reemergence of the central city as the focus of urban life, with major traffic routes moving into and out of the center of the city rather than bypassing it. Finley also suggested that instead of continuing to allow for unplanned sprawl, planning should bring about "ordered, attractive growth."

The 1961 Policies Plan for the Year 2000

The directions of controlled growth were outlined in 1961 in the dramatic publication, *A Policies Plan for the Year 2000*, by the National Capital Planning Commission and the National Capital Regional Planning Council. The Year 2000 Policies Plan presented various alternative approaches to controlled growth: (1) restricting growth in the region; (2) creating new independent cities at least seventy miles from Washington, each growing to a population of 300,000–500,000 people in the next forty years; (3) accommodating most new growth in a planned sprawl extending in all directions as low-density development; (4) dispersing of new cities throughout the region away from the urbanized center and apart from each other; (5) locating a ring of cities approximately thirty miles from the urbanized center; (6) establishing peripheral communities along the edges of the urbanized center; and (7) structuring growth in corridors along major transportation radials emanating from the central city.

WEDGES AND CORRIDORS: THE RADIAL CORRIDOR POLICY PLAN

It was the radial corridor policy plan, referred to as "wedges and corridors," that was selected as most advantageous for the city of Washington in the year 2000. Drawn along the proposed rapid transit routes and parallel highway system, the radial corridor policy plan expressed the concept earlier stated by Finley: that the central city (termed the Metro-Center) should be the primary focus or hub of the metropolitan region. The corridors were to be generated by linkages of major development centers, each corridor or spoke to be separated by wedges of open countryside. In design this would produce something similar to the idealized nineteenth-century radial transit city, a snowflake pattern

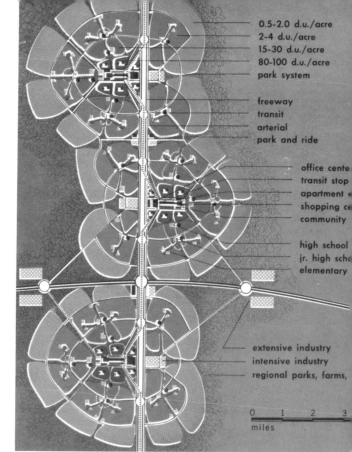

Diagrammatic View of the Urbanized Corridors, Shown in the Year 2000 Policies Plan, 1961

Diagrammatic View of the Open Wedges and Developed Corridors, Shown in the Year 2000 Policies Plan, 1961

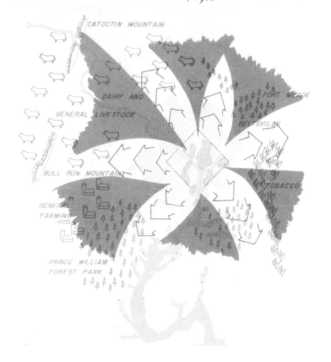

where open space was readily accessible to the urban and suburban population. The wedges and corridors plan was magnified beyond the scale of the earlier configuration but absorbed its values.

As diagrams of the radial corridor plan show more specifically, the radials would embrace clusters of public buildings and services, private office buildings, shopping centers, a mixture of house and apartment types, industrial complexes, schools, and community centers, all linked by the urban "greenways" made popular in Philadelphia redevelopment planning. Contrasting to these urban centers, the wedges of open space would reflect the private agricultural emphases that still prevailed in the region, from the tobacco lands around Mitchellville in Prince George's County to the dairy and livestock grassland in the Piedmont. These wedges of open space would also reflect the largely undeveloped tracts of federal land including the Agricultural Research Center in

The Radial Corridor Plan As Shown in the Year 2000 Policies Plan, 1961

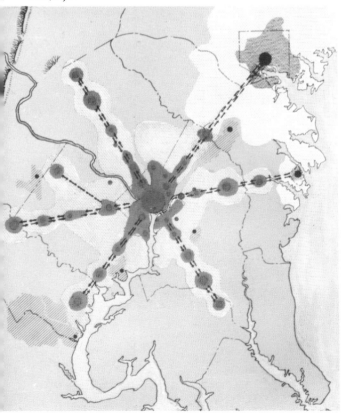

Beltsville, Maryland, and Dulles International Airport in Chantilly, Virginia. In order to secure these green wedges, the Year 2000 Policies Plan urged designation of the lands as rural in perpetuity by outright acquisition, tax concessions, and zoning as well as by concentration·of·future development in the densely populated corridors.

Metro-Center. In over-all design, the importance of the central city in giving the wedges and corridors metropolis its identity was acknowledged in the Policies Plan for the Year 2000 by designating the central area of the District of Columbia as "Metro-Center." This center was defined as the historic L'Enfant city, the area for which Pierre L'Enfant had prepared his original city plan. Metro-Center thus was bound on the north by Florida Avenue and on the south, east, and west by the Potomac and Anacostia Rivers.

Leaving aside, for the moment, the immediate problems of suburban growth and sprawl and turning to the central city, the Year 2000 Policies Plan recognized both the special jurisdiction of the federal government within the District of Columbia and the role of downtown Washington as a federal employment and commercial center. The plan noted the traditional monumentality of public buildings and the emergence of larger commercial office buildings.

What most caused the emphasis on central Washington was its role as the primary location of federal employment. The Year 2000 Policies Plan applauded the monumental public office buildings as consistent with their purpose. The plan recommended, however, that in order to provide for sheer growth, new buildings should "make more efficient use of ground area; they could be developed at densities as much as twice those of 1960 without exceeding today's height limitations." This statement laid to rest a perpetual bugaboo—building height. The plan proposed locations within the central business area for new public and private office buildings to be constructed densely in small clusters or cells of buildings organized about plaza designs. Starting with the Mall as Washington's unique and "most remarkable physical feature," the plan called for development of the historic major diagonal avenues and the vicinities

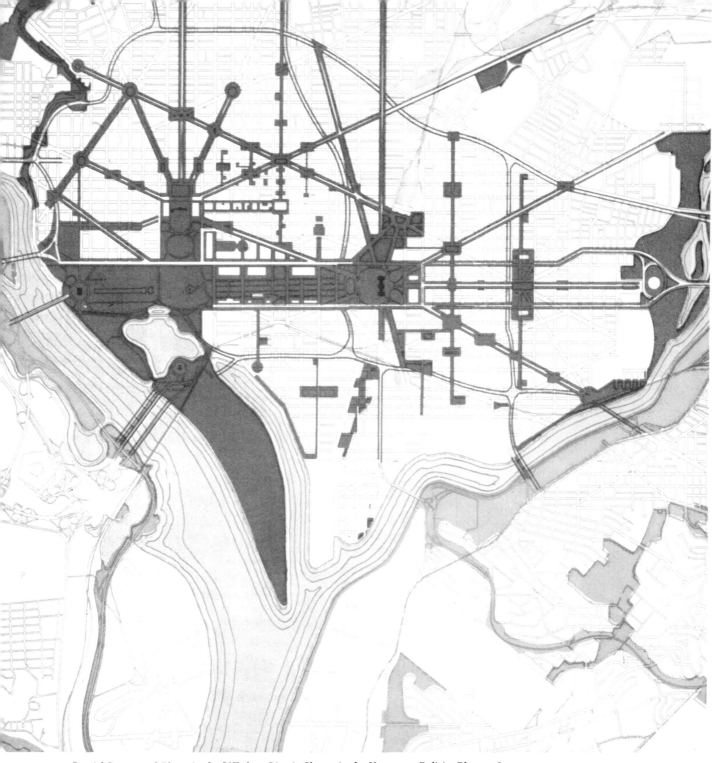

Special Streets and Places in the L'Enfant City As Shown in the Year 2000 Policies Plan, 1961

of L'Enfant parks as "Special Streets and Places." These special places were defined by their historic origins, by the existing mature trees, and by the broad dimensions of the places themselves.

In planning for the diagonals, new ideas were put forward. Why not design these thoroughfares as more than vehicular routes? Why not capture the colorful street environment exemplified by the Paris boulevards, with wide sidewalks, landscaping, varied shopping opportunities, and distinctive apartment buildings? The plan suggested that the central business district—another special place—should ideally incorporate a greater mixture of uses than offices and stores. In order to provide greater accessibility to this regenerated downtown, the Year 2000 Policies Plan retained the Inner Loop freeway proposed in the Planning Commission's 1950 Comprehensive Plan, and viewed extensions into the suburbs along the corridors as compatible with the emerging rail rapid transit system.

Accomplishments and Influences. The Year 2000 Policies Plan accomplished its purpose. It stimulated the many planning jurisdictions of the area. A fruitful debate commenced to define matters of common interest. Large portions of the wedges and corridors planning was embraced in Maryland, and—with modifications due mainly to topography—in Virginia as well. The bold and simple diagram implanted itself on the popular imagination and, widely supported by civic groups, survived new challenges by the Council of Governments for as long as fifteen years. In downtown Washington, redevelopment and the location of federal buildings received support from the plan but were less consistently responsive to it. The plan nonetheless was a major influence in the design of the Metro rail system and in special project planning for Pennsylvania Avenue and other limited sectors of the city. Most of all, the Year 2000 Policies Plan influenced future planning by the National Capital Planning Commission. Washington had indeed received no comparable shaking up since the McMillan plan of 1901–1902.

METROPOLITAN REGION: MARYLAND AND VIRGINIA

The impact of the Year 2000 Policies Plan was most pronounced in the metropolitan region. For the first time, a structure was suggested combining the much-desired qualities of order, open space, and mobility. The plan's wedges and corridors scheme fitted in well with the topography and traditions of growth in suburban Maryland. Nevertheless, in disregard of the plan, pressure existed among developers (who held land in the potential wedges) to establish additional corridors or permit the ad hoc filling in of the wedges. On the other

hand, Virginia's topography and growth was in form less compatible with the wedges and corridors scheme. The stream valleys of Virginia penetrated the area in concentric circle patterns around the central area, and dense corridors had already developed along Virginia's Route 7 from Leesburg to Alexandria and along Glebe Road.

To realize the vast wedges and corridors design, it was clear that all planning elements had to be included—zoning, regulation of new subdivisions of land, transportation networks, public works, and the allocation of funds. The regional growth configurations of the Year 2000 Policies Plan also required more immediate action to regulate development of heavily populated corridors, including the new town centers, highways, the completion of the mass transportation system—and the preservation of 300,000 acres of open space required to separate the corridors. Policies worked out jointly between the National Capital Planning Commission and the National Capital Regional Planning Council additionally involved economic analyses, development plans, and studies of legal, administrative, and fiscal arrangements. In this way, new forms of development planning were superseding the older and simpler regulations of land use that had constituted planning for the past half-century.

A WORK PROGRAM FOR THE DISTRICT OF COLUMBIA

Substance and method changed together, in no part of the region more dramatically than within the District of Columbia, where the new planning agenda outlined in the Year 2000 Policies Plan was translated into a work program during the next decade. Widespread discussion and increasing participation was most spectacularly illustrated in the continuing debate over highways and the social effects of highway development. Projected studies included a citywide analysis of housing and environmental conditions, the objective being to design a range of housing for all income levels and family sizes. Other studies were projected for building and design standards for future development compatible with Washington's traditions; the coordination of mass transit stops, federal office buildings, and other focal points of high-density development with the over-all revitalization of Metro-Center and the creation of uptown employment centers;

and the design of open space as essential to upgrading and preserving the character of residential neighborhoods.

New Beginnings in the Early Sixties

In general terms of comprehensive planning and policy changes, the Year 2000 Policies Plan exercised influence on development in the still-growing areas of the District of Columbia between Metro-Center and the District line. These outlying areas of the District did not receive the same emphasis as did the special places inside the Metro-Center. Moreover, the proposed Inner Loop freeway and its extensions were laced through large areas of the outlying area or "in-between space." This feature of highway planning was deplored in 1962 by the Planning Commission's new chairwoman, Elizabeth Rowe. A lifelong District resident who had grown up in what came to be known as the Adams-Morgan area and now a resident of Cleveland Park, Rowe had first become concerned with city planning during her term of service on President Eisenhower's D.C. Auditorium Commission from 1955 to 1958. During this commission's study of an architectural model of the site in Foggy Bottom later occupied by the Kennedy Center, she noticed the "spaghetti" (her word, used on interview) of bridges and approaches planned to span the city and affect many settled areas.

The National Capital Planning Commission. When appointed to the commission in 1962, Elizabeth Rowe found that her idyllic view of the city as a collection of neighborhoods, defined by tree-lined streets and handsome buildings, put her sympathies in sharp contrast with previous planning policies espoused by the commission's executive director, William E. Finley. These earlier policies called for well-designed highways; higher densities in inner city areas such as the Southwest and along the intended radials of the Year 2000 Policies Plan; intensive redevelopment of the Georgetown waterfront and rehabilitation and redevelopment in the Adams-Morgan area; and construction of monumental complexes of packaged living, places like Columbia

Citizens of Washington Demonstrate against Highway and Freeway Construction, Early 1960s

Plaza and the Watergate that combined office buildings with apartment houses, shops, hotels, and recreation facilities. In contrast, Rowe exemplified social concern, a sense of continuity with the past—and a growing opposition to highways' ripping through neighborhoods or any similarly drastic altering of the District's strongly defined neighborhoods and edges. Rowe shrank from the ad hoc planning of the city by means of highways, currently the best-financed government program. She described modern high-rise buildings as belonging to the "vertical ice-tray school of architecture." As counterbalance, she established historic preservation as an active concern of the Planning Commission's work.

Differences between Rowe and Finley arose over new planning policies to be adopted by the commission. Although as executive director Finley was responsible for hiring and supervising commission staff—and for daily operation of commission activities — Rowe, as chairwoman, and the other nine members of the commission were responsible for adoption of planning policies. Thus, inevitable differences contributed to Finley's resignation from the commission in October 1962. Wilmer C. Dutton, Jr., was then appointed executive director of the commission. Dutton was a former executive director of the American Institute of Planners, a planner with experience in several American cities, and a five-year resident of University Park in Prince George's County. Dutton's quiet administrative style was in marked contrast to the style of his predecessor.

The Joint Committee on Landmarks. In an effort to save long-cherished institutions and activities as well as structures, Rowe launched major studies of historic preservation by experts like Carl Feiss. The effort culminated in 1964 in the establishment of the Joint Committee on Landmarks. This committee is now jointly sponsored by the National Capital Planning Commission, the Commission of Fine Arts, and the District of Columbia government, and it continues to function as a good example of interagency cooperation. In this as in other instances, Washington was trail breaking in an area of urban conservation that only a few much smaller towns had explored. Historic preservation found general acceptance only after federal legislation establishing it was passed in 1966.

The Ad Hoc Committee on Federal Office Space. Increased preoccupation with historical values of the city's architecture was marked by creation of the Joint Committee on Landmarks. This preoccupation was further exhibited by the National Capital Planning Commission's work with the Kennedy administration to improve the quality of public architecture. Suggestions made by Secretary of Labor Arthur Goldberg produced the Ad Hoc Committee on Federal Office Space to study federal space requirements. As part of its review of this general topic, the committee issued a report entitled "Guiding Principles for Federal Architecture." These principles were intended for nationwide application, but because of the concentration of federal buildings in Washington, had particular importance for the capital city. The first principle was that public architecture should reflect the "dignity, enterprise, vigor, and stability of the American National Government," with attention paid to regional traditions in architecture and the fine arts. Second, any attempt at promoting an "offi-

cial style" must be avoided. Third, the site for the building and its relationship to its surroundings should be the first design consideration. These "Guiding Principles," interpreted by Karel Yasko, Supervising Architect of the Public Buildings Administration, served to redirect the design of subsequent public buildings in many American cities. Public buildings in Washington —as, for example, the double Y-shaped structure for the Department of Housing and Urban Development designed by Marcel Breuer—set new civic standards for architectural design.

LAFAYETTE SQUARE

Continuity with older urban structures as well as design of new buildings was stressed during the Kennedy years in Washington. This rational duality was perhaps best exemplified by Lafayette Square, forecourt of the White House. The square itself was characterized by surviving nineteenth-century residential buildings, particularly on Jackson Place, as well as by Latrobe's Decatur House and Saint John's Church. It was on Lafayette Square that several presidents had proposed to locate a new building for the executive office staff. A succession of architectural designs had, in fact, been proposed for this site. McMillan Commission ideals had been reflected in Cass Gilbert's design for the Treasury Annex and the United States Chamber of Commerce building. The constituency for this classical redevelopment of the square had evaporated, however, and the solution proposed by Delos Smith for the Brookings Institution was no more appealing. The project supported by the Eisenhower administration was Henry R. Shepley's five-story Georgian version of a modern office building; this equally failed to arouse enthusiasm.

Most briefly stated, what was at issue here was the character of the White House. It could be seen as a public building, a palace, or—as most Americans traditionally thought of it—a private residence. Which of these interpretations prevailed would be determined by development of the buildings around Lafayette Square. The issue of Lafayette Square redesign had been fully discussed with restoration of the White House during Harry Truman's presidency; as time went on, there was growing pressure for resolution. Into this situation

President and Mrs. Kennedy stepped. The advice of their friend William Walton, chairman of the Commission of Fine Arts, together with architectural assistance of the San Francisco designer John Carl Warnecke contributed to the final solution.

The design for redevelopment of Lafayette Square retained every historically recognized building around the square—and beyond, to include the old Court of Claims Building, originally built to house the Corcoran Gallery of Art and now restored as the Renwick Gallery of the Smithsonian's National Collection of Fine Arts. New buildings on Lafayette Square were planned to be located at the edge of the bowl formed by Lafayette Park and its surrounding low buildings. Among these new structures are the Executive Office Building and the Court of Claims, relocated to the east side of the square. Refurbishing of the square was at the same time undertaken by the National Park Service.

The total redevelopment of this large and strategically situated area provided a statement more influential than written directives. Redevelopment of Lafayette Square was, in fact, a turning point in the adaptive use of older buildings and more sympathetic recognition of urban continuity. It was also the beginning of a policy of mixed use for public buildings.

PENNSYLVANIA AVENUE

Redevelopment of Pennsylvania Avenue, the historic one-and-a-half-mile route connecting Capitol and White House, reflected continuing concern with the city's environmental design. On the initiative of Secretary of Labor Arthur Goldberg and his able assistant Daniel Patrick Moynihan, the White House in 1962 established the President's Council on Pennsylvania Avenue and appointed a blue-ribbon panel to serve on this council. Nathaniel A. Owings, council chairman, provided the leadership necessary to produce strong and imaginative recommendations. As a member of both this body and the National Capital Planning Commission, Seattle architect Paul Thiry was in a position to contribute not simply the ideas of an experienced urban designer but the realistic insights provided by his official responsibilities on the Planning Commission. The April 1964 Report of the President's Council on Pennsylvania Ave-

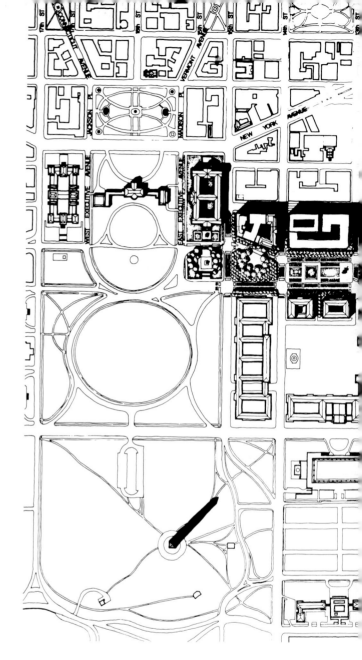

nue, as accepted by President Lyndon Johnson, was the start of a continuing effort to rehabilitate the historic "Grand Avenue" originally visualized by L'Enfant.

The 1965 Brown Book

Management of the Planning Commission's further detailing of the regional policies contained in the Year 2000 Policies Plan was largely directed by Charles H. Conrad, Wilmer Dutton's successor as executive direc-

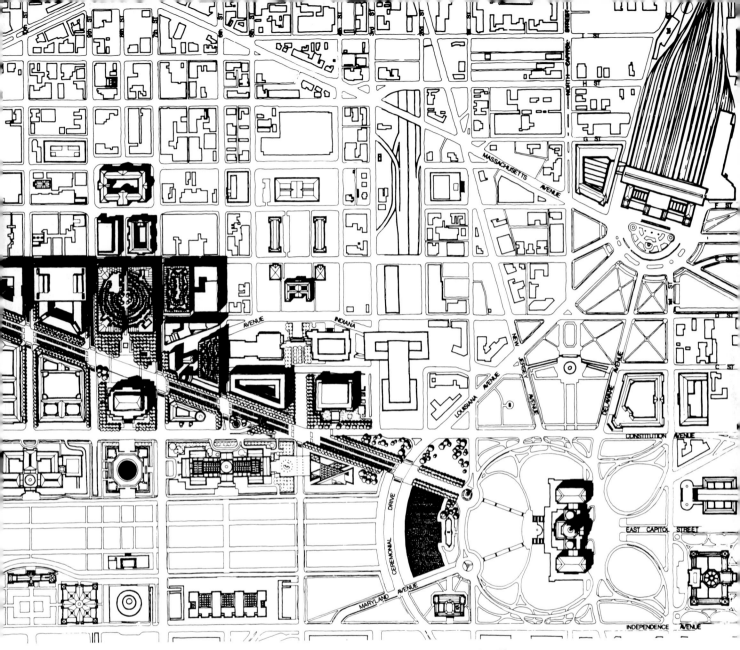

Pennsylvania Avenue Design by the Pennsylvania Avenue Development Corporation: Illustrative Site Plan, 1977

tor of the commission. A member of the commission staff from 1951 on, Conrad was appointed executive director of the commission in 1965, having served as deputy director under both Dutton and Finley in the critical years from 1958 to 1965 when the Year 2000 Policies Plan and the commission's subsequent elaboration of it were being formulated. This elaboration took the form of a series of reports and plans, each conveying its measure of further commitment by the commission. These follow-up reports also displayed Conrad's understanding of both the powers and the limitations of the

agency as it sought to influence future growth of the capital city.

The first of these reports came out in 1965, when the National Capital Planning Commission issued *1965/ 1985: Proposed Physical Development Policies for Washington, D.C.*, also called the "Brown Book." Whereas the Year 2000 Policies Plan was a statement of proposed policies applicable to the entire region, the Brown Book was a more detailed statement of proposed policies that focused on the District of Columbia. An exercise in full-fledged comprehensive planning in many

View from the Treasury Building down Pennsylvania Avenue As It Looks Today

dimensions such as the city had not seen even in 1950, this 1965 plan or "resource paper" provided policies to guide and structure the commission's preparation of the Comprehensive Plan. A first step toward a different future, the Brown Book was a "kite-flying exercise," designed to elicit public response. The plan presented a "physical conception of the city, indicating the kinds of things that might be built and their spatial arrangement." The city was portrayed as simultaneously playing three well-articulated roles: as the capital city, as the residential, constituent city, and as the center of the large metropolitan region. Given the range of buildings, places, and topography to be found in Washington, the 1965 policies guide sought to offer a wide choice of "satisfactory living environments" based on the strengthened individuality of each section of the metropolitan city. Living environments were described in detail by plans that worked from citywide design elements such as the riverfronts and conservation of the ridge line surrounding the flat historic center.

Special Streets and Places. Actualizing policies set forth by the Year 2000 Policies Plan and expressed indirectly in earlier plans, the 1965 plan treated the District as a collection of distinct special places, from the grand and historical Mall, as well as Georgetown and the Federal Triangle, to less-known neighborhoods such as Cleveland Park, Brookland, and Brightwood. Special streets included Pennsylvania Avenue, then under study by the President's Council on Pennsylvania Avenue, boundary streets such as Florida Avenue, and functional movement and connective streets. The city's edges gave the city its special ecological character, notably along the two urban rivers. More than a hundred and fifty years of interaction between man and a unique set of natural factors had produced the modern city and made possible the evolution of special planning concepts. With this historic interaction as background, the Brown Book established the basis for recognition of these concepts in future Comprehensive Plans.

Model Showing the New Design of Pennsylvania Avenue from the White House to the Capitol, as Proposed by the President's Council on Pennsylvania Avenue, 1964

Given these concepts and concerns as well as emerging growth patterns in the metropolitan region, how then was growth to be accommodated in the District? Were there "dead spots" that could be replanned and redeveloped to conform to the architecture and design of the city? In its affirmative answer to this second question, the 1965 Brown Book showed graphically where new development might take place. Turning away from suburban dispersal or even a corridored metropolitan structure, the Brown Book envisioned federal bureaus as located *within* the boundaries of the L'Enfant city. Master plans were sought for federal installations.

The Brown Book urged federal officials to consider sites for new buildings along South Capitol Street so as to fill in the ambiguous area between the Capitol and the now-obsolescent Navy Yard. These proposed new buildings were to be collectively named the South Capitol Federal Quadrangle and were planned to accommodate about 50,000 employees, less than the number housed in the new federal buildings group south of Independence Avenue. Smaller cellular groups of public buildings were suggested for the declining area at the intersection of Eleventh Street and New York Avenue, NW, as well as in several so-called Uptown Centers along the city's major transportation lines. The Brown Book recommended

Illustrative Site Development Plan for the South Capitol Street Area As Shown in the Proposed Comprehensive Plan, 1967

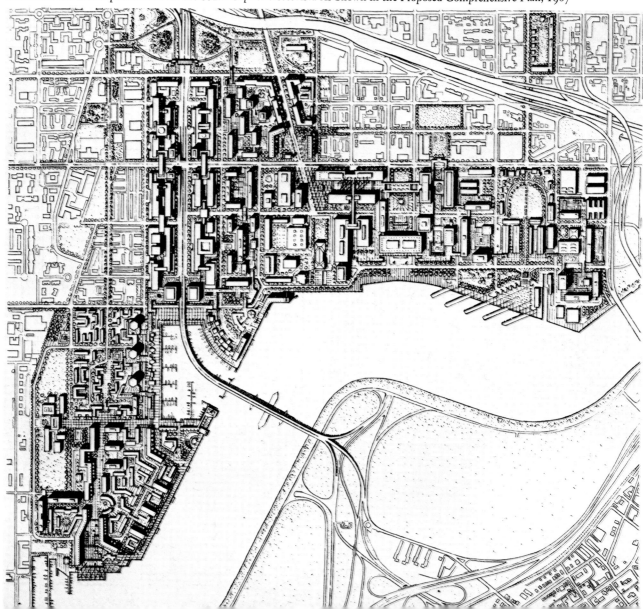

Perspective View of the Proposed South Capitol Federal Quadrangle, 1965

Illustrative Site Development Plan of the Projected International Center in the West End As Shown in the Proposed Comprehensive Plan, 1967

RCHITECTURAL STUDY
HE PROPOSED INTERNATIONAL CENTER

that private commercial development should be concentrated in what it called the Central Employment Area (the downtown retail center and its extension to the north) as well as in certain specified locations uptown.

In addition to these suggestions for official and commercial growth, the Brown Book suggested as a policies guide that the checkered West End—the area between Washington Circle and Dupont Circle—be dedicated to a completely new International Center, as distinct in its urban design as the historically defined "special places." Other areas suggested as opportune for redevelopment included the old Bolling Airfield with its dwindling airport functions; the National Training School site (later the site for the Fort Lincoln new town); a massively overhauled and reused Navy Yard; a new landscape design for the Watts Branch Parkway in Anacostia; a restructured Sixteenth Street consistent with proposed freeway and rapid transit construction; and a high-density office and apartment cluster on the old Connecticut Avenue Bureau of Standards site.

Comprehensive planning could not devise solutions to such operating programs as housing or employment, but it could create better coordinated conditions for those programs, contribute to better understanding, and advance program priorities. Beyond acknowledging that physical design did affect social behavior, the Brown Book report did not directly address the social issues of housing, the poor, and crime. What it did that was notable was to focus on the lived-in city as this city had not been thought of since the Planning Commission's earliest years and the Olmsted-Eliot plans for strengthening neighborhood identity. Hopefully, the improved neighborhoods identified in the 1965 plan would produce heightened feelings of community identity and consciousness that in turn would begin to deal with the city's social problems.

THE WASHINGTON SKYLINE STUDY

After issuance of the Brown Book as the basis for further work and discussion on the city's Comprehensive Plan, the National Capital Planning Commission produced or commissioned the development of detailed area plans that mainly reflected a growing concern with urban design and the city's natural environment. One of the earliest of these specialized studies was the *Washington Skyline Study* produced by Chloethiel Woodard Smith & Associates in 1965. Viewing the rapid change in the central city tempered primarily by the height limitation and by zoning regulations and directly influenced by the chaotic growth of office clusters throughout the metropolitan area, Smith suggested that it was time for urban design rather than controls and regulations. The office-building boom could be seen in any compass direction from Sixteenth and K Streets, NW. This growth as well as the high-rise sprawl throughout the region's subcenters could be accommodated in the future, Smith believed, by "selective height increase" and "immediate legal action to protect existing open space." For the new tall buildings ranging from 90 feet to 260 feet, Smith suggested they be situated in clusters and "so related to the monumental core of the city and the established street pattern that they protect the scale of the historic core, but allow for growth." Since the skyline was more than a silhouette, the juxtaposition of buildings against each other and against the green backdrop of hills required retention of what Smith called the "Skyline Path." This path followed roughly the route of the earlier proposed Fort Drive along Civil War fort sites, except that to the north the path followed Florida Avenue. While Smith's proposals for selective siting of tall buildings ran against the overwhelming sentiment for a forever horizontal city—and a suspicion that, once broached, the height limit would crumble altogether—the plan did refocus on the natural topography that underlay development of city and region. Smith's plan also went significantly beyond limited concerns with particular landmarks.

THE LANDSCAPE IDENTITY STUDY

Another kind of environmental determination was evoked in the conception of the metropolitan area as a unique landscape. This idea was put forward in Ian McHarg's study prepared for the National Capital Planning Commission in 1967 and titled *Toward a Comprehensive Landscape Plan for Washington, D.C.* The ongoing process of man's interaction with natural resources characterized the city as a growing and adapting organism. In the tracing of geological formations, the

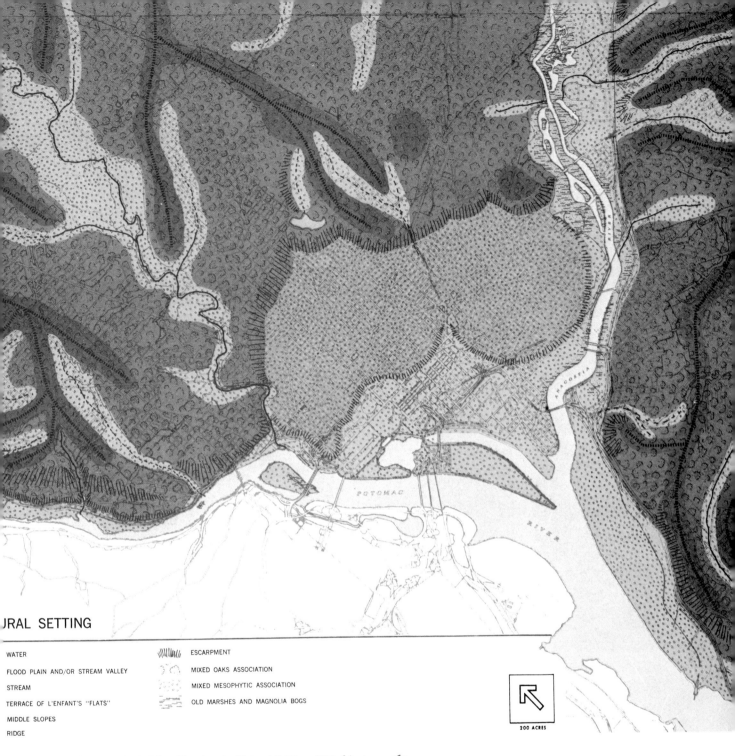

Landscape Identity Study Map, Showing the Natural Setting of Washington, 1967

region's past was pushed back to the Pleistocene. Terraces were produced in this early age, cut by "steeply dissected valleys; and two confluent rivers . . . surrounded by a backdrop of low hills" offered the natural boundaries of the precapital city, in the words of the report. The varied soils were seen to offer a wide variety of plant ecology utilized in both formal and bucolic man-made landscapes. The city holds many vestiges of

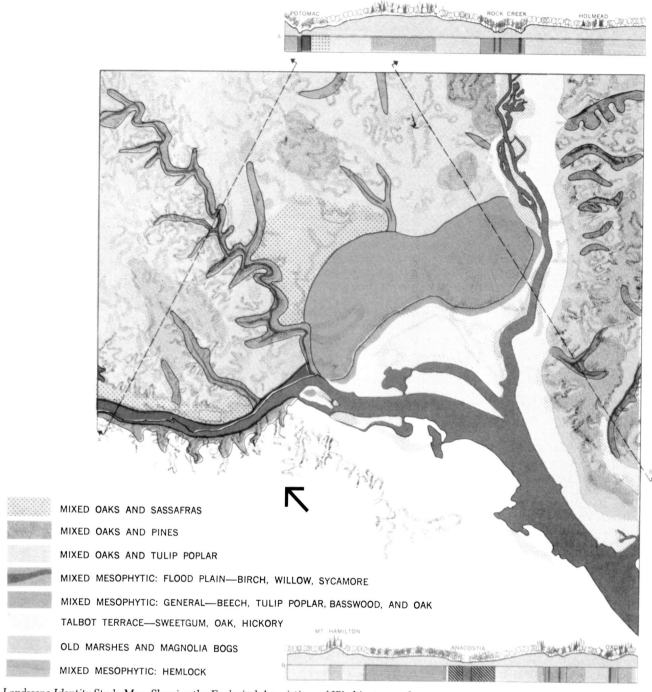

MIXED OAKS AND SASSAFRAS

MIXED OAKS AND PINES

MIXED OAKS AND TULIP POPLAR

MIXED MESOPHYTIC: FLOOD PLAIN—BIRCH, WILLOW, SYCAMORE

MIXED MESOPHYTIC: GENERAL—BEECH, TULIP POPLAR, BASSWOOD, AND OAK

TALBOT TERRACE—SWEETGUM, OAK, HICKORY

OLD MARSHES AND MAGNOLIA BOGS

MIXED MESOPHYTIC: HEMLOCK

Landscape Identity Study Map, Showing the Ecological Associations of Washington, 1967

this preurban topography, enhanced now by architectural embellishments such as the Shrine of the Immaculate Conception and the National Cathedral on the District's highest summits. McHarg ascribed the genius of the L'Enfant plan to the designer's careful "reading [of] the subtleties of land form," and recommended that the city rediscover and reinterpret the waterways, wooded hills, and ridges of the natural setting within the L'Enfant city, thereby offering a "most dramatic contrast between calculated artifice and nature." McHarg's topographic study and Smith's skyline study thus reinforced and provided details for the Planning Commission's increasing attention to landscape and skyline identity as elements of urban design.

The 1967 Green Book

Portions of the landscape study were translated into planning policies in the National Capital Planning Commission's *Proposed Comprehensive Plan for the National Capital*, the "Green Book," published in 1967. As part of a general approach emphasizing social problems, physical planning, and design, this proposed plan sought to detail the broad policy emphasis of the 1965 Brown Book policies guide, and to orchestrate social objectives in terms of urban environments. While addressing social problems of low-income Washington residents, the plan reaffirmed the commission's commitment to the city's economic health earlier voiced in policies for the new Southwest, and reaffirmed also the determination to attract and retain middle-income families in the District.

LANDSCAPE AND THE DISTINCT COMMUNITIES

The Green Book stated that qualities of the city's landscape could be experienced by residents of the city. Ideally, the topographic setting once seen by the perceptive observer would strengthen identity and the sense of belonging, and thus spark interest in the city's future. The visual experience was available—to residents and visitors—from many vantage points, "in panoramic form from hilltop parks; from the upper floors of office buildings; and at close-up from sidewalks and front porches." The topography could be experienced by "strollers and by occupants of vehicles traveling up to a mile a minute." This communication of natural and man-made values could be made clearer by more emphasis on identifying special streets and places, and by identifying and strengthening the distinct communities. The plan said that "most areas have positive characteristics and distinctive features that can be retained and exploited through design." Important to the social city, the Green Book proposed no radical surgery. "Washington's distinct communities should be preserved in order to give direction to the processes of conservation and regrowth now at work within the residential sections of the city." As a recognition of these existing distinct communities, the plan incorporated a map outlining the boundaries and names of each neighborhood. (And in testimony to strong community identity, the correct location of neighborhood boundary lines was promptly contested at every neighborhood meeting where the map was discussed.)

TRANSPORTATION

To achieve mobility within the District, a balanced transportation system was proposed: improvement of the extant thoroughfares, construction of the rail rapid transit system, development of a parking scheme. Attractive and inviting entrances to subway stations were proposed, and in order to provide for proximity of transportation, work, cultural facilities, and shopping opportunities, the plan proposed high-density construction at many stations. The 1967 Proposed Comprehensive Plan stated transportation guidelines and more decisively reversed the highway and automobile infatuation that had so influenced (and been accommodated by) planning for over forty years. "Construction of a highway system capable of carrying all peak-hour traffic without congestion would preempt too much land, destroy too many homes, produce too great a change in the overall character of the city, and would cost too much both in terms of initial investment and in the reduction of the city tax base." The plan accepted congestion at peak hours, and allowed planning for future highways to be "determined by other criteria" instead of maximum accommodation. It anticipated that the Metro rapid transit system would carry a large share of the commuter load traveling to and from downtown Washington.

EMPLOYMENT AND HOUSING

According to the 1967 Green Book, between 1965 and 1985 there would be an increase of from 130,000 to 170,000 federal, civilian, and military personnel in the National Capital Region. The plan proposed that total federal employment, including these new as well as existing federal employees, should continue to be concentrated in the L'Enfant city. Until 1985, the proposal concluded, the existing federal employment distribution ratio of 60 percent in the District of Columbia and 40 percent in the region should be continued; furthermore, new federal employment in Maryland and Virginia

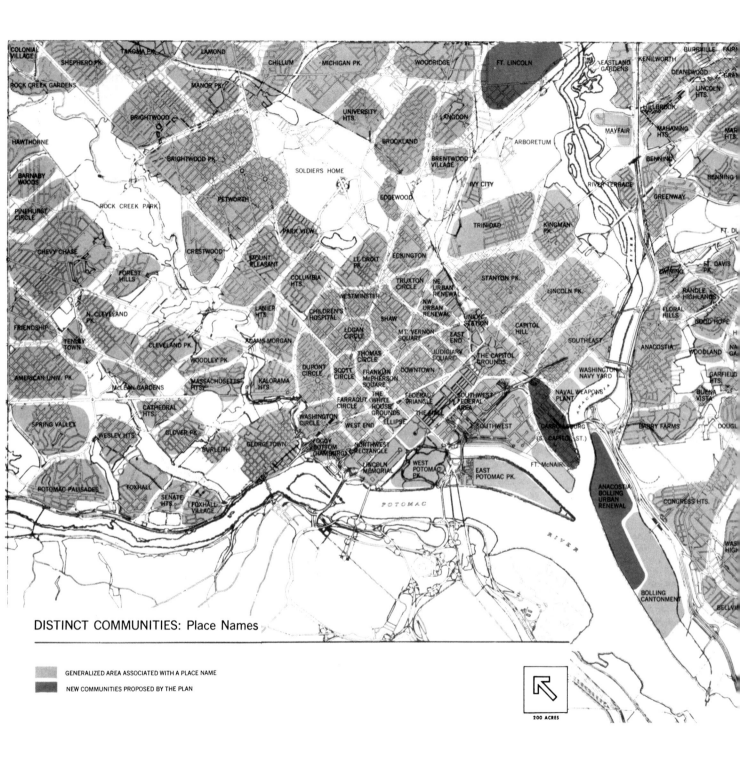

DISTINCT COMMUNITIES: Place Names

GENERALIZED AREA ASSOCIATED WITH A PLACE NAME

NEW COMMUNITIES PROPOSED BY THE PLAN

200 ACRES

Washington's Distinct Communities, 1967

304

should be allocated according to specific program criteria. Anticipating development of the Metro rail system, the 1967 Proposed Comprehensive Plan also emphasized that most new federal employment should be deployed so as to maximize patronage by federal employees of the rail rapid transit system.

In addition to employment, the 1967 Green Book stressed housing. It reviewed several areawide strategies, none of them new. Given the growth of metropolitan perspectives, it considered some assumption of regional responsibility for housing, linked perhaps to the suburban home-building boom and the growing diversification of suburbia. The Green Book also proposed acceleration of federal funding for public housing. Older proposals for systematic and coordinated enforcement of building codes were also put forward. With a concern for more than dwellings, the Green Book called for a more comprehensive concept of residential neighborhoods to embrace schools, parks, playgrounds, libraries, physical facilities, as well as police and fire protection and other public services.

PROJECT PLANNING

The 1967 Proposed Comprehensive Plan outlined several proposals for specific development projects such as that for Pennsylvania Avenue as recommended by the President's Council on Pennsylvania Avenue, launching a complex of public buildings and visitor facilities between Judiciary Square and Union Station, and an expansion of the Planning Commission's earlier suggestions for an International Center in the West End. By proposing such limited developments, the Green Book contributed to the understanding that, in part, implementation of Comprehensive Plans is accomplished through detailed phasing schemes and localized planning.

New plans for a revitalized downtown were suggested in the strengthening of Mount Vernon Square and its radial avenues into a transition area between the downtown and the residential city. The 1967 Proposed Comprehensive Plan extended proposals in the 1965 Brown Book for development along South Capitol Street to include the previously isolated Buzzard Point and Navy Yard area. Also proposed was a new linkage with the Southwest and a restored relationship between Capitol

Hill and the waterfront. This proposed development project focused attention on the quality of the city's entire waterfront, and included proposals for a long promenade extending from Kingman Lake and Anacostia Park–West Bank through the Navy Yard to Fort McNair, through the Southwest waterfront and East and West Potomac Park facing the monumental core, west through the Watergate, and then to a redeveloped Georgetown waterfront. In redirecting the city to the river, in the context of residential, commercial, and recreational uses, the 1967 plan intended to provide new vistas of the metropolitan city and reintroduce residents to the original orientation of the L'Enfant city.

REGIONALISM

The Green Book worked from the assumption that the variety of the city's natural and man-made landscape now extended beyond the built-up District of Columbia into the developing region. The District would be affected by the region's willingness to absorb added population and to accept the central city as the dominant employment center. For the region's wedges and corridors emanating from the central city, the National Capital Planning Commission reiterated in the Green Book its support of the Year 2000 Policies Plan, with some modifications in the proposed transportation network. Much of the success of the restructuring scheme would depend on the actions of jurisdictions beyond the boundaries of the District. The suburban counties now controlled the design of most entrances to the city, and these entrances were of no little significance. The attitudes of commuters and visitors toward the capital city would inevitably be fashioned by what they saw as they daily approached the District line.

While continuing toward greater precision in the detailing of planning policies and programs, the 1967 Green Book also offered a more comprehensive definition of the cityscape, natural and man-made, and placed greater emphasis on the city as a visual experience.

Most significantly, the Green Book set the stage for step by step action on its various elements as these were to be presented to the Planning Commission and the Washington community.

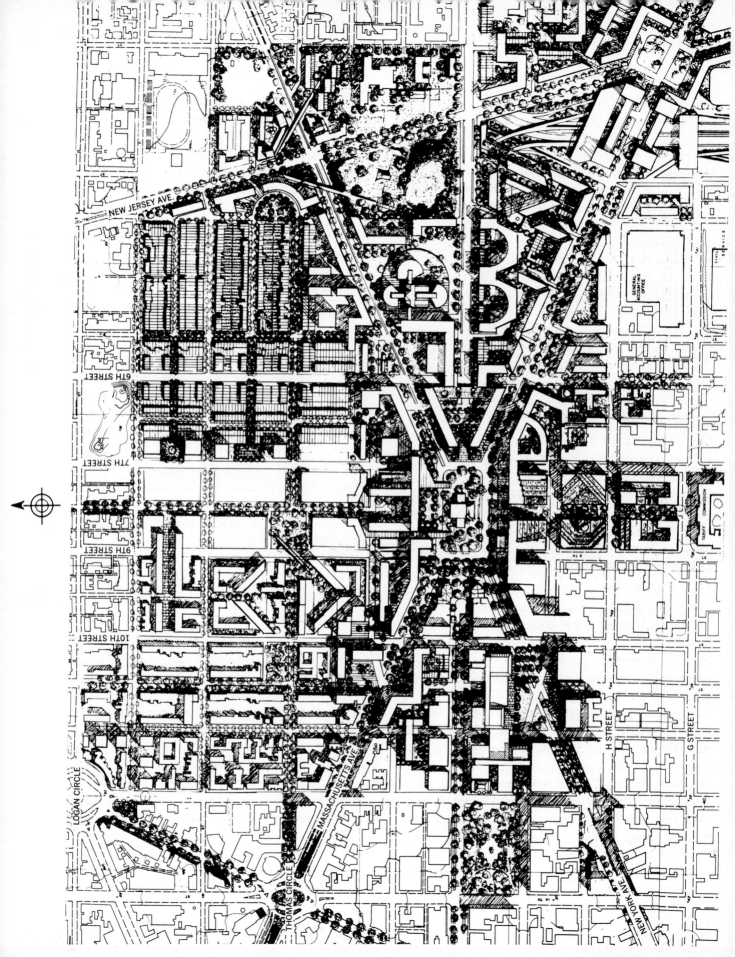

NEW JERSEY AVE.

6TH STREET

7TH STREET

9TH STREET

10TH STREET

LOGAN CIRCLE

THOMAS CIRCLE

MASSACHUSETTS AVE.

NEW YORK AVE.

H STREET

G STREET

CIVIL SERVICE

GENERAL ACCOUNTING OFFICE

TARIFF COMMISSION

The Red Book: The Continuing Comprehensive Plan

Following intense public discussion of the 1967 Proposed Comprehensive Plan or Green Book, the National Capital Planning Commission refined and revised the 1967 proposals. These revised proposals are now incorporated into four major chapters of the current Comprehensive Plan or Red Book—goals, general land use objectives, parks and recreation facilities, and transportation. These elements were adopted by the Planning Commission between 1968 and 1970; they address Washington as capital city, residential city, and central city of the large metropolitan region. As related to the District of Columbia, the basic intent of the current Comprehensive Plan is to plan for improvement of the quality of life and not for significant increases in population or development densities.

Long-Range Goals. Comprehensive Plan goals specify a city offering its residents choices among various environments, various employment opportunities, efficiency in land use, healthful living conditions, adequate public facilities, individual and special neighborhoods, and a visually attractive urban experience. These goals seek to relate the physical city to contemporary urban ideals of social justice and environmental quality.

Land Use Objectives. In its land use objectives, the Planning Commission continues to advocate the open and horizontal green city by preserving, in the words of the Red Book, "features unique to the District's individual communities." Land use objectives provide for employment, institutions, parks, residential development, and community groupings of public and commercial services, all within a context of round-the-clock usage of the city in and near the Central Employment Area. High-density development is proposed to be concentrated in this central area as well as in what are called Uptown Centers, with predominantly moderate density of residential and mixed uses in adjacent areas. It is hoped, thus, that a walk-to-work living pattern will emerge. These moderate densities as planned also serve as transition areas between high-density and low-density areas. The plan points out, however, that beyond simple land-use geometry, "the character of residential development—height, density and type—should be related to the relative accessibility, geographic setting, historical context, and existing patterns of each area, and, most importantly, to the needs of the people residing in the city."

Parks and Recreation Facilities. Policies covering parks and recreation facilities are viewed as influencing the attractiveness of neighborhoods, and the stated goal is to raise the standard of local parks to that of the national parks located within the District. In the tradition of the Olmsted-Eliot neighborhood centers, multipurpose service delivery centers are proposed, ranging from large and varied district centers to school-associated community centers, to small and intimate neighborhood centers.

Transportation. In the area of transportation, the current goal is a balanced, integrated system, combining highways, rail rapid transit, and parking facilities. While rejecting the Three Sisters Bridge (across the Potomac above Georgetown) and related freeways—and indeed rejecting any new freeway proposals—the Planning Commission recommends completion of the connecting links to the existing freeway system. The commission sees the future of the transportation system determined by land use patterns and largely affected by major public and private building programs, over which it possesses significant influence and coordinating powers.

NEW DEVELOPMENTS IN CITY BUILDING: CRYSTAL CITY

With an eye to the future as well as the present, the Planning Commission has had to recognize the importance of contemporary large-scale developments in the rapidly growing metropolitan areas. Almost in spite of planners' efforts, the activities of private speculators in the 1960s offered formidable challenges. A "packaged living" center developed around the commercial structures built in Rosslyn in the late 1950s. This same phenomenon was even more explicit in Crystal City, a development spawned by National Airport and new expressways. Located along the highly visible Virginia shore, Crystal City had the physical elements of a city—apartments, offices, hotels, shopping, recreation, all un-

Telephoto View of the Westgate Office Building Complex at Tyson's Corner, 1977

relieved by any civic, social, or humanistic grace. The complex was developed by Washington's largest builders, Cafritz and Tompkins, on a flat tract of largely reclaimed land just south of the Pentagon, conforming to plans of the Arlington County Planning Commission that located high-density development along the Jefferson Davis corridor. Unified by a vast network of underground malls—described as "territecture"—Crystal City offered a self-contained way of living in convenience and safety.

It was asserted that these new neighborhoods, termed by the *Washington Post* "omnibuildings," avoided the "sterility of one-use districts like downtown Washington, or much of the suburbs." It could be said, indeed, that the design of developments like Crystal City defined a new sterility. The high densities of people on the fifty acres of land led some urbanists to fear apathy and disaffection among residents. Architects viewing the project have questioned whether the complex truly functions as a whole or whether it is a disjointed collection of buildings. Unredeemed by even topographic irregularities, as for example at Rosslyn, the regulated monotony of Crystal City seems a crushing blow to the spirit. Whatever one thinks about urban design, this much has become clear. Developments at the scale of Rosslyn, Crystal City, and the Watergate oblige planners to examine the over-all effectiveness of their work in terms of the new building technology.

In any case, the glass office towers that populated Rosslyn and Crystal City expunged any hope that outlying new office buildings would be patterned after architectural traditions of the capital city itself. Outside the jurisdiction of the District of Columbia, the precast concrete façades took over. Squat towers repeated the commercialization of the central city, along Connecticut Avenue, and K, L, and M Streets in the northwest. Limited only in height, these structures were part of the office-building boom occurring in cities across the nation. In Washington they were for the most part the work of speculative investors and also reflected the clustering of national organizations in the capital.

Similar office groupings formed about the region's major thoroughfares, especially adjacent to the Capital Beltway, as in Westgate at Tyson's Corner. These far-flung office centers offered an urban life-style removed from the central city, so that people could commute between home and work entirely within the suburban context. This change was especially striking in Fairfax County where the beltway created, for the first time in history, a north-south route cutting across the traditional corridors leading to the south and west from Alexandria and Washington. Built at larger scale than the earlier regional shopping centers, these suburban subcenters were conspicuous in altering the traditional landscapes as well. They had not, however, been anticipated and their locations were more often fortuitous than planned. The result was seen over and over again in environmental insecurity and the unexpected drain on limited essential public services.

CONTINUITY OF PLANNING FOR THE NATIONAL CAPITAL

The impressive sequence of plans and publications—from the Year 2000 Policies Plan to the Red Book or Comprehensive Plan for the National Capital—forcefully demonstrates the continuity of planning. The decade-long effort, between 1958 and 1968, called attention to the city's strengths that were derived from L'Enfant—its wide streets, orderly pattern, open spaces, respect for the natural setting, and strategic sites for buildings. Nor did the Planning Commission shrink from the negative impact of the city upon visitors—worn-out housing and crumbling neighborhoods, shabbily maintained streets and neglected public places, blocks of downtown Washington transformed into "monotonous walls." Planning addressed these problems as well. There was also a call for removal of the wartime temporary buildings that still cluttered the city's parks and the Mall, and a fresh emphasis on historic preservation that would accomplish its objectives by making great old buildings part of new plans, and by joining development to preservation. The city so described was polynucleated, no longer to be expressed in a single downtown. In each of this city's several centers provision was made—in plans and projections—for commercial uses to contribute to "24-hour" vitality and varied use. The new freeways were located so that basic L'Enfant intentions would not be violated, and the integrity of the distinct communities would be recognized. Parking was provided as part of expressway planning. Priority at last was given to mass transportation needs. Long-deferred concern with civic amenity was expressed in a rejuvenation of park values, greatly stimulated by the efforts of Mrs. Lyndon Johnson. City streets were to some extent relandscaped; new bus shelters and trash containers made their appearance, and there was a fresh design of graphics throughout. While the city advanced toward regional planning and advocated excellence in design throughout the entire region, there still remained the specific difficulty of jurisdictional competition at the Potomac's shoreline and the need for a firm stand in favor of the central location of new federal office buildings. In sum and in principle, the concept of a national capital city as a physical model of urban excellence was reaffirmed, even if translation of this goal into practice and reality remained in many cases elusive.

Urban Design: Overlook Park at L'Enfant Plaza in the New Southwest

CHAPTER XIV   THE REDEVELOPMENT THEME 1945–1976

The Redevelopment Theme 1945-1976

Urban Renewal: Divergent Views

Postwar Washington faced all the problems of contemporary urban America—rapid growth, decentralization of population and employment, polarization of social classes, expanding mobility, and the rest. Its role as the federal city gave Washington a significant concentration of employment as well as the monumental landmarks by which it is known—but out along the beltway it was hard to distinguish Washington from any other large metropolitan area of the United States. The city's uniqueness, in short, did nothing to relieve it of the necessity of facing and resolving urban problems of the day.

Washington's urban history and its long-established planning arrangements were an important strength in understanding and dealing with these problems; the city was early represented in most of the federal aid programs that benefited other cities. One of the most important federal aid programs was urban redevelopment—urban renewal, as it was redefined in the Eisenhower administration. The earlier idealism of the public housing movement was associated now with the more comprehensive goals of urban reconstruction, the building of more viable and attractive central business districts and core cities, and the more unified and effective guidance of suburban and metropolitan development. Insofar as the urban problem at mid-century was seen as a matter of urban röt induced by the steady drift to the suburbs, urban renewal sought to offer home-owning families an inner-city alternative.

STABILIZATION VERSUS RADICAL REDEVELOPMENT

Postwar Washington viewed federally funded redevelopment as an opportunity to reverse the outward-bound suburban movement and revitalize the city. Nonetheless, when Washington embarked on redevelopment of the Southwest, the community found itself divided. On the one hand, the National Capital Planning Commission as framer of redevelopment plans believed that stabilization was the area's priority need; on the other hand, housing and redevelopment federal officials, the Federal City Council (a private organization representing the progressive downtown business community), and the Redevelopment Land Agency, which was responsible for implementing the redevelopment plan, believed that more drastic urban surgery was required. The stabilizers came on as conservatives. They argued that Southwest Washington was occupied by walk-to-work blue-collar workers who were employed on the waterfront, in warehouses and produce markets, or at Union Station. They made the case for improving the housing conditions of these families but leaving them where they were—and leaving their jobs there, too. By contrast, the federal housing and redevelopment officials and the Federal City Council pushed for more radical large-scale clearance, relocation of the existing population, and design of a large, new, and different community that would give an urban alternative to suburban living, in terms of school and community life as well as housing. Because the federal officials had the money, their views largely prevailed.

The radical redevelopment authorized by the 1949 Housing Act led some planners to expect that the removal of decayed housing and the creation of new communities in new physical surroundings would establish the inner city as an alternative attractive enough to retain or lure back the middle class. But the houses that were to have been occupied by families in such a turnaround trend were filled instead with quartets of Capitol Hill clerical workers or congressional committee staff members, and the swimming pools and tennis courts echoed to the voices of a largely transient population. Tourist attractions, hotels, waterfront restaurants, and other limited commercial uses emerged as the characteristic business activities in the area. Relations between the residents occupying new developments and the occupants of existing public housing (in addition to certain slum properties to the east) remained troubled despite conciliation efforts of a dozen new churches and community institutions.

Even before the results of redevelopment were fully realized, the course of redevelopment thinking altered. The 1954 Housing Act provided for redevelopment planning to include the retention and rehabilitation—rather than removal—of existing structures. This con-

servation approach was strengthened over the years and expanded to include retention of existing community facilities and general community character.

The Elbert Peets Renewal Plan for the Southwest

The Southwest quadrant of Washington was one of three possible redevelopment areas in the inner city designated by the National Capital Park and Planning Commission after the demise—previously discussed—of Barry Farms and Marshall Heights as potential projects. The 1950 Comprehensive Plan labeled much of the small Southwest quadrant and large areas in the Northwest and Southeast quadrants as possessing high concentrations of "obsolete dwellings," overcrowding, and other potential threats to public health. When these separate conditions were overlapped, however, the Southwest emerged as the principal initial target area for renewal.

The Neighborhood Rehabilitation Approach. In 1951, the landscape architect and urban designer Elbert Peets was commissioned by the Planning Commission to prepare a renewal plan for the Southwest. An eminent historian-interpreter of the L'Enfant plan, Peets drew up a "neighborhood plan" providing for retention of the Southwest area as predominantly low income, with rehabilitation of many existing structures and a careful weaving in of low-rise new buildings. Peets was strongly attracted to the Southwest as a distinctive and historic area, with characteristic old street trees and row houses. Peets's plan closed many streets to through traffic and reoriented the remodeled houses to gardens in the interior of blocks previously filled with alley dwellings, stables, and shacks for coal and wood. The houses themselves would be saved, being reequipped and given new settings with a fresh neighborhood character. In the spirit of the wartime Goodwillie plan, the Peets plan did not propose drastic alterations to the appearance of the neighborhood. Rather the aim was a gradual process of rehabilitation that would entail minimal relocation problems. In view of the active, busy privately financed rehabilitation efforts that had already transformed Georgetown, and the initiation of similar efforts on Capitol Hill, the Redevelopment Land Agency acknowledged in its *Annual Report* for 1952 that "the [Southwest] area, though blighted to a considerable degree, does contain many individual structures susceptible to the Georgetown kind of rehabilitation." The report hailed the Peets plan for its faithfulness to L'Enfant. But in the eyes of the Redevelopment Land Agency, the Peets plan, in its focus on leaving the area much the way it was, belonged to the rehabilitation brand of redevelopment—and for this the agency could not justify the spending of public funds.

The Justement-Smith Plan for the Southwest

In the following year, 1952, the Redevelopment Land Agency requested Louis Justement and Chloethiel Woodard Smith, the younger architect-planner whose strongly expressed views about reshaping the city had received wide circulation in her writings and in exhibitions, to explore the more radical alternative of large-scale redevelopment, an approach in line with Justement's well-known redevelopment philosophies. Reminiscent of Daniel Burnham's legendary adjuration to "make no little plans," the Justement-Smith plan aimed at a "whole process of rebuilding the city in a purposeful and accelerated fashion." The written plan in its introduction acknowledged the novelty and challenge of such an opportunity, as well as the absence of prior experience to serve as any guide. When redevelopment was approached under such unrestricted circumstances, it was expected that it would "release and stimulate progress" beyond the borders of the redevelopment area. Other sections of the city would theoretically follow in a chain reaction, proffering their own plans for redevelopment and construction. Ideally the plan would be detailed enough to provide a basis for attracting developers, but yet allow "scope for the maximum of individual initiative and imagination on the part of subordinate levels of planners and architects." The creation of "new and greater realty values" and the health of the business community, especially the building industry, were primary motivations in the plan's recommendations. The new residential areas planned in the redeveloped section of Washington were to be attractive enough to bring back the suburbanites who had fled the city. As the planners pointed out, the process of dispersal coupled with the inability of the historic ten-mile square District to annex suburban territory (and thus maintain a large affluent tax base) made the specter of the bankrupt city very real.

The broad and original concepts outlined by the Justement-Smith plan included a new entrance or "front door" esplanade to the Southwest, along Tenth Street, overpassing the railroad tracks and the planned expressway. The entrance was planned to link the formerly isolated quadrant with the cultural facilities along the Mall, most notably the original Smithsonian Building. "The view down Tenth Street to the channel, uninterrupted by buildings, over-passing the highway, bordered by parks on the east and a wide planted park set back along the west, would provide an inviting entrance leading to main east-west access avenues to residential areas and to the attractive waterfront drive leading to Fort McNair." The functional success of this new artery was dependent on its connection with Maine Avenue, which parallels the Washington Channel. Engineering problems created by topographic conditions were never fully resolved, and so the connection was not totally realized.

High-Rises, Townhouses, and the Corner Store. The new residential city was to be formed about groups of buildings, high-rise apartments and townhouses like those in Georgetown with front and back yards. According to the plan, "each group of buildings must be carefully studied later to take the greatest advantage of the various sites, orientations to sun, prevailing winds and views, provision of maximum privacy for each family unit, best use of open space, etc." The arrangement of building groups would necessitate closing off many of L'Enfant's streets. Low-income housing was to be maintained in the existing public housing area, in correct proportion to what the plan's authors saw as a "well-balanced central urban area."

A strip of high-rise apartments would be developed along the extant waterfront, traditionally the center of the Southwest quadrant's commercial and recreational life. The plan also called for the small "corner grocery" type of store and public or semipublic buildings located along the main residential avenue to provide "welcome breaks in the design and scale of residential buildings." In the juxtaposition of private enterprise and public benefits, the plan held the promise of a "richly varied and human urban area." Some of these values were echoed in the townhouse areas of Capital Park where Smith translated ideas into architectural terms through design treatment of parking and public open spaces. There was no wide-scale application of these values, however, because they proved too elusive to survive the bureaucratic conflicts and neighborhood packaging to which future decisions concerning the new Southwest were subjected. Thus, underinvestment in the public sector produced an almost wholly residential character instead of the more diversified and lively urban atmosphere originally intended. Not even the corner grocery survived.

The Southeast/Southwest Freeway. Intended to cut across this newly molded quadrant was an expressway designed to connect the Fourteenth Street Bridge with South Capitol Street. In relation to the proposed 1950 Comprehensive Plan's inner circumferential route, the freeway would serve as the first stage of this central thoroughfare. The freeway would not only serve as a means for carrying through traffic above the "central congested part of the city," but it would also allow residents within the Southwest access to the rest of the city. Rather than cutting through the quadrant as tentatively outlined in the 1950 Comprehensive Plan, the Justement-Smith plan suggested that the freeway should bound and define the residential area to be developed. When the artery was later built, it became that boundary and separated the new federal buildings complex south of Independence Avenue from the residential area.

Attracting Capital. In the tradition of the McMillan plan, the Justement-Smith sketch of proposed development provided no restrictive design but rather a stimulative range of possibilities. *It was a concept plan.* On a

Elements of Architectural Drama at Town Center in the Redeveloped Southwest

more practical level, the sketch was intended to help the Redevelopment Land Agency to attract developers and to market the redeveloped land. Unlike the "conservative" Peets plan that offered no new dramatic images, the Justement-Smith plan aided in convincing financial interests that the Southwest quadrant's reputation as a low-rent housing area would be completely altered as a result of the redevelopment.

Yet, for all of its modernism, the Justement-Smith plan was most likely inspired by traditional attractions of the quadrant, by its river orientation, and by the elements of architectural drama—vistas of the Capitol dome and monumental buildings, and neighborhood groupings deriving from L'Enfant's design. Moreover, the Justement-Smith plan incorporated the City Beautiful element of a green protected river's edge, and concern (reminiscent of the early Planning Commission days) with neighborhood parks and identities.

The Southwest Redevelopment Work of the Planning Commission and the Redevelopment Land Agency

The Planning Commission–sponsored Peets plan and the Redevelopment Land Agency's Justement-Smith plan had in common their reliance on the Southwest quadrant's past life-style. For the rest, the divergence of philosophies was marked, and this prompted the Planning Commission to name Harland Bartholomew to study and assess the two plans and make recommendations to both the commission and the Redevelopment Land Agency. Bartholomew agreed with Peets's emphasis on retaining the quadrant as a low-income residential area because of the convenience to employment centers for those who could least afford to own automobiles— and because relocation problems would be minimized. Peets's brand of rehabilitation was by the same token more difficult to define as a redevelopment project and was thus questionable in terms of justifying federal financing. While the Justement-Smith plan responded positively to those who believed there was a need for dramatic action and expression of idealism through extensive redevelopment, Bartholomew questioned the

success of attempts to transform the area completely. He also pointed out the acute relocation problems and the loss of industrially zoned land, as well as the expensive rearrangement of the traditional business thoroughfares along Fourth and Seventh Streets.

The Planning Commission's Compromise Report. In order to reconcile the two plans, the National Capital Park and Planning Commission issued a compromise report in November 1952. In this report, written with the assistance of Peets, and drawing on recommendations of the earlier report by Harland Bartholomew, the commission restated its responsibility under the Redevelopment Act of 1945 to prepare and adopt the "general framework or guide of development" which the Redevelopment Land Agency was then supposed to execute. The 1952 compromise report approved large areas for clearance, but recommended replacement by low-rise buildings that would follow in form and location the old row-house configurations. This compromise report by design avoided the "extremes of idealism— such as the complete wiping out of this area and of its replacement by a forest of multi-story apartments—and, on the other hand . . . the extreme of expediency—such as replacement or face-lifting of the existing development." The reduction in emphasis on rehabilitation was supported by the highly influential American Public Health Association's Housing Appraisal Technique that assessed more than half of the living units in the Southwest quadrant to be substandard and ripe for replacement. Although the Planning Commission was reconciled to demolition of overwhelming numbers of structures, the report reiterated that the area was steeped in "historic and sentimental interest" both in its street plan and architecture. To preserve these values, the Planning Commission sustained its conviction that the quadrant should remain a moderate to lower income area. The commission also reaffirmed its long-held concern to design neighborhoods, not individual structures. The compromise report agreed to the desirability of the Tenth Street Mall or esplanade but expressed reservations about the interchange between the terminus of the new mall and Maine Avenue. Based on this report, a final redevelopment plan was prepared.

The Role of the Redevelopment Land Agency. Final adoption of the redevelopment plan for the Southwest was only the beginning of a long, obstructing legal and administrative process for which there were no precedents or useful guides. Moreover, time itself added complexity as altered redevelopment philosophies and policies stressed a more conservation-oriented approach as opposed to radical reconstruction.

It was with the invitation—issued in 1953—to developers to submit plans for the Southwest that the Redevelopment Land Agency began its legislated responsibilities of assembling land, demolishing buildings, preparing sites, and then disposing of the land. Almost immediately, lawsuits flooded the District courts, challenging the agency's powers of condemnation. In a dragged out process, leaving many plots of land vacant over several years, the litigation route led to the Supreme Court. In the landmark October 1954 decision in *Berman vs. Parker*, the high court upheld the right of the Redevelopment Land Agency to condemn—in the public interest—land occupied by "miserable and disreputable housing."

Reference Map of Urban Renewal Project Areas in the District of Columbia, 1957

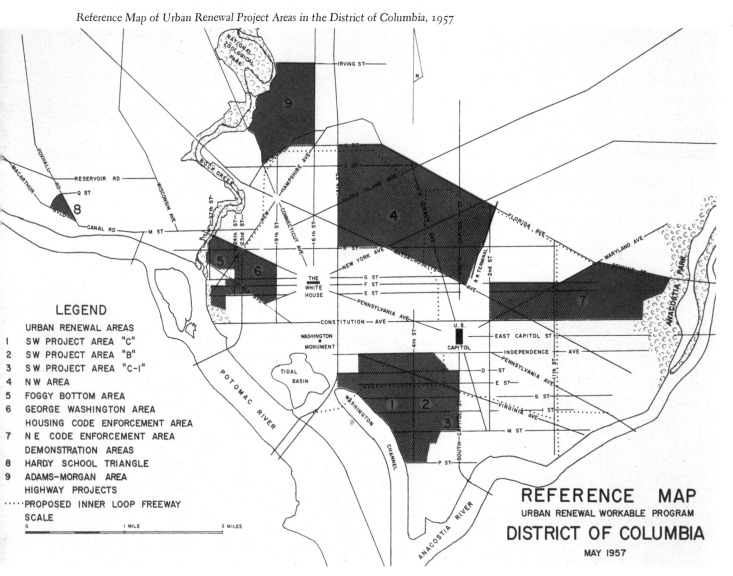

LEGEND

URBAN RENEWAL AREAS
1 SW PROJECT AREA "C"
2 SW PROJECT AREA "B"
3 SW PROJECT AREA "C-I"
4 N W AREA
5 FOGGY BOTTOM AREA
6 GEORGE WASHINGTON AREA
HOUSING CODE ENFORCEMENT AREA
7 N E CODE ENFORCEMENT AREA
DEMONSTRATION AREAS
8 HARDY SCHOOL TRIANGLE
9 ADAMS-MORGAN AREA
HIGHWAY PROJECTS
••••• PROPOSED INNER LOOP FREEWAY
SCALE
0   1 MILE   2 MILES

REFERENCE MAP
URBAN RENEWAL WORKABLE PROGRAM
DISTRICT OF COLUMBIA
MAY 1957

Zeckendorf Proposals for Southwest Washington Redevelopment, 1955

MAJOR PROJECT AREAS IN THE SOUTHWEST QUADRANT

Even before the legal battles were resolved, the Southwest was divided into three major areas. *Project B*, a small rectangular piece of land in the far northeast corner of the quadrant, was separated as a demonstration area to be developed first and in full view of the Capitol. James Scheuer and Roger Stevens, principal developers of Project B, were responsible for one of the major developments there, high-rise apartment buildings and row-house groupings in the large Capital Park complex. *Project C-1*, located just south of Project B, was to be developed as a light industrial enclave. *Project C* was the largest area, extending from the waterfront to the western boundaries of Projects B and C-1.

THE ZECKENDORF PLAN FOR PROJECT C

As the smaller projects demonstrated the success of the redevelopment procedure, the future of Project C was assured. Covering the entire quadrant from the waterfront to the boundaries of the two smaller projects, Project C was the platform for the creative planning to

come. The flamboyant New York real estate developer, William Zeckendorf, representing the firm of Webb and Knapp and recruiting the technical guidance of architects I. M. Pei and Harry Weese, took charge of the vast Project C. The detailed plan was developed between 1954 and 1959 and was based on the general plan approved in 1952. The detailed plan was largely a response to the spirit of the Justement-Smith plan. Zeckendorf envisaged the new Southwest as a showcase of unusual architectural beauty. Zeckendorf's Southwest was to be entered via a Tenth Street Mall and was to be inhabited by 4,000 families of varying incomes. There was to be a modern town center as well as enlarged waterfront restaurants and marine activities, and a cultural complex.

Zeckendorf's Tenth Street Mall itself took off from the vision of the Justement-Smith plan. The mall or esplanade in the Zeckendorf plan was described as a "wide and impressive span, flanked by stately government buildings." Contrary to its earlier proposed function as an entrance linked directly with the waterfront

319

The Southwest Waterfront Area, Late 1960s

along Maine Avenue, this mall would terminate "in a circular overlook providing motorists or pedestrians a grand view of the waterfront and residential Southwest Washington." Parallel to the Mall and just east of it, the cultural complex or plaza—as proposed by President Eisenhower's Auditorium Commission—was to be developed on nineteen and a half acres. This cultural complex was intended as a unified cultural and entertainment center, similar in concept to what was in fact later developed as the Kennedy Center for the Performing Arts in Foggy Bottom. Zeckendorf's concept of the plaza was even more than this, however. Zeckendorf saw the plaza as perfectly situated for a central tourist center, a complex of restaurants and other visitor-oriented establishments that would allow the tourist "to savor the best of America's cultural flavor and entertainment talent. . . . In short, the plaza is envisioned as a cultural center for Washington, the nation, and perhaps even the world." The waterfront in Zeckendorf's design would assume more dramatic proportions than those of "cramped" market stalls. Zeckendorf planned that the waterfront marinas, markets, and restaurants would extend the length of the channel north of Fort McNair (the Army War College site) and act as a terminus of strategic vistas from various vantage points

in the quadrant. The residential community would be housed in eight-story elevator buildings or in town-houses. Just as the new mall would provide a new vista, so the high-rise apartments would be visually designed and distributed "to achieve a balanced diversity of visual appeal and to maintain an openness to light and air," especially fronting the Washington Channel. The townhouses would be organized about residential squares beneath which extensive parking space was planned. These square open spaces were to serve as the common front yard for the abutting houses (much in the tradition of London's private parks), and were touted as providing "a suburban spaciousness for in-town locations." In addition, each house had its own small back yard, and many apartments their own balconies. The town center as proposed would incorporate both shopping center and community facilities—churches, parks, libraries, and community houses—and thus serve as a unifying link between the separate residential clusters.

Residential Clusters Built in the Southwest. The final format for residential clusters was determined less by Zeckendorf's plan than by individual developers who flocked to the Southwest after the collapse of Zeckendorf's real estate empire. They completed what he had begun. Design competitions were held by some of the developers, as for example by Charles H. Tompkins in the design for Carrollsburg Square won by the Washington firm of Keyes, Lethbridge and Condon. Although the prizewinning design was praised for its "humane character," the panel of judges feared that consistent use of high-rise buildings and townhouses organized about parklike plazas "could lead to an overdone Southwest style for residential developments." This consistency in residential accommodations was broken somewhat by retention of historic buildings: Wheat Row, the Barney House, the Washington Lewis House, and the Law House, as well as several old churches.

Federal Office Buildings on Independence Avenue. The problem of the design and land use north of the expressway was solved in 1954 by approval for the General Services Administration to construct new government office buildings along the frontage of Independence Avenue. The government had already constructed several facilities in the area, most notably the large Agriculture Department Buildings, the Bureau of Engraving and Printing, the Department of Health, Education and Welfare, and the Railroad Retirement Building. A government warehouse located within the bend of the railroad tracks was later transformed into the General Services Administration Regional Office Building. The Southwest Urban Renewal Plan designated six sites along the south side of Independence Avenue and north of the railroad for public buildings. Facilities were developed on these sites for the new Department of Health, Education and Welfare Building and the Food and Drug Administration between Sec-

Model Illustrating Carrollsburg Square Development, 1965

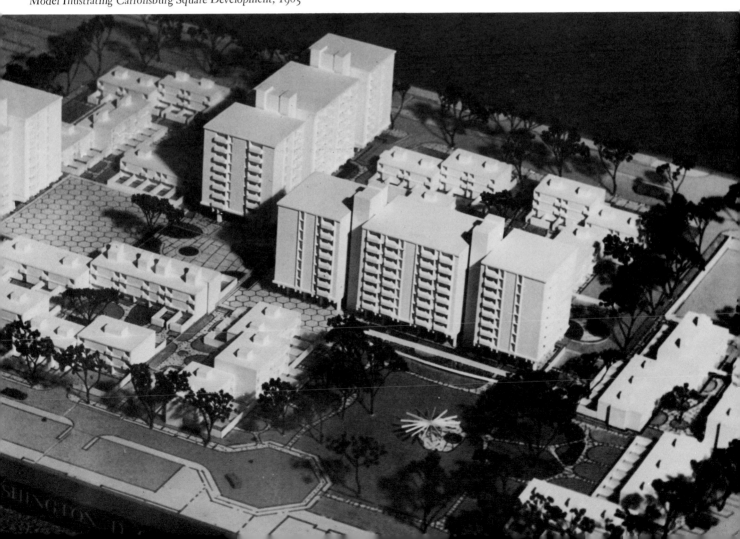

View of the Federal Office Building Complex along Independence Avenue, Showing (foreground) the Tenth Street Mall under Construction, Late 1960s

The Tiber Island Complex in Washington's Redeveloped Southwest, 1960s

ond and Third Streets; Federal Office Building No. 6 between Fourth and Sixth Streets; the Federal Aviation Administration Building housing this major agency and offices of the Department of Transportation; the Forrestal Building at the entrance to the Tenth Street Mall and what is now called L'Enfant Plaza. Later, on the south side of the railroad, a site was acquired for the Department of Housing and Urban Development Building designed by Marcel Breuer, a set piece for the new architectural policies of the Kennedy administration.

The flat triangle of land south of the railroad and north of the expressway was filled in by the large office building designed by Edward Durell Stone and leased to the Department of Transportation, the United States Postal Service Headquarters Building on the west side of the new mall, and the privately developed hotel-office building complex east of the new mall. In the completion of this triangle, the boundary between the residential area to the south of the expressway and the employment area to the north was fulfilled architecturally as well as functionally. From the planning viewpoint perhaps the most interesting feature was the un-

derground arrangement, a shopping mall and garage complex with a small theater. The principal shortcoming, as with the rest of the city south of Independence Avenue, was the absence of any reasonable mass transportation arrangement and—considering the 90,000 jobs scheduled for the area—anything resembling a transit terminal. Although the Southwest grouping as a whole was never conceived of as an element of the monumental core in earlier Comprehensive Plans, except for a small area referred to as the Southwest Triangle in the 1930s, the filling in of the southern border of the mall provided a stronger public setting to the new museum buildings that line the south side of the mall: the circular Hirshhorn Museum and Sculpture Garden and the two-block-long National Air and Space Museum.

Rehabilitation and Redevelopment Projects Elsewhere in Washington

The coupling of redevelopment with slum clearance was most clearly advanced in the example of the new Southwest. When demolition activities were at their peak, however, consideration was given again to an alternative method of redevelopment—i.e., rehabilitation. As early as 1948, the Planning Commission studied what was popularly called the "Baltimore plan." The logic of the Baltimore plan followed from the premise that obsolete, rundown housing was primarily the result of unenforced or ineffective building codes. Thus, the solution to such housing was to enforce the code and hold property owners responsible for maintaining their own buildings. Another mechanism for supporting rehabilitation efforts was the 1954 Housing Act, which allowed federal funds to be applied to rehabilitation projects in urban renewal districts.

"NO SLUMS IN TEN YEARS"

It was too late to apply this growing acceptance of rehabilitation in the Southwest since most of the old row houses were already demolished. The code enforcement method was included, however, in the 1955 study commissioned by the District commissioners and entitled *No Slums in Ten Years*. Written by James W. Rouse and Nathaniel S. Keith, it was primarily concerned with Washington's role as a national demonstration city. The report listed twenty different steps planning and governmental bodies should take in order to rid Washington of slums. These steps included code enforcement, study committees, special "fight blight funds," and new administrative procedures.

Applauding the dynamic concepts that fostered the new Southwest, the report also acclaimed private rehabilitation efforts in Georgetown, Capitol Hill, and Foggy Bottom. The report captured the spirit of the optimistic postwar decade (when problems appeared soluble by the application of vigorous governmental pro-

grams), and outlined further redevelopment areas. Surprisingly, it suggested the resurrection of the politically unfeasible Barry Farms and Marshall Heights proposals. Lest it be criticized for omissions, the report also suggested areas in all quadrants of the city save the already progressing Southwest. Optimistically, the report left the reader with this final thought: "Washington can become the country's first major slumless city—an appropriate and exhilarating role for the Nation's Capital."

New Status of the Redevelopment Land Agency. As part of the District government reorganization following enactment of the District of Columbia Self-Govern-

Aerial View of the Foggy Bottom Area Prior to Redevelopment, Early 1960s

The Columbia Plaza Complex in Redeveloped Foggy Bottom, 1970s

ment and Governmental Reorganization Act of 1973 (the Home Rule Act), the status of the Redevelopment Land Agency was changed from that of an independent federal agency to an agency of the District government. Subsequently, as a part of further reorganization, on 3 July 1975 the Redevelopment Land Agency and other housing and community development agencies within the District government were merged into a new department—the District of Columbia Department of Housing and Community Development.

Foggy Bottom. Foggy Bottom, with its brewery, gas works, and coal yards, was a popular area because of its proximity to George Washington University and nearby medical facilities. It was close also to government offices in the Northwest Rectangle, the federal office building precinct bounded by E Street, NW, on the north, by Constitution Avenue, NW, on the south, by Seventeenth Street on the east, and by Twenty-third Street on the west. Row houses located in Foggy Bottom were of modest working-class dimensions, since the dwellings had developed close to the industrial establishments

along the Potomac. Rehabilitation of these houses proceeded under private initiative, so that the neighborhood went about "unslumming itself" in the Georgetown tradition. Moreover, studies had been carried out in Foggy Bottom along the route of that area's portion of the inner circumferential route. Like a set piece of the two methods of redevelopment, slum removal and rehabilitation, the vast Columbia Plaza complex highlighted Foggy Bottom's new status. Columbia Plaza, the area's only urban renewal project, is a "packaged living" complex of high-rise and low-rise apartments, an office building, and a shopping mall. This development, meant to attract middle- to high-income dwellers, is a symbol of redevelopment for the affluent "24-hour" population. It was to be a place, that is, where people live, work, and play.

Adams-Morgan. Other redevelopment projects of the rehabilitation brand emerged in the following years. In 1961 Adams-Morgan was adopted (by the Planning Commission, but not the District commissioners) as a redevelopment area after much private initiative had al-

Streets For People: Gallery Place, a Special Pedestrian Mall in the Downtown Urban Renewal Area, 1977

ready promised a revitalized neighborhood. Plans for the area were dropped four years later, however, when residents opted for a self-renewal approach. This was understandable, for as Adams-Morgan residents looked toward the new Southwest, they could see money-making developers, demolition of important landmarks, planning of suburban-type plazas, high-density development, and extensive relocation of residents.

Bolling-Anacostia Tract. The Bolling-Anacostia Tract was designated an urban renewal area in 1967 when the air traffic functions of the Air Force base were relocated. Although the Planning Commission developed various conceptual plans for building a new neighborhood on the site, Congress later deleted the tract from the commission's jurisdiction, and directed the Department of Defense to construct military housing and other facilities according to its own designs.

Fort Lincoln. The new town of Fort Lincoln on the former site of the National Training School is currently being developed. Adopted by the National Capital Planning Commission and approved by the District of Columbia Council in 1972, the Fort Lincoln Urban Renewal Area Plan represents an incorporation of the many revisions in redevelopment thinking since 1949 as well as the historical evolution of planning in the city contained in the Planning Commission's comprehensive and specialized planning reports. The plan for Fort Lincoln emphasizes the strengths of the natural topography, views, and the environmental amenities offered by the natural woodlands as well as the historical sites and events that should be recognized by developers. As a planned community, Fort Lincoln is to have as its primary objective the "creation of an attractive and racially, socially, economically, and functionally inclu-

326

sive community of approximately 16,000 persons." It is being developed as a self-contained community, a neighborhood that will attract outsiders to its town center, its parks and trails, and itself be linked with the rest of the city by a transit shuttle to the nearest Metro station. Provisions for community malls, playgrounds, and schools provide additional elements in creating an attractive area.

OTHER URBAN RENEWAL AREAS

The redevelopment spirit of rehabilitation and small-scale renewal, both aimed at providing new communities for low- and moderate-income residents, characterized redevelopment activities after the mid–1960s. Urban renewal areas designated in the Northwest quadrant include Northwest 1 (just west of North Capitol Street), Fourteenth Street, Shaw (just north of the downtown area), and the downtown itself. Urban renewal areas in the Northeast quadrant include H Street and Northeast 1 (just east of North Capitol Street).

Northwest 1. The National Capital Planning Commission, in consultation with the Redevelopment Land Agency, designated an urban renewal area west of Union Station and North Capitol Street. In terms of successful meshing of new and rehabilitated structures, Northwest 1 could claim the 227–unit Sursum Corda development, and Sibley Plaza (sponsored by the National Association of Home Builders), as well as rehabilitation of substantial blocks of row houses within the area.

Detail of Site Model of an Early Fort Lincoln Development Plan, 1968–69

View of Northwest 1 Redevelopment Area along North Capitol Street, Early 1970s

The Program for Bates Street. One urban renewal proposal that attempted to integrate the objectives of neighborhood conservation and rehabilitation was described in *A Program for Bates Street*, proposed in 1969 but not yet implemented. Working closely with the neighborhood residents of a two-block area that was part of the Shaw School Urban Renewal Area, the proposal addressed the problem of Washington's thousands of row houses—structurally sound but obsolescent in plan and services. The interiors of blocks were proposed to be opened up, play space provided, streets redesigned for living, all as a background to the reorganization of individual houses to admit sun and air to previously dark interiors and achieve more convenient layouts. The possibility of demolishing some existing houses and incorporating some new construction in the form of public housing was also examined. This possibility was a promising exercise in smaller-scaled redevelopment, with less clearance and moderated impact on social structures. Moreover, this possibility was realistically conceived in terms of Washington's characteristic street plan and housing types. The program was to be carefully phased to avoid relocation and was in fact aimed at relocating the same population in the old neighborhood. Given the fact that nearly all new housing starts were located in the surrounding suburban communities—and that there was a need in the District to conserve and re-

use the existing housing stock—alternatives such as those explored in the Bates Street proposal seemed to foreshadow a promising future in terms of urban continuity. While not directly expressive of a historic preservation effort, the Bates Street proposal provided support for a technique through which this future objective could be

Row Houses along Bates Street in the Shaw School Urban Renewal Area, Late 1960s

realized in areas that, unlike Georgetown or Foggy Bottom, lacked the resources to "unslum" themselves on a house-by-house basis and pay all the costs involved.

URBAN RENEWAL AND THE 1968 CIVIL DISTURBANCES

Urban renewal, or what is today termed community development, persists in playing an active role in the continuous process of reshaping the city, but in a more subdued and socially oriented mode as compared to the extravagantly overoptimistic redevelopment in the early 1950s. The idealistic claim that Washington could become a slumless city within a decade has given way to a realistic and evolving process which includes an accommodation of those who have the least resources—and a recognition of their concerns and aspirations. An example of community development may be seen in reconstruction efforts in the Seventh Street corridor.

The assassination of the Reverend Martin Luther King, Jr., on 4 April 1968 precipitated widespread civil disturbances in major cities across the nation. In Washington, disturbances were concentrated in the major black commercial centers: H Street, NE, Seventh Street, and Fourteenth Street. The resulting loss of homes and jobs was matched by the destruction of property and the larger disruption of community services, and indeed damage to the morale of the entire city. As in the earlier civil disturbances in the Watts district of Los Angeles, it was immediately clear now in Washington also that the task of reconstruction would not be easy nor would reconstruction plans find any ready consensus.

Within hours after the beginning of the crisis, which continued in Washington from April 4 through 8, the National Capital Planning Commission commenced a detailed survey to determine the extent of damage. The commission also began to formulate an outline plan for reconstruction. Thus, by April 9 it was possible to report that estimated property damage totaled $13,330,556. The report of the survey published by the Planning Commission localized the areas damaged and categorized the buildings affected according to the degree of damage (from zero to 10 percent, from 11 to 50 percent, and more than 50 percent). The survey also sorted the damage as between 909 commercial establishments and 283 dwellings. A subsequent analysis by the commission raised the initial estimates to 1352 affected businesses involving damage to 645 buildings. Total property damage was calculated at $57.6 million, a figure that included the value of looted and burned inventories of goods as well as real property damage. Nearly half of the damage was in the Seventh Street corridor, that historic route that long ago had connected the Potomac port to the Baltimore turnpike. The Planning Commission report, *Civil Disturbances in Washington, D.C., April 4–8, 1968, A Preliminary Damage Report*, was an immediate response to Mayor Walter Washington's call for "positive action programs and a full mobilization of local and federal resources to assist in rebuilding the damaged sections of the District."

In addition to preparation of planning data such as real property maps, assessment and insurance records, air photos, and field inspections, meetings were held by planners with many community groups. The aim was to search for a reconstruction strategy. By 28 August 1968, the cooperating agencies of the District of Columbia and the National Capital Planning Commission were able to publish a second report, *Alternative Approaches to Rebuilding*, addressed specifically to the three major concentrations of damage. This report took into consideration a wide spectrum of views expressed in the community. A parallel survey was also put forward by the Metropolitan Washington Board of Trade.

Public agencies during the disturbances had shown the values of metropolitan organization of police, fire, and other emergency services. Immediate needs for housing those left homeless—and caring for those left unemployed—were met with a similarly impressive degree of regional emergency organization. At the same time, preparations for longer-range reconstruction efforts were initiated. In many respects, the entire response was similar to that experienced by cities after earthquake, flood, or other widespread disruption.

The political issues embedded in reconstruction plans had roots in the wide variety of expectations held by different elements in the community. These were only partially recognized in the City Council's report of 10 May 1968, entitled *Rebuilding and Recovery of Washington, D.C., from the Civil Disturbances of April, 1968*. What the City Council made clear was the evi-

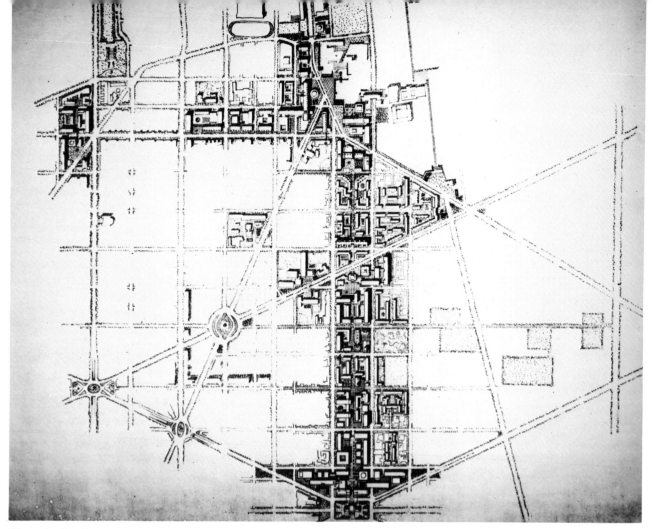

Illustrative Site Development Plan of the Historic Eighth Street Cross Axis, Showing Proposal for Redevelopment along Seventh and Eighth Streets After the Civil Disturbances, 1968

dence brought out in public hearings that "the lack of housing, employment and other opportunities for ghetto residents were . . . the basic factors contributing to the disturbances." Yet public opinion alone clearly could not resolve the differences between short-term aid and long-term redevelopment; between using the reconstruction opportunity to advance fundamental reforms and simply rebuilding the ghetto as it had been. Over all, there was a pervasive if less clearly expressed view that the opportunity for fundamental changes in land use, transportation, recreational open space, and other physical characteristics of the damaged areas should not be thrown away.

Of the many experiences that could be examined during the ensuing decade after the 1968 disturbances, redevelopment of the Seventh Street corridor is probably the most representative as well as the most illuminating.

Following closely the initiatives and plans of the National Capital Planning Commission, and the articulation of community development objectives, the Redevelopment Land Agency worked in close coordination with departments of the District government. Three new housing developments with a total of 400 dwelling units were completed by 1976 and construction had started on 245 more, with an additional 50 rehabilitated units. The Seventh Street environment was greatly improved with mini-parks and new street lighting. Many new community facilities were added and others are now in progress. Among the additional renewal areas established as the outcome of planning for reconstruction of the riot-torn sections of the city are the Shaw School Urban Renewal Area and the Downtown Urban Renewal Area.

CHAPTER XV THE METROPOLITAN REGION THEME 1945–1976

The Metropolitan Region Theme 1945-1976

Dispersal and Decentralization

From Washington's beginnings, city and region had been integrally related. President Washington saw the city set in the Potomac corridor to the west. L'Enfant designed the city with a shrewd eye to its larger riverine setting. But the Constitution's specification of a city "not to exceed ten miles square" left the dilemma of a separate city in the broader region. Before the Civil War the city had reached beyond its limits for its water supply, and from above Great Falls the great aqueduct marked the first regional service. The ring of Civil War fortifications in effect pushed out the boundaries of the city. This was particularly significant in Virginia, where the 1846 retrocession of District jurisdiction south of the Potomac was negated in the 1860s by wartime military occupation so that residents of this area found themselves "between the lines." After the Civil War, many properties acquired for military reasons remained in federal hands, a conspicuous example in full view of the city being the lands of General Robert E. Lee at Arlington; here, later on, a national military cemetery, an experimental farm of the Department of Agriculture,

and other federal establishments would be located.

This historical background to the ultimate regional city was a fortuitous nineteenth-century patchwork. With the McMillan Commission in 1901, however, rational planning embraced the metropolitan view of the city that stretched from Great Falls to Mount Vernon, and proposed unification of this larger area by parkways and recreational uses of the land. Inspiration came from the contemporary (if aborted) plans for metropolitan Boston, undoubtedly communicated by Frederick Law Olmsted, Jr., a member of the McMillan Commission. The park proposals for Washington would indeed be realized, although only after a period of more than a third of a century. And if the immediate focus of the McMillan Commission's interest was in the monumental core of the capital city with its building sites and parks, the larger urban framework and the longer chronological view were also evident.

With establishment of the National Capital Park and Planning Commission in 1926, the regional city was reaffirmed. The parkway to Mount Vernon can be regarded as a regional counterweight to the city-centered Federal Triangle. The planner Charles Eliot enunciated many regional themes, but the decisive steps to give

Setting of the Metropolitan Regional City, Shown in an Oblique Aerial View of the Anacostia River Basin, 1966

them effect were the creation of planning agencies in the contiguous suburban counties with which cooperative relations could be initiated, and the grant-in-aid machinery of the Capper-Cramton Act that provided important leverage for Planning Commission regional programs. Through Planning Commission review of regional park plans, moreover, unified planning for drainage, subdivision control efforts, and implementation of transportation planning were made possible. Even before World War I, establishment of the Washington Suburban Sanitary Commission had provided for systematic development of water and sanitary sewers on a regionwide basis. All in all, Washington was ahead of other cities in these respects.

BEYOND THE DISTRICT LINE

Sporadic location of federal establishments beyond the District boundaries entered a new phase under pressures of World War II. Led by the siting of the Pentagon, the Naval Medical Center, the Beltsville Agricultural Research Center, the Naval Ordnance Laboratory at White Oak, Maryland, and other major centers of employment, a spate of so-called temporary buildings on temporary sites followed. Many were destined to become permanent facilities, as the facility in Suitland, Maryland. Under wartime conditions, these locations were roughly determined by existing transportation and in-place utilities, by availability of housing, or by feasibility of supplying these necessary services at a time when all such efforts were rigorously limited and controlled. The suburban pattern thus fostered was a campuslike federal installation located on a major transportation artery, surrounded by new communities of single-family homes. This was followed by the filling in of open land by additional residential development, commercial centers, schools, and other local government services.

The intense pace of wartime and postwar development—for, contrary to the expectations of many planners, there was at this time neither a turndown in population growth nor abatement in building and development—relentlessly drove Washington toward metropolitan government and its dilemmas. In Washington, unlike other American cities, annexation of surrounding suburbs to the central city struck against the legal barriers of the Constitution and the Residence Act. Creation of metropolitan agencies proceeded in the Maryland counties, but Virginia lagged, and no regionwide cooperation emerged.

THE INTERCONTINENTAL BALLISTIC MISSILES THREAT

It was at this confused juncture in the immediate postwar years that Washington was obliged to face its vulnerability to attack by intercontinental ballistic missiles armed with atomic warheads, and seriously to consider urban dispersal as a means of defense. Top-secret studies, such as Project Lincoln's analysis of Manhattan, demonstrated a general urban vulnerability. This fact of life had been suggested very clearly by experience with guided missiles in the closing months of World War II; the lessons of Hiroshima and Nagasaki could not be forgotten. British experience with shadow capitals in wartime, and the forced decentralization, also during the war, of many nonessential agencies from Washington to other parts of this country, presented themselves as tested solutions. Federal contract allocation could motivate firms that were willing to move to dispersed locations, and fast amortization rewarded such moves with significant tax reductions. While the problem of civil defense was immediate and nationwide, and many strategic centers equaled Washington in both importance and vulnerability, the nation's capital presented greater opportunities to execute new civil defense plans as a demonstration for the rest of the country.

On 16 December 1950, a national emergency was declared because of this recognized threat of atomic attack. Legislation was proposed for the relocation of sensitive government agencies. According to bills introduced in the House and Senate, cross sections of the government's vital systems were to be dispersed in eight facilities comprising a total of 40,000 employees. These facilities were to be constructed in a radius outside of but accessible to the city, and were to be built of special materials resistant to blast and atomic fallout. One such facility was built for the Atomic Energy Commission; the location selected was in Germantown, Maryland. To complement this planned dispersal of sensitive agencies into the greater Washington metropolitan area, the Bureau of the Budget proposed removal of about 25,000 employees to decentralized locations totally outside of Washington in other parts of the nation. The 1950 proposals, in short, attempted to provide for a systematic dispersal policy within the context of purposeful planning.

REACTION AND RESPONSE IN THE SUBURBAN COUNTIES

The Pentagon experience in Arlington had dramatically demonstrated what happens when a major installation is suddenly constructed in the suburban landscape without planning or preparation. In response to the legislative proposals for dispersal, residents in the counties adjacent to Washington could envision what the results might be in their respective suburban areas. During the 1950 congressional hearings on this dispersal legislation, county residents testified on the probable effects of such construction and fielded suggestions for more comprehensive planning. Dismissing the potential economic benefits and added jobs in rural Loudoun County, the "Washington milkshed," for example, Mrs. Robert S. Pickins, chairwoman of the Loudoun County Planning Board, testified: "When the government moves in, school burdens increase; water problems and sewage problems increase; and the change in the economy is very disturbing."

Professionals committed to regional planning recommended that the government study the effects on housing patterns, on roadways and highways, on urban and rural communities, and on the public utilities necessary to support additional growth. The simplistic suggestion that large office structures should be separated by open spaces—which would soon be filled in by housing—was not sound planning. The regional planner Clarence S. Stein insisted in a strong statement to the congressional Committee on Public Works that no dispersal of federal installations "should be attempted without providing both housing and full community facilities, including markets and schools, for the major part of the personnel."

Even jurisdictions not immediately affected by the proposed legislation were apt to be involved indirectly. Arlington County, site of the controversial Pentagon, did not anticipate any further federal installations within its boundaries. Hearing testimony suggested that even so "Arlington will be directly affected by the proposed dispersal" in the burdens thrown on transportation routes and facilities, water supply, and sanitation. Facilities in the District and Virginia would necessarily be affected, it was predicted, because "all routes across the Potomac into the District of Columbia pass through the county."

DISPERSAL AND CIVIL DEFENSE

Planning for the eight dispersed facilities was further complicated, as the legislative hearings revealed, by questions of whether an atom bomb attack would occur during working hours when office buildings were crowded with people or at night when these buildings were virtually empty. There was no way to know whether atom bomb attacks would be focused at the center of the target area or in the vicinity, and therefore safety could not be presumed for the proposed twenty-mile radius. Other questions also were raised. Would eight facilities spread out in the counties but linked by highways be truly convenient to each other and to the District in the event of emergency? Would larger bombs necessitate an even larger radius from point zero? Could government really function by mechanical communication systems, or would face-to-face conferences still be necessary? Leaving aside the uncertain defense justifications for dispersal, some government officials regarded the proposed eight facilities as investments in relieving congestion in the central city. Planners of this decentrist persuasion were quick to pick up the theme. Quite apart from the issue of atomic war, they pointed out, there was still the unresolved problem of overconcentration of government buildings in the downtown area.

Although no legislation would emerge from the 1950 hearings, the government's dispersal policy itself was furthered by executive action, culminating in Executive Order 11035, dated 9 July 1962, establishing a continuous review of locations for public buildings. Fear of atomic attack on the city continued to pervade building location policies for most of the 1950s, but acceleration of weapons technology later on shifted the focus of concern from passive civil defense considerations to the doctrine of countervailing weapons.

336

Recentralization

Strategic dispersal was seen in the location of the Atomic Energy Commission at Germantown, Maryland, the Central Intelligence Agency at Langley, Virginia, the National Bureau of Standards at Gaithersburg, Maryland, and the National Security Agency at Fort Meade, Maryland. Other smaller movements took place and highly secret installations such as the stand-by "underground Pentagon" near Camp David (at Blue Ridge Summit, Pennsylvania) were created in this period. The dispersal movement declined as more powerful weapons appeared. At the same time, the inconvenience of outlying locations was voiced increasingly. This awareness coincided also with increasing interest in central city revitalization.

SPLENDID ISOLATION REVISITED

The effectiveness of federal office buildings sitting in splendid isolation out in the suburbs forced planners to reconsider recentralization. The supposed proximity of home to work was more an idealization than a reality; in fact, employees at dispersed installations often commuted many miles from equally dispersed residential areas elsewhere in the region. Although located close to urbanized centers, as in the case of the United States Geological Survey in Reston, Virginia, the dispersed installations simply could not offer the convenience of the central city. Despite the many connecting highways, in practice there was little face-to-face communication with other agencies or indeed with other facilities of the same agency. Since little or no public transportation existed between the installations and the city or other

Dispersal of Federal Installations, Shown in the Location in Virginia of the United States Geological Survey at Reston, 1977

suburban areas, most employees were forced to use the automobile.

The dispersed installations were inconvenient for out-of-towners to get to; agencies were forced, therefore, to hold meetings and conferences in the central city. There was the constant need to attend upon Congress. Finally, as weapons technology advanced and eventually nullified the early 1950s policy of dispersal, civil defense needs reached beyond the limited scope of building location. In an atmosphere of detente, moreover, there seemed to be no need to sacrifice the efficient day-to-day functioning of centralized government to plans for civil defense. And in fact, in spite of the long historical experience of medieval walled cities, it may be observed that military considerations have usually proved a poor basis for city building and urban design.

The National Capital Regional Planning Council and the Council of Governments

Since dispersal and suburban growth could not be rationalized on grounds of defense, a coordinating and planning body was needed to deal with over-all questions of metropolitan growth. In 1951, Director of Planning of the Maryland–National Capital Park and Planning Commission Fred Tuemmler suggested that the National Capital Planning Commission should try to coordinate federal and local interests. Although this commission was itself facing reorganization under the leadership of its executive director, John Nolen, Jr., it did serve to coordinate efforts of the suburban planning agencies to establish a regional planning mechanism.

THE NATIONAL CAPITAL REGIONAL PLANNING COUNCIL

Regional concerns were institutionalized in 1952 in the federally funded and sponsored National Capital Regional Planning Council. This council was established by the National Capital Planning Act of 1952 (Public Law 82-592), which provided for the reorganization of the National Capital Park and Planning Commission as the National Capital Planning Commission. Composed of ten members representing the local planning commissions, including two members of the National Capital

Planning Commission, this new council was supplied with a planning staff attached to the Planning Commission and was instructed to pursue regional studies and to prepare a regional plan. Thus, the council reviewed the plans of the local planning jurisdictions, especially those of the "subregional agencies": the Maryland–National Capital Park and Planning Commission, the Northern Virginia Regional Planning and Economic Commission, and the National Capital Planning Commission.

It was in the initiation of studies that the National Capital Regional Planning Council was most effective. Under the directorship of Paul C. Watt, the council produced graphic studies of employment, land use, and public utilities patterns, all extremely useful information for the individual planning agencies. Another major contribution of the council, in its short history, was the Mass Transportation Survey, a study undertaken jointly with the Planning Commission. That study was presented to the congressional Joint Committee on Washington Metropolitan Problems and became the basis for the rapid transit legislation which provided for construction and operation of the Metro system. Other contributions were the council's General Development Plan of 1956 and the Regional Development Guide of 1966. With the Planning Commission, the council formulated the Year 2000 Policies Plan. The council also supported the Joint Open Spaces Project, as well as new procedures for selecting sites for federal and District facilities, and land-use planning for the city's river edges.

But even as the National Capital Regional Planning Council was going forward with its studies and formulation of a regional plan, Executive Director Watt admitted in 1958 that the "only power the Council has resides in the persuasiveness of the logic of its works." Nevertheless, Watt thought that since suburban agencies had participated in making the regional plan—much of it an aggregation of local plans—suburban governmental powers would be used to effect it. An assessment made in the following year stated the belief, however, that the council "had fallen short of the desired objectives. . . . The Regional Council does not appear to have developed a regional point of view, but on the contrary has functioned as a sounding board to reflect the narrower viewpoints of individual jurisdictions. It has strengthened particularism rather than surmounted it."

The Regional Planning Council had, in other words, failed to constitute a cohesive regional force. By presidential Reorganization Plan Number 5, in 1966, the council was abolished. Despite its weakness, the council can be seen to have formalized—for the first time since the voluntary coordinating committees of the Park and Planning Commission's early years—the vast metropolitan regional scope of the national capital. This was a decisive step toward regional coordination, taken forward in 1957 by formation of the Metropolitan Washington Council of Governments.

THE METROPOLITAN WASHINGTON
COUNCIL OF GOVERNMENTS

Another outcome of interest in regional matters was the Washington Metropolitan Regional Conference. Founded in the mid-1950s to promote voluntary cooperative action among the metropolitan counties and special-purpose regional organizations, the conference—which was renamed the Metropolitan Washington Council of Governments, or COG, in 1957—sought to formulate policies and coordinate views on a wide range of intergovernmental social and economic issues. Although the planning interests did not surface until regional planning responsibilities of the National Capital Regional Planning Council had been transferred to the Council of Governments and the National Capital Planning Commission in 1966, the conference from the beginning did establish governmental coordination procedures. This, too, was an important step forward.

The Council of Governments continues to concern itself with designing areawide standards for health and social services, public safety, human welfare, salary schedules, waste disposal, and purchasing procedures. Recent planning has focused on a reexamination of the Year 2000 Policies Plan. This reexamination contains no independent land-use studies or other new planning data. Its direction has rather been procedural. In 1974, over a decade after the Year 2000 Policies Plan was issued, the Council of Governments predicted, in the words of its reexamination, that unless the multi-

farious planning decisions affecting development in the region were enforced through strategic location and timing of water and sewer lines, "by the year 2000 the wedges would be filled in and the region would become a 'spread city.'" The Council of Governments said that the Year 2000 Policies Plan could be realized only by very careful and vigilant growth management. The council also criticized the original 1961 plan as being too concerned with urban form and not cognizant enough of other factors that influence growth, such as taxation, business cycles, financing, and the strata of governmental decisions. The plan, it was said, was not explicitly social-minded. Despite this critical reexamination of the Year 2000 Policies Plan, however, no planning alternatives have been offered, and the Council of Governments continues to study the policies plan to seek better means for structuring growth.

Regional Growth and the Suburban Planning Agencies

Preoccupation with suburban growth had generated popularity for the Year 2000 Policies Plan during the 1960s. In the suburbs, public interest focused on the proposed development corridors, however, and overlooked the plan's basic assumption of urban centrality and its proposals for reinforcement of this traditional pattern. In a concept or policies plan this could be overlooked, but the development process necessitates phasing and coordinating city and suburban growth. The Year 2000 Policies Plan appeared to reflect ideas of the Planner Hans Blumenfeld of Philadelphia, who formulated the wedges and corridors theory, insisting upon simultaneous recognition and accommodation of the forces of concentration and dispersal. The scheme also closely resembled the contemporaneous development of the so-called finger plan in Copenhagen. At the time, this pattern was in the mainstream of urban planning, and popularity of the corridors concept has continued into the present.

The Metropolitan Growth Policy Program. Without actually retracting the wedges and corridors scheme, the Council of Governments has raised new planning questions in its most recent pursuit of a Metropolitan Growth Policy Program. The current need to establish land-use controls, allocation of scarce resources, and equal responsibility for the burdens of growth throughout the region have forced the development of new planning tools. In its 1975 report, the Council of Governments recommended the constant monitoring of employment and migration, which together are regarded as the "key drivers of growth in the region."

SUBURBAN GROWTH IN MARYLAND

Reconciling these issues depends on the work not only of suburban agencies but also of regional agencies. For the Maryland–National Capital Park and Planning Commission, suburban growth was reflected in the continuing enlargement of its jurisdiction. This commission issued a new Comprehensive Plan in 1962, and in principle adopted the wedges and corridors scheme two years later. The various levels of decision making in county planning—from county councils to ad hoc planning by the Washington Suburban Sanitary Commis-

sion—have dealt the scheme many blows, leading to the Council of Governments' prediction of a "spread city" with development covering the county. Yet on the whole the planning concept still stands, strengthened in Montgomery County by open space provisions that have created an agricultural zone, reinforced by five-acre minimum subdivision requirements and an adequate public facilities ordinance, as well as by the strong provisions of capital budget planning. Intensification of environmental concerns, including air and water pollution, are potential new molders of county policy. Environmental interests have led to new zoning categories and subdivision philosophies that include open space. The concept of providing for parks has escalated from the early stream-valley ribbons to large regional parks, green belts around new development, neighborhood parks, and park-school combinations. Whether planning in suburban Maryland should continue to emanate from the bicounty commission, represented in the Council of Governments, or should develop into a stronger Maryland regional role is still a question.

Nighttime View of a New Town: Columbia, Maryland

View of the Mount Vernon Estate, Showing the Potomac River Location in Northern Virginia, 1977

VIRGINIA'S RESPONSE TO THE YEAR 2000 POLICIES PLAN

Literal, diagrammatic acceptance and implementation of the Year 2000 Policies Plan has been more difficult in Virginia, given the concentric stream valleys and existing development in Loudoun, Fairfax, Arlington, Alexandria, and Prince William Counties as well as the many independent cities. In Northern Virginia, the planning activities of Fairfax County have become extremely important because of its large size and its proximity to the District. Fairfax County has been a member of the Northern Virginia Planning District Commission since 1948. Like the Maryland–National Capital Park and Planning Commission, the Virginia commission was established to adopt a regional plan and aid planning agencies in the various constituent jurisdictions. It prepared a plan in 1965 which espoused a wedges and corridors growth pattern extending through existing concentric development into the still-rural areas of Loudoun and Prince William Counties. The ·plan was adopted in principle by all the major jurisdictions except the more densely settled Fairfax County. Planning functions of the Northern Virginia Planning District Commission have become obscured by the question of whether it or the Council of Governments is responsible for regional planning in Northern Virginia, and also by refusal of some jurisdictions to endorse its programs. Despite a late start and various administrative uncertainties, a steady evolution of planning philosophies has occurred in Northern Virginia, closely mirroring that in Maryland: infatuation with growth is giving way to environmental concerns, control of growth, prudent land use, and development of more flexible planning tools.

RIVERS, BRIDGES, AND HIGHWAYS: FRAME AND FULFILLMENT

The image of Washington today, as at the beginning, is framed by its rivers. Those great uniters of the metropolis, the Potomac and the Anacostia, were once the urban foci of the capital city. When new land routes preempted the river as the chief artery, the river became

Model of a Redevelopment Proposal for the Georgetown Waterfront, 1973

the city's "backyard," where industrial activities and high density threatened its open character. Other changes to the river were dictated by deforestation and cultivation of lands, for these practices allowed earth to be washed into the rivers with every rainfall and also caused agricultural wastes to flow past the city, drastically affecting the environment and depositing loads of silt when the river currents slowed. Reclamation of the river flats and a new appreciation of river edges by the McMillan Commission and then the National Capital Park and Planning Commission focused attention on the gateway aspects of bridges and land as well as the water routes into the city, and inspired acquisition over the next half-century of the scenic riverside gateway—the George Washington Memorial Parkway.

While fulfillment of these entrances to the capital

city created a stabilized aesthetic riverfront as far as the District's boundaries, the prolific growth of bridges and highways during the post–World War II era brought new hazards. Along the rivers, strategic areas such as Georgetown and what is now called Bolling-Anacostia were poised for new and more intensive development. In order to plan for this vital environmental and recreational resource, the National Capital Planning Commission in 1972 published the comprehensive study, *The Urban River*, a detailing of Comprehensive Plan policies. This study argued for restoration of the river's historic character and suggested new design treatments. The Planning Commission's 1976 study, *Shoreline Acquisition and Development Policies and Programs*, was a further detailing of Comprehensive Plan policies.

Perhaps the most critical if unique area of the urban

river was Georgetown, with the obsolescent but still operative Whitehurst Freeway that had earlier stimulated extensive high-rise construction along K Street and also in the Foggy Bottom area. Spurred by a presidential directive to prepare a plan for the Georgetown waterfront, the National Capital Planning Commission and the District of Columbia Department of Transportation sponsored the Georgetown Waterfront Area Study. In January 1975, the consultant's final report recommended replacement of the elevated freeway with a cut-and-cover depressed thoroughfare, and called for extension of the traditional scale and urban design of Georgetown north of M Street down to the waterfront.

THE QUALITY OF URBAN LIFE

As the metropolitan city blends into the surrounding region, the larger geographical framework appreciated by the city's founders has been realized. The position of the city in the Atlantic seaboard megalopolis has resulted in the rapid development of the Baltimore-Richmond corridor extending to the north and south. This is evidenced by new rapid rail lines interconnecting the area. Transportation, water supply, sewage and solid waste disposal, and recreation have all become important regional issues as the cities in this entire area must share out the limited resources and services. As a result, greater responsibilities have been accepted by the states, and by the federal government through the National Capital Planning Commission, the central federal planning agency for the National Capital Region. To deal with metropolitan growth issues, new strategies have been invoked. Preservation of open space for the purpose of structuring metropolitan growth has become an important goal. The original Year 2000 Policies Plan required that more than 300,000 acres of land be held from development—far more than would be required for parks and recreational use. Through the years, the ecological and environmental significance of such open areas has been reinforced. In cities, attention is focused on social and economic problems and strategies for resolving them. It is in the metropolitan areas, however, that the challenges of urban growth and resulting harmful effects on the environment have been most strongly felt.

East Coast Megalopolis, 1977

The New Washington

Quality, Quantity, and Growth: Which Way Washington?

Future Washington is more likely to be a creature of change than of growth, a trend demonstrated by the fact that for more than twenty years the District of Columbia has actually lost population. Earlier extravagant expectations for a metropolitan area of eight million people by the end of this century have since been drastically revised by demographic behavior. Now options facing the central city are stated more in terms of improving the quality of life than of accommodating larger numbers. More considered voices in Congress have for years been saying that bigger is not necessarily better, that many of Washington's problems are self-inflicted in the heedless pursuit of progress—with the federal establishment underwriting the bill. In the suburban counties an active interest in limiting and controlling growth has taken the form of building moratoriums, many of them related to the limited capacity of local utility systems. Under these conditions future population levels are realized in self-fulfilling prophecy. Still, the most important factor affecting growth pat-

terns in the District of Columbia and throughout the National Capital Region is the federal establishment. Although the federal establishment remains the fundamental source of city and regional character, image, business activity, and cultural life, there may be a limit to the extent of federal employment in the Washington area. More and more the view is accepted that prosperity does not depend upon growth, any more than the quality of urban life is to be measured wholly by the crude indicators of numbers employed and incomes earned.

Self or Symbol? However one defines growth or city-building difficulties, Washington suggests measurable success in the chief problem, maintaining the metropolitan city itself as a unity and securing from one historical period to another continuity over nearly two centuries. This has been done in the face of sustained and large-scale rapid growth. It has at all times required the weaving together of federal and local interests in the city. It has also required recognition of the local commercial and social interests of the indigenous community as well as the larger political, national, and international interests of the federal government. And

Federal Presence: Aerial View up Seventh Street and the Parallel Eighth Street Cross Axis, Looking North from the Federal Center along Independence Avenue, SW

345

even while it serves as a sounding board for bureaucratic factions, Washington has steadfastly acknowledged the fascination of citizens with their capital city.

Typical or Ideal? Whether this city should expect to be a model American city, the ideal to which other cities should aspire, or whether it should seek to be typical of American cities, *a good example of the kind,* is another Washington dilemma. This question, impossible to deal with in the abstract, is very real when the city faces problems such as regulation of building heights, design of the regional rail transit system, or control of Potomac River pollution. Generally, over the years, proponents of the model city have prevailed, but then the question arises of deciding upon the urban ideal. The design of the Arlington Memorial Bridge illustrates how the pendulum of taste and culture has swung to and fro over the decades—from an entirely functional, proposed engineering solution, complete with double decking and trolleycar tracks, to the monumental sym-

Downtown Washington Design and Development: Illustrative Site Plan, 1974

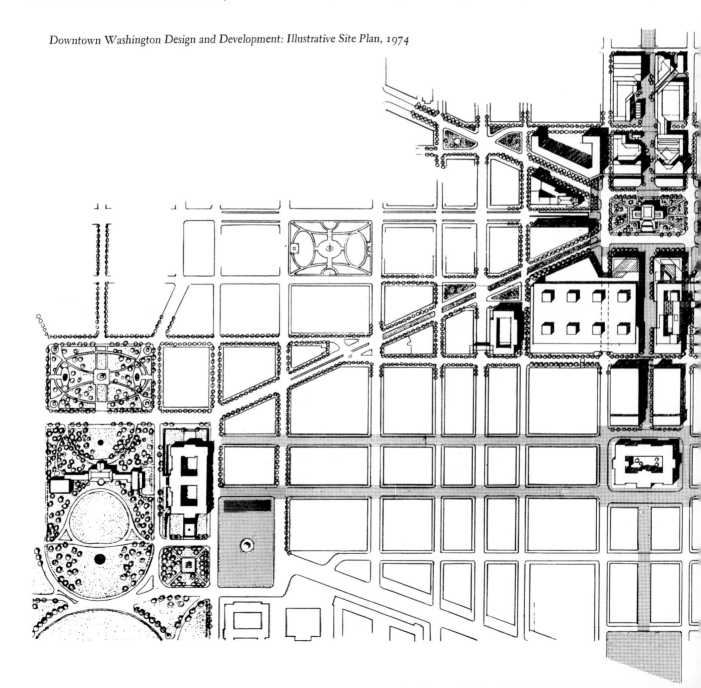

bol that was eventually built. The supremacy of the model city proponents suggests how the Washington Monument came to completion as a granite obelisk that defied anything dreamt of in Egypt or Rome, instead of following the federal design conceived by Robert Mills to incorporate columns and sculpture. It also explains how Congress can settle itself into architectural surroundings that, whatever one thinks of the design of the Library of Congress and the Madison Building, do exemplify grand ideals.

To raise the question of the typical or the ideal is to invite an answer based on the city's architecture. For the first hundred years, the city found the nation's best architects and put them to work. Federal buildings and monuments are the clearest evidence of these accomplishments, and there are notable private buildings of all sorts as well. It can be offered as a general observation that neither is the work done in Washington the best work of the architects concerned, nor does the city offer the boldest architectural advances and experiments

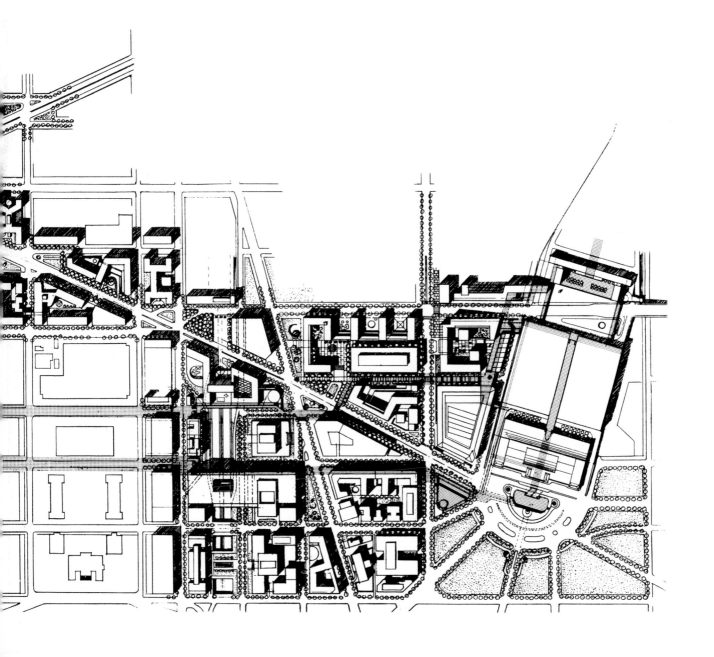

—although, again, there are notable exceptions, from Renwick's Smithsonian Institution "Castle" to Saarinen's Dulles International Airport.

WASHINGTON'S URBAN PRECINCTS

Washington has also shown the ability to develop viable urban precincts. Once you get there, Capitol Hill somehow *works* as a community of 15,000 people. Washington's international sector—foreign embassies and chanceries, the State Department, the Agency for International Development, the United States Information Agency, the World Bank, the International Monetary Fund, the Inter-American Development Bank—has generated a satisfactorily related complex of cosmopolitan shops, foreign-language bookstores, clubs, gourmet restaurants, international banks, and other services, in addition to hundreds of specialized consulting firms, newsgathering services, and other secondary reflections of the primary agencies. This is city life at its best, keen and comprehensive specialization, close-knit communities, face-to-face encounters, a distinctive character, individuality within a pattern of infinite variety. Even the street vendors offer quiche and pâté, sidewalk restaurants abound, and when weather permits the parks are filled with midday throngs picnicking alfresco on the green. In the Bourse district of Paris or the Inns of Court in London, similar precincts, marvels of efficiency and amenity, have grown and developed over the years; Washington, with its rapid growth, is perhaps lucky to have achieved what it has.

Contemporary Scene along East Capitol Street on Capitol Hill

348

Federal Establishment and Regional Center: Two Cities or One?

Most visible in the regional capital city is the location of federal enclaves that define the national interest. These enclaves, typified by the United States Geological Survey at Reston and the Naval Ordnance Laboratory at White Oak, low and blandly designed office buildings surrounded by acres of automobiles, are hardly to be distinguished from federal regional centers throughout the United States. In the Washington area, however, they are significant factors in the distribution of employment, the demand for highways and mass transportation—and their impact on the local economies. Their location raises questions of accessibility to those having business to do with the agencies, of intercommunication with other government branches, of national security. They also raise the questions of a federal city capable of operating as an organic and unified whole, and of the over-all relationship of the federal establishment to the metropolitan region.

Some aspects of this relationship are easily recognized. One certainly is historical continuity with the urban past, with the city's topographical features and formal design, its fixed location of Capitol and executive establishment, its monuments and parks. Another is the network of communications and urban services that support both the federal establishment and the Washington community, and are (like the aqueduct and the beltway) increasingly the product of federal financing and federal decision-making. But of the greatest importance, both to the federal government and the Washington community, is the accommodation and resolution of future demands by the federal government.

The Deliberately Created Capital City. Two other national capitals in this hemisphere, Ottawa and Mexico City, also are federal districts like Washington, illustrating the same profound concern with symbolic and urban appearance, the national interest in capital city growth and size, and an administrative form of government different from what is found elsewhere in the nation. None of these cities shows brilliant success in its concerns and efforts. Yet the problem of capital cities is worldwide, in both new nations and those that have elected to abandon former colonial capitals. Nothing suggests that their interests and their concern with symbol and national identity is any less positively expressed than in Washington. Nor is Washington as a deliberately created capital city unique, as reference to Canberra and New Delhi or Brasília and Chandigarh illustrate.

FEDERAL CITY AND DISTRICT OF COLUMBIA: A RECIPROCITY OF SIGHT?

Dominant since 1791 when L'Enfant first attempted to formulate a considered relationship between the federal elements of the city and its constituent core, the federal interest has urgently needed redefinition. This is now being undertaken in terms of planning for growth and change, for new institutional arrangements of federal, local, and metropolitan planning in the far-flung regional city of three million people. L'Enfant had captured the prominent hilltops and ridges for federal sites, and interconnected them by his famous "reciprocity of sight" along avenues that followed ridges and terraces, to create an urban landscape in which the formal and the picturesque had been blended. His proposals for a municipal center or the mile-long shopping street east of the Capitol are but two among many illustrations of L'Enfant's awareness of the urban functions of the capital city. As the city has evolved, however, and particularly as the federal establishment has grown and its demands for accommodation have become more varied, the national interest has changed in both character and extent. Life here has flowed beyond the original Washington City up into the surrounding hills, and has expanded far beyond the limits of the District of Columbia, beyond even that more modern boundary, the Capital Beltway. Decisions that allowed and governed this growth have not consistently governed its effects; thus, the need for rational and continuous comprehensive planning has long been felt.

THE 1974 REORGANIZATION OF PLANNING

The 1974 reorganization of planning in Washington reflected the parallel development of home rule that since 1961, in stages, gave the District a form of elected

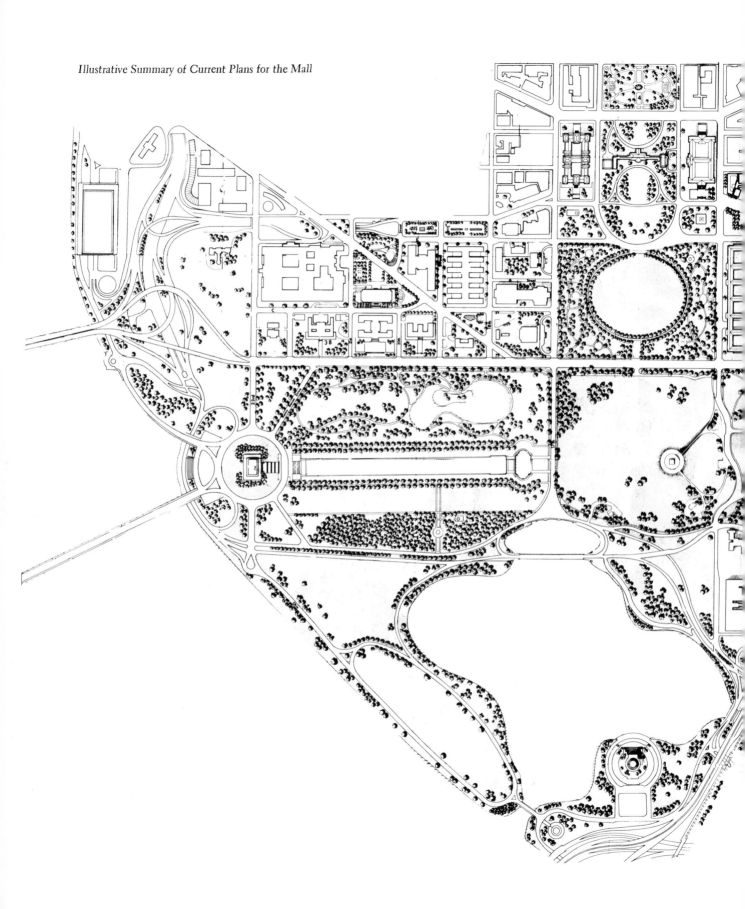

Illustrative Summary of Current Plans for the Mall

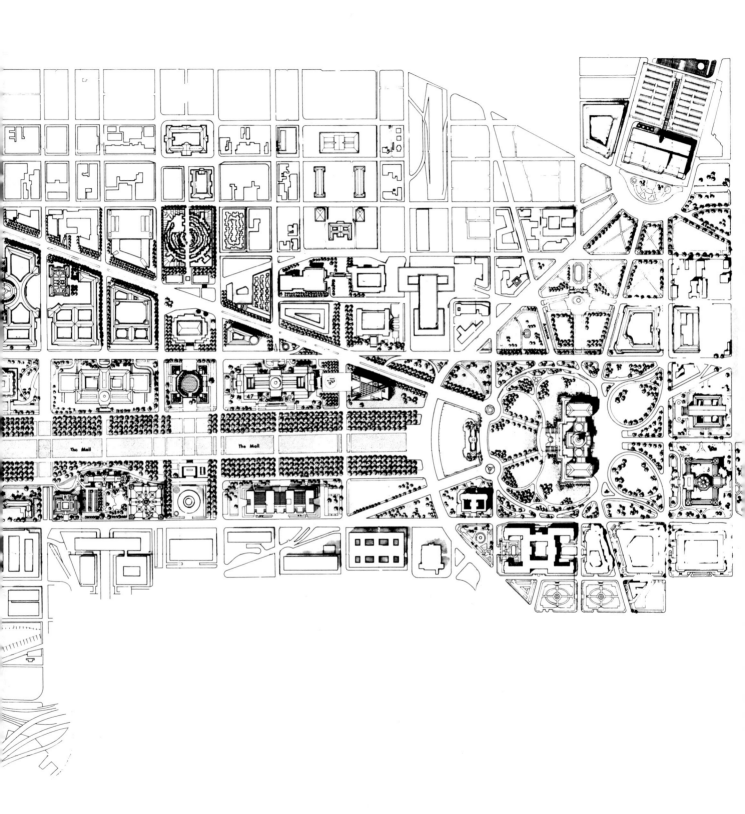

government with a mayor and council, an elected school board, representation in Congress, and three electoral votes for president and vice-president. Reorganized planning arrangements produced in the District a planning agency designed to give the new local government support to address its own special problems of redevelopment, housing, and social planning. The regional planning program, which had always been based upon intergovernmental cooperation, had for several years been established as a function of the Washington Metropolitan Council of Governments. Here primary responsibility had been located for suburbanization, metropolitan growth, and coordination, as well as the voice of suburban interest. To deal with the federal interest in the District and region, a third agency exists: the reoriented National Capital Planning Commission. With this commission, perhaps most of all, rests responsibility for continuity of planning for the city. Within the context of the original 1791 L'Enfant plan and the 1901–1902 McMillan plan, this continuity is being maintained by identification of the federal interest in the development of regional planning policy; by review of federal building projects and master plans—and District government building projects and master plans—within the central area of Washington; and by preparation and adoption of federal elements of the Comprehensive Plan and a federal regional capital improvement program.

Comprehensive Planning in Washington

That the national capital city could command the services of the best professionals—often at fees lower than in other cities—and that it could confer or in some cases even establish professional prestige and leadership has been proven again and again as the National Capital Planning Commission has utilized the services of leaders of the planning establishment. The Washington planning program has proved equally able to identify and command the services of outstanding architects, landscape architects, and engineers. While there is a significant tendency to experiment and innovate, this planning program has consistently maintained leader-

ship in its field and in a remarkably large number of instances is both the first and the most successful in initiating planning advances. Of course, it deals less with aspects of planning addressed to problems that do not happen to exist in Washington (such as heavy industrial facilities) and deals more with programs, such as parks and the location of public buildings, that are of special importance to the national capital city. The planning program has ventured discreetly into many areas of social concern, even if it was obviously handicapped—prior to 1973—by the peculiar system of nonrepresentative local government. Yet it has pioneered boldly and consistently in regional planning arrangements, in engineering services, in highways and transportation, in parks and parkways, and in other sectors of planning and urban life. If a consistent theme or motive for these characteristics is to be found, it is in the source of the planning program's legitimacy—the role of the federal capital city.

CURRENT COMPREHENSIVE PLANNING

One important aspect of the 1973 Home Rule Act is the provision for the National Capital Planning Commission and the mayor to "jointly establish procedures for appropriate meaningful continuing consultation throughout the planning process for the National Capital." Thus, local interests are to be given an opportunity to be heard within the context of federal priorities for the nation's capital.

One of the first areas where there must be "appropriate meaningful continuing consultation" is in the planning effort to further detail the Comprehensive Plan for the National Capital, formerly the sole responsibility of the Planning Commission. Elements of the Comprehensive Plan pertaining to local concerns such as detailed land-use plans for specific nonfederal areas of the city are to be prepared now by the District of Columbia government, adopted by the City Council, and reviewed by the Planning Commission as to federal interest and inclusion in the Comprehensive Plan. If any such element is determined to affect adversely the federal establishment or other federal interests, it may be vetoed by the commission. The success of this process will depend upon clear channels of communication, an understand-

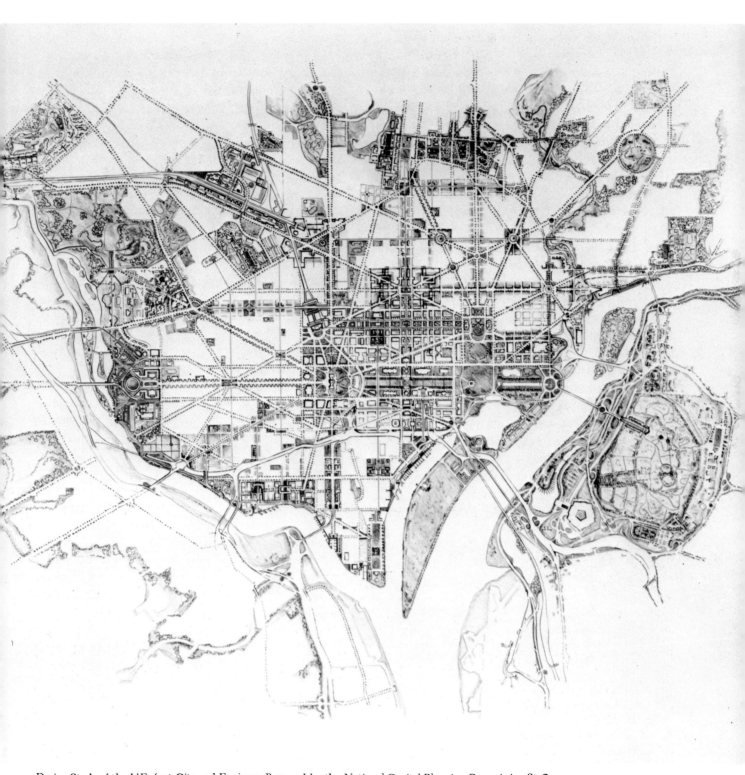

Design Study of the L'Enfant City and Environs, Prepared by the National Capital Planning Commission Staff, 1977

ing of both federal and local needs and priorities, and a willingness to work toward resolution of any differences.

The District government's new Municipal Planning Office has begun working on development of local District of Columbia planning goals and a local District of Columbia land-use plan. Identification and development of additional local Comprehensive Plan elements is a part of the future agenda for the District government. These may include housing, economic, and transportation elements, an environmental element, and social elements such as recreation and open space, public safety, social services, education, health, and history and culture.

As part of its initial efforts to implement the new comprehensive planning process, the National Capital Planning Commission has identified and is giving priority to the preparation of seven federal elements of the Comprehensive Plan: Federal Goals for the National Capital Region; Foreign Missions and International Agencies; Federal Employment Plan and Program; Federal Land Use Plan; Federal Open Space Plan and Program; a Plan for the L'Enfant City and Environs; and a Visitor Facilities Plan and Program. Additional federal elements of the Comprehensive Plan have been identified and will be prepared as resources permit and priorities are set. These include a Postal Facilities Plan and Program and a Federal Historic Preservation Plan and Program. As part of the comprehensive planning process, the National Capital Planning Commission is continuing to identify and describe other federal elements. Concurrently, the Municipal Planning Office is also in the process of identifying appropriate District elements of the Comprehensive Plan. Together, these efforts represent a basic commitment to continuous comprehensive planning for the nation's capital. While providing a policy framework for future decisions regarding physical development and social and economic vitality, the comprehensive planning process allows for changes and additions to that framework—changes and additions due to new priorities and new needs.

Tourism and the Televised Image

In conveying its image, modern Washington has failed to deal successfully with one of the city's most important and distinctive activities, tourism. Washington draws some twenty million visitors annually. The national aspect of the capital city is best seen through their eyes and their experiences. For many visitors Washington is the struggle of the charter bus against the congestion of the central city—and evening's exhaustion at a beltway motel. For millions of high school students, the experience is further travestied by cafeteria meals and improvised dormitory accommodations. Hurried schedules allow little time for exploration beyond the conventionalities of postwar Washington and its familiar monuments. The indigenous city is lost behind white marble façades, as the monumental city is lost behind colored metal walls of parked automobiles. To discover and interpret the city means more than this. The Washington tourist usually sees the obvious rather than the discoverable: the Kennedy Center, not Wolf Trap; the cherry blossoms around the Tidal Basin, not the spring floral display at Dumbarton Oaks. Few civic lessons are learned in Washington by those on their first visit, little more than the art of the high Renaissance is learned by day-tripping tourists in Venice. Even so, more modest goals are possible to realize.

The 1950 Guide Map. In 1950, the historical-minded American Institute of Architects held its annual convention in Washington, recreating and experiencing a lively appreciation of their 1900 meeting, just a half century earlier, which had launched the modern phase of the city's planning and led to the work of the McMillan Park Commission. The guide map prepared for the 1950 occasion showed an architect's view of the city. This city, concentrated in the old river-bottom area, maintained L'Enfant's central composition, now reinforced by the Federal Triangle, as its principal feature. On the Virginia side, the 1950 guide map showed only the Pentagon, National Airport, and features of Arlington National Cemetery, and in Maryland, but a single reference, this to the Naval Medical Center in Bethesda. South of Independence Avenue, only the

Washington's Popular Image: A View of the Capitol

Department of Agriculture and the Federal Security Agency were considered worth depicting. In its selection of buildings of architectural interest, the 1950 guide map showed the apogee of Classical Revival architecture as it had developed from 1900 on and now stamped a capital city about to enter seriously upon its modern architectural adventures. Only a suggestion of this modern trend had appeared in the architecture of the State Department Building and the West Central Heating Plant overlooking Rock Creek. The 1950 guide map hardly gave a hint of the suburban development that was taking place. This development had just begun to reveal architectural expression in new housing, schools, churches, and shopping centers, and would soon be elaborated in office buildings, industrial parks, and buildings of local and federal government agencies. All that was to come about in the quarter century that has followed.

Now a new expectation and anticipation of the capital city has come with the global village created by television. Around the nation and around the world, Washington's formal image is known to millions. People travel to reassure themselves of the reality of the images they have already seen. Their experience is hardly measured by the days they stay and the dollars they spend even if the Washington visitor is officially defined as one who spends four hours or more in the city, enough time to make some mark on the local economy by buying a meal or taking the bus. This crude formula burlesques the dichotomy of Washington, the contrast between the visitors' city and the indigenous city.

THE SMITHSONIAN INSTITUTION AND
WASHINGTON'S CULTURAL ESTABLISHMENT

In the heart of Washington, between the Capitol and the White House, a massing of cultural institutions has appeared that in its unmatched quantity and quality responds both to the national capital city's annual flood of tourists and visitors and to its cultivated indigenous

The Patriotic Image: A Telephoto View of the Washington Monument Grounds, July 1976

population. The geographical center of this cultural massing is the Mall, a plan for which has been approved by the National Capital Planning Commission. At the heart of it is the Smithsonian Institution, a museum complex greatly proliferated from its original red sandstone Norman Gothic "Castle" on the Mall, and now represented by such components as the National Museum of Natural History, the National Museum of History and Technology, the National Gallery of Art, the Freer Gallery of Art, the Hirshhorn Museum and Sculpture Garden, the National Air and Space Museum, and, in areas near the Mall, by the National Collection of Fine Arts and the Renwick Gallery, and the National Portrait Gallery. This impressive grouping is reinforced by historical and literary resources centered at the Library of Congress, the Folger Shakespeare Library, and the National Archives, and facilities for the performing arts located in the Kennedy Center overlooking the Potomac River. To these resources Washington has also added specialized institutions such as Ford's Theatre, the Phillips Collection, the Corcoran Gallery of Art, the Textile Museum, the Museum of African Art, and the Dumbarton Oaks collections of Byzantine and Pre-Columbian art. At the edges of the city there are new cultural facilities, notably the Wolf Trap Farm concert center. Most of these have burgeoned since 1960, expressing not only the size and rapid growth of the city but a new and highly visible cosmopolitanism.

DESTINY AND DEFINITION: MODERN WASHINGTON

The 1976 July Fourth celebrations on the Mall and along the Potomac provided a paradigm, an illustration by the tourism sector of the Washington economy, of the relationship between federal and local interests. Provided also was an anticipation in the present of what future growth promises—its problems as well as its delights. In the past, only the experience of wartime Washington had allowed a similar shock of anticipation of what future growth might hold for the city.

As the city moves toward its destiny, it has found in the redefinition of the federal interest its principal urban challenge. This the National Capital Planning Commission approaches on a case-by-case basis from which nothing is excluded. In this sweeping and continuing evaluation, no aspect is ignored: the location of employment, the configuration of urban systems, urban design and architecture, housing and community organization, public services and amenities, historic preservation, and much more. This new identification of the federal interest measures the impact of the national government and its decisions on the regional economy. The integration of views is expressed in the preparation and adoption of federal elements of the Comprehensive Plan for the new, regional Washington, the worthy successor to nearly two centuries of the most continuing urban planning effort of any city in the nation.

PHOTOGRAPHIC ESSAY: FACES AND FORMS OF WASHINGTON

Farragut Square

East Potomac Park

Rock Creek Parkway at the Q Street Bridge

Confluence of Rock Creek and the Potomac River

Beach Drive in Rock Creek Park

Key Bridge and the C & O Canal

Rock Creek Park Foot Bridge

Potomac River Signage

360

Curved Q Street Bridge

Rochambeau Bridge at Fourteenth Street

Duke Ellington Bridge over Rock Creek Parkway at Calvert Street

Pierce Mill at Park Road and Tilden Street, NW, in Rock Creek Park

C & O Canal Barge at a Georgetown Lock

Tenleytown Street Scene near Fort Reno

Along Connecticut Avenue

P Street near Rock Creek Park

Street Scene: A Block Party at Thirteenth and R Streets, NW

Mobility at the JFK Playground, Seventh and P Streets, NW

Balustraded Stair That Carries Twenty-second Street in Kalorama to Higher Levels

Norman Water Tower at Fort Reno

The Boathouse at the Foot of Virginia Avenue

Aerial View of the National Cathedral

Telephoto View of "The Cairo" (Completed in the 1870s), and the National Shrine of the Immaculate Conception in Northeast Washington

Telephoto View, Georgetown University

Temperance Fountain and Apex Liquor Building at Pennsylvania Avenue and Seventh Street, NW

Detail of Lafayette Park Sculpture, Showing Figures of Rochambeau and Portail

Statue of Benito Juárez at Virginia and New Hampshire Avenues, NW, Showing (background) Columbia Plaza

Statue of Benjamin Franklin at Pennsylvania Avenue and Tenth Street across from the Old Post Office

Equestrian Statue of Bishop Francis Asbury, and a Clustering of Churches at Sixteenth and Mount Pleasant Streets, NW

Aerial View of the
Capitol's West Front,
Showing the Grant
Memorial and the
New Reflecting Pool

The Non-Federal Presence: Aerial View of the New Washington

Bibliographic Essay

Bibliographic references in this essay are keyed to the text by chapter and section under rubrics that are identical to subheads used in the text. Sources of direct quotations are identified in the text by author or document name and are cited fully in this essay. Background materials not presented in the text are occasionally incorporated here in the form of historical content notes. At the end of this essay (at pp. 402–3) there is a section on sources consulted: general sources, bibliographies, annual reports, manuscript collections, iconographic collections, and personal interviews.

Signed content notes are initialed as follows: Charity V. Davidson, Frederick Gutheim, Antoinette J. Lee, and Ruth W. Spiegel.

Prologue: The Washington Plan in Past and Present

THE L'ENFANT PLAN: TIMELESSNESS AND PERSISTENCE

A brilliant analysis of the meaning of the major elements of L'Enfant's plan is presented in J. P. Dougherty, "Baroque and Picturesque Motifs in L'Enfant's Design for the Federal Capital," *American Quarterly* 26 (March 1974).

A Note on Thomas Jefferson's Sketches for the New Capital City, 1790–91

In 1790, Thomas Jefferson drew a small grid, encompassing 1500 acres at the juncture of the Potomac and the Anacostia Rivers (the site of Carrollsburg), to develop his thoughts on the plan for the new capital city. While Philadelphia—the autochthonous American city—provided the immediate inspiration for the right-angled streets shown in this drawing, Jefferson hoped to avoid the monotony of its streetscape by varying the distances between buildings and streets. Fully versed in the functional requirements of an urban center, Jefferson allocated to commerce the fourteen blocks facing the deep waters of the Anacostia; to government purposes, the four blocks facing the Potomac. The rest of the city was to develop on the inland blocks. The sketch shown here is reproduced from "Proceedings to be

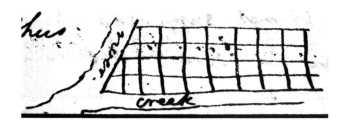

had Under the Residence Act," 29 November 1790, Thomas Jefferson Papers, Library of Congress Manuscript Division.

Following L'Enfant's survey between Rock Creek and Tiber Creek, Thomas Jefferson refocused his planning thoughts on a site facing the confluence of Tiber Creek and the Potomac River where Hamburg and the "Key of Keys," the rocky projection guarding the upper channel of the Potomac, were located. For this site Jefferson drew an elongated grid—with the commercial waterfront much con-

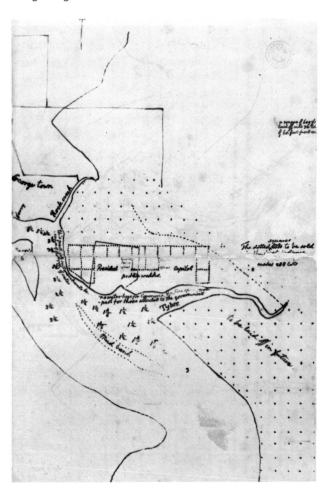

tracted from his November 1790 sketch—to encompass four city blocks along the Potomac. Most important for the spatial relationships and the "genesis of L'Enfant's great mall" was the location of the President's House and the Capitol and their connection along a strip of land by the Tiber, "public walks" as Jefferson labeled it. Although in area this plan appears to be constricted in comparison with the area later covered by L'Enfant's plan, Jefferson actually was envisioning a city commensurate with Philadelphia. The planned city size is shown here by the widely separated "dotted squares" denoting blocks "to be laid off" and sold in lots at some time "in future." This drawing of the elongated grid is reproduced from a manuscript (no title, no date, although likely March 1791), Thomas Jefferson Papers, Library of Congress Manuscript Division.

REVOLUTION, REASON . . . AND ARCHITECTURE

On the swelling of neoclassical art by which L'Enfant was motivated, see Hugh Honour, Neo-Classicism (Baltimore, 1968), who quotes DuFourny; see also Peter Collins, Changing Ideals in Modern Architecture (Montreal, 1967). On the mathematics of the age and the scientific and cultural milieu that created its architecture and city planning, see Brooke Hindle, The Pursuit of Science in Revolutionary America, 1735–1789 (Chapel Hill, 1958); Helen Rosenau, The Ideal City in Its Architectural Evolution (London, 1959), and Social Purpose in Architecture, Paris and London Compared, 1760–1800 (London, 1970); and Helen M. Fox, André Le Nôtre: Garden Architect to Kings (New York, 1962).

HISTORIC CITY AND CONTINUING PLAN

A Note on the Philosophy of Architecture in Washington

On Washington's distinctive identity, the philosophical question posed by the L'Enfant plan is whether the capital city's deviation from the gridiron plan of most American cities detracts or adds to Washington's value. Should the capital have been more typical or more exceptional? The question takes many forms. Henry Stern Churchill, architect-planner who has been engaged in Washington on several occasions (including service as planner of the George Washington University campus, where he had to struggle with the gridiron), argues in his book The City Is the People (New York, 1961) that the Washington plan was alien in conception and was retained over the years only by the exertion of reactionary special interests reflecting continuing alien elements. Of these the most important and influential were the exponents of formal, academic, eclectic architecture, most of whom were trained in the Ecole des Beaux-Arts tradition.

374

Lewis Mumford, The Culture of Cities (New York, 1938), has described Washington as the last and greatest example of the baroque model of the city—and then castigated this urban form because of its autocratic objectives and the equally autocratic means required for their realization. In the subsequent rewriting and amplification of Mumford's work, published in 1961 under title of The City in History, an entire section on the city was added by Mumford. This may be taken as rendering obsolete the 1938 historical interpretation, although the idea that antidemocratic forces in the early republic were faithfully reflected in the princely, imperialistic forms of the baroque city is suggested also by Sibyl Moholy-Nagy, Matrix of Man (New York, 1968).

Several reviewers of John W. Reps's extensive examination of the L'Enfant plan and that plan's revival in the 1901–1902 plan in Monumental Washington: The Planning and Development of the Capital Center have labored this view. Of these reviews, that of Alexander R. Butler, a humanist and historian at Michigan State University, is perhaps the most incisive; see "Review of Recent Books," Maryland Historical Magazine 62 (December 1967). Although Professor Butler does not sufficiently distinguish the original L'Enfant plan from the 1901–1902 plan, his view of the plan can be restated to say that it was (1) an expression of the "Imperial-Roman-Versailles-Baroque-American supercolossal aesthetic"; (2) a plan of "grandiose size, pomposity, vastness and emptiness"; and (3) "a relic of an aesthetic more akin to dictatorial despotisms than to modern democracies."

Reps's work itself—John W. Reps, Monumental Washington: The Planning and Development of the Capital Center (Princeton, 1967)—is fundamentally a monograph on the 1901–1902 plan of the McMillan Commission. Professor Reps has written an excellent introductory chapter on the L'Enfant plan. Appreciating the greatness of the plan, its scale, design, topographical emphasis, and the discretion with which its formal elements were employed, Reps recognized its flaws. The flaws he summarizes as follows—the distance between the President's House and the Capitol which negates L'Enfant's hoped for "reciprocity of sight" between the two most important elements of his city; and the unresolved conflicts between the so-called gridiron and the radial avenues, as represented in awkwardly shaped bits of land at the intersections. Reps's measured conclusion is that "this was a great city plan conceived in an incredibly short time by one of the most remarkably talented persons of his era." On the whole, objections to the L'Enfant plan are less important today than they must have been at the end of the eighteenth century. Indeed in the following two centuries, as the city and its principal

Detail of the Lincoln Memorial

buildings took on Victorian scale, and the speed and volume of modern traffic reflected the larger metropolitan city and its technology, L'Enfant's plan seems even to have anticipated the new conditions. The marshy, natural riverfront—between Carrollsburg and the proposed Naval Column at the mouth of the Tiber—has subsequently become an important park by the application of reclamation techniques that were unavailable in L'Enfant's time. The conflict between the gridiron and the radial networks could have been adjusted by the further design effort which L'Enfant identified but lacked the time to accomplish.

One of the most sophisticated and brilliant analysts of the L'Enfant plan, Elbert Peets, himself a landscape architect and profound student of the history of urban design, has most impressively reconstructed the city conceived by L'Enfant as quite different and separate from the city that was actually built; see Paul D. Spreiregen, ed., On the Art of Designing Cities: Selected Essays of Elbert Peets (Cambridge, Mass., 1968). Peets's critique centers, too, upon the conflict between the gridiron and the radial elements of the plan "without sufficient inter-adjustment." In Peets's words, "the radial and diagonal avenues have their identity, beauty, and dignity sapped away by the constant intrusion, often at very acute angles, of the gridiron streets." Peets's second criticism is of L'Enfant's failure to provide effective plazas with shapes and functions that compare with the great plazas characteristic of the late Renaissance and even of the eighteenth century. Both of these are, again, faults of an incomplete sketch, and Peets himself is inclined to minimize objections in his final estimate of L'Enfant's plan. "What makes [L'Enfant's] vision a work of true creative imagination, compelling our homage and repaying our closest study, is that it is articulated, organized, pulled strongly

375

yet suavely together, into a single work of art of unparalleled magnitude.

"*No greater hurt could be done to L'Enfant*," Peets continues, "*than to accept without question every detail of his plan and to acclaim as beautiful every part of the imperfect realization of it which the vicissitudes of history have assembled. . . . But that vision was one of unprecedented daring; its author, without experience himself and with almost no opportunity to learn from the experience of others, had the most limited means of foreseeing its effect in reality; it was formulated and put on paper in a very brief time; the control of its realization, a process in which numberless refinements would have been worked out, was taken from him; the greatest part of it was embodied in brick and stone during a period and by a society probably unequalled in paucity of artistic feeling.*"

CHAPTER I:

The Planned Central City 1790–1800

THE NEW NATIONAL CAPITAL CITY AND ITS POTOMAC SITE

For Ada Louise Huxtable's transcendent description of Washington, see the architecture section of *Washington: The New York Times Guide to the Nation's Capital*, ed. Alvin Shuster (Washington, D.C., 1967). For the origins of the "district" concept, see Louis Dow Scisco, "A Site for the Federal City: The Original Proprietors and Their Negotiations with Washington," 1956, Columbia Historical Society Manuscript Collection. This paper was later shortened and published in *Records of the Columbia Historical Society, 1957–59* (Washington, D.C., 1961). On selection of the Potomac site, see Constance McLaughlin Green, *Washington, Village and Capital, 1800–1878* (Princeton, 1962). Green's treatment of the decisions to create, locate, and plan the national capital city is fully documented, and tightens up the more discursive treatment earlier offered by W. B. Bryan, *A History of the National Capital*, I (New York, 1914). Although there is no designation of a name in the Constitution's reference to the "seat of the government," it was anticipated as early as 1791 that the capital city would be named for George Washington; see Elizabeth S. Kite, *L'Enfant and Washington, 1791–1792* (Baltimore, 1929). The commissioners began using the name Washington in January 1794, according to Bryan. To George Washington himself, it was always referred to as the "federal city."

The natural topography—and its abundance—that presented itself to L'Enfant is described in W. L. McAtee, *A Sketch of the Natural History of the District of Columbia*

Equestrian Statue of George Washington at Washington Circle

(*Bulletin of the Biological Society of Washington* 1; Washington, D.C., 1918). Early settlement of the area is sketched by Bryan; see now also Robert L. Humphrey and Mary Elizabeth Chambers, *Ancient Washington: American Indian Cultures of the Potomac Valley* (Washington, D.C., 1976). "Paper towns"—towns established in law but in fact never developed—are described by John W. Reps, *Tidewater Towns: City Planning in Colonial Virginia and Maryland* (Williamsburg, 1972), and by Fairfax Harrison, *Landmarks of Old Prince William* (Berryville, 1964). On the reference to Philadelphia as a "green country town," Samuel Hazard, *Annals of Philadelphia, 1609–1682* (Philadelphia, 1850), cites William Penn's fifteenth instruction to his commissioners charged (in 1683) with laying out the city of Philadelphia "that it may be a green country town which will never be burnt and always be wholesome." This is quoted by Anthony N. E. Garvan, "Proprietary Philadelphia as Artifact," in Oscar Handlin and John Burchard, eds., *The Historian and the City* (Cambridge, 1963); see also Edmund N. Bacon, *Design of Cities* (New York, 1967).

PIERRE CHARLES L'ENFANT

The biographies of L'Enfant are thorough and encyclopedic. They include H. Paul Caemmerer, *The Life of Pierre Charles L'Enfant, Planner of the City Beautiful, the City of Washington* (Washington, D.C., 1950), and Eliza-

376

beth S. Kite, *L'Enfant and Washington, 1791–1792* (Baltimore, 1929). While brief, Fiske Kimball, "L'Enfant," *Dictionary of American Biography*, offers one of the best appreciations of L'Enfant's architectural design and his role as a traditionalist rather than an innovator. For the reference to Laugier's *Essai sur l'architecture*, see Helen Rosenau, *Social Purpose in Architecture, Paris and London Compared, 1760–1800* (London, 1970).

A Contextual Note on "Worthy of the Nation"

The floating appraisal, "worthy of the nation," apparently goes back to the beginnings of Washington, and is sufficiently general to have been employed in other contexts—at least as early as 1824 when, in discussion of the founding of the National Gallery of Great Britain, the Chancellor of the Exchequer expressed hope for the "establishment of a splendid Gallery . . . worthy of the nation"; see Homan Potterton, A Guide to the National Gallery (London, 1975). Lieutenant Montgomery C. Meigs, the Army Engineer who built the Washington aqueduct, voiced the phrase in 1852 or 1853 in support of this project. "Let our Aqueduct be worthy of the nation," Meigs wrote in his report to Congress. This is cited in Albert E. Cowdrey, "Design for a City: The U.S. Army Engineers in the Building of the Nation's Capital" (MS, Historical Division, Office of the Chief of Engineers, Washington, D.C., 1974). No direct documentation of Meigs's report is given but references are supplied to (a) Weigley, Quartermaster General of the Army, 61; (b) Warren T. Hannum, "Water Supply of the District of Columbia," Professional Memoirs: Corps of Engineers, U.S. Army 4 (1912); (c) Edwin A. Achmitt and Philip O. McQueen, "Washington Aqueduct," Military Engineer 41 (1949); and "The Washington Aqueduct, 1852–1952" (MS, Washington District, Corps of Engineers, 1953). The apparent date of the Meigs report is 1852 or 1853. Of the many references to the phrase "worthy of the nation" as applied to Washington, this appears to be the earliest in point of chronology. Although it refers not to the city but to the aqueduct, the presentation strongly suggests that Meigs was not originating the phrase but echoing its currency in the larger urban context.

Idealized Bird's-Eye View of Washington, Shown in an Engraving by Kimmell and Foster, 1865

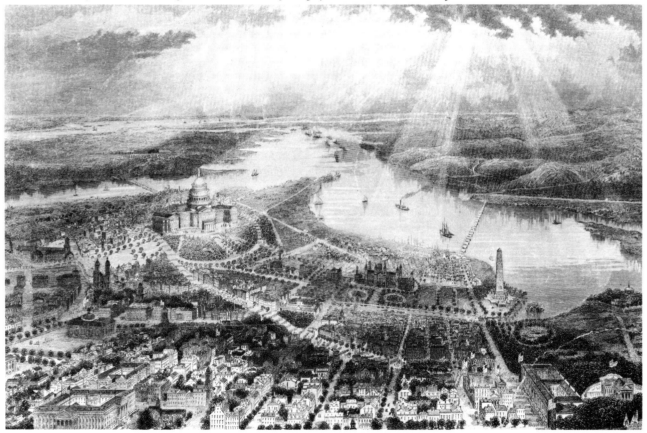

It was President Grant, however, who gave the phrase its strong, explicit relationship to the national capital city by sustaining the point in his many messages to Congress; see H. Paul Caemmerer, A Manual on the Origin and Development of Washington (Washington, D.C., 1939). Grant's commitment to making the national capital city "worthy of the nation" and his role as a steadfast friend of the capital city is further substantiated in the biography by his grandson, Ulysses S. Grant III, Ulysses S. Grant; Warrior and Statesman (New York, 1969). While more detailed documentation of the use of the phrase, "worthy of the nation," in reference to Washington's role as a capital city would be of interest, it is clear that the ideal was enunciated very early, that it inspired the city's builders in their most vigorous efforts, and that it still brightly illuminates the efforts of contemporary urban designers. A.J.L.

THE LAND AND THE WATERCOURSES

Henry Fleet's "Brief Journal" is reproduced in Edward D. Neill, *Founders of Maryland* (Albany, 1876); the passage quoted here is given in Fairfax Harrison, *Landmarks of Old Prince William* (Berryville, 1964). The drainage patterns of the Potomac area, the creeks, branches, and tributaries of the river as well as the springs, wells, and other sources of water, has been reconstructed by Garnett P. Williams, a geomorphologist and sedimentarian on the staff of the U.S. Geological Survey (see his "Historical Washington's Vanishing Waterways," *Records of the Columbia Historical Society*, forthcoming), and is expected to enlarge substantially the earlier work on this subject by Paul M. Johnston: U.S. Geological Survey, "Geology and Groundwater Resources of Washington, D.C., and Vicinity," Water Supply Paper No. 1776, Washington, D.C., 1964; and "Groundwater in the Washington, D.C., Area and a Brief History of the Public Water Supply," *Journal of the Washington Academy of Sciences* 52 (1962). Copies of the Johnston articles are shelved in the Columbia Historical Society library, Washington, D.C.

TRAVELERS' DESCRIPTIONS OF EARLY WASHINGTON

Quotations from the La Rochefoucauld-Liancourt journals are from the 1974 translation by Professor and Mrs. David J. Brandenburg, *The Voyage in the United States of America, 1795, 1796, 1797*, excerpts of which (containing descriptions of the federal city) are published in the *Records of the Columbia Historical Society, 1973–74* (Washington, D.C., 1975). I am indebted to the Brandenburgs for the opportunity to read their manuscript. For the Weld, Twining, and Baily excerpts, see W. B. Bryan, *A History of the National Capital*, I (New York, 1914). The preexisting towns of Alexandria (founded 1749) and Georgetown

(1751) were assimilated into the District of Columbia by 1791, and by this date both were thriving ports widely described and commented on by travelers. As negotiations commenced with proprietors of the land where the federal city was to rise, these proprietors were generally Georgetown residents.

L'ENFANT'S SURVEY: MARCH 1791

The details of L'Enfant's operations are provided in his letters and reports to President Washington, Jefferson, and the commissioners, and in the local press; see Elizabeth S. Kite, *L'Enfant and Washington, 1791–1792* (Baltimore, 1929); *Records of the Columbia Historical Society* 2 (Washington, D.C., 1899). For Washington's instructions to L'Enfant mentioned in the president's letter to Deakins 2 March 1791, see Kite, and there also see Washington's 31 March 1791 letter to Jefferson. The research of Louis Dow Scisco, as noted above, is published in the *Records of the Columbia Historical Society, 1957–59* (Washington, D.C., 1961). James Craig's "New Town" is described in A. J. Youngson, *The Making of Classical Edinburgh* (Edinburgh, 1966). For George Washington's diary entries on his negotiations with the proprietors in Georgetown, see John Clement Fitzpatrick, ed., *The Diaries of George Washington, 1732–1799* (Boston, 1925), IV.

L'ENFANT'S MEMORANDUM: URBAN DESIGN, LANDSCAPE IMAGE, AND A STRATEGY FOR DEVELOPMENT

On L'Enfant's sketch plan of 22 June 1791 and his accompanying memorandum, see Elizabeth S. Kite, *L'Enfant and Washington, 1791–1792* (Baltimore, 1929).

THE L'ENFANT PLAN: BEGINNINGS OF BUILT WASHINGTON

The commissioners wrote to L'Enfant instructions about naming the city Washington and numbering and lettering the streets, east-west streets to be numbered from the Capitol, north-south streets to be designated by letters of the alphabet. For this communication from the commissioners to L'Enfant dated 9 September 1791, see Edward S. Delaplaine, *The Life of Thomas Johnson* (New York, 1927). Lee Otis Colbert, "The Earliest Maps of Washington, D.C.," *Military Engineer* 41 (1949), outlines the details of the L'Enfant manuscript map of 1791, the Ellicott map of 1792, the James R. Dermott map of 1797–98 defining the public lands, and Nicholas King's plats of 1803 produced by the city's first surveyor. On the speculative boom and its effect on the character of the early city, see Allen C. Clark, *Greenleaf and Law in the Federal City* (Washington, D.C., 1901). Also see Talbot F. Hamlin, *Benjamin Henry Latrobe* (New York, 1955), for favorable reference

C & O Canal Scene

to Thomas Law and his real estate activities—as well as for a rare glimpse of Thomas Jefferson's shortcomings as an architectural designer. For Elbert Peets's essay, "The Lost Plazas of Washington," see Paul D. Spreiregen, ed., *On the Art of Designing Cities: Selected Essays of Elbert Peets* (Cambridge, Mass., 1968).

CHAPTER II:

The Port City 1800–1860

Filling in the physical city of Washington with a cultural and intellectual life is discussed in James Sterling Young, *The Washington Community, 1800–1828* (New York, 1966); the first chapters provide a remarkably keen insight into the effects of the city's plan on the social community as well as on the political community centered around the Capitol. Young also explores the isolation of the legislators from the rest of the city; the creation of Washington "at a distance" from the rest of the nation he sees as evasive and an effort to escape the scrutiny of the nation. Young is far from clear, however, that this consequential effect was a deliberate objective of the city's plan.

In the absence of a detailed history of the port activities that verified the original river-orientation of the city, one must draw upon a number of specialized histories. For descriptions of the natural landscape of early Washington as well as the vast environmental changes that later registered the presence of the federal establishment, see Margaret Bayard Smith, *The First Forty Years of Washington Society* (New York, 1906). The expectation that the Southwest quadrant along the Washington Channel would become the most prosperous area of the embryonic city is discussed in Herman R. Friis and Ralph A. Ehrenberg, "Nicholas King and His Wharfing Plans of the City of Washing-

ton, 1797," *Records of the Columbia Historical Society, 1966–68* (Washington, D.C., 1969); see also Allen C. Clark, *Greenleaf and Law in the Federal City* (Washington, D.C., 1901).

On Carrollsburg, see in the Martin Luther King Memorial Library, Washington, D.C., in the vertical files s.v. Waterfront, the article by William M. Birth. For Bryan's reference to "cultivated gardens," see his *History of the National Capital*, II (New York, 1916). The port, milling, and canal activity that generated considerable prosperity in antebellum Georgetown is described in Constance W. Werner, *Georgetown Historic Waterfront* (Washington, D.C., 1968). The lively river traffic that plied the waters of the Potomac and the Eastern Branch and linked together tidewater settlements is noted in John Sessford, "The Sessford Annals," *Records of the Columbia Historical Society* 11 (Washington, D.C., 1908), while the Letter From the Governor and Council of Maryland Transmitting a Report of the Commissioners Appointed to Survey the River Potomac (Washington, D.C., 1823) testifies to the hazards and uncertainties of river navigation caused by the "vicissitudes of the seasons." Richard Mannix, "Albert Gallatin in Washington," *Records of the Columbia Historical Society, 1971–72* (Washington, D.C., 1973), records the rhythm of life in the young city—the social seasons, the muddy roads, and the embryonic neighborhoods situated on high ground.

A Historical Note on the Potomac Company and the Potomac Canal

The idea of a Potomac canal was popular even before the Revolution. The state of Virginia chartered an unsuccessful canal company as early as 1772. Another company (variously known as the Potowmack Company, the Potowmack Navigation Company, the Potomac Canal Company, or

The Latrobe Gate at the Navy Yard in Southeast Washington

simply, the Potomac Company) was chartered by Virginia in 1784 and by Maryland in 1785, with George Washington as its president (1785-89). This company intended to improve the Potomac's river bed by removing obstructions wherever practical and to build a series of short canals around the falls and the unimprovable sections of the river. This system, known as sluice navigation, was the standard method used in England during the late eighteenth century. The Potomac Company began levying tolls on the improved sections in 1799, and by 1802 five canal links, ranging from fifty yards to two miles in length, were complete. This system was navigable only during floods and freshets. The canal limped along until 1821, when a joint committee of the Virginia and Maryland legislatures investigated the Potomac Company and found that the company had not fulfilled the proviso in its charter that it provide "navigation for boats carrying fifty barrels of flour even in the driest seasons." The company was disbanded in 1822.

Additional plans to improve the most unsatisfactory sections of the so-called Potomac Canal between Little Falls and Georgetown were drawn up even while the Potomac Company was still in existence. Benjamin Latrobe's Plans and Sections . . . , prepared in 1802, was such a proposal. Latrobe's canal was never built, but the route he laid out was almost identical to the one along which the Chesapeake & Ohio Canal was constructed nearly twenty-five years later. C.V.D.

BUILDING THE CITY: FIRST FOUR DECADES

For Margaret Bayard Smith's remarks, see The First Forty Years of Washington Society (New York, 1906). For Joel Barlow's vision of the city of communication, see John Dos Passos, The Ground We Stand On (Boston, 1941). See also Mary Mitchell, "Kalorama: Country Estate to Washington Mayfair," Records of the Columbia Historical Society, 1971-72 (Washington, D.C., 1973). Latrobe's remarks are quoted in Talbot F. Hamlin, Benjamin Henry Latrobe (New York, 1955); see there also Hamlin's description of the Van Ness residence designed by Latrobe. Mitchell reproduces the view painted by Charles Codman. The original painting is on display in the Jefferson Room, Department of State, Washington, D.C. On particular residences, see now George McCue, The Octagon (Washington, D.C., 1976).

On Hadfield's confrontation with the "rogues" responsible for the construction of public buildings, see G. L. M. Goodfellow, "George Hadfield," Architectural Review (London) 138 (July 1965). For Robert Mills's statement about "good common buildings, which was a desideratum in architecture" and his allusion to the hydraulic cement used in the Treasury Building arches, see Helen Mar Pierce Gallagher, Robert Mills: Architect of the Washington

Modern Construction of Streets For People Pedestrian Mall along Historic Eighth Street in front of the Patent Office Building (Now the National Portrait Gallery)

Monument 1781-1855 (New York, 1932), where there is considerable discussion of Mills's philosophy on the design and construction of public buildings. The National Capital Planning Commission's study, Downtown Urban Renewal Area Landmarks, Washington, D.C. (Washington, D.C., 1970), describes Mills's arch construction, used by him also in the Patent Office as "an innovation in engineering at the time." For Robert Dale Owen's remarks on the Post Office, see his Hints on Public Architecture (New York, 1849). The most complete work on the Chesapeake & Ohio Canal is Walter S. Sanderlin, The Great National Project: A History of the Chesapeake & Ohio Canal (Baltimore, 1946); see also his article, "The Maryland Canal Project: An Episode in the History of Maryland's Internal Improvements," Maryland Historical Magazine 45 (1950).

WASHINGTON PANORAMA: THE YEAR 1840

On the retrocession movements initiated by Georgetown and Alexandria, see W. B. Bryan, A History of the National Capital, II (New York, 1916). Constance M. Green, Washington, Village and Capital, 1800-1876 (Princeton, 1962), succeeds in visualizing the physical and social city of the 1840s and cites travelers' accounts that substantiate this panoramic view. See also the first edition of the guidebook by George Watterston, A Picture of Washington (Washington, D.C., 1840), the first good guide to the city and an unambiguous source on the physical city in the year 1840.

THE MALL AND THE MONUMENTAL CORE

Robert Mills's letter to Robert Dale Owen on the "Proposed Smithsonian Institute" is quoted in Helen Mar Pierce Gallagher, Robert Mills: Architect of the Washington Monument (New York, 1935). Daniel D. Reiff, Washington Architecture, 1791-1861: Problems in Development (Washington, D.C., 1971), offers thorough documentation of the city's major residential and public buildings, illustrated in excellent photographs.

Downing's plan for the Mall comprised both a written and a graphic portion. For the excerpts from the written portion, quoted here, see Wilcomb E. Washburn, "Vision of Life for the Mall," Journal of the American Institute of

Architects 47 (March 1967). The physical evolution of the Capitol Building and the grounds surrounding it are discussed in two articles in the *Records of the Columbia Historical Society, 1969–70* (Washington, D.C., 1971): "The Capitol," by Philip Van Doren Stern, and "The Capitol in Peril? The West Front Controversy from Walter to Stewart," by Charles C. McLaughlin.

A Historical Note on the Columbian Institute and the Botanic Garden

The United States Botanic Garden located at the foot of Capitol Hill is the descendent of the Columbian Institute's early efforts. President Washington suggested as early as 1796 that a national botanic garden be established, but the idea was not acted upon until the early 1800s. The role of the short-lived (ca. 1820–25) Washington Botanic Society in setting up the botanic garden is uncertain, but by 1818 the first president of the Columbian Institute was urging that the institute—a group of Washingtonians who met to discuss the natural world—assemble a collection of native plants which "might be useful in medicine and dye-making."

In 1820 Congress passed legislation which made it possible to lease public land to private parties willing to develop public gardens or parks. One of the first, and possibly the only, grant made under the provisions of this act was that of five soggy acres at the eastern end of the Mall to the Columbian Institute for a botanic garden. The institute's founders had hoped that this group would become the Washington counterpart to Philadelphia's American Philosophical Society, but by 1826 the Columbian Institute was dying, and with it, the botanic garden. A few Washingtonians continued to visit the garden over the next two decades, but on the whole, the surviving specimens were ignored and neglected.

United States Botanic Garden on Independence Avenue, SW

Telephoto View of the Modern City and the McMillan Reservoir

Interest in the idea of a botanic garden was renewed in 1842, when the Wilkes Exploring Expedition returned from South America and the islands of the South Pacific with rare plant specimens. The Wilkes specimens were originally set up in and around the Patent Office (today the Smithsonian Institution's National Portrait Gallery and National Collection of Fine Arts), but in 1850, the specimens were moved to greenhouses on or near the site of the Columbian Institute botanic garden. The United States Botanic Garden is now under the jurisdiction of the Architect of the Capitol.
C.V.D

THE CITY'S WATERWAYS AND THE DESIGN
OF A MODERN WATER SUPPLY

The route of Washington's water supply and technical aspects of its original design are covered in Albert E. Cowdrey, "Design for a City: The U.S. Army Engineers in the Building of the Nation's Capital" (MS, Historical Division, Office of the Chief of Engineers, Washington, D.C., 1974), and Philip O. McQueen, "The Washington Aqueduct, 1852–1952" (MS, Washington District, Corps of Engineers, 1953). Further insight into Meigs as a designer is provided in Harold K. Skramstad, "The Engineer as Architect in Washington: The Contributions of Montgomery Meigs," *Records of the Columbia Historical Society, 1969–70* (Washington, D.C., 1971). W. B. Bryan describes construction of the water supply routes and support structures in *A History of the National Capital*, II (New York, 1916); see there also descriptions of the spread of public institutions beyond the District boundaries. The status of the capital city's waterways and shipping trade just prior to the Civil War can be gauged from the *Annual Report of the*

Secretary of the Treasury for the years 1850–60. The *Annual Report of the Secretary of War* for 1883 presents a ten-year survey of improvements to the Potomac River. See also at the Columbia Historical Society, Washington, D.C., the file of newspaper clippings on riverfront improvements. A.J.L.

TOWARD A MORE COSMOPOLITAN CITY: THE 1850S

For the commentary on Washington "gentry," see W. B. Bryan, *A History of the National Capital*, II (New York, 1916); see there further details on the armory. The importance of tourism to nationwide interest in the capital city cannot be overestimated nor can the impression the city makes on tourists be ignored. Roughly coinciding in its beginnings with the inauguration of rail travel (in 1835, when the Baltimore & Ohio Railroad reached Washington) and flooding in at the time of the Civil War, tourism is best documented in the publication of literally hundreds of guidebooks. Most influential among the early guidebooks are those done by George Watterston: *A Picture of Washington* (1840), *A New Guide to Washington* (1842), *New Guide to Washington* (1847–48). For a more complete list of Washington directories and guidebooks, see Constance McLaughlin Green, *Washington, Village and Capital, 1800–1876* (Princeton, 1962). I am indebted to Francis Donald Lethbridge for the opportunity to examine what must be the largest private collection of Washington guidebooks. F.G.

CHAPTER III:

The Civil War 1860–1865

WASHINGTON IN WARTIME: THE MILITARY CITY

On this period of Washington history, the Columbia Historical Society, Washington, D.C., calls attention to two little-known volumes in its collection: The condition of Washington during the war is discussed in Colonel George A. Armes, *Ups and Downs of an Army Officer* (Washington, D.C.: By the author, 1900). A strategic view of Washington's defenses is reflected in A. N. Waterman, "Washington in the Time of the First Bull Run," *Military Essays and Recollections of the Commandery of Illinois, Military Order of the Loyal Legion* 2 (1894). On the efforts of the capital city to provide modern municipal services to meet emergency wartime needs, see the *Journal of the 61st Council of the City of Washington* (Washington, D.C., 1863–64) and the *Journal of the 62nd Council of the City of Washington* (Washington, D.C., 1864–65), also at the Columbia Historical Society. For contemporary descriptions of the abatis and city fortifications, see in the Martin Luther King Memorial Library, Washington, D.C., Washingtoniana Division, the vertical files s.v. Civil War.

A Historical Note on Colonel Albert Myer
and the Signal Corps

Albert James Myer was born in Newburgh, New York, in 1829. He entered the army as an assistant surgeon in 1854 and was posted to Texas. While there he became interested in the development of a system of visual signals as an alternative to the telegraph. A military board was created in 1858 to consider Myer's suggestions, and two years later Congress passed an act providing for one signal officer, but no signal corps, in the army. Myer was appointed to this post of signal officer, which carried the rank of major, and was ordered to New Mexico to serve in the campaign against the Navajo.

Shortly after the outbreak of the Civil War, he was ordered to Washington to organize and command what, in 1863, was to become the United States Army Signal Corps. Myer established a signal school near what is today the junc-

Civil Wartime View of Georgetown from Mason's Island

tion of Massachusetts and Wisconsin Avenues, NW, to train signal corpsmen in his "wig/wag" system and code. This system, which Myer had perfected in New Mexico, utilized a single flag in a series of proscribed positions. The size and color of the flag varied according to the distance the signal had to be sent (the greater the distance, the larger the flag) and the color of the background behind the signaler (a white flag if the signaler were silhouetted against a dark background, and a red flag if in an open area or against a light background). At night, signals were sent by means of two lanterns, one placed at the feet of the signaler as a point of reference while the other was moved according to the same pattern as a flag. Myer published his code in 1864 in *A Manual of Signals: For the Use of Signal Officers in the Field.*

When the Signal Corps was reorganized by Congress in 1866, Myer was made chief signal officer with the permanent rank of colonel. He continued as chief signal officer until his death in 1880.   C.V.D.

WASHINGTON IN WARTIME: THE CIVILIAN CITY

George Rothwell Brown, *A Not Too Serious History* (Baltimore, 1930), delineates in anecdotal style the social city and the public accommodations generated by the massive influx of soldiers. Graphic documentation for the nearly self-sufficient fortress city is provided in Stanley P. Kimmel, *Mr. Lincoln's Washington* (New York, 1957), and in the issues of *Harper's Weekly* that span the war years. For social history of the period, see Mary Mitchell, *Divided Town* (Barre, Mass., 1968), which presents a picture of divided loyalties in Georgetown. This theme is pursued at the imaginative level in Alan Tate's novel, *The Fathers* (London, 1938).

An Orthographic Note on Tenleytown

The spelling for the modern Tenleytown section of northwest Washington has varied over the decades. The area is named for the original Tenally family, but officials— census takers and tax assessors—varied in their spelling of the name. The most popular spelling prior to the nineteenth century, and probably even before the Civil War, was "Tenallytown"; certainly this is the spelling preferred by long-time residents of the area. A third spelling, "Tennallytown," also occasionally appears. See further Judy Helm, "Study on Tenleytown," in preparation.   C.V.D.

The Civilian City: Commemorative Plaque at Fort Stevens

The city for its symbolic value in the Union cause is clearly perceived by Margaret Leech in *Reveille in Washington* (New York, 1941), a remarkable history of the effects of the Civil War on the city. In this work, moreover, events are closely tied to the scale of the neighborhoods and widely dispersed public enclaves that the city then presented. For an authentic and anecdotal visualization of how Washington looked to the viewer in 1865, see the pictorial map and guidebook, T. Loftin [Snell], *Stranger's Guide to Washington, D.C.: The City as Mr. Lincoln Knew It, 1865* (Washington, D.C.. By the Author, 1967).

CHAPTER IV:

The Postbellum City 1865–1900

THE WINDS OF PEACE: DEMILITARIZED CITY

Samuel C. Busey, *Pictures of the City of Washington in the Past* (Washington, D.C., 1898), and *Personal Reminiscences* (Washington, D.C., 1895), offer a personalized view of the postwar city in transition as it was expanding beyond the District boundaries into the metropolitan region. On Washington's social seasons, see "A Nation in a Nutshell," *Harper's New Monthly Magazine* (March 1881). For the description of Washington as the "paradise of a poor man with brains," see Henry H. Glassie, "Victorian Homes in Washington," *Records of the Columbia Historical Society, 1963–65* (Washington, D.C., 1967). The 1875 *Harper's* article referred to in the text is "New Washington," *Harper's New Monthly Magazine* (February 1875).

PUBLIC WORKS: THE ARMY CORPS OF ENGINEERS

The essential documentation of federal contributions to the city's development is provided by the annual reports of the Corps of Engineers. In these reports, each of the supervisory personnel relates his efforts to tame and make navigable the waters of the Potomac and the Anacostia, to provide the city with a clean, clear, modern water supply, to reclaim the malarial flats and also floodproof the city, and to protect the increasingly scarce cultural and historical resources of a city experiencing rapid change. Happily, many of the key Corps figures in this era possessed a keen interest in the historical roots underlying these environmental issues. A preliminary analysis of the Corps's role in the Victorian city is offered in Colonel Alan J. McCutchen, "A Historical Summary of the Work of the Corps of Engineers in Washington, D.C. and Vicinity, 1852–1952" (MS,

Washington District, Corps of Engineers, 1952), which is organized around specific structures and natural phenomena, and Albert E. Cowdrey, "Design for a City: The U.S. Army Engineers in the Building of the Nation's Capital" (MS, Historical Division, Office of the Chief of Engineers, Washington, D.C., 1974), which traces the career of the Corps through the sequence of time. On the water supply responsibilities of the Corps, see Philip O. McQueen, "The Washington Aqueduct, 1852–1952" (MS, Washington District, Corps of Engineers, 1953). The Meigs letter to Michler, dated 27 July 1867, describing European streets is printed in full as Appendix T-2 to the 1867 *Annual Report of the Chief of Engineers.*

THE TERRITORIAL GOVERNMENT OF WASHINGTON: 1871–1874

On this period of Washington history, and especially the brief but influential career of Alexander R. Shepherd, see William M. Maury, *Alexander "Boss" Shepherd and the Board of Public Works* (Washington, D.C., 1975), and also the earlier version published in the *Records of the Columbia Historical Society, 1971–72* (Washington, D.C., 1973). See also Maury's "The Territorial Period in Washington, 1871–1874" (diss., Division of Experimental Programs, George Washington University, Washington, D.C.), especially for information on public improvements in the Northwest quadrant of the city. In addition, some of the notable designers in this period are discussed in Harold K. Skramstad, "The Engineer as Architect in Washington: The Contribution of Montgomery Meigs," *Records of the Columbia Historical Society, 1969–70* (Washington, D.C., 1971). On the over-all condition of sewers, public utilities, and street pavement in the city at the end of the third quarter-century, see "New Washington," *Harper's New Monthly Magazine* (February 1875).

On Orville Babcock, see, in addition to the *Dictionary of American Biography*, the *Annual Report of the Chief of Engineers* for the years 1871–77, when he was in charge of public buildings and grounds. See also Donald J. Lehman, *Executive Office Building*, General Services Administration Historical Study No. 3 (Washington, D.C., 1970). On Alfred B. Mullett's government career, see the *Annual Report of the Supervising Architect of the Treasury* for the years 1863–74. Lawrence Wodehouse's comment on the State, War and Navy Building is in his article "Alfred B. Mullett and His French Style Government Buildings," *Journal of the Society of Architectural Historians* 31 (March 1972).

THE NEW MUNICIPAL GOVERNMENT: BY COMMISSION

On the role of the District government in the city's physical evolution, see the annual reports of the commissioners of the District of Columbia.

McMillan Reservoir

THE WATER SUPPLY FOR WASHINGTON, ABUNDANT AND CLEAR

A Note on Historical Documentation

The development of the city's water system is not reliably discussed at length in any of the general secondary sources for this period of Washington history. A great deal of information is contained, however, in readily available printed primary sources such as the annual reports of the Chief of the Army Corps of Engineers. The annual reports of the Water Registrar (pre–1887) and the Water Superintendent (post–1887) contained in the annual reports of the Engineer Commissioner of the District of Columbia also provide a wealth of information. In addition, the District of Columbia government has maps of the water distribution system for the period after 1871.

A discussion of the condition of the city's sewer system is contained in a report issued by a presidential committee in the mid–1880s. A series of official reports to Congress prepared by the city government prior to construction of the filter plant (ca. 1905) discusses the condition of the water itself as well as the supply system. During the 1930s, a report to establish the capital cost basis of the water system was prepared under the direction of the Engineer Commissioner and submitted to Congress. Informally referred to as the Shingler Report, this document contains historical information on costs, dates, and justification for additions and improvements to the city water system. Like the Shingler Report, House Document No. 480, prepared jointly by the Office of the Engineer Commissioner and the Corps of Engineers during the 1940s, contains historical information on development and expansion of the system for Washington. C.V.D.

RECLAMATION OF THE RIVER FLATS AND THE CREATION OF PUBLIC PARKS

For a contemporary view, see "Improvement of the Potomac Flats," *Scientific American* 65 (19 September 1891). For Waring's findings, see "A Report of Mr. George E. Waring, Jr., on the Improvement of the Sanitary Condition of the Executive Mansion," as printed in the *Annual Report of the Chief of Engineers* for 1882. For Frederick Law Olmsted's statement of his position on a "comprehensive scheme" for the Mall, see his letter to Mr. V. Hammond Hall, 28 March 1874, Olmsted Papers, Library of Congress Manuscript Division. For discussions of the Olmsted plan for the Capitol grounds, see Charles C. McLaughlin, "The Capitol in Peril? The West Front Controversy from Walter to Stewart," *Records of the Columbia Historical Society,* 1969–70 (Washington, D.C., 1971); Albert Fein, *Frederick Law Olmsted and the American Environmental Tradition* (New York, 1972); and Laura Wood Roper, *FLO, A Biography of Frederick Law Olmsted* (Baltimore, 1973). On Theodore A. Bingham, see the entry in *Who's Who in America, 1930–31* (Chicago, 1932), and the *Annual Report of the Chief of Engineers* for the years 1897 to 1903 when Bingham was in the Office of Public Buildings and Grounds. See also John W. Reps, *Monumental Washington* (Princeton, 1967).

A Historic Preservation Note on Mount Vernon

It was the location of Mount Vernon along the Potomac that influenced selection of the Potomac site, just upriver, for the nation's capital. George Washington's homesite continued to be a major attraction for waterborne traffic even after the president's death. By the 1840s, steam ferryboats offered service to Mount Vernon, and the plantation

The Mansion at Mount Vernon, 1866

Telephoto View of the Clock Tower of the Old Post Office

was transformed into a tourist attraction. The nation's continuous interest in Mount Vernon—and the patriotic vision of Ann Pamela Cunningham—served to save the mansion and grounds from possible development as a resort hotel and to establish it in 1858 as one of the first historic preservation achievements in the land.

PUBLIC BUILDINGS IN THE CENTURY'S LAST DECADES

The history of the Renaissance-styled Library of Congress building is traced in four articles in *The Quarterly Journal of the Library of Congress* (October 1972): Helen-Anne Hilker, "Monument to Civilization: Diary of a Building"; John Y. Cole, "The Main Building of the Library of Congress: A Chronology, 1871–1965"; "Album"; and "Smithmeyer & Pelz: Embattled Architects of the Library of Congress." See further John Y. Cole, "A National Monument for a National Library: Ainsworth Rand Spofford and the New Library of Congress, 1871–1897," *Records of the Columbia Historical Society,* 1971–72 (Washington, D.C., 1973). Federal public buildings and structures testified to the government's commitment to Washington as the capital city and directly influenced the configurations of growth in the region. For an important study of evolving philosophies of public design, see Joanna Schneider Zangrando, "Monumental Bridge Design in Washington, D.C., as a Reflection of American Culture, 1886–1932" (Ph.D. diss., George Washington University, 1974). The General Services Administration has sponsored several excellent histories of key federal buildings of this era under the learned authorship of Donald J. Lehman: *Pension Building,* General Services Administration Historical Study No. 1 (Washington, D.C., 1964), and *Executive Office Building,* Study No. 3

(1970). See also Gail Karesh Kassan, "The Old Post Office Building in Washington, D.C.: Its Past, Present and Future," *Records of the Columbia Historical Society, 1971–72* (Washington, D.C., 1973).

For the observation on the streetcar system, see "New Washington," *Harper's New Monthly Magazine* (February 1875). For further observations on Washington's residential architecture and the eccentricities of the L'Enfant cross streets, see the following sequence of articles in *Harper's New Monthly Magazine*: "State and Society in Washington" (March 1878), "A Nation in a Nutshell" (March 1881), and "A Glimpse of Some Washington Homes" (March 1885). For the quotations from Tanya Edwards Beauchamp, see the article "Adolph Cluss: An Architect in Washington during Civil War and Reconstruction," *Records of the Columbia Historical Society, 1971–72* (Washington, D.C., 1973).

RESIDENTIAL WASHINGTON AND THE GROWTH OF SUBURBS

On the Dupont Circle area, see further in the Martin Luther King Memorial Library, Washington, D.C., Washingtoniana Division, the vertical files s.v. Residential Sections–Dupont Circle. See these same files s.v. Mount Pleasant. In general, these files provide an excellent source for primary materials on residential areas in Washington.

HIGHWAY LEGISLATION IN THE 1890s

On the streets of Washington, see further in the Martin Luther King Memorial Library, Washington, D.C., Washingtoniana Division, the vertical files s.v. Streets. The highway plans prepared by the Engineer Commissioner of the District of Columbia in response to the 1893 Highway Act (27 Stat. 532), and issued in 1895 and 1897, can be found in bound form at the Cartographic Division of the National Archives, Record Group 351, "Records of the District Surveyor's Office." Additional insights into the artifacts of the city are provided by the papers prepared in the graduate seminars in American Material Culture offered annually under the aegis of the Smithsonian Institution's Office of American Studies, Wilcomb E. Washburn, Director.

CHAPTER V:

The McMillan Plan 1901–1902

TURN OF THE CENTURY: THE PROMISE OF AMERICAN CITIES

John W. Reps describes in detail the pre–McMillan Commission plans for the Mall area, most notably plans offered by Franklin W. Smith, Theodore Bingham, and Samuel

Parsons, Jr., in *Monumental Washington: The Planning and Development of the Capital Center* (Princeton, 1967).

1900: THE AMERICAN INSTITUTE OF ARCHITECTS' CONVENTION IN WASHINGTON

Discussion of Washington architecture and planning by members of the American Institute of Architects is published in the *Proceedings of the 34th Annual Convention of the American Institute of Architects* (Washington, D.C., 1900). This volume of *Proceedings* includes discussion by Cass Gilbert, Edgar Seeler, C. Howard Walker, Paul Pelz, George Oakley Totten, H. K. Bush-Brown, Joseph C. Hornblower, and Frederick Law Olmsted, Jr., as well as the opening remarks of McFarland and Peabody, as quoted here in the text. Glenn Brown, *Memories, 1860–1930* (Washington, D.C., 1931), provides a highly personalized view of the "revival" of the L'Enfant plan, the role of the American Institute of Architects in its "crusade" to improve civic art, the work of the McMillan Commission, and the array of political and design figures who secured the Beaux-Arts traditions in Washington up to World War II.

Documents related to the McMillan plan include Glenn Brown, comp., *Papers Relating to the Improvement of the City of Washington* (Washington, D.C., 1901); Charles Moore, ed. and comp., *Park Improvement Papers* (Washington, D.C., 1903); and William V. Cox, comp., *Celebration of the One-Hundredth Anniversary of the Establishment of the Seat of Government in the District of Columbia* (Washington, D.C., 1901). For additional background on Cass Gilbert, see his *Reminiscences and Addresses* (New York, 1935). Glenn Brown's plan for the capital is described by him in "A Suggestion for Grouping Government Buildings: Landscape, Monuments, and Statuary," *Architectural Review* (Boston) 7 (August 1900), reprinted in the *Proceedings of the 34th Annual Convention of the American Institute of Architects* (Washington, D.C., 1900). For Charles Moore's view of Washington as a "world standard," see Moore's unpublished memoirs, National Archives, Washington, D.C., Record Group 42, Section 66, "Records of the Commission of Fine Arts."

1901: SENATOR MCMILLAN AND THE SENATE PARK COMMISSION

Senator McMillan's carefully worded statement on the formation of the Senate Park Commission is contained in the official report: U.S., Congress, Senate, Committee on the District of Columbia, *The Improvement of the Park System of the District of Columbia*, 57th Cong., 1st sess., 1902, S. Rept. 166. This report incorporates a complete description of the proposed plan, excerpts of which are quoted here in the text. The original report continues to make good reading on the city of Washington as it would become and the aesthetic prescriptions to which it would respond. On the roles played by individuals on the McMillan Commission and for anecdotal materials, the following biographies have been consulted and quoted: Thomas S. Hines, *Burnham of Chicago, Architect and Planner* (Oxford and New York, 1974); Charles Moore, *Daniel H. Burnham, Architect, Planner of Cities*, 2 vols. (Boston and New York, 1921), and *The Life and Times of Charles Follen McKim* (Boston, 1929); Charles Lewis Hind, *Augustus Saint-Gaudens* (New York, 1908); Louise Tharp, *Saint-Gaudens and the Gilded Era* (Boston, 1969); *The Reminiscences of Augustus Saint-Gaudens*, ed. Homer Saint-Gaudens, 2 vols. (London, 1913). There is no biography as yet of Frederick Law Olmsted, Jr., but the work of Sibley Jennings at the Commission of Fine Arts promises at last a study of this much-overlooked designer, a man long overshadowed by the accomplishments of his father.

THE GRAND TOUR AND THE CITY OF THE FUTURE

The route of the European tour that provided Old World inspiration and clarification of architectural and design sources for commission members is recorded by Charles Moore in the first volume of his biography of Daniel H. Burnham (Boston, 1921), as well as in his biography of McKim (Boston, 1929). John W. Reps, *Monumental Washington: The Planning and Development of the Capital Center* (Princeton, 1967), covers the negotiations between Alexander Cassatt and Burnham, as well as the work of William T. Partridge in the New York office of the commission.

1902: THE COMMISSION'S REPORT AND
THE MODELS OF WASHINGTON

The official report is titled *The Improvement of the Park System of the District of Columbia* (57th Cong., 1st sess., 1902, S. Rept. 166).

An Exhibition Note on the Senate Park Commission Models of Washington

The pair of scale (1 inch = 80 feet) models of Washington designed and constructed by George Carroll Curtis in 1901–1902 for the McMillan Senate Park Commission have enjoyed an exceptionally long and useful life. These models, now the property of the Commission of Fine Arts, were selected for inclusion in the bicentennial exhibition, The Federal City: Plans & Realities, sponsored jointly by the National Capital Planning Commission, the Commission of Fine Arts, and the Smithsonian Institution and exhibited in the Smithsonian's Great Hall beginning 22 February

Original Preparation of the McMillan Commission Models of Washington, 1901–1902

1976. By the early 1970s, Curtis's models had found their way to storage in a hangar at National Airport, and were by this time in vast disarray. Two restorers worked for an entire year to reassemble the models, like giant jigsaw puzzles, detail by detail, building by building, tree by tiny tree. A two-thirds section of each of the two original models was restored for display. The exhibition labels for the models read as follows: Washington, Existing Conditions, 1900, and Washington, Proposed Changes, 1902. For photographs of these models, see p. 123.   R.W.S.

The comprehensive parks design that was translated by Frederick Law Olmsted, Jr., onto the Washington landscape was derived from the Boston Metropolitan Park Commission by Charles Eliot and Sylvester Baxter. Details are affectionately recorded by the former's father, Harvard President Charles W. Eliot, in *Charles Eliot, Landscape Architect* (Boston, 1902).

THE GRAND PLAN FOR THE MALL

Key sources for the design standards to which the commission members subscribed include Glenn Brown, *Memories, 1860–1930* (Washington, D.C., 1931), and Charles Moore's unpublished memoirs, National Archives, Washington, D.C., Record Group 42, Section 66, "Records of the Commission of Fine Arts." Moore's memoirs are an especially rich source on the personal qualities of commission members; see Moore's memoirs also for insight into the political maneuverings of the commission.

For the critical reference to the "pantalooned statue," see the *Washington Post*, 8 October 1907. For Grant's statement and additional background on preservation of the L'Enfant plan, see Ulysses S. Grant III, "The L'Enfant Plan and Its Evolution," *Records of the Columbia Historical Society, 1932* (Washington, D.C., 1932). Public Law 1036 on Mall development and the role of the National Capital Park and Planning Commission is documented in *Statutes at Large* 45, ch. 708, 619 (1929).

THE 1901–1902 PLAN: REACTION AND RESPONSE

The historical record traces comment and criticism of the McMillan plan. Initial enthusiasm for the plan was tempered by the reality of specific building projects, the first group of which were under way by 1908 and could be seen by the *Evening Star* as costly beyond the nation's means. The Mall element of the plan, so said the *Star*, was likely to be as "bare and hot as the Desert of Sahara," the straight-lined formality of the design was "grim," and the new commission that advocated the plan was seen as "self-appointed." The newly conceived Mall and its formal plantings, in the eyes of those still faithful to the curving concealments and surprises of Downing, were seen as the work of "tree-butchers and nature-butchers."

The initial constituency of the plan had passed from the scene by the 1920s, to be succeeded by the more discriminating objectivity of the urban design historian Elbert Peets, the first to write about the McMillan plan in the longer perspective; see now Paul D. Spreiregen, ed., *On the Art of Designing Cities: Selected Essays of Elbert Peets* (Cambridge, Mass., 1968). Peets was succeeded by John W. Reps, whose *Monumental Washington* (Princeton, 1967) described the McMillan plan as the "first and greatest essay in civic design of the American twentieth century." In his standard history of city planning in the United States, Mel Scott, *American City Planning Since 1890*, 2d edn. (Berkeley, 1971), found the principal achievement of the plan to be the city's central core, fatally outmoded by the automobile so as to become a "historical artifact, an elaborate set piece immune to the whims of time and chance, a sacrosanct expression of the national past and the national destiny" untouched by the realities of national history or geography. In his biography of Daniel Burnham, Thomas S. Hines, *Burnham of Chicago, Architect and Planner* (Oxford and New York, 1974), recognizes the plan as "a major renewal effort" to replace an "eclectic and textured homogeneity [with a] homogeneous uniformity."

This catalog of characterizations could be considerably expanded, but it is clear that no one has yet taken full

The Jefferson Memorial

measure of the McMillan plan. As for the City Beautiful formula itself, see further Charles Mulford Robinson, *Modern Civic Art, or The City Made Beautiful* (New York and London, 1903). To evaluate the McMillan plan in light of later City Beautiful schemes, see Ira L. Bach, "A Reconsideration of the 1909 Plan of Chicago," *Chicago History* 2 (Spring–Summer 1973), and "The City Beautiful and the San Francisco Fair," in Kevin Starr, *Americans and the California Dream* (New York, 1973).

CHAPTER VI:

Toward Metropolis 1902–1926

THE PLAUSIBLE PATTERN AND A QUEST FOR NEW PLANNING

The annual reports of the Chief of the Army Corps of Engineers provide the essential background to the widening de facto planning responsibilities of the federal government prior to the Corps's absorption—along with the office of the superintendent of the State, War, and Navy Department buildings—in 1925 into the independent office of Public Buildings and Public Parks of the National Capital. The 1925 legislation is 43 Stat. 983.

URBAN PARK DEVELOPMENT: THEORY
AND PRACTICE IN WASHINGTON

The best general introductions to urban park development for the early decades of the twentieth century are found in Mel Scott, *American City Planning Since 1890*, 2d edn. (Berkeley, 1971), and John W. Reps, *Monumental Washington* (Princeton, 1967). Information on specific projects is best obtained from primary sources, including the Minutes and *Annual Report of the Commission of Fine Arts* for the years 1910–26; the Minutes of the National Capital

Park Commission for the years 1924–26; the *American Civic and Planning Annual* of the American Planning and Civic Association; and the annual reports of the Chief of the Army Corps of Engineers.

PUBLIC ARCHITECTURE: CONSTITUENT BUILDINGS AND ORCHESTRATED URBAN FORM

The philosophy and importance of the eclectic nationalized style and of the Classical Revival in Washington can best be gleaned from manuscript sources, especially the records of federal agencies concerned with design in the city. These include Minutes and the *Annual Report of the Commission of Fine Arts* for the years 1910–26; the Minutes of the National Capital Park Commission; annual reports of the Public Buildings Commission; records of the Office of the Supervising Architect of the Treasury; and the manuscript diaries of Edward Bennett. Issues of the *American Civic and Planning Annual* also contain substantial material. For serial articles on individual projects and architects, see the *Avery Index to Architectural Periodicals*, 15 vols., 2d edn. (Boston, 1973).

CIVIC DESIGN: FIRST QUARTER OF THE CENTURY

The *Annual Report of the Commission of Fine Arts* for 1910–26 emphasize the aesthetic aspects of the official city but allow for transmittal of many McMillan plan recommendations into the work schedules of the National Capital Park Commission and the National Capital Park and Planning Commission.

A Historical Note on the Term "White Lot"

According to tradition, the White Lot was so named because of a white-washed wooden fence that surrounded it. This area, roughly equivalent to the present Ellipse, is bounded by Constitution Avenue, Seventeenth and Eighteenth Streets, and the White House grounds. One of the major problems that had confronted the Quartermaster Corps in Washington during the Civil War was the storage of supplies, particularly livestock, for the army's use. The creating of this White Lot as a holding area for cattle awaiting slaughter was a typical solution to supply problems, though the area's name persisted in common usage long after the problems and the war were over. C.V.D.

RESIDENTIAL DEVELOPMENT: HOMES AND HOUSES IN CITY AND SUBURB

For details on the private development of the city, see further in the Martin Luther King Memorial Library, Washington, D.C., Washingtoniana Division, the vertical files s.v. Residential Sections. For the reference to Waverly Taylor, for example, see the vertical files s.v. Residential

Sections—Foxhall; on the electric railroad to Glen Echo, see Residential Sections—Palisades. An exhaustive survey of Massachusetts Avenue as exemplary of gracious Washington architecture is published by the Commission of Fine Arts, *Massachusetts Avenue Architecture*, 2 vols. (Washington, D.C., 1973–75). On the Larz Anderson House, see further James Orr Denby, *The Society of the Cincinnati and Its Museum* (Washington, D.C., 1967); Rita Reif, *Treasure Rooms of America's Mansions Manors and Houses* (New York, 1970); Herbert P. Weissberger, "Notes on Anderson House," 1971 (typewritten).

The Larz Anderson House As It Looks Today

An Architectural Note on the Larz Anderson House

Larz Anderson III was born in Paris in 1866. After being educated at Harvard, he entered the United States diplomatic service, serving first as the second secretary at the American legation in London (1891) and then as the first secretary at the American embassy in Rome (1894–97). Anderson served in the Spanish American War as a captain and assistant adjunct general of volunteers, and then resumed his diplomatic career. He was appointed minister to Belgium in 1911 and ambassador to Japan 1912–13. He resigned from the diplomatic service prior to the outbreak of World War I. During the war, Anderson was very active in volunteer relief work in Washington, D.C., and traveled extensively. He died in 1937, and was buried in Saint Mary's Chapel at the National Cathedral in Washington.

Between 1902 and 1905, Anderson and his wife, Boston heiress Isabel Weld Perkins, built the fifty-room Late-Renaissance-Revival–styled house at 2118 Massachusetts Avenue, NW. Designed by the Boston architectural firm of Little & Browne, the house was a center for local and international society until Anderson's death. Anderson's great grandfather had been one of the founders of the Society of the Cincinnati, and in 1939, Mrs. Anderson donated the house and most of its furnishings to the society for a national headquarters. C.V.D.

CHAPTER VII:

The Year of Decision 1926

LEGITIMIZATION OF PLANNING: METROPOLITAN CITY, NATIONAL CAPITAL

For documenting national and local advancements toward creation of professional planning bodies, see the annual reports of the Washington Board of Trade, the Commission of Fine Arts, the United States Chamber of Commerce, and the American Civic and Planning Association. Locations of these reports are listed under manuscript sources at the end of this Bibliographic Essay. For the John Nolen, Sr., summarizing work on citizens' groups, see the report of the 1924 National Conference on City Planning, "The Importance of Citizens' Committees in Securing Public Support for a City Planning Program."

For the early work of Harlean James, see her *Land Planning in City, State and Nation* (New York, 1926). The 1923 remarks by Colonel C. O. Sherrill are quoted in the *Evening Star*, 2 May 1923. John M. Gries and James Ford edited the proceedings of the thirty-one committees that constituted the influential President's Conference on Home Building and Home Ownership; see especially the volume entitled *Planning for Residential Districts* (Washington, D.C., 1931), where photographs of sections of Washington are used to illustrate the best and the worst of the national housing picture. President Herbert Hoover traced the development of his personal interest and commitment to housing and planning issues in Washington in *The Memoirs of Herbert Hoover: The Cabinet and the Presidency, 1920–1933* (New York, 1952). For the Civic Development Department's statements on planning, see United States Chamber of Commerce, *The National Chamber's Civic Work* (Washington, D.C., n.d.). For the Washington Board of Trade's view of itself as a voluntary and unofficial organization, see *Nation's Capital Magazine* (November 1930).

LEGISLATION FOR COMPREHENSIVE PLANNING: THE ACTS OF 1924 AND 1926

The act creating the National Capital Park Commission in 1924 (43 Stat. 463) represents the first initial step toward a planning body, legislated two years later with the 1926 act providing for the National Capital Park and Planning Commission (44 Stat. 374). Rationale for this 1926 act is illustrated in the Minutes of the National Capital Park Commission, on file at the National Capital Planning Commission. They testify, among other things, to the low levels of funding and the shortcomings of park acquisition powers without a comprehensive planning context in which to act.

THE PUBLIC BUILDINGS ACT OF 1926: THE FEDERAL TRIANGLE PROJECT

The development of the Federal Triangle and changing justifications for the project can be studied through the *Annual Report of the Public Buildings Commission* for the years 1922–32. The articles in the *Federal Architect* published from July 1930 through year date 1946 by the Association of Federal Architects under the spirited editorship of Edwin B. Morris of the Treasury Department reflect the changing tastes in civic design at the federal level. The diaries of Edward H. Bennett are in the office of Edward H. Bennett, Jr., Chicago, Illinois. For the addresses delivered at the 25–26 April 1929 conference at the United States Chamber of Commerce, see *The Development of the United States Capital*, 71st Cong., 1st sess., H. Doc. No. 35, 1930. For Andrew Mellon's statement on responsibility to the McMillan plan, see Andrew W. Mellon, "A Unified Plan for Public Buildings," *American Civic and Planning Annual* (Washington, D.C., 1930). For Bennett's notes on modern "blunt" architecture, see the diarial entry for 13 April 1931. See there also the quoted remarks of President Hoover.

Philip Sawyer, "The Design of Public Buildings," *Architectural Forum* 55 (September, 1931) outlines the difference in design between public and private architecture, with the "economy" characteristic emphasized in the Federal Triangle. Mellon's suggestion to Bennett on the "harmonious design" for the Federal Triangle are quoted in

Portion of the Federal Triangle along Constitution Avenue at Fourteenth Street, Early 1940s

Edward H. Bennett's article, "The Architecture of the Capital," in *The Development of the United States Capital,* 71st Cong., 1st sess., H. Doc. No. 35, 1930; see there also Bennett's view (cited here in the text) of the plazas' unifying function in the Federal Triangle. The rationale behind the civic center element of City Beautiful design as represented by the Federal Triangle is developed in Warner Hegemann and Elbert Peets, *The American Vitruvius: An Architect's Handbook of Civic Art* (New York, 1922). For the remark of John Russell Pope on the role of the Board of Architectural Consultants, see the miscellaneous papers accompanying the diaries of Edward H. Bennett in the office of Edward H. Bennett, Jr., Chicago, Illinois, dated to 21 September 1931. The annual reports and Minutes of the National Capital Park and Planning Commission covering the 1930s shed considerable light on the commission's entry into Federal Triangle planning *after* this planning was well under way. These documents also highlight the rising issues of traffic, parking, and design that compromised Bennett's plan for the Apex Building of the Triangle composition.

CRISIS AND CRITIQUE: EVALUATIONS AND SECOND THOUGHTS

For Karl K. Hardy's remarks on the soundness of the Federal Triangle building program, see his "Economic Justification for the New Public Buildings," *American Civic and Planning Annual* (Washington, D.C., 1932).

CHAPTER VIII:

The Early National Capital Park and Planning Commission 1926–1933

PLANNING IN THE NATION'S CAPITAL

The work schedules of the National Capital Park and Planning Commission are recorded in detail in the Minutes of the commission covering the years studied, and are summarized for public inspection in the commission's annual reports for the years 1927–32. These documents are on file at the National Capital Planning Commission, Washington, D.C. For correspondence describing the commission members as "men of the widest experience," see Louis C. Cramton to Mr. H. M. Lord, Director of the Budget, 29 January 1929, Louis C. Cramton Papers, Library of Michigan History, University of Michigan, Ann Arbor, Michigan. For Charles Eliot's remarks on his "strong sense" of history and his job as a professional planner, see the newspaper article dated July 1931, Charles Eliot II Papers, Graduate School of Design, Harvard University, Cam-

Aerial View of the North Side of the Capitol

bridge, Massachusetts. The anecdote about Harlean James's viewing Eliot as "that kid" was recounted to the author in a personal interview with Charles Eliot II, Cambridge, Massachusetts. Statements by Eliot, U.S. Grant III, and Major Carey Brown to the House Committee on the District of Columbia are quoted in *The Work of the National Capital Park and Planning Commission,* Final Report of the House Committee on the District of Columbia, 70th Cong., 1st sess., 10 March 1928. A similar collection of statements to introduce the commission to the national planning profession were made to the National Conference on City Planning; see the report, *The Development of the National Capital and Its Environs* (Boston, 1928).

THE AUTOMOBILE

For the views of J. C. Nichols, see his article, "Economic Saving in City Planning," in the report of the National Conference on City Planning, *The Development of the National Capital and Its Environs* (Boston, 1928). The molding of residential development to the natural topography as articulated by Nichols is illustrated in promotional literature found in the neighborhood files, Martin Luther King Memorial Library, Washington, D.C., Washingtoniana Division. For Harland Bartholomew's résumé of street development, see the *Annual Report of the National Capital Park and Planning Commission,* 1928. Annual reports of this commission are on file at the National Capital Planning Commission, Washington, D.C. On the special interest maps prepared by the commission, see the newspaper article dated July 1931, Charles Eliot II Papers, Graduate School of Design, Harvard University, Cambridge, Massachusetts. See this collection also for the statement on Georgetown and Boston's Beacon Hill as quoted in the section on Housing in this chapter.

HOUSING

The statements of Colonel Ulysses S. Grant III about Wesley Heights are quoted in *The Work of the National Capital Park and Planning Commission*, Final Report of the House Committee on the District of Columbia, 70th Cong., 1st sess., 10 March 1928. For the description of Spring Valley, see in the Martin Luther King Memorial Library, Washington, D.C., Washingtoniana Division, the vertical files s.v. Residential Sections—Spring Valley. For John Ihlder's housing proposal, see his article "A Housing Program for the District of Columbia," in National Capital Park and Planning Commission, *Reports and Plans, Washington Region: Supplementary Technical Data to Accompany Annual Report* (Washington, D.C., 1930).

PLANNING FOR PARKS AND PARKWAYS

For the views of T. H. MacDonald on the road to Mount Vernon, see the Minutes of the National Capital Park and Planning Commission for December 1926. For the views of Milton Medary, see his article, "The Aesthetic Value of City Planning in the National Capital," in the report of the National Conference on City Planning, *The Development of the National Capital and Its Environs* (Boston, 1928). For Charles Eliot's report on the park system, see the Minutes of the National Capital Park and Planning Commission for December 1926; see also the 1927 Annual Report.

PUBLIC BUILDINGS: LOCATION, DESIGN, AND CONCENTRATION

Architectural control over new development adjacent to key federal lands and enclaves as mandated by the 1930 Shipstead-Luce Act (*Public Law 71-231*) is discussed in *The Shipstead-Luce Act: Rules and Regulations* (Washington, D.C., 1938). Representative Cramton's reference to "artificial beauties such as monuments, boulevards, and pretentious buildings" occurs in a letter from Cramton to Mr. H. M. Lord, Director of the Budget, 29 July 1929, Louis C. Cramton Papers, Library of Michigan History, University of Michigan, Ann Arbor, Michigan. See this same collection for materials covering the prelude to the Capper-Cramton Act. These papers discuss the acute environmental issues at stake and reveal the high levels of support for the work of the National Capital Park and Planning Commission.

A Topographical Note on the Key of Keys

The "Key of Keys"—or "Quay of all the Quays," as the variant title and spelling go—was a large rocky projection jutting into the Potomac approximately at the foot of the Naval Observatory on Twenty-third Street, NW. During the eighteenth century, this projection was a popular land-

*Telephoto View of the Area around the Historic Key of Keys
As It Looks Today*

ing point for river traffic—hence the name Key of Keys. According to tradition, some of General Edward Braddock's troops landed here in 1755, and then marched west along the Frederick Road to Fort Cumberland. This story has never been confirmed, but the rock was often referred to as "Braddock's Rock." During the 1790s, it was decided that the rock would make excellent foundation stone. This site was the source, in fact, for much of the stone used for foundation walls in the Capitol and the White House. Some of the rock was still extant in the early 1830s when the Chesapeake & Ohio Canal was extended to meet the Washington City Canal, and it became necessary to blast away a large piece of this rock to clear the right of way for the canal and its towpath. C.V.D.

REGIONAL PLANNING AND COOPERATION

Documentation for planning activities in the suburban Maryland counties is found in the Maryland–National Capital Park and Planning Commission Minutes for 1927 to 1930, and the *Twenty-Fifth Annual Report—Anniversary Edition, 1927–1952* (Silver Spring, 1952), as well as in newspaper articles on file at local libraries: at the Montgomery County Library, Rockville Branch, see issues of the *Sentinel* dated 10 December 1926, 7 January 1927, 4 February 1927, 6 May 1927, 20 June 1930; *Evening Star* (Washington), 10 November 1926; at the Maryland–National Capital Park and Planning Commission library, see *Riverdalian*, 26 January 1927, 2 March 1927. See also Roland W. Rogers, "A Park System for the Maryland Washington Metropolitan District," *City Planning* (January 1931); Irving C. Root, "Planning Progress in Maryland Washington Metropolitan District," *City Planning* (January 1931). Additional source materials are letters to E. Brooke Lee (Democratic political leader of Montgomery County), dated 1926–27, Maryland–National Capital Park and Planning Commission library, Silver Spring, Maryland. The legislation creating the Maryland–National Capital

Park and Planning Commission is Sec. 17, chap. 448, Acts of the General Assembly of Maryland, 1927.

For Eliot's remarks about the close relationship between the two planning commissions, see *The Work of the National Capital Park and Planning Commission*, Final Report of the House Committee on the District of Columbia, 70th Cong., 1st sess., 10 March 1928. For the reports of the Washington Region Water Supply Committee and the Washington Region Drainage and Sewerage Committee, see National Capital Park and Planning Commission, *Reports and Plans, Washington Region; Supplementary Technical Data to Accompany Annual Report* (Washington, D.C., 1930). Eliot's penultimate remarks on planning needs are reported in the Minutes of the National Capital Park and Planning Commission for June 1933. Certain planning activities in the suburban Virginia counties are also reflected in this body of Minutes.

CHAPTER IX:

The New Deal in Planning 1933–1941

THE SHIFT FROM COMPREHENSIVE PLANNING TO
SHORT-TERM GOALS

On the need to reorganize the National Capital Park and Planning Commission as well as the need for a Comprehensive Plan, see the American Planning and Civic Association Papers, Wisconsin State Historical Society; see also Papers of Frederic A. Delano, Harland Bartholomew, and U. S. Grant III, Architecture and City Planning Collection, Olin Library, Cornell University, Ithaca, New York. Charles Eliot's 1927 memorandum, "Union Square and the Mall," is included as Appendix A to the Minutes of the National Capital Park and Planning Commission for October 1933. See there also the statement and suggestions of Henry V. Hubbard quoted here in the text. In the same Minutes for October 1933, see also Appendix B, John Nolen, Jr., "Program and Policies for Progressive Improvement of the Mall and Adjacent Areas," for the views of Nolen as quoted in the text.

For Olmsted's views on the Jefferson Memorial, see the "Memorandum Report by Frederick Law Olmsted on Proposed Sites for a Memorial to Thomas Jefferson in the National Capital," included as Appendix A in the Minutes of the National Capital Park and Planning Commission for August 1935. For the views of the Commission of Fine Arts on the Jefferson Memorial, see Appendix B in the same Minutes, the "Memorandum with Reference to Proposed Sites for a Memorial to Thomas Jefferson in the National Capital," signed by Gilmore D. Clarke and William T.

Partridge. The controversial confrontation of architectural classicism with the modern movement is best illustrated by discussions presented in Henry Hope Reed, *The Golden City*, 2d edn. (New York, 1971), and Christopher Tunnard and Henry Hope Reed, *American Skyline* (New York, 1953).

INFLUENCE OF THE PLANNING COMMISSION

The new federal programs that mushroomed in response to emergencies of the Depression—and overwhelmed plans previously developed by the National Capital Park and Planning Commission—are discussed in the Minutes of the commission for the years 1933–41, the period covered by this chapter. The 1934 traffic study referred to in the text is by Charles Herrick, "General Conclusions from the Employees' Transportation Survey, 1934," included in the Minutes of the commission for January 1935. The "grab-bag" statement is from Harold L. Ickes, "Warnings Against Further Encroachment upon the Parks and Playgrounds of the National Capital," included as Appendix F in the Minutes of the Park and Planning Commission for October 1941. For Frederic Delano's letter of resignation and the statement of the American Planning and Civic Association as quoted in the text, see the association's Papers, Wisconsin State Historical Society; see also Papers of Frederic Delano, Architecture and City Planning Collection, Olin Library, Cornell University, Ithaca, New York.

A Note on the 1939 Exhibition on "Washington: The Planned City without a Plan"

Had not ten young architects organized an exhibition at the national convention of the American Institute of Architects in Washington in 1939, that convention might have been remembered only by the architects. In fact, however, a group of young architects led by Alfred Kastner and Chloethiel Woodard staged an exhibition entitled: "Washington: The Planned City without a Plan." Kastner and Woodard, both on the Committee on Housing and City Planning of the Washington Chapter of the American Institute of Architects, wrote an accompanying essay, "Social Function of the Architect." In this essay, the authors expounded on the modern democratic city, quoting the wisdom of Lewis Mumford and Frank Lloyd Wright. In casting aside the City Beautiful ideal, they saw the McMillan plan in Washington as well as the river drives along the Schuylkill River in Philadelphia as "typical of the escapism" of an earlier time. Philadelphia, they said, was planned with beautiful commuting strips so that the affluent could drive between work and home shielded from the "oceans of slums." They described Washington's more recent planning as "equally futile. The new federal buildings form a federal island which pulls traffic through the Washington downtown area. For both examples the formula is equally simple: be effective to sightseers, concentrate your efforts in the smallest possible area, and forget the total picture as much as you can. . . . The plan of Washington in 1939 is obsolete and inappropriate."

These harsh words were followed by the authors' suggestions for a remedied approach to planning: competitions on master plans and sectional plans should be held to dramatize the issues to the public; other professions such as medicine and sociology should have a collaborative role on planning problems; a City Planning Institute ought to be created to serve as an educational and political body "which would stimulate the average citizen to active participation in the rational development of the city"; and a City Planning "Museum" should be established to educate the citizenry and professionals, since such education was "necessary to develop political action for city planning."

This blistering attack on the planning agencies in Washington, particularly the National Capital Park and Planning Commission, was spread beyond the boundaries of the District as the exhibition traveled around the country. Soon after the convention closed, a special meeting of the Planning Commission was held. The president of the Washington Chapter of the American Institute of Architects, Philip Schreier, disclaimed any endorsement of the exhibition and maintained that many members of the chapter objected strenuously to it. Woodard was unable to formulate precisely what her criticisms were of Washington planning, but argued that her exhibition and essay were "done in the spirit of 'let's talk about it.'" The Planning Commission staff listened sympathetically, explaining that much of the commission's weakness stemmed from lack of funds, small staff, the need to cope with the immediate problems posed by the Depression—and now the rumblings of another world war. (For further details, see Alfred Kastner and Chloethiel Woodard, "Social Function of the Architect," paper presented in connection with the exhibition, "Washington: The Planned City without a Plan," included as Appendix D in the Minutes of the National Capital Park and Planning Commission for October 1939.)

MULTICENTERED REGIONAL CITY

For the report of John Nolen, Jr., on building site shifts, in particular the Department of Agriculture's Arlington Experimental Farm, see the Minutes of the National Capital Park and Planning Commission for October 1933, Appendix B. For actions of the commission surrounding selection and planning for the Pentagon site itself, see the Minutes for 20 March 1941, 31 July 1941, 18 September 1941, and 20 March 1942. For the press release referred to in the text,

see the Minutes of the Commission of Fine Arts, on file (indexed) at the commission's office in Washington, D.C. For Harold Ickes's warnings about the Pentagon site, see his "Warnings Against Further Encroachment upon the Parks and Playgrounds of the National Capital," included as Appendix F in the Minutes of the National Capital Park and Planning Commission for October 1941. Other documents important for their anticipation of urban regional diffusion include the Maryland State Planning Commission report, *Baltimore-Washington-Annapolis Area* (Baltimore, 1937), and the National Resources Planning Board report, *Regional Factors in National Development*, by John M. Gaus (Washington, D.C., 1938).

Photographs during this period attain increased significance as documentation. In addition to general iconographic collections listed at the end of this Bibliographic Essay, there are also iconographic records of the New Deal agencies. These records are now deposited in the Library of Congress Prints and Photographs Division. The photographs dating to the 1930s are of large quantity and high quality.

A Note on Washington's Early Airport History

Samuel Milner, a historian at the Federal Aviation Agency, has investigated Washington's early airport history, beginning with the privately owned flying field built by Henry Berliner near the Virginia end of the Fourteenth Street Bridge. Commenced in 1927, this airport—later called Hoover Airport—accommodated scheduled service as well as private flights. The airport (and also the amusement park adjacent to it) were reached by streetcar from Twelfth Street and Independence Avenue. Hoover Airport could

National Airport, 1976

also be reached via Military Road. Across this highway, on the site of a former racetrack, a second privately owned commercial airport was established after 1928, largely on filled land. This hazardous situation was ultimately resolved by the consolidation of the two airfields into one, called Washington-Hoover or more properly Washington Municipal Airport. Washington Municipal Airport was Washington's only airport until the opening of National Airport at Gravelly Point in 1941. See further Constance McLaughlin Green, Washington, Capital City, 1879–1950 (Princeton, 1963), and especially for maps, Herman R. Friis, Geographical Reconnaissance of the Potomac River Tidewater Fringe of Virginia from Arlington Memorial Bridge to Mount Vernon (Washington, D.C., 1968). Concerning the extensive brickyards along the Virginia shore, see William B. Clark and Benjamin L. Miller, "The Physiography and Geology of the Coastal Plain Province of Virginia," Virginia Geological Survey Bulletin 4 (1912). See also Fairfax County Board of Supervisors, Industrial and Historical Sketch of Fairfax County, Virginia (Falls Church, 1907).

CHAPTER X:

World War II and Postwar Years 1941–1952

STATISTICS OF GROWTH

The measure of the city's wartime and postwar growth is traced in District of Columbia Department of Highways, "Twenty-four Years of Progress in Highway Development, 1924–1948," mimeographed (Washington, D.C., n.d.). For the Planning Commission's recommendation on temporary federal office buildings, see the Minutes of the Special Committee to Consider Sites for Office Buildings, 22 December 1941, included as Appendix A in the Minutes of the National Capital Park and Planning Commission. For the reference to the "small village" of blacks that was relocated from the Pentagon site in Arlington over to Anacostia, see Herman R. Friis, Geographical Reconnaissance of the Potomac River Tidewater Fringe of Virginia from Arlington Memorial Bridge to Mount Vernon (Washington, D.C., 1968). This "small village" settlement appears to have had origins dating to the Civil War era. For the 1942 Goodwillie report and plan, see Arthur Goodwillie, The Rehabilitation of Southwest Washington as a War Housing Measure: A Memorandum to the Federal Home Loan Bank (Washington, D.C., 1942).

POSTWAR PLANNING AND LEGISLATION

For the statements of Alfred Bettman, the Cincinnati lawyer and planning expert, see the Minutes of the National

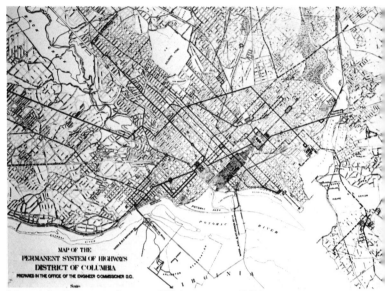

Map of the Permanent System of Highways, 1911 Edition

Capital Park and Planning Commission for February and April 1943. For the views of Louis Justement, influential in the early phases of post–World War II redevelopment, see his New Cities for Old: City Building in Terms of Space, Time and Money (New York and London, 1946). For discussion on the 1945 District of Columbia Redevelopment Act and the 1949 Housing Act (63 Stat. 420), see correspondence dated 1941–53 in Papers of the American Planning and Civic Association (later Urban America), Social Action Archives, Wisconsin State Historical Society. Also see correspondence dated 1941–55, Papers of Frederic Delano, Harland Bartholomew, and U. S. Grant III, Architecture and City Planning Collection, Olin Library, Cornell University, Ithaca, New York.

On the urban philosophy current in the 1930s and forties, see Frank Lloyd Wright, Disappearing City (New York, 1932), and Eliel Saarinen, The City—Its Growth, Its Future (New York, 1943). For Louis Justement's 1944 statements on advanced city planning, see the Minutes of the National Capital Park and Planning Commission for May 1944. On Barry Farms and Marshall Heights, see the records of the Redevelopment Land Agency, whose project files, newspaper clippings, and annual reports are in the library of the District of Columbia Department of Housing and Community Development, Washington, D.C. The "Study of Barry Farms Area," Parts I and II, are included in the Minutes of the National Capital Park and Planning Commission for November 1944. For the "Study of Marshall Heights Area," see the commission Minutes for April 1945. The Greiner-DeLeuw report is appended to the commission Minutes for December 1946 and March 1947.

THE 1950 COMPREHENSIVE PLAN

The *1950 Comprehensive Plan for the National Capital and Its Environs* is contained in five published volumes: *Washington: Present and Future, A General Summary of the Comprehensive Plan for the National Capital and Its Environs,* Monograph No. 1 (April 1950); *People and Land,* Monograph No. 2 (June 1950); *Housing and Redevelopment,* Monograph No. 3 (June 1950); *Open Space and Community Services,* Monograph No. 4 (June 1950); and *Moving People and Goods,* Monograph No. 5 (June 1950); on rapid transit, see *Moving People and Goods,* and for the "obsolete, blighted, and satisfactory" categories, see *Housing and Development.*

METROPOLITAN CITY AT MID-CENTURY

For general background on the year 1950, see the Minutes of the National Capital Park and Planning Commission so dated. See also the series of monographs published by the commission, *Washington: Present and Future* (Washington, D.C., 1950).

DEVELOPMENT IN SUBURBAN VIRGINIA

For the statement of John Nolen, Jr., opposing high-rise buildings, see the Minutes of the National Capital Park and Planning Commission for January 1942. On the projected development adjacent to Arlington National Cemetery, see the Letter from Gilmore D. Clarke, chairman of the Commission of Fine Arts, to General Ulysses S. Grant III, dated 9 May 1945, included in the Minutes of the National Capital Park and Planning Commission for May 1945. As to the Planning Commission's suggestions for Springfield, see the Minutes for March 1948.

PLANNING FOR GROWTH IN THE MARYLAND COUNTIES

For wartime and postwar developments in suburban Maryland, see the Brookings Institution study, *The Government of Montgomery County, Maryland: A Survey* (Washington, D.C., 1941). See also *Looking Forward* (Silver Spring, 1942), a report dated 19 October 1942 on progress made to that time by the Maryland–National Capital Park and Planning Commission, including an outline of work to be undertaken in future by the commission and its staff. For additional background materials on Maryland development, see the Mary P. Vinton Collection in the Municipal Room at the Montgomery County Public Library, Rockville Branch, for the years 1950–65. For the statement of M. Bond Smith quoted here in the text, see the Minutes of the National Capital Park and Planning Commission for December 1949; for Tuemmler's statement, see the Minutes for September 1946.

CHAPTER XI:

The Turnaround 1952–1960

REGIONAL PLANNING AND THE NATIONAL CAPITAL PLANNING COMMISSION

The National Capital Planning Act, 66 Stat. 781 (1952), reorganized the planning agency into the National Capital Planning Commission, created the National Capital Regional Planning Council, and outlined the responsibilities of each organization. For the legislative and administrative history of the Planning Commission, see now *Planning Washington 1924–1976: An Era of Planning for the National Capital and Environs* (Washington, D.C., 1976).

REDEVELOPMENT AND THE TURNAROUND TREND

The 1955–56 study on rezoning (cited in the text) prepared for the Washington Zoning Revision Office by Harold M. Lewis, the New York consultant, produced the following planning reports: "General Background and History of Zoning in the District of Columbia," January 1955; "Population and Employment in the District of Columbia," March 1955; "Height and Bulk of Commercial Buildings in the District of Columbia," September 1955; "Density of Residential Population," December 1955; "Relation of Assessed Value to Zoning," January 1956; "Off-Street Parking and Loading," April 1956; "A New Zoning Plan for the District of Columbia," November 1956; "Land Use in the District of Columbia," June 1956. A doctoral dissertation on Washington's early redevelopment program is in preparation by William Barnes, Syracuse University.

TRANSPORTATION

For the Mass Transportation Survey, several reports were produced by consultants in the period 1955–59, but the over-all findings were summarized in the *Transportation Plan, National Capital Region: The Mass Transportation Survey Report* (Washington, D.C., National Capital Planning Commission and National Capital Regional Planning Council, 1959). The specialized consultant reports and the summary reports are on file at the National Capital Planning Commission library in Washington, D.C. The work of the Joint Committee on Washington Metropolitan Problems is detailed in the staff reports to the 85th Congress and 86th Congress, 1958–60, and the hearings conducted by the Joint Committee in 1958.

METROPOLITAN WASHINGTON: CITY, SUBURB, AND REGION

On Rosslyn, see G. Brian Kelly, "Rosslyn: Double Decker City Rises beside Potomac," *Christian Science Monitor,* 1967 (offprint).

VEHICLES OF CHANGE

The source of the Frederick Law Olmsted, Jr., quotation is the McMillan Commission report, *The Improvement of the Park System of the District of Columbia*, 57th Cong., 1st sess., S. Rept. No. 166, 1902. Annual reports of the National Capital Park and Planning Commission were published annually from 1927 to 1932. From 1932 on, records of commission activities are contained in the Minutes. Annual reports and Minutes of the National Capital Park and Planning Commission are on file at the National Capital Planning Commission, Washington, D.C.

A Note on the History of the Bridges at Fourteenth Street

The first effort to bridge the Potomac at the foot of Fourteenth Street, NW, came in 1809 when the Washington Bridge Company constructed a wooden toll bridge there. Almost a mile long, this bridge had a draw at each end to minimize obstruction of river navigation. Known as the Long Bridge, it was never a financial success. When the British invaded Washington and burned the government buildings in 1814, President Madison and some government officials fled to safety in Virginia via this crossing. The Virginia end of the Long Bridge was fired by American forces, and repairs were not completed until 1818.

Fourteenth Street Bridge Complex

The federal government bought the Long Bridge from the bridge company for $47,000 in 1831, after several of the bridge's spans had been carried away by ice and flood waters. Reconstruction required four years to complete. The new bridge was damaged by ice again in 1836, 1841, 1856, 1860, 1863, 1866 and 1887, but portions of the 1836 bridge survived until 1906. The Long Bridge gained prominence during the Civil War, and in 1863, a parallel bridge was built just downstream. In 1870, the Baltimore & Potomac Railroad also began using the crossing.

Congress finally authorized the bridge's removal in 1901, and approved the construction of a new Highway Bridge and a railroad bridge. The railroad crossing was taken up by the Pennsylvania Railroad, and in 1903 the Pennsylvania Bridge Company won the bid to construct the Highway Bridge; this truss bridge was opened in 1906.

The Highway Bridge was extensively renovated in 1929, but the tremendous growth in automobile traffic soon made this structure obsolete. Congress authorized the construction of two new highway bridges in 1947. The Rochambeau Memorial Bridge opened in 1950 and the George Mason Memorial Bridge in 1962. A third span between these two was completed in 1971. In common usage, the entire complex of bridges is called "the Fourteenth Street Bridge."
C.V.D

HIGHWAY AND EXPRESSWAY PLANNING: THE COMPREHENSIVE VIEW

Background to the development of the highway system in the District of Columbia and environs is provided in District of Columbia Department of Transportation, "Twenty-four Years of Progress in Highway Development, 1924–1948," mimeographed (Washington, D.C., n.d.).

REGIONAL PLANNING: DEVICES OF COORDINATION

For summaries of the Greiner-DeLeuw report, see the Minutes of the National Capital Park and Planning Commission for December 1946 and March 1947.

THE MASS TRANSPORTATION SURVEY

For the survey and its recommendations, see the hearings of the Joint Committee on Washington Metropolitan Problems, 85th and 86th Cong. (1958–60). One of the published reports of the Joint Committee, *A Discussion Guide to Washington Area Metropolitan Problems* (Washington, D.C., 1960), includes a transportation section with bibliography.

THE REGIONAL METRO SYSTEM

Further development of the Metro rail system can be traced through the National Capital Transportation Agency, Recommendations for Transportation in the National Capital Region (Washington, D.C., 1962). Note that the National Capital Transportation Act of 1965 (79 Stat. 664) authorized the creation of a regional system, the Washington Metropolitan Area Transit Authority, and allowed for the phasing out of the original Agency.

A short history of Metro from the 1950s to late 1969 is sketched by William J. Murin, *The Evolution of Metro* (Washington, D.C., 1970). Murin notes that two important landmarks in the design of the system are these reports: *Transit Development Program for the National Capital Region*, 88th Cong., 1st sess., H. Rept. No. 1005, 1963, and National Capital Transit Authority, *Rapid Rail Transit for the Nation's Capital—Transit Development Program, 1965* (Washington, D.C., 1965).

The Capital Beltway in Maryland between Silver Spring and Kensington

THE CAPITAL BELTWAY

Transportation studies on the Capital Beltway include *The Socio-Economic Impact of the Capital Beltway in Northern Virginia* prepared by the Bureau of Population and Economic Research, University of Virginia, Charlottesville, in cooperation with the Virginia Department of Highways and the U.S. Department of Transportation, Bureau of Public Roads (Washington, D.C., 1968), and Wilbur Smith and Associates, *Maryland Capital Beltway Impact Study: Final Report, Washington Standard Metropolitan Statistical Area and Maryland Counties* (Silver Spring, 1968).

CHAPTER XIII:

New Agendas in Policies and Comprehensive Plans 1960–1968

THE PICTURE WINDOW AND OTHER SYMBOLS OF GROWTH

Four major planning reports form the primary source for this chapter: *A Policies Plan for the Year 2000*, published by the National Capital Planning Commission and the National Capital Regional Planning Council (Washington, D.C., 1961); the "Brown Book" or *1965/1985: Proposed Physical Development Policies for Washington, D.C.*, published by the National Capital Planning Commission (Washington, D.C., 1965); the "Green Book" or *The Proposed Comprehensive Plan for the National Capital*, published by the National Capital Planning Commission (Washington, D.C., 1967); and the ongoing Comprehensive Plan, known as the "Red Book." Under the full title, *Comprehensive Plan for the National Capital, Adopted Pursuant to the National Capital Planning Act of 1952*, as amended, this plan was published by the National Capital Planning Commission in 1968, and elements of the plan were at that time first adopted. The document is published in binder format to facilitate the incorporation of modifications and additions to the Comprehensive Plan. For the view of the city on the move, see the magazine article on "The Capital: Washington Reborn," *Time*, 17 November 1961. For the views of Allan Temko, see "Capital's Growth Crisis Seen as Global in Scope," *Washington Post*, 12 August 1962. On the remarks of William Finley to the Washington Building Congress, see the *Washington Post*, 16 November 1958. *The Crack in the Picture Window* was the title of Washington writer John Keats's critique of suburbia, based largely on the experience of Montgomery County, Maryland.

Suburban Development in Northern Virginia, Seen from Shirley Highway, 1972

THE 1961 POLICIES PLAN FOR THE YEAR 2000

For background on the wedges and corridors plan for metropolitan growth, see the essays written by Hans Blumenfeld and edited by Paul D. Spreiregen in *The Modern Metropolis: Its Origins, Growth, Characteristics, and Planning* (Cambridge, Mass., and London, 1967).

NEW BEGINNINGS IN THE EARLY SIXTIES

For biographical notes on Elizabeth Rowe, William Finley, Wilmer Dutton, and other members and executive directors of the National Capital Planning Commission, see *Planning Washington 1924–1976: An Era of Planning for the National Capital and Environs* (Washington, D.C., 1976). "Guiding Principles for Federal Architecture" is contained in the Report to the President by the Ad Hoc Committee on Federal Office Space, 23 May 1962. The monthly column, "Washington Perspective," in *Progressive Architecture* for the years 1953–58 traces planning necessities and federal architecture in the capital city. See also Frederick Gutheim, "Urban Space and Urban Design," in Lowden Wingo, ed., *Urban Space* (Baltimore, 1963).

The reports documenting the evolution of Pennsylvania Avenue design proposals are the Report to the President by the Ad Hoc Committee on Federal Office Space, 23 May 1962; see there the much-quoted declaration that "Pennsylvania Avenue should be lively, friendly, and inviting, as well as dignified and impressive." The *Report of the President's Council on Pennsylvania Avenue* (Washington, D.C., 1964) provides the fundamental and detailed statement of the plan put forward in the 1960s. Immediate steps to implement the plan are traced in the *Report of the President's Temporary Commission on Pennsylvania Avenue* (Washington, D.C., 1967); see also later reports of the Pennsylvania Avenue Development Corporation. Efforts to redesign Pennsylvania Avenue were visualized in the Library of Congress exhibition, *The Grand Design*, and especially in the exhibition catalog (Washington, D.C., 1967).

THE 1965 BROWN BOOK

For the landscape identity study referred to in the text, see *Toward a Comprehensive Landscape Plan for Washington, D.C.*, prepared for the National Capital Planning Commission by the firm of Wallace, McHarg, Roberts, and Todd (Washington, D.C., 1967). This study is often referred to as the McHarg report.

THE 1967 GREEN BOOK

For useful commentary on urban design in Washington, see the writings of Ada Louise Huxtable in the *New York Times* and those of Wolf von Eckardt in the *Washington Post*.

THE RED BOOK: THE CONTINUING COMPREHENSIVE PLAN

For the *Washington Post* article on Crystal City, see Phil Stanford, "Crystal City—A Self-Contained World," *Washington Post*, Potomac Magazine, 15 March 1970.

CHAPTER XIV:

The Redevelopment Theme 1945–1976

URBAN RENEWAL: DIVERGENT VIEWS

For general background, see the Minutes of the National Capital Park and Planning Commission for the years 1945 on. Microfilm graphic records are cataloged and shelved at the Planning Commission in Washington, D.C. Early textual records other than the Minutes and meeting transcripts are stored at the National Archives, Washington, D.C.

Picture Windows in the New Southwest

THE ELBERT PEETS RENEWAL PLAN FOR THE SOUTHWEST

Initial plans proposed for redevelopment of the Southwest include the Peets plan dated 15 April 1952 and the November 1952 plan prepared by Elbert Peets and the Planning Commission staff, *The Redevelopment Plan for the Southwest Project Area B* (Washington, D.C., 1952). For the Goodwillie report and plan, see Arthur Goodwillie, *The Rehabilitation of Southwest Washington as a War Housing Measure: A Memorandum to the Federal Home Loan Bank Board* (Washington, D.C., 1942).

THE JUSTEMENT-SMITH PLAN FOR THE SOUTHWEST

The Justement-Smith plan of May 1952 is entitled *Rebuilding Southwest Washington: A Report to the District of Columbia Redevelopment Land Agency* (Washington, D.C., 1952).

THE SOUTHWEST REDEVELOPMENT WORK OF THE PLANNING
COMMISSION AND THE REDEVELOPMENT LAND AGENCY

The Harland Bartholomew compromise report of May 1952
referred to in the text is *Redevelopment Plans for the
Southwest Survey Area in the District of Columbia*, prepared under the direction of the National Capital Park and
Planning Commission for the District of Columbia Redevelopment Land Agency (Washington, D.C., 1952). For
the Zeckendorf plan, see—in the files at the District of Columbia Department of Housing and Community Development—Webb and Knapp, Inc., "The Urban Renewal Plan
for Project Area C," March 1956. The relocation of major
portions of the old Southwest's population was studied by
Daniel Thursz in *Where Are They Now* (Washington,
D.C., 1966). The report referred to in the text is James W.
Rouse and Nathaniel S. Keith, *No Slums in Ten Years: A
Workable Program for Urban Renewal* (Washington,
D.C., 1955), prepared for the commissioners of the District of Columbia.

REHABILITATION AND REDEVELOPMENT PROJECTS
ELSEWHERE IN WASHINGTON

Background for major redevelopment areas in Washington
other than the Southwest is provided in the project files
and annual reports of the Redevelopment Land Agency
(now the District of Columbia Department of Housing
and Community Development). See there especially *Urban
Renewal Plan for the Fort Lincoln Urban Renewal Area*
(Washington, D.C., 1972), and *A Program for Bates Street*
(Washington, D.C., 1969).

On the Seventh Street corridor reconstruction, see further
the report of the Redevelopment Land Agency, *Washington Goes Forward, 1968–1976* (Washington, D.C., 1976),
and the report of the Metropolitan Washington Board of
Trade, "The Board of Trade Riot Response Project,"
Report No. 1, prepared by Robert Gladstone and Associates, April 1968 (mimeographed). See also the article,
"City Pushes to Meet Deadline on Plan to Rebuild Riot
Areas," *Washington Post*, 23 July 1968.

CHAPTER XV:

The Metropolitan Region Theme 1945–1976

DISPERSAL AND DECENTRALIZATION

The debates surrounding the effects of dispersal of federal
facilities in the Washington metropolitan area are recorded
in hearings before the House Committee on Public Works
on H.R. 9864, 81st Cong., 2d sess., 8 December 1950; before the Subcommittee of the Senate Committee on Public
Works on S. 4232, 81st Cong., 2d sess., 13, 14, and 18
December 1950 (see here the Pickins and Stein remarks
quoted above in text); and before the Subcommittee on
Public Buildings and Grounds of the House Committee on
Public Works on H.R. 1728, 82d Cong., 1st sess., 5, 6,
and 8 February 1951 (see here the statement of the Arlington County Board). The issue of decentralization of federal
office buildings is studied in Coleman Woodbury, ed., *The
Future of Cities and Urban Redevelopment* (Chicago,
1953).

RECENTRALIZATION

For expression of the renewed emphasis on the central city,
see especially the writings of Paul Thiry, member of the
National Capital Planning Commission 1963–74 and editor
of the *Journal of the American Institute of Architects'* spe-
ial issue, vol. 39, no. 1 (January 1963), *Washington in
Transition*; see there also Morton Hoppenfeld, "A Metro
Center for the Year 2000." Among the reports done by the
Federal City Council, Washington's version of the so-called
executive coalition, see *Progress Through Citizen Action*
(Washington, D.C., 1957), and *Action Report for Downtown Washington* (Washington, D.C., 1959). See also the
1961 report, *Downtown Progress: Action Plan for Downtown*, done by the National Capital Downtown Committee,
Inc., and subsequent reports also published by this committee.

THE NATIONAL CAPITAL REGIONAL PLANNING COUNCIL AND
THE COUNCIL OF GOVERNMENTS

For the statements of Paul C. Watt, director of the National Capital Regional Planning Council, see *Washington
Metropolitan Area Transportation Problems*, Hearings before the Joint Committee on Washington Metropolitan
Problems, 85th Cong., 2d sess., 22 and 23 May, and 11
June 1958. For the assessment of the Regional Council
quoted in the text, see *Meeting the Problems of Metropolitan Growth in the National Capital Region*, Final Report
of the Joint Committee on Washington Metropolitan Problems, 86th Cong., 1st sess., S. Rept. No. 38, 31 January 1959.

A synoptic view of the metropolitan region can be gained
from the annual reports of the National Capital Regional
Planning Council and the Metropolitan Washington Council of Governments. These annual reports are on file for
study at the library of the National Capital Planning Commission and the library of the Council of Governments,
both in Washington, D.C. For a later review of the Year
2000 Policies Plan, see Metropolitan Washington Council
of Governments, *Re-examination of the Year 2000 Policies
Plan*, 2 vols. (Washington, D.C., 1974).

For the Council of Governments' recent study of metropolitan growth, see *Metropolitan Growth Policy Program* (Washington, D.C., 1975). The library of the Washington Center for Metropolitan Studies contains a specialized collection of reports and other material on regional structure, growth, planning, and government. On planning activities in the Maryland suburbs, see the following documents: Allied Civic Group, Inc., *Survey of Montgomery County: Report and Recommendations of Government Operations Committee* (Silver Spring, 1962); The Institute of Public Administration, *The Regional Planning Role of the Maryland–National Capital Park and Planning Commission* (New York, 1962); the annual reports of the Maryland–National Capital Park and Planning Commission for the years from 1957 on; special reports and statements of the Montgomery County Citizens Planning Association (in particular, *Background on Montgomery County Planning Problems*, 26 February 1962; *Report on Issues*, 20 April 1962; Statement of Ramsey Wood, 28 February 1963) on file at the Montgomery County Public Library, Rockville Branch; Ladislas Segoe Associates, *Preliminary Report—Survey and Review of Organization and Activities of the M–NCPPC* (October 1956); the Mary P. Vinton Collection in the Municipal Room at the Montgomery County Public Library, Rockville Branch; Madeline Baker, "Politics of Planning in Montgomery County" (M.A. diss., George Washington University, 1966); and Charles Puffenbarger, "Montgomery County Planning: A Study in Politics" (M.A. diss., George Washington University, 1963).

Virginia's planning activities have been less coordinated with other planning agencies in the metropolitan area. See the annual reports of the Northern Virginia Regional Planning and Economic Commission, the Fairfax County Planning Commission, and the Northern Virginia Planning District Commission, most of which are available in the Virginiana Collection, Fairfax County Public Library. For the reference to Megalopolis, see Jean Gottman, *Megalopolis: The Urbanized Northeastern Seaboard of the United States* (Cambridge, Mass., and London, 1961).

Recent reports published by the National Capital Planning Commission—in addition to published modifications and additions to the Comprehensive Plan for the National Capital—reflect the conservation approach to the city's future development and a concern with environmental quality emphasizing natural features and landmarks of the built environment; see the *Quarterly Review of Commission Proceedings* published from 1974 on. See also *Downtown Design and Development* (Washington, D.C., 1974); and *The Urban River* (Washington, D.C., 1972), which proposes general policies and programs for implementing Comprehensive Plan policies. *Shoreline Acquisition and Development Policies and Programs* (Washington, D.C., 1976) is a further detailing of policies and programs for implementing Comprehensive Plan policies. An argument for continuation of the traditional scale of Georgetown across its waterfront is made by the Georgetown Planning Group, *Georgetown Waterfront Area Study*, prepared for the Planning Commission and the District of Columbia Department of Transportation. This study includes three reports: *Phase I Report: Development Concept Alternatives* (Washington, D.C., 1972; *Phase IIA Report: Preliminary Development Plan and Program* (1973); and *Consultants' Final Report: Recommended Development Plan and Program* (1975).

Contemporary Telephoto View from the Washington Cathedral

Sources Consulted

GENERAL SOURCES

Detailed studies and contemporary interpretations of the city in light of new research is published in the *Records of the Columbia Historical Society* (Washington, D.C.). In this continuing series, 49 individual volumes have been published since 1897; vol. 1 was published in 1897, and vol. 49 (covering the years 1973–74) was published in 1976. These volumes do not follow a consistent numbering system on the book spines, although there is internal consistency in numbering. For clearest presentation to researchers, references to these volumes are given here as follows: vols. 1–28 are cited by volume numbers and year date of publication; from vol. 29 forward, only the years covered and year date of publication are shown. The society also maintains a manuscript collection just now being cataloged. References to this collection are identified by Columbia Historical Society Manuscript Collection and year date.

Classic Washington histories are: Wilhelmus Bogart Bryan, *A History of the National Capital from Its Foundation through the Period of the Adoption of the Organic Act*, 2 vols. (New York, 1914–16), which skillfully traces the city's history to 1878 and provides a remarkable emphasis on the physical format of the city; and Constance McLaughlin Green, *Washington*, 2 vols.: *Village and Capital, 1800–1878* (Princeton, 1962), and *Capital City, 1879–1950* (Princeton, 1963), which assesses the evolving social atmosphere in juxtaposition with development of the political and cultural city; and John Clagett Proctor, ed., *Washington Past and Present: A History*, 5 vols. (New York, 1930). For an additional rich source of information, see the "Articles on Early Washington" written by John Clagett Proctor for the *Sunday Star* for the run of dates from 22 January 1928 to 7 September 1952. These articles are on file at the Martin Luther King Memorial Library (D.C.P.L.), Washingtoniana Division, in Washington, D.C. For the most extensive visual documentation of Washington architecture, see now the Dunlap Society publication, *The Architecture of Washington, D.C.*, 2 vols. (Essex, N.Y., 1976–77). Vol. 1 presents slides and microfiche on ten major buildings in Washington; vol. 2 deals with the Capitol and the Federal Triangle.

Broad studies of the physical region include an interpretation of the larger region that has defined and nurtured the city, advanced in Frederick Gutheim, *The Potomac* (New York and Toronto, 1949; rev. ed. with added illustrations, new section on Washington, bibliographic updating, New York, 1968; paperback ed. from original plates, New York, 1974). A graphic description and interpretative view of the Washington topography is explored by the National Capital Planning Commission, *Toward a Comprehensive Landscape Plan for Washington, D.C.* (Washington, D.C., 1967). John W. Reps, *Tidewater Towns: City Planning in Colonial Virginia and Maryland* (Williamsburg, 1972), describes and compares the many human settlements that formed along the tidewater rivers and inlets. In *Monumental Washington: The Planning and Development of the Capital Center* (Princeton, 1967), Reps presents a history of the ceremonial/governmental core of the city, with particular emphasis on the L'Enfant plan and the McMillan Commission plan. Washington in context with the growth of the planning profession nationwide can be evaluated in Mel Scott, *American City Planning Since 1890*, 2d ed. (Berkeley, Los Angeles, and London, 1971), which also offers a provocative analysis of the McMillan Commission plan as exemplary of the City Beautiful movement.

An introduction to the city of Washington is also provided by several guidebooks: Washington Metropolitan Chapter of the American Institute of Architects, *A Guide to the Architecture of Washington, D.C.*, ed. Hugh Newell Jacobsen, rev. ed. (New York, 1974); U.S. Works Progress Administration, Federal Writers' Project, *Washington, City and Capital* (Washington, D.C., 1937), which meshes history, critique, and tours. For the city as expanded over its bridges, see Donald Beekman Myer, *Bridges and the City of Washington* (Washington, D.C., 1974). The most recent guidebook, planned around 25 walking tours, is *Washington on Foot*, ed. Allan A. and Carol Hodges, 2d ed. (Washington, D.C., 1977). For a list of earlier guidebooks and Washington directories, see Constance M. Green, *Washington, Village and Capital, 1800–1876* (Princeton, 1962).

BIBLIOGRAPHIES

Recent bibliographies offer an introduction to the study of Washington. Perry G. Fisher, *Materials for the Study of Washington* (Washington, D.C., 1974), provides incisive and often witty commentary on many basic sources, including planning studies, novels, and specialized histories. An emphasis on the development of the physical city and urban planning is provided in Anne Llewellyn Meglis, *D.C. Redevelopment Land Agency Presents a Bibliographic Tour of Washington, D.C.* (Washington, D.C., 1974). The National Capital Planning Commission, *Bibliography of Studies and Reports on the District of Columbia and the Washington Metropolitan Area* (Washington, D.C., 1967), lists contemporary reports covering the topics of population, economics, land use, housing, and visitors and tourism.

ANNUAL REPORTS

The published annual reports of the following agencies were consulted: National Capital Park and Planning Commission, Commission of Fine Arts, Army Corps of Engineers, Board of Commissioners of the District of Columbia, Maryland–National Capital Park and Planning Commission, Metropolitan Washington Council of Governments, District of Columbia Redevelopment Land Agency (now a part of the Department of Housing and Community Development of the District of Columbia), Public Buildings Commission, and Office of the Supervising Architect of the Treasury.

MANUSCRIPT COLLECTIONS

In the course of this study, the following manuscript collections were consulted:

Records of the National Capital Park and Planning Commission, National Archives, Record Group 42, Section 328.

Records of the Commission of Fine Arts, National Archives, Record Group 42, Section 66; Charles Moore's unpublished memoirs are included herein.

Papers of the American Planning and Civic Association, Social Action Archives, Division of Archives and Manuscripts, Wisconsin State Historical Society, Madison, Wisconsin.

Diaries of Edward H. Bennett, office of Edward H. Bennett, Jr., Chicago, Illinois.

Minutes of the National Capital Park Commission for the years 1924–26, National Capital Planning Commission, Washington, D.C.

Minutes of the National Capital Park and Planning Commission for the years 1926–52, National Capital Planning Commission, Washington, D.C.

Records of Jesse C. Nichols, including papers and short biographies, J. C. Nichols Company, Kansas City, Missouri.

Papers of Louis C. Cramton and Charles Moore, Library of Michigan History, University of Michigan, Ann Arbor, Michigan.

Papers relating to Frederic A. Delano and John Ihlder, Franklin Delano Roosevelt Library, Hyde Park, New York.

Papers of Frederic A. Delano, Harland Bartholomew, the American Planning and Civic Association, and Ulysses S. Grant III, Architecture and City Planning Collection, Olin Library, Cornell University, Ithaca, New York.

Papers of Henry V. Hubbard, Frederick Law Olmsted, Jr., and Charles Eliot II, Graduate School of Design, Harvard University, Cambridge, Massachusetts.

Papers relating to Frederick Law Olmsted, Jr., office of Olmsted Brothers, Brookline, Massachusetts.

Papers of Oscar Stonorov and materials relating to the Corcoran Gallery of Art 1950 Sesquicentennial Exhibition,

Archives of Contemporary History, University of Wyoming, Laramie, Wyoming.

Papers of Frederick Law Olmsted, Sr., Huntington Library, San Marino, California.

Papers of William W. Wurster, office of Wurster, Bernardi and Emmons, San Francisco, California.

Papers of Frederick Law Olmsted, Sr., especially those relating to the United States Capitol grounds, Library of Congress, Manuscript Division, Washington, D.C.

ICONOGRAPHIC COLLECTIONS

The following public sources in Washington, D.C., were consulted for illustrative material: at the Library of Congress, the Geography and Map Division, which holds many original maps dated to the eighteenth and nineteenth centuries, and the Prints and Photographs Division; the Washingtoniana Division of the Martin Luther King Memorial Library, District of Columbia Public Library System; the Columbia Historical Society; the United States Chamber of Commerce; the National Capital Planning Commission; the National Archives; the District of Columbia Department of Transportation; and the District of Columbia Redevelopment Land Agency (now a part of the Department of Housing and Community Development of the District of Columbia government). For additional sources, see Chalmers M. Roberts, *Washington, Past and Present* (Washington, D.C., 1949–50).

Several private collections have also been consulted: in Washington, D.C., the Bernstein and Kiplinger collections, and at George Washington University, the Wright collection; in New York, at the New York Public Library, the Stokes collection.

PERSONAL INTERVIEWS

The following individuals who played key roles in the planning of Washington graciously submitted themselves to taped interviews and thus provided a personal dimension to this book: Horace M. Albright, Sherman Oaks, California; Harland Bartholomew, St. Louis, Missouri; Charles Conrad, Washington, D.C.; Wilmer C. Dutton, Jr., Riverdale, Maryland; Charles W. Eliot II, Cambridge, Massachusetts; William E. Finley, Miami Lakes, Florida; Colonel E. Brooke Lee, Damascus, Maryland; Mrs. James H. Rowe, Jr., Washington, D.C.; and Paul Thiry, Seattle, Washington. Additional interviews were conducted with members of the National Capital Planning Commission staff.

The historical studies in this series are a part of the National Capital Planning Commission Bicentennial Program, and under the direction of Samuel K. Frazier, Jr., Study Director, were conducted and written by Frederick Gutheim, AIP, consultant to the Commission; Mr. Gutheim was assisted by Antoinette J. Lee. Staff support was provided by Donald F. Bozarth, Carol A. Hodges, George H. F. Oberlander, and Leo Schmittel. A major staff contribution was made by Donald E. Jackson. Charity Vanderbilt Davidson of the joint District of Columbia/National Capital Planning Commission Historic Preservation Office also made a significant contribution. The index for this volume was prepared by Barbara S. Kraft.

The National Capital Planning Commission and the Smithsonian Institution Press acknowledge with gratitude the assistance of the following individuals and organizations in providing graphic materials: Ms. Betty M. Culpepper and Mr. Alexander Geyger, Washingtoniana Division, Martin Luther King Memorial Library; Ms. Anne Meglis, District of Columbia Department of Housing and Community Development; Ms. Carol Manka, District of Columbia Department of Transportation; Mrs. Nancy C. Taylor, joint District of Columbia/National Capital Planning Commission Historic Preservation Office; Mrs. Susan Kohler, Commission of Fine Arts; Mr. Ronald Grim, Cartographic Division, National Archives; Messrs. Leroy Bellamy and Sam Daniel, Division of Prints and Photographs, Library of Congress; Messrs. Robert A. Truax and Perry G. Fisher, Columbia Historical Society; the National Gallery of Art; the National Park Service; the Smithsonian Institution; the Chamber of Commerce of the United States of America; Downtown Progress, Inc.; Washington Metropolitan Transportation Agency; the Mount Vernon Ladies' Association of the Union.

The Commission and the Press further acknowledge the assistance of the following individuals and institutions in supplying nongraphic materials: Mary and Donald F. Lethbridge; Ms. Dorothy S. Provine, Civil Archives Division, National Archives; Franklin Delano Roosevelt Memorial Library, Hyde Park, New York; Mr. Edward H. Bennett, Jr., Chicago, Illinois; The Burnham Library and The Art Institute of Chicago, Chicago, Illinois; Library of Congress; Wisconsin State Historical Society, Madison, Wisconsin; Graduate School of Design, Harvard University, Cambridge, Massachusetts; Library of Michigan History, University of Michigan, Ann Arbor, Michigan; Columbia Historical Society, Washington, D.C.; Washingtoniana Division, Martin Luther King Memorial Library (D.C.P.L.).

Acknowledgment is also accorded additional individuals and institutions listed above under Manuscript Collections and Iconographic Collections consulted in the preparation of this book.

Page numbers refer to the text and the illustrations.

Health, Education and Welfare Department
  Building, 321, 323
Heaton, Arthur, 154
Hegemann, Werner, 176
Height of Buildings Act of 1910, 234
Henderson, Mrs. John B., 144
Henry, Joseph, 53, 65
Herndon, 107
Herrick, Charles, 221
Hickey Hill, 143
Highway Act of 1893, 109, 111, 386
Highway Act of 1898, 111, 188
Highway Commission (1895), 170
Highway Improvement Plan of 1944, 239
Highway Planning Survey (1939), 273
Highway Plan of 1893, 187, 188, 189, 192,
  273
Highways: suburban development, 208, 209,
  226, 247, 265, 273–82; World War II
  construction, 225, 230; urban, 240, 241,
  316; planning, 261, 303, 307, 386, 397.
  See also Street system
Highways, Department of, 277
Hill, James G., 147
Historic preservation, 97, 188–89, 292, 293,
  309, 354
Hitchcock, Henry-Russell, 220
Hoban, James, 44
Holmes Run, 209
Home Builders, National Association of,
  234, 327
Home Building and Home Ownership Con-
  ference (1931), 163–64, 390
Home Owners' Loan Corporation, 232
Home Rule Act of 1973, 352
Hookers' Division, 69, 78–79
Hoover, Herbert, 163–66 *passim*, 172–79
  passim, 390
Hoover, Kenneth M., 261
Hoover Airport, 221, 394
Hopkins, Mrs. Archibald, 191
Houdon, Jean Antoine, 3
Housing: apartment buildings, 108–9, 164,
  265–66, 396; mentioned, 57, 190, 191,
  221, 291
Housing Act of 1949, 234, 235–36, 238,
  246, 314
Housing Act of 1954, 314, 323
Housing and Community Development,
  District of Columbia Department of, 325
Housing and Home Finance Administration,
  235
Housing and Urban Development Depart-
  ment Building, 293, 323
Howard University, 70, 78, 95
Howe, George, 175
Hoxie, Richard L., 90

Hubbard, Henry V., 212, 218, 219, 393
Hunting Creek, 57
Huxtable, Ada Louise, 13, 376
Hybla Park airfield, 221

Ickes, Harold, 216, 222–23, 225, 393, 394
Ihlder, John, 164, 166, 187, 190–91, 234, 392
Indian Head Highway, 230
Inner Loop Freeway, 291, 316
Intercounty Belt Freeway, 247
Interior: Building, 156; Department of, 216,
  224
Internal Revenue Service Building, 176, 182
International Sector, 348
International Style Exhibit of 1933, 220
Interstate Commerce Commission Building,
  176

Jadwin, Edgar, 198
James, Harlean, 161–62, 180, 390, 391
Jeffers, T. C., 219
Jefferson, Thomas, 2, 3, 14–45 *passim*, 130,
  160, 373–74, 379; Memorial, 135, 146,
  180, 201, 219–20, 388, 393
Jenkins Hill. *See* Capitol Hill
Johnson, Lady Bird (Mrs. Lyndon), 310
Johnson, Lyndon, 294
Judiciary Square, 47, 87, 98, 102, 181, 182,
  305
Justement, Louis, 166, 234, 235, 315–17,
  319, 395, 399
Justice Department Building, 150, 176, 182

Kalorama, 19, 45, 103, 144, 155, 156, 380
Kastner, Alfred, 393–94
Kearney, James, 93
Keith, Nathaniel S., 324
Kelsey, Albert, 151
Kendall, Amos, 57
Kennedy, Jacqueline, 294
Kennedy, John F., 294
Kennedy Center, 292, 354, 356
Kennedy Stadium, 287
Key Bridge, 10, 194, 215, 263
Keyes, Lethbridge and Condon, 321
Key of Keys, 204, 374, 392

Kidwell, John L., 93–94
Kidwell's Meadows, 93
Kimball, Fiske, 18, 27, 219, 220, 377
King, Martin Luther, Jr., 329
King, Nicholas, 1, 39
Kingman Lake, 142, 305
Kite, Elizabeth, 17
Klingle Street Bridge, 107
Köllner, August, 50
Kutz, Charles W., 141, 160

Labor Department Building, 150, 176
Lafayette Square: buildings on, 46, 147,
  149, 165, 166; planning, 126, 136, 293–
  94; mentioned, 82, 87, 103, 125
Landmarks, Joint Committee on, 293
Landscape design, 27–28, 54–55, 82–84,
  117, 121–22, 127–28, 380
Land speculation: colonial towns, 16; Federal
  period, 21, 23, 33, 40, 41; waterfront, 40,
  94; Civil War, 68; during territorial gov-
  ernment, 102–3; Marshall Heights, 237;
  office buildings, 309
Land use planning, 353–54
Langdon, J. G., 120, 170
Langley, 225
Langley, Samuel, 221
Lansburgh, Mark, 235
La Rochefoucauld-Liancourt, 21, 378
Latrobe, Benjamin, 3, 19, 43–47 *passim*,
  293, 380
Laugier, Père Marc-Antoine, 18
Law, Thomas, 33
LeDroit Park, 63, 107
Lee, E. Brooke, 206–7
Lee, Robert E., 86, 333
Lee plantation, 69, 223
Legislative Group, 174, 203
Lehman, Donald, 88
L'Enfant, Pierre Charles: architectural influ-
  ences on, 2, 3, 17, 20, 120–21; commis-
  sions, 16, 17, 18, 376–77; personality, 19;
  city surveyor, 22, 98; dismissal, 36; tomb,
  xvi; mentioned, 1, 13, 21, 39, 40, 132, 289
L'Enfant plan: origins, 2–3, 13; and McMillan plan, 17–18, 119–20, 133, 152, 240;
  survey and map, 22–35 *passim*, 77, 98,
  373, 378; street system, 25–26, 31–32,
  109, 111, 188, 271, 386; landscape design,
  27–28; alterations to, 44, 46, 47, 77; the
  Mall, 51–52, 53, 116, 218; military preparedness provisions, 61; commercial centers, 76; parklands and recreation, 76, 94,

R

Ten-mile square boundary (Federal District), 2, 13–14, 19, 95, 156, 185, 287, 333, 356
Territorial government, 84–88, 384
Thiry, Paul, 294, 400
Thorn, F. M., 77
Thornton, William, 41, 44, 46
Thoroughfare Plan of 1930, 273
Three Sisters Bridge, 307
Tiber Creek, 2, 14, 20–27 passim, 40, 76, 78, 81, 126, 374
Tiber Island, 323
Tidal Basin: construction, 93; recreational use, 128, 129, 143, 144, 167; Jefferson Memorial site, 219, 220; mentioned, 96, 126, 219, 323
Tompkins, Charles H., 321
Topography: site, 22, 65, 124, 249, 376; and planning, 291, 300–302, 303; maps, 31, 83; neighborhoods, 77, 106, 108, 207, 391; and development, 111, 187, 189; mentioned, 15, 19, 21, 33, 93
Totten, George Oakley, Jr., 116, 147, 166
Tourism, 167, 354–56, 382
Townsend, Richard H., 155
Transportation Department Building, 323
Treasury Department: Buildings, 43, 47, 62, 63, 128, 149, 175; mentioned, 85, 88, 172, 180
Trowbridge and Livingston, 151
Truman, Harry, 293
Tuemmler, Fred, 338
Turnaround trend, 259, 313, 314, 396
Twining, Thomas, 21, 93
Tyson's Corner, 270, 278, 308, 309

Union Square, 126, 129, 216
Union Station, 121, 130, 131, 151, 161, 218, 232, 305, 314
Uniontown. See Anacostia
Urban design: influenced by, 3, 18, 113, 116, 140; theories, 4, 27, 176, 194, 220, 289–90, 300, 390; applications, 133–34, 143–46, 153, 189–90, 192–94, 263, 265; commissions, 174, 186; deficiencies, 178–79, 180, 309. See also Boston Metropolitan Park System
Urban Land Institute, 275
Urban renewal: planning, 232, 313–23, 399; rehabilitation vs. demolition, 323–29; areas, 325, 326–29. Se also Barry Farms; Marshall Heights; Redevelopment
Usher, John P., 68

Van Ness house, 45–46, 380
Vaux and Olmsted, 115
Versailles, 2, 18, 27
Virginia, 95, 107, 156, 206, 333, 396. See also under Suburbanization
von Ezdorf, Richard, 88, 98

W

Wallach School, 101
Walker, C. Howard, 116
Walker, George, 23
Walter, Thomas V., 47, 55
Walter Reed Army Medical Center, 202
Walton, William, 294
War Department: new building site, 203, 223; mentioned, 65, 68, 88. See also Pentagon (War Department Building)
Waring, George E., 92
Warnecke, John Carl, 147
War of 1812, 43, 44, 397
War Services Committee, Chamber of Commerce, 164
Washington, George: plans Federal District, 1, 2, 14, 24, 82; statues of, 3, 99, 376; and L'Enfant, 17, 23, 27, 28, 31; business interests, 42, 380; bicentennial of, 196; mentioned, 1–31 passim, 97, 130, 160, 333
Washington, Walter, 329
Washington Airport, 221
Washington Building Congress, 287
Washington Board of Trade: and suburbanization, 109; District Centennial, 115, 116; function, 166–67, 390; city-planning role, 167, 169, 170, 238–39, 329
Washington Canal Company, 44–45
Washington Channel, 125, 142–43, 315, 379
Washington Common, 129, 219
Washington estate, 223
Washington Grove, 210
Washington Hotel, 163, 182
Washington Lewis House, 321
Washington Metropolitan Problems, Joint Committee on, 262, 338, 396
Washington Metropolitan Regional Conference, 339
Washington Monument: construction, 51, 71; Mills's design, 52; views from, 53, 152; grounds, 63, 86–87, 125, 127–28, 143, 179, 201; Brady photographs, 67; men-

tioned, 2, 144, 218, 219, 347, 356
Washington Municipal Airport, 221, 224, 225, 394
Washington Region Water Supply Committee (1929), 209–10
Washington Suburban Sanitary Commission (1916), 206, 207, 335, 340
Washington Zoning Revision Office, 259
Waterfront development, 33, 92, 129, 130, 240, 245, 272, 305, 320, 342, 401
Watergate, 292, 305, 309
Water supply system: quality of, 47, 56–57, 90–91, 381–82, 384; aqueducts, 48, 76, 82, 90, 95, 107–8, 333, 377; sources and regulation, 120, 206, 209–10, 393; studies of, 377, 378, 384; mentioned 39, 56–57, 106, 114, 335. See also Drainage
Watt, Paul C., 338, 400
Watts Branch Parkway, 300
Webb and Knapp, 319
Weese, Harry, 319
Weld, Isaac, Jr., 21
Welsbach mantle, 105
Wesley Heights, 154–55, 189–90
West, Benjamin, 3
West Central Heating Plant, 355
West End, 299, 300, 305
Western Market, 76
Wheat Row, 41, 104, 321
Wheeler, Harry A., 164
White, Stanford, 155
White House. See President's House (White House)
Whitehurst, H. C., 239
Whitehurst Freeway, 240, 272, 274, 343
White Lot, 151, 389
White Muslin Palace of Aladdin, 62
Wicomico-Sunderland escarpment, 19, 24, 26, 45
Wilkes Arctic Expedition, 54, 381
Willard Hotel, 68, 163, 182
Williamsburg, 120
Wilson, James, 131
Wilson, John M., 95
Wilson High School, 194
Winder Building, 65
Wodehouse, Lawrence, 88
Wolf Trap Farm, 354, 356
Wood, Waddy B., 156
Woodley Park, 104
Works Progress Administration, 215
World's Columbian Exposition (1893): urban design influence, 113, 116; Burnham's job with, 118; influences McMillan Commission, 120, 133–34; mentioned, 111, 164, 175
World War "tempos," 150, 151, 172, 204,

The text of this book is set in "Electra," a type face cut from designs drawn for the Mergenthaler Linotype Company by W. A. Dwiggins, the American type designer, in 1935. The type face falls within the "modern" family of type styles, but is drawn to avoid the extreme contrast between thick and thin elements. Chapter heads are set in Onyx, an elongated fat face, designed for American Type Founders by Gerry Powell in 1937. Major subheads are set in Century Nova Italic, designed for American Type Founders by Charles Hughes in 1966.